M000187600

LOOKING
TOWARD
ARARAT

Republic of Armenia

LOOKING TOWARD ARARAT
ARMENIA IN MODERN HISTORY

Ronald Grigor Suny

INDIANA UNIVERSITY PRESS
Bloomington and Indianapolis

PUBLIC LIBRARY
Rochester, NH 55804

© 1993 by Ronald Grigor Suny
All rights reserved

No part of this book may be reproduced or utilized in any form or by
any means, electronic or mechanical, including photocopying and
recording, or by any information storage and retrieval system, without
permission in writing from the publisher. The Association of American
University Presses' Resolution on Permissions constitutes the only
exception to this prohibition.

The paper used in this publication meets the minimum requirements of American
National Standard for Information Sciences—Permanence of Paper for Printed
Library Materials, ANSI Z39.48-1984.

 ™

Manufactured in the United States of America

Library of Congress Cataloging-in-Publication Data

Suny, Ronald Grigor.
    Looking toward Ararat : Armenia in modern history / Ronald Grigor
Suny.
        p.   cm.
    Includes bibliographical references and index.
    ISBN 0-253-35583-4 (cloth : alk. paper). — ISBN 0-253-20773-8
(paper : alk. paper)
    1. Armenia (Republic)—History. 2. Armenia (Republic)—History—
Autonomy and independence movements. I. Title.
DK687.S86   1993
956.6'2—dc20   92-19420

1   2   3   4   5   97   96   95   94   93

56.62
u74L

To my wife, Armena Marderosian,
and my daughters,
Sevan Siranoush Suni and
Anoush Tamar Suni

Contents

Preface

As a new independent Republic of Armenia is established among the ruins of the Soviet Union, Armenians are rethinking their history—the processes by which they arrived at statehood in a small part of their historic "homeland" and the definitions they might give to the boundaries of their "nation." Both a victim and a beneficiary of rival empires, Armenia experienced a complex evolution as a divided or an erased polity with a widespread diaspora.

Rather than promoting a notion of Armenians as a nation from primeval to present times, the essays gathered here, written during the last several decades, are preliminary explorations of the construction of modern Armenian identity and nationhood. They discuss the cultural and social transformations and interventions that created a new sense of nationality in the nineteenth and twentieth centuries. The making of a nation is seen here as involving both outside impositions and acts of self-realization by the Armenians themselves.

In Part I images of Armenians by others are examined alongside internal Armenian representations of self. The social, cultural, and intellectual influences on the formation of a secular intelligentsia are considered in the context of imperial impositions, revolutionary opportunities, and externally dictated programs for "modernization."

Ideas of antiquity and shared origin and perceptions of uniqueness and value combined with the experiences of dispersion, genocide, and regeneration to forge an Armenian nation in Transcaucasia. As Caucasian Armenians plan their political independence from the moribund Soviet Union, they, like other Soviet peoples, reject any positive evaluation of the transformations imposed on them by the Communist regime. Yet, as the essays in Part II attempt to demonstrate, Armenians in Armenia can be seen to be the recipients of an indelible inheritance from that hard passage. Finally, it is shown that while the limits of the Armenian nation at times excluded the diaspora, in this moment of state renewal they have been expanded to take in that half of the nation that lives beyond the borders of the republic.

The openness of the present and the inability of historians and other analysts to predict the possible futures has encouraged me to rethink some of my conclusions in earlier published versions, and here and there I have changed some language, clarified some points, and adjusted some of my thoughts. The basic thrust of the individual pieces and the overall project, however, remains essentially the same. They are offered, not as answers to the question of identity, but, hopefully, as part of the debate; not as an effort to recover some lost essence of Armenianness, but as an attempt to participate in the construction of a new sense of ethnicity. This new kind of ethnicity, to follow the path taken by the sociologist Stuart Hall,

> is constructed in history, it is constructed politically in part. It is part of narrative. We tell ourselves the stories of the parts of our roots in order to come into contact, creatively, with it. So this new kind of ethnicity—the emergent ethnicities—has a relationship to the past, but it is a relationship that is partly through memory, partly through narrative, one that has to be recovered. It is an act of cultural recovery.[1]

Acknowledgments

The introduction and chapters 6, 13, and 14 are published here for the first time. The others have been previously published as follows:

Chapter 1: in Richard G. Hovannisian, ed., *The Armenian Image in History and Literature* (Malibu, CA: Undena, 1981), pp. 105–37.

Chapter 3: *Armenian Review* XXXVI, 3/143 (Autumn 1983), pp. 18–34.

Chapter 4: *Armenian Review* XXXII, 2/126 (June 1979), pp. 134–51.

Chapter 5: *Armenian Review* XXXIII, 1/129 (March 1980), pp. 30–47.

Chapters 2, 7, 8, 9, and 11: in *Armenia in the Twentieth Century* (Chico, CA: Scholars Press, 1983), the published versions of the John and Haigouhie Takajian lectures delivered at Columbia University in 1981.

Chapter 10: *Armenian Review* XLII, 3/167 (Autumn 1989), pp. 1–19.

Chapter 12: *Michigan Quarterly Review* XXVIII, 4 (Fall 1989), pp. 481–506.

Several friends, relatives, students, and colleagues have read and commented on the original essays, and I would like to thank Geoff Eley, Richard Hovannisian, Dikran Kouymjian, Vincent Lima, Maude Mandel, Linda Suny Myrsiades, Norman Naimark, and Khachig Tololyan for their suggestions and criticisms. A particular expression of gratitude goes to Ara Sarafian and Stephen Rapp, my research assistants, who were diligent in finding new material and keeping me alive to new questions. As always, this work has benefited from the joy that my family has provided me, and in gratitude for the time that they have allowed me to take from them I dedicate to Armena Marderosian, Sevan Siranoush Suni, and Anoush Tamar Suni this attempt to rethink the heritage we share.

Transliteration and dating

With some exceptions made to conform to more familiar usage, words and names have been transliterated from Russian, Georgian, and Azerbaijani according to the Library of Congress systems, with a few modifications. Armenian transliteration is based on the system adopted by *The Armenian Review*, which is based on the east Armenian dialect used in the Russian Empire, Iran, and the independent and Soviet republics of Armenia. Consistent with Georgian practice, Georgian words, even titles of books and newspapers, have not been capitalized, though personal names have. Names have been given in the transliteration appropriate to the nationality of the person, e.g., the Armenian form Shahumian rather than the Russian Shaumian.

Unless otherwise noted, dates before February 1, 1918, which refer to events in Russia or Transcaucasia, are given in the Julian calendar, which was thirteen days behind the Gregorian calendar of the West in the twentieth century, twelve days behind in the nineteenth century, eleven days behind in the eighteenth century, and so on.

LOOKING
TOWARD
ARARAT

Introduction:
From National
Character
to National Tradition

> There can be no identity without memory
> (albeit selective), no collective purpose without
> myth, and identity and purpose or destiny are
> necessary elements of the very concept of a
> nation.—Anthony D. Smith[1]

Precariously positioned at the furthest reach of Christiandom in the classical
and medieval ages and situated by modern cartographers at the very edge of
Europe, Armenia has historically been both victim and beneficiary of rival
empires. As the Soviet Union began its rapid disintegration, the smallest union
republic, now governed by a democratically elected national movement, declared itself prepared to chart its own course between East and West. The
Armenian government assumed the legitimacy of its independence and full
statehood on the basis of a confident claim to antiquity as a nation and "its
historic responsibility for the destiny of the Armenian people."[2] Citizenship
in the new republic was granted, not only to all living within its borders, but
to those Armenians in the diaspora who wished to exercise that right. Along
with a new state, a new concept of nationhood was being invented for the
world's Armenians. Identity and affiliation had become vital political issues,

and once again the question of who Armenians are was raised both in Armenia and abroad.

In the wake of the collapse of the Soviet empire, a profound unease about Armenia's future accompanied the hope that an independent democracy could survive in the Caucasus. The long past of the Armenians provided mixed lessons of a people under constant threat from larger neighbors but able to survive between and within rival imperialisms. But that history, poorly known by many Armenians, was itself a field of contestation between official historians forced to conform to state dictates and the needs of nationalists to recover their own understandings of the Armenian experience. In the West the history of Armenia and of the Armenians in the modern age has yet to be written. On the one hand, it has fallen victim to the Russocentric biases of Sovietologists and been subsumed under a general history of the USSR that neglects the particulars of distinct nations. On the other, within the field of Middle Eastern studies, the story of the Armenians, a people who effectively were removed from the bulk of their historic homeland, ceased to be of interest to those who concentrated on the victors, the founders of the Turkish republic and the successor states of the Ottoman Empire. Even for the few scholars who dealt professionally with Armenian history, the modern experience was marginal to their study of the golden ages of Armenia's past, the empire of Tigran the Great or the fifth-century foundations of Armenian Christian culture. There was little interest in studying this people beyond its moments of greatest unity and influence.

As long as history was conceived largely in national and political terms, the story of a stateless, dispersed people seemed of lesser importance. For the long centuries from the fall of the last Armenian kingdom in 1375 until the genocide of 1915 the slate was blank, and even the tragedies of the twentieth century remained unexplored by dispassionate analysts.[3] A double isolation afflicted the official historiography of Soviet Armenia, which suffered both from enforced ideological constraints and a persistent tendency to turn inward, to explore Armenian rather than more universal social scientific concerns.

Often directed toward an ethnic rather than a broader international or scholarly audience, Armenian historical writing has been narrowly concerned with fostering a positive view of an endangered nationality. Popular writers and activist journalists both in the diaspora and Armenia handed down an uncritical historical tradition replete with heroes and villains, and scholars who might otherwise have enriched the national historiography withdrew from a field marked by unexamined nationalism and narcissism. Criticism has been avoided as if it might aid ever-present enemies, and certain kinds of inquiry have been shunned as potential betrayals of the national cause. Though this small book is no substitute for the fundamental archival and interpretative work that must be done by scholars in order to reconstruct a critical historiography of the Armenians, the essays collected here are an attempt to rethink the modern history of the Armenians and to promote an integration of the somewhat isolated historiography of Armenia into more general theoretical and historical concerns. The assumption behind the collection is that only with the aid of conceptual tools from other disciplines and historical fields can unquestioned certainties and mythologies be challenged. Perhaps with the critical exploration of the Armenian past and present, historians of modern Armenia can provide some assistance in the ongoing struggles over identity and the meaning of the Armenian experience.

I

As a people scattered in dozens of countries and living in permanent danger of assimilation or acculturation—if not annihilation—the Armenians in the nineteenth and twentieth centuries (and probably much farther back) have been engaged in an unending discussion of what constitutes an Armenian. What is far less problematic for larger nations with their own state institutions has been central to the discourse of modern Armenians: What is Armenianness? Who is in the group, who should be excluded? Is this historic people defined by its ancient language, which many who call themselves Armenian can no longer use, or by their unique Christian faith, which many if not most Armenians in the world do not practice? Is it a sense of history, a national consciousness that they share, or a way of life? If it is a matter of shared values, should we look for the answers to these questions in the received texts of Armenian literature and historiography or in the anthropology of living communities?

The discussion of Armenian national identity has been hobbled by its inward focus, its rejection of comparative approaches and acquaintance with theories of ethnicity. The question has been posed with part of the answer already known: that the Armenians of today are essentially the same people that migrated into eastern Anatolia in the sixth century B.C. Armenians are a people who have existed in one form or another for at least 2,600 years, not only in their putative homeland but in countries around the globe. For all that time there has been a people called Armenian (*Hai* in their own language), and their most enduring feature seems to be that in spite of countless adversities they managed the singular feat of surviving with their language, church, and sense of nation intact.

The survival and continuous linguistic, religious, and physical existence is undeniable, but concentration on survival exclusively or primarily has led to unfortunate intellectual practices. Both historians and nonspecialists have held that the Armenians have been guided in all times and places by a single ideological motivation, that of self-determination or freedom or, after 314, preservation of their particular form of Christianity. Heroes and villains have been defined in their relation to those fundamental goals. The notion of a single explanatory formula for all of Armenian history or a unifying theme of purpose that links the Urartians to Tigran the Great, to the Bagratids, to Cilicia, to the genocide of 1915, and to Soviet Armenia, one suspects, is more a literary conceit than an accurate description of Armenia's complex, uneven, and fragmented history.

The idea shared by many Western and Soviet historians alike of a single purpose in Armenian history, whatever it might be in various accounts—survival, freedom, keeping the faith, independence—is closely tied to another unexamined assumption, that there has been through all time an Armenian "spirit," an immutable essence that has always characterized the Armenians. The very constancy that makes up the Armenian nature in such accounts is a reading back of the present national existence or consciousness into the whole past. Here is a simple historical teleology: the past leads to a foreordained present, the making of the modern Armenian nation.

Armenia is set against the "other," the *otar,* the outside world, and left out are the ways Armenians have been different in different times and different from one another at the same time.[4] The divisions among Armenians—for instance, among those who preferred the Gregorian Church, those westernizers who favored the Greek or Latin, and those earlier who sided with the Iranian Great Kings or Rome against the local Armenian dynast—illustrate not a single people with a clear national sense but rather an intricate, multifaceted society with conflicting loyalties, some to one great noble clan, others to an external power. Without much distortion modern readers of the medieval histories of Armenia easily depict the defenders of the Christian church as the national heroes, while those Armenians who sided with the Iranians are traitors. These early medieval histories lend themselves to such reinterpretations, for clerical historians, often clients of certain noble houses, represented those who defended the church or the just claims or particular nobles as patriots. While I would not go so far as to argue that my namesake Vasak Suni, the villain in Eghishe's account of the Armeno-Iranian wars of the fifth century, should be considered a national hero in the same sense as Vardan, the defender of the Armenian church against the attacks of the Sassanian king Yazkert, nevertheless Vasak's actions had not yet come to have the valence they would carry once the church was inextricably linked with the Armenian people.[5] A more contextualized reading of the events of 451 might note that in the "feudal-dynastic" social system of fifth-century Armenia, in which different noble houses moved back and forth between alliances with rival empires, the claims of a specifically Armenian versus Persian loyalty were far less imperative than they would become in the nineteenth or twentieth centuries.

An essentialist view of Armenians—that as a people they have always and everywhere possessed a core of discernible, ethnically determined qualities—has been for political nationalists the basis for their political ideology: the continuous existence of the Armenians as a historic people, their origins in the Armenian plateau, arms them with the right of self-determination, nationhood, and a historically sanctified claim to the territories that constitute Armenia. Because this view of Armenian history plays such an important political role for Armenians (as homologous views play for Georgians, Azerbaijanis, Turks, and other peoples), any attempt to dispute it, to decompose the collection of beliefs that make up this reading, must be done with care and sensitivity, with full awareness that such an investigation may be perceived as an attack on the very soul of the nation.

II

Whatever the advantages of such an organic view of history for nationalism, Armenian essentialism has reinforced exclusiveness, ethnic isolation, and divisiveness within the community. What is being proposed in these essays is a more open understanding of nationality, one determined equally by historical experiences and traditions and by the subjective will to be a member of a nation. A distinction is drawn between a national essence or spirit, features that do not stand up to historical analysis, and a national tradition, a cluster of beliefs, practices, symbols, and shared values that have passed from generation to generation in constantly modified and reinterpreted forms. Parts of this historical tradition are appropriated by each generation for its own purposes. For Armenians these traditions are in part the product of Armenian authors, from the great fifth-century historians through the *patmahair* (father of history) Movses Khorenatsi to Mikayel Chamchian and the poets, novelists, pamphleteers, and scholars of the last two centuries. They are also the result of lived experiences, which are then incorporated into the living tradition and the self-definition of the people. Elites, particularly intellectuals and political activists, construct the idea of nation and its attributes; teachers, journalists, and politicians carry it to the broader strata of the population; but common folk also shape the national tradition through their own ethnic traditions, their responses to the "word" from above.

Traditions do not necessarily reflect historical reality accurately but are always a selection that make up a preferred view of a people's past. Passed down without much reflection, and in part the conscious creation of innovators who select, embellish, and ritualize parts of the preferred past, these "invented traditions" gain influence and lasting power when they resonate something in the population. Nationality may be constructed, an "imagined community," but it is far from ever an imaginary community without roots in ethnographic and historic experiences.[6]

In the Armenian case, history has been a broken trail, and many lost stories and traditions had to be recreated or replaced. No nations, not even those like the English whose traditions seem to have survived over long periods of time and where archaic institutions appear still vital, have in fact preserved their history without loss and recreation. Memory is fallible even in situations where state structure, archives, and official historians help preserve the written record. Armenians were an extreme example of a people that had lost touch with previous phases of their civilization as states fell or fell apart, as populations migrated or were moved. In the absence of the state, continuity was maintained by the literate clerical elite. Yet the national literature was known to only a few, even as it continued developing in isolated monasteries, and Armenia as an idea or living concept was lost at times for the mass of the Armenians. Clerical intellectuals periodically rediscovered the ancient roots of the Christian people of eastern Anatolia and attempted to carry that knowledge back to the people. A key role was played by a small number of Catholic monks in Venice and Vienna, the Mekhitarists, who energetically revived Armenian learning at the end of the eighteenth century.[7] Rather than inventing Armenian traditions out of whole cloth, the Catholic fathers reprinted the nearly inaccessible works of the early medieval Armenian historians and wrote their own histories based on them.

The importance of this recovery cannot be exaggerated. Though its effects turned out to be far different from the originally religious mission of the Mekhitarist monks, their work did nothing less than lay the foundation for the emergence of secular Armenian nationalism. Yet that new national understanding was built on particular sources that the national writers constantly shaped and reshaped. In the subsequent development of the national tradition the emphases of the clerics were given new accents, but the writers constantly circled back to themes that had their origin in the classical Armenian texts. Robert W. Thomson, a scholar who has spent much of his life bringing the Armenian classic historians to an English-reading audience, has eloquently described the importance of these works for Armenians in other ages.

> [T]hree works stand out as being of very special importance. The *History* of Agathangelos, which describes the conversion of Armenia to Christianity; the *History* of Moses Khorenats'i, which describes the origins of the Armenian nation and its early history down to the time of Mashtots, inventor of the Armenian script; and the *History* of Elishe, which describes the resistance of Christian Armenians to religious persecution in the fifth century. Other histories may be of greater interest to modern scholars as sources for understanding Armenian culture in certain periods of change—that of Faustos Buzand, for example, which describes fourth-century Armenia and the conflicts between church and traditional pagan society. But Agathangelos, Moses Khorenats'i, and Elishe have a particular place in Armenian tradition as enshrining the received account of Armenian history: Armenia, a small country but of great antiquity where many many deeds have been performed (Moses); a nation converted to Christianity before others, where God's grace has been manifested (Agathangelos); a people steadfast in their faith, true to their ancestral traditions, and ready for martyrdom should larger and stronger empires attempt to suppress Armenian liberties (Elishe).[8]

Among the most consistent themes that can be isolated in the Armenian tradition are the convictions that Armenia is of great antiquity and value and that it has a special historic role to play. The very recording of the Armenian experience by Armenian authors from the fifth century to the present testifies to their belief that they hold a special place despite their small numbers. About the eighth century Moses Khorenatsi put it modestly, "Although we are a small country and very restricted in numbers, weak in power and often subject to another's rule, yet many manly deeds have been performed in our land worthy of being recorded in writing."[9]

Armenia's antiquity was a claim to a privileged position in the human story. Armenian origins were said to go back to Hayk, son of Torgom, great-grandson of Japeth, son of Noah himself. The Bagratid princes and kings of the eighth through eleventh centuries claimed to be of Jewish origin, related to King David, and, thus, linked to God's chosen people. In their own view Armenians were not just one Christian people but the people of the first Christian state; not just converts in the early fourth century but the recipients of the word of God from the apostles Thaddeus and Bartholomew.

The antiquity of the Armenians is well attested in the historical record. The first recorded reference to Armenia (Armina) dates to c. 520 B.C., in the inscription of Darius I at Behistun, which speaks of the Persian king conquering the Armenians with great difficulty in three battles. Thereafter Armenians are mentioned in the classical sources Herodotus, Strabo, and Xenophon. Speakers of an Indo-European language, the proto-Armenians migrated into eastern Anatolia, the Armenian Plateau, in the mid-sixth century B.C., just after the fall of the Urartian Empire. There they mingled with the indigenous peoples and eventually came under the sway of the great Persian empire of the Achaemenids to the east.

Modern Armenians trace their origins back to this ancient ethnogenesis. Perhaps there are genetic connections between this ancient people and some today living in Soviet Armenia, but having lived in a region of volatile East-West migrations, invasions, conquests, and brutal exterminations, modern Armenians are more the product of ethnic intermingling than they are the pure biologic heirs of Urartu. Their language is connected but also distant and different. In terms of basic culture and social structure, the two most fundamental aspects of a people, the differences between the original Armenians and the present ones are far greater than any similarities. What links the pagan Armenians of the Iranian frontier to the urban dwellers of Erevan or the farmers of Fresno is the idea that they are the same people, a sense of solidarity and communality that is the basis of any nation.

Up to the reign of the great king Tigran (95–55 B.C.), Armenians were in the process of original social and linguistic formation. The Proto-Armenians became an identifiable group with their own Iranian-style tribal structure and borrowed paganism. An almost exclusively rural society with minimal state organization, Armenians were ruled by a warrior class, an elite of pagan priests, and a rough kind of kingship. Insofar as there was political organization, it was highly decentralized with great autonomy for the emerging nobles.

By the time Rome expanded into eastern Anatolia and Caucasia, in Tigran's reign, this basically Iranian culture and society had taken on features of the Hellenic West. State structures, still rudimentary, were more developed. Trade with distant markets flourished, and urban life probably took on greater importance, though Armenians still did not have the feature that would stereotype them in modern times: the character of tradesmen and merchants. Though earlier Xenophon had noted that Armenian horses were valued far and wide, most trade for much of Armenian history was in the hands of outsiders. Armenians remained largely a peasant population with a small elite of nobles (*nakhararner*) and warriors loosely bound to their king. Even under Tigran, when Armenia briefly became a multinational empire, the state authorities had to contend with the persistence of more ancient forms of social organization—the clan loyalties built into the *nakharar* system.[10] These divisions among Armenians were a much more potent determinant in their fate than the relatively weak institution of kingship.

In no sense should ancient Armenia be seen as approaching a nation-state in the modern sense. A cluster of principalities (*nakhararutiunner*) that fought one another fiercely, the Armenian feudatories often allied with non-Armenian powers against their fellow Armenians. The story of the Arab patronage of the Bagratid family is a familiar one, as is the affiliation of the Mamikonians with Byzantium. Though political solidarity was weak among Armenians, there was a commonality of language, an attachment to territory, and fierce devotion to the national religion, first pagan, later Armenian Christian. Religion, whether the amalgam of Iranian and Greek deities that formed Armenian paganism or the particularized form of moderately monophysite Christianity that the Armenian Church adopted, was the primary identification of this people, coinciding roughly with the linguistic and territorial community.

By the early fourth century A.D., when the Armenian king Trdat led his people to Christianity (314 A.D.), Armenians can be said to have formed a unique, identifiable ethno-religious community, or what Anthony D. Smith calls an *ethnie*. The authors of the next century already testify to the possession of a complex of myths, memories, values, and symbols that fits Smith's notion of *ethnie*.[11] Their community was distinguished from those of their neighbors by a collective name; they shared a common myth of descent and history, a distinctive culture, language, and religion, all of which created a sense of solidarity and kinship.[12] The boundaries of their church coincided with the linguistic cultural community. Even as Armenians turned their cultural face to the West and adopted the universalistic religion of the Christians, they particularized it, made it their own, and defiantly distinguished themselves from the powerful Greek Orthodox empire to the west.

As the easternmost outpost of Christianity, Armenia took on a special role in the preservation of the faith, but for Armenians themselves rather than Christianity in general they fought to preserve the unique faith of the Armenians. Only during the Crusades did Armenians join in a wider movement of pan-Christian defense. Their usual stance was as a small, isolated nation, suffering and being martyred for Christ. From the battle of Avarayr (451) on, Armenians have been ready, in their view, to sacrifice themselves, like the Maccabees of ancient Israel, for the greater glory of God. In more modern times sacrifice has been directed at more mundane ends, but the sense of martyrdom has remained intact. As Leonardo Alishan has written, "Martyrdom became for the Armenians, as it had become for the Jews before them, an attempt to escape history, to rise above it, and by placing the historical event in a religious context, to reinterpret it and redefine 'victory'."[13]

The Armenians are not the only people in the world to commemorate, indeed celebrate, a battle lost as a great moral victory, but they certainly have done it longer than almost anyone else. For 1,500 years the one great day of the religious calendar has been Vardanants, the anniversary of the defeat and death of Saint Vardan and 696 men at Avarayr. Though the Persians won on the battlefield, the sacrifice that preserved Armenia for Christianity is seen as a victory. "The main problem is the preservation of Armenian traditions (*awrenk'*)," writes Thomson, "which include religious practices but are more comprehensive than the term 'religion' in a modern sense. For Ełishe, in the long run it is better to die than to compromise these traditions; to defend them and die for them is an act of spiritual virtue."[14] In subsequent centuries popular retelling of the Vardanants story would alter its meaning, until modern nationalists would see the sacrifice made for nationhood, for independence from foreign domination and cultural assimilation.[15] Much of the original religious meaning would be fused with the national, and in the hands of anticlerical revolutionaries the underlying theme of the necessary struggle and the need for sacrifice would be transformed into the violent politics of the twentieth century.

Premodern Armenians conceived of themselves primarily as a religious community, and much of what we take to be nationality today was contained in religious identification in earlier times. In the long years of Ottoman rule, that basically religious identification was institutionalized in the Armenian *millet,* the political formation through which the Armenians were governed indirectly by the sultan through the Armenian patriarch at Istanbul. Rather than language or ethnicity, religion defined a people (*millet*) in the Ottoman world.[16] In the Russian Empire as well, the Armenians were united into a single religious community under the religious and educational authority of the Catholicos at Echmiadzin. But with the emergence of a new national consciousness that emphasized the ethnic culture of the common folk, the vernacular languages of ordinary speech, and the need to engage the modern world politically, the very concept of the Armenians as a religious community was challenged by the more Western notion of secular nationality. At a time when most Armenians were poor peasants who knew little about their past, except the fragments passed down in the oral tradition and the religious messages of the clergy, the efforts, first of the Mekhitarist fathers and later of patriotic agitators, to "revive" lost traditions met with a frustrating silence. First, philologists, grammarians, and historians wrote for the small elite who could read and might have some interest in rather esoteric intellectual endeavors. But already the Mekhitarists reached out by opening schools, presenting plays, and providing a model of energy and dedication that inspired succeeding generations of patriots, even as they rejected the original religious (in this case Catholic) impulse of their forefathers.

By the fourth decade of the nineteenth century, intellectuals, both in Russia and Turkey, were shifting to an anticlerical, secular nationalism. No longer willing to discuss cultural and political issues in the language of martyrdom and sin, men like Khachatur Abovian, Mikayel Nalbandian, Stepan Vosgan, Grigor Otian, and Nahapet Rusinian, and later Rafael Patkanian, the novelist Raffi, and the journalist Grigor Artsruni, articulated a new vision of a historic Armenian nation, one with a history that stretched back millennia. Raffi wrote: "O fathers! O forefathers! I drink this glass, but not as a toast to your remains. Had you built fortresses instead of monasteries with which our country is full; had you bought guns and ammunition instead of squandering fortunes on holy urns; had you burned gunpowder instead of perfumy incense at the holy altars, our country would have been more fortunate than she is today. . . ." The Western Armenian Otian, not to be outdone by his Russian-Armenian colleagues, proclaimed: "Each hood of a *vardapet* (unmarried priest) hides a devil!" Stepan Vosgan, a participant in the revolutions of 1848 in France, exhorted his comrades in 1859: "Rally around the concept of *Haiastan* [Armenia] and not that of religion."

The claims of the secular patriots were a challenge to the most sacred of Armenian traditions and an attempt to create a new one. As extreme as their words were, however, the break with the past was not as complete as they may have thought. Sacrifice and dedication to the idea of Armenia remained central to their inspiration, but now it was to a concept of an Armenian nation rather than to an Armenian religion. Enlightenment remained a major concern, not, however, in terms of the light of God but of Western learning, modern science, the ideals of the French Revolution and the Russian intelligentsia, of revolution, freedom, and even socialism.

The revolutionary nationalists rejected one of the most common and unquestioned views of Armenian history, the one thing every Armenian knows if he or she knows nothing else: that the church was the institution that held the Armenians together through their long and troubled passage. This unifying theme of Armenian historiography survived the anticlericalism of the secular patriots, and even today many writers have been unable to liberate themselves from the evident truths of this version. Without inflicting bodily harm to this cherished notion, it is important to note that before the church was founded, Armenians existed for one thousand years. The church could be and has been both a unifying and divisive factor in Armenian life. Itself often divided, as it is today, the church has experienced schism, dissolution, corruption, and interference from rich and powerful community leaders. The exclusive hold of the Apostolic Church over Armenians has been threatened both by Catholic and Protestant missionaries from without and from Romanizing influences from within. Yet even when three or four rival centers of church power contended with each other for paramount influence, the traditions that the church upheld continued. Again, one might emphasize, rather than because of some ethnic essence or particular institutions, the Armenians continued through the preservation and renewal of their cultural tradition.

In those periods when Armenians managed to establish a political existence, as in the 300-year-long Cilician period (eleventh through fourteenth centuries) or the seventy years of Soviet Armenia, the Armenian political leaders, kings, and *nakhararner,* rather than the church, played the major role in consolidating and promoting the fortunes of the Armenians. The extraordinary importance of the church should more properly be limited to those long centuries and those places distant from the homeland, particularly in the diaspora and in the Ottoman *millet* system, where national political authorities ceased to function among Armenians and the church maintained the culture of its people. Ancient peoples survived into our centuries, not because of genetic superiority or the survival of their states, but because their cultures survived.[17] In this sense genocide, the killing of a people, may be less a threat to survival of an ethnicity than ethnocide, the systematic destruction of a culture.

The making of nations is far less the gathering together of peoples of like complexion than it is the promotion of common traditions and the solidification of culture. Nationality formation is an open-ended process, never fully complete, moving back and forth between consolidation and consciousness, assimilation and loss of cohesion. Awareness of historical experience remains the only guarantee against dissolution. As Milan Kundera said, "A small nation can disappear and knows it." In our century Armenians have come to the very brink of extinction, but instead of succumbing to despair and cultural nihilism they have incorporated even the most extreme of experiences, genocide, into their national tradition. In the late twentieth century the tragedy of 1915 along with a renewed identification and attachment to the homeland have become the major themes in the constantly changing national consciousness of diaspora and homeland Armenians.

PART ONE

IMAGINING ARMENIA

1 Armenia and Its Rulers

The assumption by many patriots among the Armenians is that a militant expression of national pride is the *sine qua non* for the survival of this small people as a nation. For such Armenians, nationalism—that is, the feeling of primary loyalty to one's ethnic group—is equivalent to virtue, and those, particularly among their ethnic brethren, who question this dedication to the "cause" are suspect as true Armenians. Whatever the last refuge of the scoundrel may be (and in my opinion patriotism has as good a claim as any), for Armenians universally their own sense of security about what constitutes being Armenian is constantly being challenged by counterclaims from the larger states in which the Armenians find themselves and by confusion about the historical experience of their own people. Armenians are a peculiar people; first, they form a nation (or at least a nationality) that lives within another nation; and second, they are a people often proud of their heritage about which they have not got the foggiest notion. A strident nationalism has been for many a compensation for rootlessness and a substitute for historical knowledge.

Nationality, nation, national consciousness, nationalism—all terms difficult to define with any rigor or consistency—have been discussed by social scientists as the products of the great transformations of the late eighteenth and nineteenth centuries. One of the most respected and innovative thinkers working on the questions of nationality and nationalism, Karl W. Deutsch, links the formation of nations to the historical process of political integration that increases communication on various levels among the members of an ethnic group.[1] Like other communication theorists of nationality, Deutsch begins with the social and technological processes that worked to mobilize individuals through increasing their possibilities and abilities to communicate with one another. Urbanization, social mobility, the rise of newspapers, the growth of education, the building of railroads and telegraph lines, and military conscription all contributed to more intense and intimate social communication. Deutsch distinguishes three levels of ethnic mobilization through the development of communication: the formation of a *people*, the making of a *nationality*, and the full creation of a *nation*. A *people* is defined as "a group of persons linked by complementary habits and facilities of communication" who gain "the ability to communicate more effectively, and over a wider range of subjects, with members of one large group than with outsiders."[2] Though language is obviously one aspect of that complementarity of communication, it is not the only one. Social habits, cultural preferences, physical proximity, and common fears and hopes also contribute to the members of a people preferring to communicate with other members of that people than with outsiders, as well as to the setting up of communication barriers with nonmembers, with those to whom Armenians refer to as *otarner* (foreigners), the Other.

This first and most basic aspect of a people—the increase in social communication that leads to identification of that people as a social group in contradistinction to others—requires the recombination of prior tribal and kinship alliances and the linking of these smaller groups together in a larger ethnic entity. Geographically a people usually occupies a larger area than a tribe, and this area is marked by a high level of economic, social, cultural, and political interdependence. In this area language is consolidated out of distinct dialects, and one dialect is selected by the literary elite as the official or orthodox form of the written language. A leading group or elite is formed in time, an elite to which most of the population defers and accepts as a model. Thus is a people created, "a community of shared meanings, or more broadly still, a group of people who have interlocking habits of communication."[3]

The second step, the formation of a nationality, is a relatively late historical development, generally reserved for the nineteenth and twentieth centuries, that is, the age of nationalism, the modern world. As Deutsch explains:

> In the age of nationalism a *nationality* is a people pressing to acquire a measure of effective control over the behavior of its members. It is a people striving to equip itself with power, with some machinery of compulsion strong enough to make the enforcement of its commands sufficiently probable to aid in the spread of habits of voluntary compliance with them.[4]

In this second step, the ethnic group becomes ethnically conscious, aware of its own importance, fearful of its own demise, anxious to provide comparative advantages to its members, willing to act in its own interests, able to organize itself into movements. A nationality is equipped with *national consciousness,* by which is meant simply the awareness of the value of a particular ethnicity, or its distinctiveness and characteristics. Under certain circumstances a nationality may also develop *nationalism*. By this I mean more precisely the political and cultural activization of an ethnic group or a leading part of that ethnic group, the mobilization of a nationality to achieve some cultural or political end, such as cultural autonomy, statehood, the recognition of its language by a government, and so on. Born of the social change and social mobility that has marked the last two centuries, nationalist movements have attempted to provide a comparative advantage for one ethnic group over competing groups. As Deutsch put it in a lecture at Harvard, nationalism is an effort to prevent an ethnic group from becoming an underclass and to promote that group to the position of a privileged class.[5]

Finally, there is yet a third step: the formation of a *nation* or perhaps a *nation-state*. For many nationalists this is the ultimate goal. In Deutsch's definition,

> A nation is a people who have hold of a state or who have developed quasi-governmental capabilities for forming, supporting, and enforcing a common will. And a nation-state is a state that has become largely identified with one people.[6]

As suggestive, even compelling, as Deutsch's model is, it is incomplete. The generation of shared meanings, feelings, and perceived interests cannot be derived directly from social processes or structures, shared experiences or felt dangers. Rather, experience is mediated and comprehended through the discourses of nationalism as they reach intellectuals, activists, and ordinary people. The making of nationalities and nations occurs in evolving social, political, and cultural contexts that smaller, colonized peoples have little power to shape; but how they interpret those contexts and give meaning to their own experiences within them are crucial to whether individuals and collectivities will consolidate around a particularistic understanding of ethnicity or assimilate into a large universalistic entity. From the time of the French Revolution the power of nationalist discourses, combined as they often have been with discourses of democracy and sovereignty, has effectively challenged rival ideas of the legitimacy of dynastically constructed empires, extraethnic religious communities, and subnational local loyalties. At the same time the construction of nationalities and nations has had to overcome other forms of affiliation and divisions of geography, dialect, religion, and class within what would become the nation.

Even the most casual acquaintance with Armenian history shows a rather dismal picture of internal division, conflict, isolation, and a monotonous litany of invasion, conquest, repression, deportation, and massacre. Armenians can console themselves with the thought that despite such horrors, they have managed to survive as a people for well over two thousand years, and unlike many of their neighbors at the beginning of Armenian history—the Hittites, the Medians, the Urartians, etc.—there is still an ethnic presence known as Armenian. Some scholars have argued, in fact, that Armenia's divisions may well have been her salvation, for few conquerors ever managed to hold sway over all of Armenia. There was always some part of the country that was relatively autonomous or independent, in which the more potent assimilationist pressures could be resisted. However, from the perspective of national consolidation, from the point of view of the formation of a nationality, Armenia's history provides more evidence of political and cultural disintegration than of national integration.[7]

As a mountainous country Armenia has been naturally divided into regions that have had little communication between them. This regional isolation has been reflected in the proliferation of classical and medieval kingdoms and principalities, in the feuds between various parts of Armenia, and in the difficulty of dynasts to establish a single, unified Armenian polity. It is also reflected in the multiplicity of Armenian dialects, some of which are incomprehensible to Armenians of other areas. Besides the two major literary languages, eastern and western Armenian, based respectively on Erevan and Constantinople dialects, Armenian writers have used other local variants: Sayat-Nova and Sundukian wrote in Tiflis dialect, Melik-Shakhnazarian in Karabagh dialect, and Patkanian in the dialect of Nor Nakhichevan. This lack of unity was particularly true for the darkest period of Armenian history, that long stretch from the fourteenth century, when the last Armenian kingdom in Cilicia was overrun and the Ottoman Turks established their rule over the bulk of Armenia, to the eighteenth century, when the liberation movement in eastern Armenia began to manifest itself.

On the eve of the Russian entry into Transcaucasia at the beginning of the nineteenth century, Armenians in Transcaucasia and Anatolia were a people divided in two major ways: geographically and by social class. Geographically, the Armenians of Armenia were divided by the frontier between the Persian and Turkish empires (which later became a three-way separation with the coming of the Russians to the Ararat Valley). But more than a geographical separation, the division into eastern and western Armenias was to have profound social and cultural effects on the peoples of these two regions (leaving Persian Armenia aside for the moment). The Armenians of Turkey, by the late nineteenth century, were significantly more "backward," that is, poorer, less well-educated, less urbanized, less aware of the outside world, than were their compatriots in Russian Armenia. Since the cities in which wealthy Armenians flourished, Constantinople and Smyrna, were hundreds of miles away from the villages of Armenia, the peasants of eastern Anatolia had little contact with their people's urban, commercial elite. The Russian Armenians, however, enjoyed a greater degree of physical security under tsarist rule than did the Anatolian Armenians who were frequently threatened by their Turkish and Kurdish neighbors.[8]

There were intellectual differences as well. In Russia, after a few generations, Armenians began to imbibe European culture through the Russian intelligentsia. They traveled north to Moscow and St. Petersburg, to Dorpat in the Baltic, and on to Germany to further their education. There was, in general, more social mobility in Russian Armenia than in Turkish Armenia, and the large cities of Tiflis, Baku, and Batumi provided an outlet for rural overpopulation. Here in the railroad workshops of Tiflis, the oil fields of Baku, and the refineries of the port of Batumi, Armenians made up an important segment of the Caucasian working class. By the early twentieth century these workers were influenced by the new radical intellectuals who had adopted socialism and nationalism as their expression of concern for the fate of their people. Caucasian Armenians thus had a relatively more secure life and somewhat easier access to urban life and Western developments than did the great mass of Armenians in eastern Turkey.

Just as in Transcaucasia, the great inroads of Western civilization in the Ottoman Empire occurred outside Armenia proper. The intelligentsia of the Turkish Armenians emerged not within historical Armenia but in the large cities of western Turkey. The western Armenian intelligentsia developed quite differently from their contemporaries in Caucasia. Young Armenians from Turkey were educated in France and Italy, influenced by Western literary movements, and developed a stronger liberal streak than the Russian Armenians. Their concerns were largely with the communities of Armenians in the cities of western Turkey and much less with their peasant compatriots in eastern Anatolia. This was a reformist intelligentsia that largely avoided the more violent revolutionary influences of the Caucasians. Interestingly enough, the Armenian revolutionary movement was imported into Turkey by Caucasian Armenians. While it is true that the very first Armenian party, the Armenakans (1885), was founded in Van, the more effective Hnchaks (1887) and Dashnaks (1890) were the creation of Russian Armenians.[9]

Besides these vertical, geographic divisions between eastern and western Armenia, there were horizontal divisions in each of these societies, class cleavages that distanced one part of society from another. Both Turkish and Russian Armenians lived in stratified societies, the elites of which were urban, cosmopolitan, educated, while the majority lived in a culture of poverty bounded by the limits of village life. One can say without exaggeration that while urban Armenians lived in nineteenth-century surroundings, Armenian villagers still lived as they had a hundred years earlier. For them there had been no French Revolution, no industrial revolution, and Western modes of life were largely unknown. The wealthy middle-class Armenians of Tiflis, Baku, Constantinople, and Smyrna, on the other hand, thrived as middlemen in societies made up of foreigners, and very often adopted the style of life and values of Europeans. This was the class with whom outsiders came into contact, and whose success in commerce and industry led to the familiar stereotype of the Armenians as wily businessmen, the "Jews" of the Middle East.

The Armenian business class provided a certain degree of political leadership to the Armenian urban communities. In Constantinople the wealthy *amiras* and *sarafs* controlled the Patriarchate, the institution through which the Armenian *millet* was governed, until challenged from below by the lower middle-class *esnafs* or craftsmen in the 1840s.[10] In Tiflis the wealthy *mokalakebi* ruled urban life through their monopolistic guilds, the *amkarebi*. In the late nineteenth century, when the Russian government extended the 1870 municipal reform to Transcaucasia, the Armenian men of property effectively took control of the city *duma* and mayorality.[11] But for all their political and economic clout, the Armenian bourgeoisie did not for the most part see itself as responsible for the welfare of the Armenian masses, the peasant majority and the new, emerging working class. Rather than developing a sense of national leadership, or placing themselves at the head of a national movement, the Armenian bourgeoisie tended to attach its fortunes to the fate of the imperial powers. Cooperation with tsarist and Ottoman officialdom had its rewards, of course, and the cautious bourgeoisie preferred to work within the existing imperial systems rather than support the growing nationalist revolutionary movements. The Hnchaks and Dashnaks found that they had to "shake down" the Armenian bourgeoisie by threatening it with terrorism in order to raise financial contributions to their cause. Thus, the familiar picture of nationalism as a product of the middle class must be modified in the case of the Armenians. Some of the earliest writings on the Armenians as a nationality came out of the business circles of the Madras Armenians in the 1770s; men like the rich merchant Shahamir Shahamirian and Movses Bagramian had called for the liberation of Armenia from foreign dominance. But more often, the businessmen of Constantinople or Tiflis, while perhaps eager for reforms, nevertheless were not enthusiastic about a nationalism that implied revolutionary struggle.

The physical, social, and psychological distance between the urban Armenian elites and the peasants was very great and was bridged only late in the nineteenth century by the small, radical intelligentsia that emerged from the middle and lower middle class.[12] In the absence of a "bourgeois" nationalism, a radical nationalism of the intelligentsia linked the future of all Armenians regardless of class or country in a common, sacrificial struggle.

The divisions among the Armenians in the nineteenth century were profound, and a cautious estimate might have been made that it would be nearly impossible to consolidate these disparate groups into a single mobilized nationality. The degree of social communication among the various parts of Armenian society was quite low for much of the century. There were no universally recognized leaders accepted by all sectors, although there was a general deference to the national church. It is, therefore, not surprising that the first national leaders came from the church—the various patriarchs of Constantinople, the Caucasian Nerses Ashtaraketsi, and most notably Khrimian Hairik.

How then did Armenians, scattered, divided, uneducated as they were, overcome their divisions and begin to consolidate as a nationality? To understand that process one must appreciate how national consolidation for a small people in the mountains of Caucasia and Anatolia was intimately connected with the developments that revolutionized European society—the dominion of market economies, industrialization, urban growth, the spread of popular education, and the rise of ethnic nationalism. The transmission of the revolutionary shifts in Western Europe to Armenians was made by Armenian businessmen who had long been in contact with Western Europe and had been among the most Europeanized elements in the Persian and Turkish empires. Armenian communities in Constantinople, Madras, Tiflis, Moscow, and elsewhere responded quickly to the new capitalist forms of doing business, to Western culture and education, and to the new awareness of ethnicity.

As an "age of revolution," the nineteenth century must be understood as more than a period of violent political change. In the century and a quarter from the French Revolution to the First World War, a series of rapid political, economic, and cultural changes took place that made the world of 1914 one of considerably more wealth, social mobility, and cultural variety than the world of 1789. These changes, as we all know, affected most immediately Western Europe and North America, but the influences of the industrial revolution, the new science, the nationalist stirrings of Western liberation movements were felt in Eastern Europe, in Russia, and eventually in the Turkish Empire. This was a century of nation-building in which new nation-states like united Germany and Italy emerged. The relatively slow-changing world of the preindustrial period gave way to a world in constant flux, and one of the products of this social change and social mobility was nationalism. Society was no longer as stagnant, no longer as predictable as it had been before the early nineteenth century. New possibilities had opened up; some people were rapidly moving up socially and economically, others were moving down. Various nationalities organized to protect themselves in this new competitive environment, to promote their interests against those of rival nationalities, and the Armenians too entered into this competitive arena and began to act to secure a place in the sun. They did this almost simultaneously with the Russians and other peoples of the Caucasus, but they acted long before their Turkish overlords were affected by the new nationalism.

At the most basic level the physical distance between Armenians, and particularly the isolation of the peasantry, lessened in the nineteenth century as new forms of transportation and communication appeared. The improvement of roads in Caucasia, and later the introduction of the telegraph and railroads, linked remote parts of the region with the cities of Baku, Tiflis, Batumi, and central Russia. At the same time the expansion of the market economy broke down the relative autarky of the village economies and brought them closer to one another and to the commerce and industry of the towns. Rural society with its limited range of trade and informal markets was transformed by the power of long-range commerce, the growing market in hired labor, and the elaborate division of labor and system of exchange associated with nineteenth-century capitalism. Mobility and intercourse changed the lives of Armenians who might never have had any contact with middlemen from the towns but now became involved in the flow of urban life. Villagers moved to town where they were hired by Armenian factory owners, and Armenian workers looked toward the paternalistic Armenian bourgeoisie for

guidance and protection. While social distinctions limited the degree of inti-
macy between the upper and lower levels among the Armenians, the new
urban scene provided the context for rival readings of this new experience.

A sense of nationality did not emerge automatically or without difficulty
from the complex and uneven metamorphosis that Armenians underwent in
the nineteenth century. People moved in a variety of directions at once—some
toward secularization and acculturation in the larger Russian world, others
toward identification with their class compatriots whether worker or bourgeois, and still others into a sense of community with other members of their
church and linguistic group. How the attitudes and preferences of different
people were shaped, how new understandings were created, cannot be understood without considering the rival interpretations that emerged from and
were imposed on the novel, multidirectional experience that people were undergoing.

According to a European proverb, "a nation is a group of persons united
by a common error about their ancestry and a common dislike of their neighbors."[13] Armenians had long felt themselves to be a distinct people, with their
own language and literature, a Christian people in a sea of Muslims. Both
family and church reinforced and maintained this sense of Armenians as a
separate ethnoreligious community. In the nineteenth century Armenian intellectuals began to articulate a new idea of what it meant to be an Armenian,
a secular myth appropriate for the "modern" world. The image of the Armenian as an ethnic rather than a religious figure, as a creature of culture with
political claims, had two principal sources, one internal, the other external.
Within the Russian and Ottoman empires nationalist poetry and prose
emerged as part of a literary and journalistic renaissance among educated
Armenians in Istanbul, Izmir, Tiflis, and Moscow. In the second third of the
century the first journals and novels in the vernacular Armenian and the first
political expressions of Armenian aspirations appeared in the popular press.[14]
The new and influential secular intelligentsia saw their role as serving the
people rather than their church or prince. Often the product of religious
schools, these young Armenians made contact with the broad intellectual
trends of Europe in Russian, German, and French universities. They returned
home to teach school, write in and edit the journals and newspapers in their
native languages, and eventually to form secret societies with grandiose plans
for the future of Armenia. These nationalist intellectuals formed the social
bridge between the middle class out of which they emerged and the Armenian
lower classes with whom they identified their own aspirations. At first the
intelligentsia was moderate in its methods, but when it encountered resistance
from Armenia's imperial masters it turned ever more radical.

The external source of Armenian consciousness came from the very imperial powers who had so long ruled the Armenians and considered them to be
among the most loyal of their subjects. The Russians and the Turks in the last
quarter of the century forced all Armenians, even those most desirous of

assimilation, to recognize themselves as a separate people by discriminating against Armenians and persecuting them. Many Armenians in the Caucasus had become Russified in the congenial rule of Alexander II (1855–1881). Uninterested in their own ethnicity, they had adopted Russian names, learned to communicate in Russian, and viewed Russian culture as their avenue toward European civilization. But as a result of the policies of the Russian government toward Armenians in the last decades of the century, Armenians were compelled to see themselves as different and to organize resistance against their own destruction. As a consequence of the need for protection, the leadership of the Armenians shifted from the church and urban bourgeois elite to the growing number of revolutionary nationalists.

It is very difficult to characterize in any precise way the nationalism of Armenians in the nineteenth century. The Armenian people, as we have seen, were fragmented along geographic, political, and class lines. The national feeling of Armenian merchants in Constantinople might be quite different from that of peasants in Karabagh or students in St. Petersburg. What can be said in a general way is that as more and more Armenians came into contact with other nationalities in the growing cities of Caucasia and western Turkey, as they felt the impact of Western concepts of nationality and nationhood, their own self-concept shifted from that of a religious community to that of a nationality with a common history and cultural constants.

Under the Ottoman *millet* system and according to the Russian *Polozhenie* (Statute) of 1836, Armenians were considered to be a religious community with special governing privileges vested in the clergy. Naturally, the new, secular view of Armenianness developed by the intelligentsia was resisted by the clergy, but intellectuals like Nikoghos Zoraian, Nahapet Rusinian, Grigor Otian, and Khachatur Abovian fought the battle on the front of language and won the right to publish, not in the classical Armenian (*grabar*) of the church as before, but in the language spoken by the people (*ashkharabar*). From its first stirrings, Armenian nationalism contained a definite anticlerical streak.

Another major characteristic of Armenian nationalism was its differential regard for the two empires in which Armenians primarily lived. Russia, despite its autocratic government and failure to fulfill the promises of an autonomous *Armianskaia oblast'* (Armenian district), was regarded as a liberator by many Armenians. Hopes had been laid on the Russians for centuries, and in the nineteenth century Russophile liberals like Grigor Artsruni, the long-time editor of the Tiflis newspaper *Mshak* (Cultivator), urged the Russians to undertake the military occupation of Turkish Armenia. The height of pro-Russian feeling was reached when the Russians defeated the Turks in the War of 1877–1878 and brought part of Armenia (Kars and Ardahan) into the Russian Empire. Even after the Russian government became openly anti-Armenian, in the 1880s and 1890s, Armenian nationalist revolutionaries refused to concentrate on fighting the Russian autocracy and instead directed their activities against the Ottoman Empire.

In stark contrast to the lingering pro-Russian feeling among Armenians, the attitude toward the Turks was one of bitter hatred if not racial contempt. There was little expectation in the second half of the century of relief from the sultan's government without outside pressure from one or more of the Great Powers. Whereas Russians were seen as Europeans, the Turks were regarded by many Armenians as an Asiatic people, an inferior and uncultured people.

A third characteristic of the Armenian nationalist image was that Armenians were European. Inspired by European thought, the Armenians adopted European nations as the model for Armenians and speculated that European support for Balkan liberation could eventually be extended to the Armenians. Armenian national aspirations, which ranged from simple amelioration of life in Turkey to autonomy or full independence (there was no programmatic agreement on ends), were intimately involved in the international competition of the European powers. In the last decades of the nineteenth century, the fate of this relatively obscure people was placed on the agenda of numerous meetings of European diplomats. The "Armenian Question" had been born.[15]

A fourth characteristic of Armenian nationalism was that after the initial literary and journalistic period, it very rapidly became revolutionary and socialist. Influenced by Russian revolutionary populism (*narodnichestvo*), young Armenians in the Caucasus formed secret circles in the 1880s to discuss the liberation of Armenians across the Arax in Turkey. In August 1887 the Hnchak (Bell) Party was founded in Geneva, and three years later the Armenian Revolutionary Federation (Dashnaktsutiun) was formed in Tiflis. Revolutionary nationalists placed themselves at the head of an all-class, all-nation movement based on individual terrorism and self-sacrifice. Their socialism proved to be unpopular among Turkish Armenians and alienated many middle-class elements in Russia and Europe. Nevertheless, the young intellectuals who formed the backbone of the movement refused to give up their allegiance to socialism, a doctrine that for them represented the most progressive European ideology available. Socialism made the Armenian cause part of an international movement, but it also created great distrust of Armenians on the part of European political leaders.[16]

For much of the last two hundred years it has seemed a natural, if not inevitable, process that various ethnic groups enter the political arena, develop nationalist ideologies, movements, and parties, and eventually, through a revolutionary struggle, "liberate" themselves from a rule of an imperial power and form their own sovereign nation-state. History seems to have blessed this development and awarded it an incontestable legitimacy. But overlooked by some observers of this process is an alternative scenario for emerging ethnic entities within a multinational empire, which we might call the "imperial idea." By this I mean the view of some "enlightened" officials and rulers, both in Turkey and Russia (as well as in other imperial states), that reforms could be implemented that would make possible the civil equality of all subjects regardless of nationality, religion, or race, that a cosmopolitan, multinational society could be developed that would both preserve the empire and guarantee the rights of subject minorities. In Turkey this imperial ideal was referred to as *Ottomanism;* in Russia it was implied in the work *Rossiiskaia* (in contrast to *Russkaia*).

First in the Hatt-i-Sherif of Gulhane of 1839 and later in the famous Hatt-i-Humayun of 1856, the Ottoman Empire, responding to British pressure, embarked on the Tanzimat (Order) reform movement. The thrust of the reforms was to establish equality among all Ottoman subjects and to end the discrimination against non-Muslims. These decrees were hardly a constitution, for no limits were placed on the powers of the sultan. Indeed, as Turkish Foreign Minister Mustafa Reshid Pasha said at the time (1841): "It would be quite impossible to govern by constitutional methods a people as ignorant and incapable of understanding its true interests as ours."[17]

Three problems arose in Turkey as a result of this kind of ecumenical reform:

1. Many Turks, particularly religious elements, resented the disturbance of the "natural order" of social hierarchy caused by these foreign innovations. Equality was French, after all, not Turkish.
2. A habit developed among the Armenians, Greeks, and other Christian minorities in Turkey "to look to Europe for support in securing the promised equality, rather than to an Ottoman government which had issued the decree only under pressure."[18]
3. Most important, the reforms were never fully applied. The Ottoman Empire seemed resistant to legislated change from above; and repeated failures led to resentment, frustration, and ultimately extralegal resistance from the minority peoples.

In theory, at least, Ottomanism remained a possibility, but in practice it was never able to overcome (1) the inertia of the political system and (2) the emergence of Turkish nationalism. In the thirty-year reign of the "Bloody Sultan," Abdul Hamid II (1876–1909), Ottomanist ideas, such as those of Prince Sabaheddin, were bypassed in favor of the nationalist ideas of people like Ahmet Riza. "Islamism" became a weapon of the state against foreign intervention and minority nationalisms.[19] Turkish nationalism, which developed in part as a reaction to the nationalism of the Christian minorities, was, like Armenian nationalism, heavily influenced by thinkers who lived and were educated in the Russian Empire. The Crimean Tatar Ismail Bey Gasprinski and the Azerbaijani writer Mirza Fath Ali Akhundzade inspired Turkish intellectuals in the late nineteenth and early twentieth centuries. Unlike Ottomanism, Turkish nationalism provided no place for the non-Turkish nationalities except one of subordination. Whereas Armenian rights and even autonomy might have been acceptable to Ottomanist liberals, it was anathema to Turkish nationalists, for it meant the disunity of their people and their country. For these young Turkish nationalists the word "Turk" took on a positive ethnic connotation that it had not had in earlier usage, and the term *millet* turned from defining a religious community to mean nation. Once Turkish nationalism became an effective political movement, a clash between it and the newly politicized Armenians was increasingly likely, even inevitable.

In the Russian Empire the attitude toward nationalities varied greatly. Peoples like the Jews or Poles suffered discrimination sanctioned by law, while Baltic Germans enjoyed a variety of privileges. For most of the nineteenth century Russification was limited to bureaucratic efforts aimed at administrative uniformity, and officials hoped that smaller nationalities would in time be peacefully assimilated into larger ones. Alexander II told the Baltic Germans in 1867: "I have always maintained that it is ridiculous to criticize someone because of his origins."[20] The emperor's tolerance toward minorities was evident in his elevation of the Armenian general Mikhail Loris-Melikov to the highest administrative post in his empire. Armenians did well through the first three quarters of the nineteenth century. Their activities as merchants received state backing, and the Armenian church was given a degree of autonomy and control over education in the *Polozhenie* of 1836. Until the 1880s it seemed possible that tsarism would tolerate ethnic diversity and avoid the pitfalls of a forced assimilation.

However, Russian nationalism was steadily growing as a political force. In the conservative newspapers and journals of Nikolai Pogodin, Mikhail Katkov, Ivan Aksakov, and others, one could read chauvinist arguments in favor of Russifying the peripheries of the empire. Even the liberal lawyer Spasovich called for "smoothing away as much as possible the mixed character which exists in the borderlands of Russia, installing uniformity in the extreme . . . in every possible way: in institutions, in language, in the church, in speech, in costume, in food."[21] Whereas before the death of the Tsar-Liberator Russification had meant only an attempt at administrative uniformity, after 1881 it came to include the Russianizing of schools and culture and a general attack on minority institutions and languages. In 1885 Armenian schools were closed by the government. In the 1890s various charitable and cultural organizations were attacked, and laws eliminated teaching in languages other than Russian. While his father had employed an Armenian to bring order to his empire, Alexander III (1881–1894) responded to vicious, chauvinistic, arguments about Loris-Melikov being an "Asiatic," not a "true Russian," and therefore untrustworthy. The emperor's lieutenants in the Caucasus made it nearly impossible for non-Russians to enter the state civil service. Finally, and most provocatively, in 1903 the state seized the properties of the Armenian church. For the Russian government under the last two tsars, the Armenians were a subversive people bent on revolution, a "fifth column" with doubtful loyalties. Whereas in the past centuries Armenians had been valued by both the Russian and Turkish states as people with international commercial relations and cultural ties to Europe, by the early twentieth century those international connections were suspect, and the Armenians were perceived as a rootless people alien to the empires in which they lived.[22]

Yet Armenian Russophilia never completely dissipated. The Artsruni tradition of looking at the Russians as potential liberators continued even through the dark years of the late nineteenth century. After the first Russian revolution (1905–1907), the liberal and pro-Armenian viceroy of the Caucasus, Vorontsov-Dashkov, helped to mend relations between the tsarist government and the Armenians. On his initiative the church properties were returned, instruction in local languages was reintroduced into schools, and the state service was once again opened to non-Russians. The liberal ecumenical tendency represented by Vorontsov-Dashkov was not unchallenged, however, and Russian nationalists continued to stir up anti-Armenian sentiments among the other Caucasian peoples. The period of governmental persecution and the growing hostility in Caucasia toward Armenians contributed to the growing support for the revolutionary movement, particularly for the Dashnaktsutiun, which led the struggle for restoration of Armenian church properties.

By the early twentieth century the Armenians of Transcaucasia and, to a lesser extent, in eastern Turkey had become a mobilized nationality. No longer a simple ethnographic conglomerate, the Armenians now had a recognized political leadership in the revolutionary parties, ever clearer aspirations (reforms, autonomy, modernization, socialism), and important allies within the empires in which they lived (Vorontsov-Dashkov and, for a while, the Young Turks). But the very process by which Armenians had achieved a degree of national cohesion and an articulated nationalism had created enormous dangers for them. Armenian nationalism and claims to territory had provoked the national hostility of neighboring peoples. The Georgian nationalists resented the material and political power of the Armenians in Tiflis and other Georgian cities. The Azerbaijanis, a people who had developed little ethnic consciousness until the early twentieth century, were mobilized by the perceived danger of armed Armenians in their midst. The Armeno-Azerbaijani battles of 1905 did much to shape ethnic hatreds in Baku and Elisavetpol. In the Ottoman Empire Turkish nationalism excluded the Armenians from the new Turkish order contemplated, and the Kurds, antagonized by the Armenian attempts to ameliorate their situation, engaged in ferocious massacres of Armenians. One nationalism begat a competing nationalism. One nationality's claims to a better position stimulated rival claims by its neighbors. The solution to these rival claims might have been a denationalized empire, but neither the tsarist autocracy nor the Ottoman state proved capable of establishing an imperial system free from chauvinism and discrimination. As the crisis developed, the conflict among the peoples of Asia Minor and Transcaucasia became entangled in the world crisis that led to World War I. The solution became the final solution—an attempt by the Turks to eliminate the Armenians physically and a design by the Russians to rule an Armenia without Armenians.

The compromising of the ecumenical imperial ideal and the resulting clash of nationalisms put the Armenians in the gravest peril of their long history. Both the Russian and the Ottoman governments were faced with an increasingly militant Armenian population with a revolutionary leadership at a time when the Armenian Question had ceased to be simply an internal problem and had become an international issue. The Russians sought to disarm the revolutionaries through police repression and a huge political trial of the Dashnaktsutiun (1912), but the Turks went much further. The "Sick Man of Europe" dealt with Armenians in an increasingly brutal manner, through military attacks, massacres, and eventually through a policy of genocide.

Historians who have dealt with the Armenian massacres have generally seen them as resulting from Turkish racism and barbarity or as being provoked by Armenian revolutionaries. I would like to argue that both of these views are simplistic and tendentious. In order to understand the causes of the Hamidian massacres of the 1890s and the genocide of 1915, one must consider a hierarchy of preceding developments:

1. The failure of reform in the Ottoman Empire eliminated the possibility of an internal, nonrevolutionary solution to the plight of the Armenians. Frustration with legal alternatives led to the formation of revolutionary parties. If one takes the view that the Armenians are to blame for what happened to them because they organized resistance, then one is simply arguing against the notion that people have the right to fight against an oppressive state and must accept whatever horrors an established government offers.

2. The activities of Armenian revolutionaries stimulated responses from Turkish authorities, which in turn provoked more resistance from the Armenians. A cycle of violence was created that involved more and more people and produced more and more victims. Foreign protest about Turkish atrocities only antagonized the Turks and encouraged the Armenians.

3. In eastern Anatolia a brutal competition for land and local power developed among the three principal peoples in the area—the Armenians, the Turks, and the Kurds. Encouraged by revolutionary leaders, Armenian villagers refused to pay the customary taxes to Kurdish tribesmen. Resistance led to repression. The Turks used the Kurds to control the area, but the Kurds used their military units, the Hamidieh, to massacre Armenians. Political disorder and unchecked military power led to chaos and the collapse of any semblance of law. A state of war existed between the Muslims and the Armenians as the government abdicated its responsibilities.

4. Finally, strategic considerations motivated the Turkish government to end the perceived Armenian threat to their northeastern frontier. During World War I, faced with the Russian Army, the Young Turks decided to disarm, uproot, transport, and eliminate the Armenians in eastern Anatolia. This policy was equivalent to the murder of a people, to genocide, and at least 600,000 to 1,500,000 Armenians perished in the death marches, executions, and battles of 1915.

War between Turkey and Russia always posed a danger to the Armenians, as well as an opportunity. Many Armenians in the summer of 1914 could remember the war of 1877–1878 when the Russians had annexed parts of Turkish Armenia and thousands of refugees had followed the tsarist troops back into Transcaucasia. Again it appeared possible that the Russian steamroller might sweep the whole of the Armenian plateau into the Romanov grasp. Armenians in Caucasia were enthusiastic about liberation by Russian troops. The Catholicos Kevork appealed to the tsar to undertake the protection of Armenian Christians in Turkey. Prominent Armenian politicians like Tiflis mayor Aleksandr Khatisian and the Dashnak Hagop Zavriev urged the formation of Armenian volunteer units to fight alongside the Russians against the Turks. But on the other side of the frontier, the Turkish Armenians were in a most exposed position. To many Turks they seemed to be a subversive force more loyal to Turkey's enemies than to the land in which they lived. The Dashnaktsutiun, meeting in congress in Erzerum, pledged that Armenians in Turkey would aid the Turks in a war with Russia, but the party refused to give any guarantee about Armenians in Russia.[23] Thus when war broke out between Turkey and Russia in November 1914, Armenians were fighting on both sides of the front.

At first the Turkish armies led by Enver Pasha did well against the Russian army of the Caucasus, advancing up to Sarikamish. Enver's plans to establish a Pan-Turkic state stretching into the Caucasus and even Central Asia seemed a realizable dream. But the bitter winter in Armenia caught the Turks unprepared, and early in 1915 the Russians pushed them back deep into Anatolia. Enver lost nearly three-quarters of his army, perhaps as many as 78,000 killed. It was at this juncture, as the Russians penetrated into Turkish Armenia, as the Russian foreign minister Sazonov told the State Duma that his government planned "the complete liberation of Armenia from the Turkish yoke," that the Young Turk triumvirate in Istanbul planned the deportation and extermination of the Armenians.

The Turkish actions against the Armenians were taken in desperation and panic. Not only were the Russians advancing in the east and the British and French navies threatening the capital, but the Armenians in Van had risen in revolt. The response of the government was brutal: on April 24, 1915, 235 prominent Armenian intellectuals and politicians were arrested and exiled. In the next few months thousands of their countrymen were thrown out of their homes and either immediately executed or sent on deportation marches into the Syrian desert. By this inhuman policy the Turks tried to eliminate a people who had lived in eastern Anatolia for nearly a thousand years before the Turks had arrived. This was their "final solution" to the Armenian Question, their last effort to secure Turkey for the Turks and save their empire. When the Russian troops reoccupied Van in September 1915 and moved into Mush and Bitlis in February–March 1916, they entered empty towns. The Armenians whom they had come to liberate were gone, many never to return. The Turks failed to save their empire or to establish a Pan-Turkic state; the Young Turk government would eventually fall. But the Armenians did not come back to the Armenian plateau. Scattered and slaughtered, they regrouped in Transcaucasia. Now a country of refugees, starvation, and disease, Caucasian Armenia was the only part of historic Armenia to survive the war with significant numbers of Armenians located on Armenian soil. It was here, around Erevan, that the Armenians would attempt to turn themselves from a nationality bereft of territory and material wealth into a nation with a secure future.

2 Images of the Armenians in the Russian Empire

Living through the dynamic social changes of the nineteenth century, the Armenians of Caucasia were not alone undergoing a complex transformation during the imperial period. Their neighbors, the Georgians and Azerbaijanis, and their conquerors and rulers, the Russians, also were beginning the transition into modern times with the concomitant evolution of intellectual life, political forms, capitalist relations, and increasingly importantly, of urban society. The images of the Armenians were changing, as were the Armenians and the viewers. Not surprisingly, images superseded one another, with newer views becoming dominant but with the older views remaining, like an afterimage, influencing what was now thought to be seen. The power of preconceptions, projections, and stereotypes shaped how Russians, Georgians, and Azerbaijanis viewed Armenians, despite changes that rendered some of the older images less relevant. At the same time, the inability of the Armenians themselves to affect their image among the non-Armenians is a pathetic reminder of how little of a small people's history depends on its own will and ambitions.

For the last two centuries the fortunes of the large majority of the Armenian people and of Armenia itself have been intimately connected to the fate of the Russian Empire and its Soviet successor. Russian policy toward the Armenians fluctuated in the imperial period from declarations of protection for fellow Christians to persecution of a newly conscious national minority. The shifts in Russian perceptions of the Armenians were contingent on both the changes in Russia's interests in Caucasia and the developments taking place among the Armenians themselves. In general, Russian images of the Armenians fell into three major types: the image of the Armenian as Christian, as commercial, and as conspiratorial. The Christian image linked the Armenians suffering under Muslim rule to their Orthodox protectors in the north; the image of the men of commerce also served for the most part to tie the Armenians to the expanding economic world of tsarist Russia; but the image of the conspiratorial revolutionary reflected a new reality, one of opposition and rebellion, which deeply alienated the Russians from their Armenian subjects. To a certain degree each of these images superseded the former in the eyes of the state, though never entirely. At the same time the state in its policies helped to sharpen one or another of these images and to accelerate the development of forces that gave the final image a dangerous reality.

The perception of a national minority by the Russian autocratic state was an extremely important political fact for that minority and could determine whether that group would benefit or suffer from the enormous power of their rulers. From the late Middle Ages Muscovy was a "service state" in which the privileges and rights of the various social estates were linked to merit as determined by the monarch. No one in autocratic Russia, not even the serf-owning nobility, held its property and privileges as a matter of natural right or by virtue of a constitution. Nobility was conferred, at least in theory, because of services rendered to the ruler. The privileges granted to merchants and townspeople were contingent on the functions they performed in the economy. No nationality held any rights to religious tolerance, ethnic autonomy, or national self-determination. All non-Russian peoples did well to heed the blunt statement of Grand Duke Vasili II on the position of subjects before the autocratic monarch: "*Vse kholopy*" (All are slaves). Whatever privileges or protection might be granted by the sovereign to a national minority or even to Great Russians themselves depended entirely on the will of the absolute ruler. Thus, the position of the Armenians was contingent on the perceptions of Russian officialdom. If, as in the mid-nineteenth century, Armenians were considered useful or virtuous, they would be rewarded with state support and new liberties. If, however, as in the last decades of the empire, they were perceived as enemies of order, their privileges and even their property were threatened.

Contact between Armenians and Russians dates back to the tenth century at the court of the Byzantine emperor Basil II. When Kiev joined the Christian world at the end of the tenth century, Prince Vladimir married Anna, the sister of Basil II. Both were members of the so-called Macedonian dynasty, which was of Armenian origin. In succeeding centuries Armenian merchants traded in Russia through their base in the Crimea, and in the later Middle Ages Armenians established themselves as traders and craftsmen in Moscow and Astrakhan. Thus, long before Russians ruled over a part of Armenia their sporadic contacts with Armenians established clearly two principal sources of Armenian identification—commerce and Christianity. These two features of the Armenians were, of course, related in a significant way. As Christians in the Muslim world, Armenians were strategically located to engage in trade with Christians outside the Turkish and Persian empires. Because they were stateless, cosmopolitan people of trade, this class of Armenians was frequently compared with the Jews. The ambivalence implied in such an image lingers with the Armenians to the present day.

In the mid-seventeenth century relations between the Russian Empire and the Armenians began to take on a new and more sustained character as Russo-Persian trade picked up and as the *meliks* (petty princes) of the Caucasus joined with the energetic Catholicos of Echmiadzin, Hakob Jughaetsi, to seek allies for a struggle against their Persian overlords. Encouraged by the decline of Safavid power, the Armenian leaders sent deputations to the Georgian king, to the Pope, the Holy Roman Emperor, the king of Poland, and finally to the Muscovite court to solicit aid in an anti-Persian campaign. The Armenian representatives, Israel Ori and Minas *vardapet,* came as suppliant fellow Christians, the victims of infidel oppressors asking to be assisted in their liberation, and it is significant that their efforts were directed to a variety of Christian courts. They made little distinction between the Catholic monarchs of Austria and Poland and the Orthodox tsar of Russia. The historians G. Ezov, Leo, N. Karamian, and Ashot Hovhannisian have argued that European aid seemed a better prospect to the Armenians than Russian assistance, but, as P. T. Harutiunian has claimed, a "Russian orientation" was already developing among some Armenian merchants in the latter half of the seventeenth century. As early as 1667–1673, the Armenian trading company of Julfa had signed a commercial agreement with the Muscovite government.[1] Armenians soon controlled the silk trade from Persia through Russia to Europe. Given that these Persian-Armenian merchants were neither independent nor free traders but agents of the Persian shah and the silk producers, Russian policy under Peter the Great was aimed at protecting, patronizing, and winning over these silk traders in order to use them to develop commerce and silk production for the benefit of Russia. Such patronage led in time to the shift of allegiance of some Armenian merchants to the Russians. Once again the Armenians as Christians and merchants made them congenial allies for Russia.

Peter's interest in the Caucasus was based on his overall commitment to the economic development of his empire. Having concluded a pleasing peace with the Swedes in 1721, he turned almost immediately to planning a campaign against the Persians along the Caspian. Aware that the Christian leaders of Georgia and Caucasian Armenia were anxious to join forces with the Russians, Peter set out from Astrakhan in July 1722. It would be wrong to conceive of the emperor as a crusader for Christian liberation, motivated primarily by his love for the unfortunate Armenians and Georgians. A secular and pragmatic ruler, Peter correctly perceived an opportunity for territorial expansion and economic rewards at the expense of a weakened Persia. But at the same time it would be a mistake to caricature the tsar as a cynical manipulator of Armenian and Georgian hopes for relief. Rather, the interests of the empire and those of the Caucasian Christians for the moment coincided, and as long as these interests were compatible Peter could act without further delay to aid his Christian allies. The historian Laurence Lockhart might overstate Peter's concerns for the Christians, but he is essentially correct in his assessment of Peter's motives:

> His aims were at first purely commercial, as he wished to divert through his own country the rich transit trade in silk and other commodities between Persia and the West through Aleppo and Smyrna. He was also anxious to obtain cotton from Turkistan for his newly founded industries. . . .
> An excellent trait in Peter's character was his wish to champion the cause of the Christian minorities in Persia, of whose trials and tribulations he had doubtless heard much from Alexander Archilovich [a Georgian prince who lived near Moscow, the grandson of Vakhtang V of Kartli] and other Georgians, as well as from Armenians.[2]

The campaign, of course, proved to be a disaster both for Peter, who lost 10,000 men, and for the Caucasian Christians, whose alliance with Russia and rebellion against Persia encouraged the Turks to invade eastern Caucasia. In 1724 Peter abandoned his Christian supporters in Transcaucasia by signing a treaty with the Ottomans partitioning the formerly Persian holdings in Caucasia and leaving most of Georgia and Armenia in Turkish hands. "Great numbers of Christians" voted with their feet to cross the new frontier and settle in the Russian areas. Clearly here were limits to Russian concerns for the Armenians, and Russian support was contingent on the coincidence of interests of the minority Christians and the Orthodox empire.

In their efforts to legitimize the present links between Russia and Armenia, Soviet historians have made much of the Russian orientation of the eighteenth-century meliks of Karabagh. But two hundred years ago the Russian option was only one of several for Armenian leaders. In the complex and turbulent politics of the late Safavid Persian Empire, the various Christian princes of the borderlands maneuvered among Persian factions, Turkish invaders, Georgian kings, and hopes for Russian and European aid. While some meliks sided with the Russians, others preferred the Persians and still others the Turks. Joseph Emin, the traveler and author of a unique enterprise to liberate the Armenians, sought a Georgian solution through the intervention of Erekle II. While in the nineteenth and twentieth centuries an image of the Armenians as depending on Russian liberators would itself become a powerful force cementing loyalty to the empire, in fact the Russian orientation was neither a consistent attitude of Caucasian Armenians nor a widespread movement among the majority of Armenians.

Still, the distinct image of Armenians as oppressed Christians longing for Russian protection did emerge ever more sharply in the eyes of the Russians in the eighteenth century. Emissaries to the court of Saint Petersburg and frequent communications reminding Russians of past pledges of assistance kept alive the image of the suppliant Christian Armenian. In a letter to the

Russian monarch, the Karabagh melik Avan-Yuzbashi affirmed boldly: "We will fight until that time when we will enter the service of the tsar, and all will perish to the last one but we will not leave Christianity; we will fight for our faith."[3] Such expressions of fidelity from a distant and exotic land inspired both policy and poetry. The first mention of an Armenian in Russian literature appeared in 1778 in an obscure poem by an obscure poet, V. Petrov, who listed the Armenian as one of the peoples who recognize Catherine the Great (1762–1796) as their "mother." The date of the poem is significant, coming four years after the Treaty of Kuchuk-Kainarji brought Catherine's first war with the Ottoman Empire to a close and affirmed the empress's right to intervene in Ottoman affairs in the interests of Christian minorities. The late 1770s and early 1780s were a time of renewed interest in the Caucasus. Catherine's jeweler, the Armenian Ivan Lazarev, built an Armenian church in Saint Petersburg (1779) and held a series of discussions with Bishop Hovsep Argutinskii and Catherine's chief minister, Prince Grigorii Potemkin, about the possibility of Armenian liberation. Around the same time painted images of Armenia were provided for aristocratic Russians by M. M. Ivanov and Gavriil Sergeev, who drew the ruins of Armenian churches and scenes of Erevan, Tiflis, and Echmiadzin. Already, a romantic vision of the Caucasus as a wild and exotic land was provided in the works of Radishchev, Derzhavin, and Zhukovskii. The Empress herself revived Peter the Great's policy of patronage and encouragement of the Armenians, and in 1779 she granted Armenians living in Russia "rights and advantages equal to the Russians." As a group considered reliable in contrast to the neighboring Muslims, Armenians were permitted to settle in the newly acquired lands along the Black Sea, in Crimea, and at Nor Nakhichevan. Catherine extended Russian protection over eastern Georgia (Kartli-Kakheti) in 1783 and recognized the existing privileges there of all social classes, including the powerful Armenian merchants. Although the supposed security offered by the Treaty of Georgievsk proved in the short run to be as ephemeral as that promised by Peter's invasion sixty years earlier, a more permanent political link would be forged two decades later. The Christian Armenians and Georgians were of great usefulness to the empress's plans for expansion to the south, as had been demonstrated in the annexation of the Crimea.[4] For the incorporation of the Caucasus, Catherine, her son Paul, and her grandson Alexander I could rely on the active cooperation of Russophile segments of the Armenian and Georgian elites.

For the Russians it was important that they had been invited repeatedly to enter Transcaucasia. They saw themselves as both liberators and conquerors—liberators of Christian peoples no longer able to defend themselves and conquerors who had brought glory to the empire by defeating the Muslim powers. The Decembrist Lachinov, a participant in the sieges of Erevan and Kars, recorded in his diary his feelings when he saw the happiness of the Armenians at the arrival of Russian troops: "I am a Russian, and my heart beats from joy that I am a Russian; and with pride I notice the respect of peoples for Russia's greatness."[5] Russian artists and poets depicted the Russian victories over the Persians and Turks as historical events of great moment and deified military heroes like Paskevich-Erevanskii. Yet the Christians of the area were ominously invisible in the poems of the period. While the Caucasian landscape was celebrated in hyperbolic verse, the Armenians and Georgians seemed not to inhabit that landscape or at best appeared as the passive recipients of the freedom brought by the Russians. Alexander Pushkin, who had joined his friends in the campaign of 1829, was a witness to the capture of Erzerum. His tone throughout his account is either indifferent or condescending toward the Armenians, though he notes coolly the enthusiasm of the Armenians for the Russians: "The Armenians noisily crowded into the narrow streets. Their little boys ran before our horses, making the sign of the cross and repeating: 'Christians! Christians!'"[6]

The new rulers from Russia referred to all the peoples of the Caucasus, regardless of nationality, as *tuzemtsy* (natives), thus playing down distinctions among them and emphasizing the distance between the Caucasians and the Russians. Although a sense of nationality or ethnicity was not yet clearly developed either among Russians or Armenians, Russian officials were aware of different ways of life and firmly believed in the superiority of the Russian way. Their consistent goal, though hesitantly approached at first, was to bring the Caucasian political and social order into conformity with the bureaucratic absolutism and serf-owning political economy of Russia proper.[7] These goals, while ultimately destructive of local political autonomy and traditional social forms, nevertheless did not affect the basic cultural, religious, and linguistic practices of the Caucasians. Russians made little effort in the early and mid-nineteenth century to proselytize their brand of Christianity, to attack frontally the social customs of the local peoples, or to force the use of the Russian language.

Russian policy was at first quite favorable toward the Armenians. The Emperor Alexander I (1801–1825) made it clear in his instruction to his commander in chief in Georgia, General Knorring, that he favored preferential treatment of his Armenian subjects:

> We ask you to take special care to win over the Armenian nation with every form of kindness. Because of the numerous people of this tribe in areas contiguous to Georgia, this is one of the most dependable means of increasing the power of these people and together with that the strengthening in general of the faith of Christians. To this end we would be pleased if, by showing as much as possible your patronage of the Ararat patriarch at the Echmiadzin monastery, you maintained friendly relations with the head of the church.[8]

Armenians had much reason to rejoice at the coming of the Russians to Transcaucasia, for the advantages brought by the Tsarist troops were considerable. Thousands of Armenian refugees from Turkey and Persia settled in the newly acquired Russian lands, and whole areas formerly occupied by Muslims were given over to Armenians. The Russian officials preferred having Christian agriculturalists settled along their frontier with the Turks and Persians. Tsarist troops provided defense against the formerly frequent Persian incursions and the continuing raids by Lezgin mountaineers. Moreover, the treaties of Gulistan (1813) and Turkmenchai (1828) not only inaugurated periods of relative peace with Russia's neighbors, but the Russian military presence made possible a long period of security and tranquillity during which Armenians could revive their flagging fortunes. Russian officials were the harbingers of a crude law and order, and they put an end to the most abusive treatment of Armenian merchants and craftsmen by the Georgian nobility. General Lazarev reported to Saint Petersburg on the violence and exploitation of the urban population:

> Often one sees people who have no means of defending themselves being completely looted. Goods from merchants, eatable products from industrialists—all are taken without payment by *baraty* (orders), given by all the princes, by all the princesses, and finally by all who have been given some position. No rank has any salary, and everyone must feed himself from his own place, and from this yet more is tolerated by the merchant and city dweller, by the inhabitant, in a word, by everyone.[9]

The urban artisan and merchant class of Tiflis and other east Georgian cities composed the first compact Armenian population with which the Russians had close and prolonged contact. The impressions of Armenians already formed by a few Russians in sporadic meetings with these eastern merchants were confirmed by the experience of Russian officers and bureaucrats in Transcaucasia. General Lazarev, one of the first Russian officers to enter Georgia, could with confidence tell his superiors that "the Armenians control most of the trade here."[10] "The merchants and *mokalaki* are almost all Armenians since the Georgians consider commerce shameful."[11] Tiflis, he noted, was governed by two Armenians, the melik and Tumanov, "who fulfill no orders but report [to the king] that everything has been done. . . . Here everything operates as it does with us in government bureaux; there everything is tomorrow; here, *ikneba*, that is, 'it will be'; and from that nothing happens."[12]

Armenians were already well established in the principal towns of Georgia by the late Middle Ages and were effectively playing the role assigned to them by the monarchs of Kartli—the merchant, the artisan, and the moneylender. But the virtues displayed by men of business long remained alien to the seignorial culture of the Georgians and the aristocratic virtues of the Russian army officers. The hostility and disdain felt by the Georgian elite toward the Armenian middle class was violently expressed by Prince Iese Baratashvili toward the end of the eighteenth century:

> Godless Armenians . . . merchants, huckstering and because of the sins
> of our king entrenching themselves in the palace . . . in defiance of the will

of God they are made lords, administrators, and *aznaurni* [nobles] in Georgia. . . . This is done only because of the impiety of kings, but look to the east, the west, south and north: Where do Armenians possess nobility? They have been dispersed by God! Is it in Man's power to reunite them?[13]

Georgian noble resentment of the Armenians stemmed from two principal sources: the fundamental cultural differences between the emerging bourgeois civilization of the urban Armenians and the traditional aristocratic values of the Georgian upper class; and the demographic, political, and economic hegemony that the Armenians exercised over Tiflis and much of the country. Georgian society, peasant and noble, was almost entirely based on an agrarian economy and the age-old relations of lords and peasants in a rural environment. The nobility usually concerned itself little with improving the agriculture that was the source of its income and preferred to live on the customary payments in labor, kind, and money that was extracted from its bondsmen. Urban culture and economy was largely foreign to the Georgians, and what trade and craft industry existed in the towns of their kingdoms was largely in the hands of the immigrant Armenians. Thus, the social division of labor between city and country was in Georgia accented by the different nationalities.[14]

The Russian aristocracy, like the Georgian nobility, had neither sympathy for men of commerce nor an inclination toward business enterprise. Instead, they developed a deep affection for Georgian nobles, particularly those who entered Russian state service. This affection was based on shared values of military bravery, chivalry, and a love of grace and largess. When Pushkin arrived in Tiflis, he noted that "the Georgian people are warrior-like. They have shown their courage under our standards. Their mental abilities will benefit from great education. They are in general happy and gregarious by custom. On holidays the men drink and stroll through the streets. Black-eyed boys sing, jump, and somersault; the women dance the lezginka."[15] But the similarities between these aristocratic elites contrasted starkly with the differences between the nobles and the middle-class Armenians. In his few references in his poetry to Armenians, Pushkin uses the Armenian as a metaphor for trickery, deception, and cowardice. In the poem "Tazit," for example, an angry Chechen father berates his son for not displaying the virtues of a Chechen warrior and revenging his brother's death: "Podi ty proch'—ty mne ne syn. Ty ne chechenets—ty starukha. Ty trus, ty rab, ty armianin!" (Get away from me—you are no son of mine. You are not a Chechen—you are an old woman. You are a coward, you are a slave, you are an Armenian!) And in the poem "Chernaia shal'" (Black Shawl), the lover with whom the narrator's Greek beauty betrays him is an Armenian!

The operating images of Armenians in Russian eyes, those of the defenseless Christian and the sly businessman, set up different responses in the policymakers of the first half of the nineteenth century. As the protector of the Armenian Christians, the tsars promoted the fortunes of the Armenian

Church, but their relations with the Armenian people of commerce were much more ambivalent. Russian economic policy toward Transcaucasia fluctuated in the early nineteenth century from supporting development as a "civilizing" measure to outright declarations that the region should be treated as a "colony" and exploited as a source of natural resources for Russian industry. The Armenian merchants who dominated the Caucasian urban economy came to be perceived as dangerous rivals to their Russian counterparts, and the state took an active role in promoting Russian competition and discriminating against local Armenian capital. Yet these efforts by officials to destroy the business monopoly of the Armenians were by and large failures, and by mid-century the government elevated the most prominent Armenian merchants, the *mokalakebi* of Tiflis, to the rank of *pochetnye grazhdane* (honored citizens) of the Russian Empire.

The services of Armenian entrepreneurs were valued by Russian officials who envisioned a prosperous and economically developed Transcaucasia; at the same time, disdain for the dirty business of business remained part of the Russian view of the Armenian commercial class. The first Russian governor of Georgia, General Tsitsianov, was disturbed by the relatively free market economy in Tiflis in which Armenians were able to manipulate prices and costs to their advantage. He ordered his officers to check that no middlemen raised prices on vital necessities in order to make exorbitant profits. He wrote: "Armenians after the Jews are the most able people [in this matter] to the general detriment of the inhabitants."[16] Three decades later an official government publication described the Armenians in this way:

> Armenians, like the people of Moses, have been dispersed about the face of the earth, gathering wealth under the weight of their rulers, unable to enjoy their own land. This is the cause of the Armenian's lack of character: he has become a cosmopolitan. His fatherland becomes that land where he can with the greatest advantage and security and through the resourcefulness of his mind make for himself profit. . . . Cleverness, wilyness—these are the essential characteristics of the unenlightened, and more so, of commercial peoples like the Armenians: any sort of deception is considered by them acceptable in buying and selling, any means for acquisition is considered legitimate. . . . In a word, where there is a possibility to obtain a profit, there without fail one finds the Armenians. Self-interestedness is the first motivator of all of their thoughts and deeds.[17]

The suspicion and mistrust of the commercial Armenian was widespread in the precapitalist political economy of pre-Reform Russia. Calculations of profit and economic efficiency rather than more customary and traditional forms of exchange made the Armenian an alien element in the relatively stagnant economic world of Transcaucasia. He was, of course, the harbinger of a new social order based on market relations and rational economic considerations, but to Georgian peasants and nobles and Russian aristocrats and bureaucrats the loyalties of the Armenian were neither to the existing way of life nor to the country in which they found themselves.

The disdain and distrust toward the commercial Armenian was tempered by the respect felt for the Christian Armenian. In the same year (1836) that the government report indicted the Armenians for their "lack of character," the government of Nicholas I granted the Armenian church the famous *Polozhenie* (Statute) by which Armenians received full freedom of worship, control over their schools, and official recognition of their institutional autonomy. During the long ministry of Catholicos Nerses Ashtaraketsi (1843–1857), Russian officials worked closely with the head of the church. Recalled from exile in Bessarabia, Nerses was cultivated by Viceroy Mikhail Vorontsov (1845–1854), who instructed his subordinates to make good use of the "faithfulness and loyalty to us of the Armenians." Catholicos Nerses, he went on, was a "strong and always prepared weapon," a man who was "able to bring order to the seminaries and schools and prepare capable priests for the future."[18] Viceroy Bariatinskii (1856–1862), somewhat at a loss when his Russophilic ally died in 1857, wrote to his sovereign of the importance of appointing a successor who could work as closely with Saint Petersburg. The Emperor Alexander II (1855–1881) replied to Bariatinskii: "Je regrette sincèrement le vieux Nersès, mais peut-être sa mort nous donnera-t-elle plus de facilité dans le reglement des affairs du clergé armenien. Le choix de son remplaçant devra etre fait avec une grande circonspection et je compte sur vous pour la présentation des candidats que le Synode convoqué devra me faire" (I sincerely miss the old Nerses, but perhaps his death will make easier the settlement of the affairs of the Armenian clergy. The choice of his replacement ought to be made with great circumspection, and I am counting on you for the presentation of candidates that the Synod when convoqued will make to me.)[19] Bariatinskii, who had cultivated the Armenian church as a means of "transmitting Russian influence into Persia and the Ottoman Empire," suggested the Armenian Patriarch of Constantinople, Mateos Chukhajian (1802–1865), as the preferred candidate.[20] The Emperor approved his choice, but unfortunately for the future of state-church relations Catholicos Mateos (1858–1865) proved to be an unwilling subordinate to Russian authority. He soon was appointing bishops without imperial approval and refused repeatedly to answer the viceroy's summons to visit Tiflis.[21] The Russian honeymoon with the Armenian church was rapidly coming to an end as the era of reform associated with the young Alexander II faded into memory.

For the minority nationalities in the tsarist empire, the first half of the reign of Alexander II has often been fondly remembered as a period of tolerance, increasing freedom, and positive reform. Between the defeat in the Crimean War (1856) and the reemergence of Russia as a great European power in the Russo-Turkish War of 1877–1878, the Armenians identified their hopes for economic progress and physical security with the Russian state. Within Russian Caucasia the Armenian bourgeoisie and its literary intelligentsia praised the positive role Russians played in Armenian affairs. From the conservative newspaper *Meghu Haiastani* (The Bee of Armenia) (Tiflis, 1858–1862) to the liberal *Krunk Haiots Ashkharhi* (The Crane of the Armenian World) (Tiflis, 1860–1866) to the Muscovite *Hiusisapail* (Northern Lights) (1858–1862), Armenian publicists sang the praises of the Russian state and particularly of the reforms of the 1860s. The Russophile liberal tendency was more forcefully articulated in the 1870s and 1880s by Grigor Artsruni's *Mshak* (Cultivator) (1872–1920), which appeared in Tiflis and dominated that city's Armenian intellectual life. Culturally the period was marked by the assimilation of many Armenians into Russian life. As one observer, A. V. Amfiteatrov, put it in referring to the years of Grand Duke Mikhail Nikolaevich (1862–1882) and Prince Dondukov-Korsakov (1882–1890), "Caucasia was Russified without Russification, and at the forefront of this natural Russianizing were, once again, the Armenians."[22] Economically, the post-Emancipation period was marked by considerable growth for the Armenians of Tiflis, Baku, and other Caucasian cities. As the market economy and capitalist industry expanded in Transcaucasia, Armenian businessmen thrived, while Georgian nobles and peasants suffered from the difficulties of adjusting to an agriculture based on "free" labor and production for the market. Although the state continued to favor the nobility in Transcaucasia, the growing economic power of the Armenian bourgeoisie was soon reflected in their control of Tiflis municipal politics. As a result of this increased economic and political visibility, the Armenians attracted new forms of hostility from those among whom they lived.

By the last third of the nineteenth century, the casual remarks of travelers, poets, and government officials about the characteristics of the Armenians had hardened into stereotyped attitudes about their inherent and racial character. Armenians were very frequently compared to the Georgians but usually with no regard for the historical developments that had distinguished these two peoples. A Russian observer, S. Maksimov, early in the 1870s echoed many other travelers to the Caucasus:

> Trade in the Caucasus is entirely in the hands of clever and calculating Armenians. Armenians are higher than Georgians in intelligence and in love for work, and for that reason there is nothing surprising in the fact that Georgian properties are rapidly falling into Armenian hands. Georgians are dependent on them just as the Poles are on the Jews and similarly feel toward them the same contempt and hatred (if not more than the Poles feel toward the Jews). The commercial Armenians reveal much cleverness, wilyness, are always ready with flattery; their thirst for profit leads them to cheating and swindling.[23]

The Russian enthographer P. I. Kovalevskii speaks of the Georgians as "merry [and] sociable," but also as noted for their "laziness, insufficient energy and enterprise, instability, lack of self-restraint, little ability in work, light-minded and superficial attitude toward business and matters at hand."[24] All of this contrasts sharply with his image of the Armenians. The British diplomat Oliver Wardrop wrote in the 1880s of his perceptions of the relations between Armenians and Georgians:

> A local proverb says "A Greek will cheat three Jews, but an Armenian will cheat three Greeks," and the Georgian, straightforward, honest fellow, is but too often cruelly swindled by the artful children of Haik. When the fraud is very apparent the Armenian often pays for his greed with all the blood that can be extracted from his jugular vein.[25]

However doubtful the accuracy of such national stereotypes described by numerous visitors to Transcaucasia, they seem to reflect something observers did see. Reported here are characteristics that have to do with the class position of the visible representatives of the various ethnic groups rather than inherent or genetic features of a whole people. Not only were there successful Georgian entrepreneurs (though far fewer than Armenian ones) equipped with the necessary business acumen, there were also Armenian peasants, both in Transcaucasia and Anatolia, who were not noted for their "cleverness, wilyness, or flattery" but who displayed attitudes and patterns of life and work much closer to their Georgian compatriots. What separated these two peoples were the positions they held in Caucasian society and the roles they played in the economy and political life. Also, the dominant elites of each nation, that group to which social inferiors deferred and looked up to for guidance and leadership, were quite different. The Armenians had long ago lost their nobility, the *nakhararutiun* of former kingdoms, and they were socially and politically dominated by the merchants and moneymen of the cities, while the Georgians had few native examples of bourgeois leadership, having instead had as models a traditional landed nobility then in economic decline. What foreign observers saw when they viewed Transcaucasian society had some basis in fact, but travelers and poets tended to generalize from their experience with the elites of Armenian and Georgian society and apply their conclusions to the whole of those peoples. The racial or ethnic stereotypes that have passed down to us are far more the product of the visibility and behavior of the dominant classes in Caucasian society than a true reflection of the nature of nationalities.

Through the 1870s Russian state interests and Armenian aspirations continued to coincide. As the growing nationalism of the Christian peoples of the Ottoman Empire turned discontent with Turkish rule into organized resistance, the Armenians of Tiflis joined in chorus with the Russian Pan-Slavs to champion the cause of Christian liberation in the Russian press and court circles. Russia once again appeared as the savior of the Armenians during and immediately after the Russo-Turkish War of 1877–1878. At the Congress of Berlin (1878) the Armenians found themselves isolated from the concert of

Europe, and when Russia was forced to give up much of her gains from the war, the Armenians, too, experienced defeat. The favorable Article XVI of the Treaty of San Stefano, which had guaranteed Russian presence in Turkey until reforms had been carried out in the Armenian vilayets, was converted into the meaningless Article LXI of the Treaty of Berlin, which called for such reforms only after the withdrawal of Russian troops.

San Stefano marked the zenith of Armenian-Russian collaboration. Within a few years the domestic and international insecurity of the Russian Empire would turn tsarist policy toward a narrow Russian chauvinism in which the aspirations of the minority nationalities would have no place. This turn was already evident in the last years of the reign of Alexander II. The increasingly violent revolutionary movement stimulated the tsar to invite the hero of the Russo-Turkish War, Count Mikhail Tarielovich Loris-Melikov (1826–1888), to head the Russian government and bring order to the empire. Generally perceived as a liberal, at least in the Russian context, the so-called dictator of the heart encountered stiff resistance from conservative and nationalist circles. When Alexander II was assassinated in 1881, Loris-Melikov became an early victim of the conservatives who rallied around the heir and convinced him that the Armenian Loris-Melikov, that "frenzied Asiatic," was a dangerous reformer. The Procurator of the Holy Synod, Konstantin Pobedonostsev, wrote to his former pupil, now the Emperor Alexander III, and told him bluntly:

> Do not keep Count Loris-Melikov. I do not believe him. He is a sly person and can still play a double game. If you give yourself over into his hands, he will lead you and Russia to destruction. He was able to work out liberal projects and to carry on a game of internal intrigue. . . . He is not a Russian patriot. Be careful, for the sake of God, Your Highness, that he does not capture your will; and do not lose time![26]

Pobedonostsev played on the emperor's suspicions of liberals and foreigners, emphasizing Loris-Melikov's Armenian "nature," his slyness, his not being a "true Russian." Here Pobedonostsev was sounding a theme—that of the Armenians as foreign, Asiatic elements—that would become ever more prominent in Russian conservative writings and would link Armenians with the Jews. From now on Armenians would often be referred to as *inorodtsy* (aliens), a term usually reserved for Jews, nomads, and a few Siberian tribes. The psychological distance between the alien Armenians and the *istinnye russkie* (true Russians), thus, was greatly increased.

For the Armenians the end of reform within the Russian Empire and the policy of conservative retrenchment coincided with a renewed European interest in the Armenian Question and an acceleration in the Armenian revolutionary struggles both in Turkey and within Russia. As a result Russians came to perceive Armenians as a recalcitrant, ungrateful, difficult-to-govern, and even disloyal people. As Armenian national consciousness swept the Caucasian and

Muscovite intelligentsia, significant numbers of educated Armenians began to experience a new sense of divided allegiance. While maintaining loyalty toward Russia, toward that nation that had protected their people from Muslim attack and opened to them the fruits of European civilization, young people more and more redirected their energies and passions toward their own nationality, developing a sense of Armenianness and a feeling of duty and obligation toward their less fortunate compatriots across the frontier in Turkey. As long as Russian policy remained flexible and open to the possibility of reform, as in the early years of Alexander II, there was little cause for conflict between most Armenians and the modernizing regime; but as the enthusiasm for reform receded within the government, the Russophilic liberalism that had characterized much of the Armenian intelligentsia through the reign of the "Emperor-Liberator" gave way in the reign of his successor to revolutionary nationalism tinged with socialism. Even though the principal thrust of this new movement was directed against the Ottoman Empire, the Russian authorities became concerned about its implications for the tsarist autocracy. The specter of separatism was raised by the police and soon engulfed the former images of the Armenians as loyal Christians and enterprising businessmen. The cosmopolitan bourgeoisie was pictured as rootless and inherently disloyal. And the differences between Armenian Christianity and Russian Orthodoxy were perceived to be much more of a chasm than earlier imagined. The church itself soon became a target of Russification. And the Armenians as a whole were more consistently seen as a conspiratorial, rebellious, treacherous nation.

The open articulation of nationalist sentiments in the Armenian press, in schools, and in the church was considered by the officials of Alexander III to constitute a danger to the autocratic monarchy and a threat to the unity of the multinational empire. As Hugh Seton-Watson has pointed out: "From the point of view of the rulers of mid-nineteenth-century Europe, nationalism was a subversive doctrine, for it introduced a new principle as the basis of the legitimacy of government. It substituted for the old legitimacy, based on monarchy by divine right, a new legitimacy based on the nation."[27] Not far below the surface of nationalism often lurked notions of popular sovereignty and nation-states.

But nationalism was a deadly double-edged sword and could be as much a danger to the ruled minorities as it was to the ruling nation. Russian nationalism mobilized the ruling Russian authorities under Alexander III to attempt to Russify through law and by force the non-Russian peoples. In a sense Russification was the further extension of the earlier policy of creating a uniform political and social order in all parts of the empire, but the administrative integration of minorities until the 1880s had never entailed an effort to eliminate the basis of ethnicity in the border areas by prohibiting education in local languages. The policies carried out in the 1880s against the non-Russian peoples were inspired by the chauvinists around the emperor—Pobedonostsev, Dmitri Tolstoi, Mikhail Katkov—and carried out by the long-serving minister of education (1882–1897), Count I. V. Delianov (1818–1897). Ironically, Delianov, a thick-headed and unquestioning servant of the autocrat, was himself an Armenian. Known to his subordinates as the "Armenian zero" (*armianskii nol'*), Delianov was unable to win the respect even of his closest associates.[28] Yet he was able to create the environment in which the image of Armenian separatists became a violent reality.

The Russification efforts began in earnest in 1885, first in the Baltic region and in Poland, and then in Transcaucasia. The zealous governor of the Caucasus, Prince A. M. Dondukov-Korsakov, ordered all Armenian parish schools closed and their replacement by Russian schools. The Caucasian authorities, under the guidance of the inspector (*popechitel'*) of the Caucasian Educational District, Kirill Petrovich Ianovskii, hoped to eradicate the Armenian "patriotism" and "populism" that they believed was spreading among Armenian students. Five hundred schools, attended by 20,000 students and employing 900 teachers, were shut down. Resistance was immediately organized in the form of secret schools, and in the wake of the school crisis there emerged a more radicalized Armenian intelligentsia. By 1886 the schools had been reopened, but their staffs had been purged and stricter state surveillance over teachers had been established. The unilateral abrogation of the *Polozhenie* of 1836 and the callous treatment of the educational system run by the church dealt a fatal blow to the Russophilia prevalent among Armenians, pushed the church further into opposition to tsarist authority, and led within a few years to the formation of the Armenian revolutionary organizations, the Hnchak and Dashnak parties.

The reaction of the Armenians to the government's Russification policies only served to confirm the impressions of state officials that the minorities harbored dangerous, subversive elements. In the fall of 1886 Pobedonostsev, after a visit to Transcaucasia, informed the emperor that "the Armenians and Georgians are seeking to free themselves from Russian culture and nourish the mad dream of the reestablishment of their national independence. Only firm power can succeed in containing and crushing this mad dream."[29]

The estrangement between Russia and the Armenians eroded the traditional Russian role of protector of Christian minorities just as the fate of the Armenians of Turkey became a major source of concern for the Great Powers of Europe. The "Near Eastern question," writes William L. Langer, "was by far the most acute and the most dangerous. In the 1880s Europe was kept on tenterhooks by the Bulgarian problem. In the following decade it was the Armenian Question that threatened to precipitate a general conflagration."[30] But just as Turkey's traditional ally, Britain, began seriously to consider the partition of the Ottoman Empire, the Russians became her defender. A complete reversal of roles had taken place between 1877 and the mid-1890s, and Armenian hopes for reform in Anatolia rested with Britain. The failure of both Russia and Britain, however, to impose reforms on the Turks in the 1880s led to the conviction on the part of young Armenians that they had to take up their national struggle in defiance of European hesitations. The Russian and European press regularly reported on the revolutionary exploits of Hnchaks and Dashnaks and on the brutal responses of the Turks. Demonstrations, like those at Kum Kapu in Istanbul (July 15, 1890) and at Bab Ali (September 18, 1895), were designed to arouse the attention of the pusillanimous diplomats and the readership of the popular press. But the activities of the revolutionaries, particularly those of the Hnchaks who had openly proclaimed their opposition to the Russian autocracy, gave added weight to the Russian image of the Armenians as congenital rebels. Any vestige of Russian state support for the Armenian cause dissipated rapidly in the wake of the insurrection and massacre at Zeitun and the occupation by the Dashnaks of the Ottoman Bank (1895). When the British pressed the sultan for reforms in eastern Anatolia following the Sassun massacres, Russia and her ally France worked behind the scenes to limit their effect as much as possible. Other British initiatives to enlist Russian help to force concessions on the Turks were also rejected. For Russians the image of the brother Christian had been effectively replaced by the image of a villainous conspirator who in his fury would undermine both the Ottoman and the Romanov monarchies. The only Armenia in which the Russian Foreign Minister Prince Lobanov-Rostovskii might be interested was in Armenia without Armenians.

The image of the Armenian as revolutionary was disseminated within the government by the state police, who were convinced that the Armenians of Transcaucasia were united in their active backing of the revolutionary activities in Turkey. Funds were being raised in the Caucasus by the sale of photographs of Armenian guerrillas in national costume.[31] Great sympathy was shown toward the arrested participants in the ill-fated Gugunian expedition of 1890. Evidence was found that students were collecting money and arms for the revolution and forming armed groups for action across the border. What concerned the police most were the widespread enthusiasm for the revolutionaries among all classes of Tiflis, and the appearance of a well-financed, international conspiracy. A police report of 1897 stated: "The idea of revolution has penetrated all the classes of Armenian society, those that have much wealth and those that have nothing. It has affected the rich merchant and the peasant, the townsman and the small shopkeeper, the intellectual class, and the most uneducated."[32] And most ominously for the church, the police concluded that though it is impossible "to prove the active participation of the Catholicos of all Armenians in the revolutionary movement, at least [we can] prove with absolute certainty his sympathies and those of the entire Echmiadzin Synod in this matter."[33] The spread of a violent socialist revolutionary movement seemed a raging plague to the gendarmerie, a virus that had affected all levels of Armenian society and turned a whole nation into enemies of the state.

The complete reversal of the Russian tradition of protecting the Christian Armenians was achieved in the wake of the Hamidian massacres of 1895–

1896. When a group of Armenians in Europe turned to the British with a petition for aid, the authorities in Saint Petersburg were so outraged that they informed the Catholicos that Armenian schools in Russia would be closed as a fitting punishment for the audacious petition. In January 1896 the Armenian church schools were once again closed, and officials made plans to seize church properties to finance a new state school system for the Armenians.[34] Under the Armenophobe governor of the Caucasus, Prince Grigorii Golitsyn (1896–1905), a wholesale attack was launched against all educational and charitable institutions of the Armenians. In 1898 the benevolent societies and libraries were closed down, and censors were ordered to prohibit publication of the words "Armenian people" or "Armenian nation." One censor, himself an Armenian, agreed that only the words "Armenian society" should be used to describe his nationality; after all, he asked, "What kind of a people are we anyway?"[35]

As the nineteenth century came to a close, the Armenians had become a pariah nation in the eyes of the very people who a century earlier had crossed the Caucasus to preserve the Christians of the region. Isolated from Russian officialdom and their neighbors, the Georgians and the Azerbaijanis, the Armenians had to withstand a violent upsurge of Russian chauvinism and Armenophobia, even as their economic power and political weight made them the incontestable leaders of Caucasian urban life. The most vocal spokesman against the Armenians was the Russian nationalist Vasilii L'vovich Velichko (1860–1904), who for two years (1897–1899) edited the semi-official Caucasian gazette, *Kavkaz* (Caucasus). His widely read anti-Armenian polemics were reprinted in the Georgian press, and when the poet-editor returned to the north he continued his diatribes in Russian journals like *Russkii vestnik* (Russian Herald). Velichko played on the hostile feelings of the Georgian nationalists to the consternation of Caucasian liberals and socialists who deplored his racist rhetoric. Armenians, wrote Velichko, "play the same role among the Georgians that plant-lice play among ants: they exploit the peace, they accumulate wealth, and only occasionally do they share this with their rulers before whom they tremble with servile fear."[36] In one article he quoted the Georgian saying *"movida somekhi, moitana skhva mekhi"* (An Armenian came and brought various misfortunes). "History has taught the Georgians," he went on, "not to trust people who have a natural tendency for spying and treachery."[37] Velichko claimed that the selfishness and ingratitude shown by the Armenians have turned the Azerbaijanis against them as well, as evidenced by the Azeri saying: "Light fire to your ten fingers like candles to show the way to an Armenian, and he will not say thank you."[38]

A political conservative and supporter of autocracy, Velichko's hostility toward Armenians had political and social bases as well as racial overtones. The Armenians were guilty in his eyes of the abominable aspiration to a constitution: "Only non-Russians want a constitution because it will create havoc for Russia."[39] He opposed the liberal reforms of the Armenian-dominated municipal government of Tiflis. When the city fathers petitioned the central government for a polytechnical institute in the city, Velichko warned in print that such a school in Tiflis would be controlled by the Armenians:

> The middle order here is the true friend of applied knowledge, which contributes more immediately to material accumulation in large amounts. Small wonder that the Armenian youth with their advantages over the Georgians strives precisely for applied science: this is in his blood, so to speak. . . . If here in Tiflis, which more and more is becoming the property of the middle order in its tribal and clannish exclusiveness, a polytechnicum is established, then, as any one who knows local life and does not wish to hide its peculiarities knows, this temple of applied science will be filled primarily with Armenian young people.[40]

Velichko tried to convince the Georgians that their natural allies were the Russians. The only solution to the problem of nationality in the Caucasus was to strengthen the Russian element: "When Russian people will be numerous in the borderlands, prosperous, strong and filled with national self-consciousness, then by itself the sphere of our language, our ideas, our spiritual and economic influence will widen."[41] For right-wing nationalists like Velichko the blurred and conflicting images of the Armenians came together in a hateful combination. Race, religion, revolution, and the materialist values of the entrepreneur all were used to depict the Armenian as an alien element.

The growing isolation of the Armenians was directly connected to the contradictory images projected on them by their rulers and neighbors. Armenians were both the mercenary, exploitative plutocrats known disparagingly as *maklak* (from *mokalake,* citizen in Georgian), as well as the feared and despised revolutionary. The merger of these two images into a general perception of the Armenian as a dangerous alien can be seen in the Georgian poet Akaki Tsereteli's verse fable "The Flea and the Fly," in which the flea convinces the fly that they should ally against the spider who is building a web to catch them. The fly (the Georgian) agrees, and the flea (the Armenian) sits on the fly and begins to draw blood. The fly grows weaker and weaker, but the flea continues to urge unity. The fly begs the flea to stop because she is dying and the spider (the Russian) is a distant threat.

In the early twentieth century Armenians were in open rebellion, not only within the Turkish Empire, but against the Russian autocracy as well. The image of the Armenian as revolutionary had become a reality as the result of the misconceived policies of the tsarist government that in two decades had squandered the Russophilic affections of their Armenian subjects. In 1903, after long deliberations, the government of Nicholas II (1894–1917) seized the properties of the Armenian church and by that act united the great majority of the Armenian people of Transcaucasia behind the radical leadership of the Dashnaktsutiun. Now the Christian Armenian and the commercial Armenian had become identified with the revolutionary in fact as well as in the projections of the Russians. To deal with the open rebellion in the Caucasus, Nicholas sent the trusted Count I. I. Vorontsov-Dashkov to serve as viceroy (1905–1916). Although the violence and rebellion lasted well into 1907, Vorontsov-Dashkov's skillful combination of liberal concessions and armed repression eventually restored a degree of stability to the Caucasus. One of his earliest and most popular measures was the restoration of the Armenian properties to the church. The active state policy against the Armenians decelerated, and the last years of imperial rule witnessed a brief, tentative restoration of the Armenian-Russian entente.

Russian opinion about Armenians, however, remained seriously divided. The Russian chauvinists attacked Vorontsov-Dashkov's policies and warned incessantly about the dangers of separatism. Nikolai Mazurenko, for example, wrote:

> The lack of confidence in the non-Russian peoples of Transcaucasia and the conviction that if not all Armenians and Georgians then the great majority of them are "irreconcilable enemies of Russia" are not false principles based on "imperial power" but are sooner the inflexible conclusion of all Russian people who have had the misfortune of experiencing themselves or seeing other Russians experience the true feelings and consistently hostile attitude toward us of these natives.[42]

A few years later a certain A. Liprandi, a member of the Russian Nationalist party, condemned Vorontsov-Dashkov's concessions to the Armenians as "anti-Russian" and stated bluntly: "The population of Caucasia, more precisely Transcaucasia, consists of different non-Russian elements, and they are all anti-state in their attitude, all filled with revolutionary separatism, and all living and breathing hatred toward Russia. Can the Russian state power depend on them? It is clear that it cannot."[43] His most bitter venom was reserved specifically for the Armenians: "Now among the Armenians there is no exception: they all to a man hate Russia and everything Russian—except of course, Russian gold—and they rave about 'free Armenia.'"[44]

While the political Right elaborated the negative images of the Armenians, liberals and the Left attempted to ameliorate ethnic tensions by reversing these images. Maxim Gorky wrote a passionate pamphlet against what he considered government instigation of the Armeno-Azerbaijani clashes in Baku in 1905. Remembering his own travels in years past, Gorky wrote:

> Having been in the Caucasus, I have seen everywhere how friendly and peacefully the Georgian works alongside the Tatar and the Armenian, and how like children they gaily and simply joke, sing, and laugh together, and how hard it is to believe that these simple noble people now stupidly and senselessly are killing one another, giving in to provocation by evil and dark forces.[45]

The idyllic picture drawn by Gorky presented an image of harmony and friendship that existed more in the hopes of internationalist socialists and liberal journalists than in the streets of Tiflis or Baku. But it was an ideal toward which the oppositional forces were willing to work, and against great odds the Left struggled against separatist nationalisms and for a multinational movement against autocracy. On the literary front Russian poets and critics contributed to a counterimage of the Armenians as a cultured people with a literature worthy of European recognition. In 1916 Gorky edited and published a collection of Armenian literature in Russian, and at about the same time the Russian poet Valerii Briusov brought out his anthology of Armenian poetry.[46] Accepting Europe as the unquestioned standard of civilization, the Russian critic and collector of Armenian literary works Iurii Alekseevich Veselovskii (1872–1919) touted Armenian literature as worthy of Russian and European attention and wrote: "It is not without reason that Armenians are called 'the Europeans of Asia.'"[47]

Perhaps the most important effort to reverse the negative images of the Armenians in government circles was made by the viceroy of the Caucasus. In his report to the tsar (1913), Vorontsov-Dashkov rejected the argument that the Armenians were congenital rebels:

> Six years ago I reported to you, Sire, with complete candor that within the borders of the Empire we ourselves created the [Armenian] problems by carelessly ignoring the religious and national views of the Armenians. . . . This population is almost exclusively rural, occupied diligently with agriculture; what is more, this kind or work is so congenial to the spirit of these people that the inhabitants of all Armenian cities remain primarily farmers. Only about one-fifth of Armenians live outside their homeland, primarily occupied in commercial-industrial enterprises and creating among the nationalists with whom they live that false impression about Armenians in general that exists among us, just as we have views about Greeks as a nationality based on Greek merchants.[48]

As he had reported in 1907 so he reaffirmed in 1913: "No form of separatism exists among Caucasian Armenians. . . . Of course, revolutionary parties exist among Armenians, as they do in Russia proper, but to speak of the revolutionary nature of the Armenian people is as strange as to suspect the Russian people of an absence of allegiance to its monarch."[49] Vorontsov-Dashkov criticized the government's attempt to incriminate the whole Armenian people through the infamous trial of 500 Dashnaks organized in 1912. The viceroy himself had not been informed by the police before they arrested nearly 1,000 Armenians in the Caucasus in preparation for the trial. As it turned out, the trial was a dismal failure for the government. The widely reported defense by prominent democratic lawyers, like Alexander Kerensky, resulted in the acquittal of all but fifty of the defendants. Like the Beilis case of about the same time, the attempt to use the semi-independent judiciary to promote the racist views of the government backfired.

As the Russian Empire entered its final crisis in the years immediately before and during World War I, the Armenians remained in a precarious and ambiguous position. The conflicting images of Christian, *commercant,* and conspirator were each taken up by different groups. Still suspect in the eyes of the highest governmental officials as conspirators and hated by the Georgians as mercenary exploiters, the Armenians nevertheless found sympathy and support in liberal and radical circles. The foreign ministry as well took up the Armenian Question once again in the last years of peace, and in concert with the major European powers approved a new program of reforms in Turkish Armenia. But once World War I broke out and Armenians found themselves in the unenviable position of inhabiting the lands between the great empires, they again became pawns of the Russians and the victims of the Turks. The rapacious imperialist appetites of England, France, and Russia, so long unable to be satisfied by a partition of Turkey, now could be satiated. Most of Armenia was given in secret to Russia in the Sykes-Picot Agreement of May 1916. But before that accord had been definitively formulated, before the Allies could defeat decisively the Young Turk regime and implement their covert plans, the Turks themselves embarked on their own version of the final solution to the Armenian Question. The death marches of 1915 emptied Anatolia of Armenians and made possible the dream of both Turkish nationalists and Russian imperialists of an Armenia without Armenians.

3 The Emergence of the Armenian Patriotic Intelligentsia in Russia

The study of nationalism in general, and that of small peoples like the Armenians in particular, was long confined to an investigation of emerging patriotic themes in literature and art or the views of nationalist intellectuals and politicians. Several decades ago many historians shifted away from a concentration on the emotional and quasi-religious states of mind described by Hans Kohn and C. J. H. Hayes to a more serious application of the insights provided by social scientists like Karl Deutsch.[1] Whereas the earlier tradition, which in its essentials went back to the eighteenth-century German originators of nationalist ideology, emphasized the "naturalness" of nationality, its inherent and organic quality, and its almost inevitable self-assertion, historians like Eric J. Hobsbawm, Miroslav Hroch, and Geoff Eley proposed that far from being natural and inevitable, nationalism was generated in a conscious political intervention by early nineteenth-century intellectuals and patriots. One of the distinctive features of early nationalist development in Eastern Europe and the Russian Empire, indeed, was the extraordinarily important role played by nationalist intellectuals in the absence of already formed nation-states in "inventing" national traditions and "imagining" national communities.[2]

The development of social communication that Deutsch and others prescribed as the basis for nationality could not in and of itself explain the changes in consciousness that led to identity with nation. Rather, such an "objective" social trend might be said to provide the social and economic context in which groups of intellectuals began their investigations into the past of their own peoples and generated ideas that then found a powerful resonance among their intended constituents. As Eley put it:

The emergence of [nineteenth-century nationalities] was no natural or logical development from a series of objective and empirically readily observable characteristics of human populations, like a common territory, language or religion. A viable or successful nationalist movement bore a far more arbitrary and less predictable relationship to existing patterns of social organization than this familiar assumption might suggest. This is not to say that a common territory, language or culture provided no basis for shared identity or consciousness, but for that consciousness to become *nationalist* in any true sense (rather than say regionalist, ethnic, religious or peasant-populist) something else normally has to happen in the form of political intervention. In other words, creative political action is required to transform a segmented and disunited population into a coherent nationality, and though potential communities of this kind may clearly precede such interventions (so that they are rarely interventions into a vacuum), the latter remain responsible for comingling the materials into a larger collectivity.[3]

It was a short, but difficult, step from recognizing the creative role of individuals in the invention of nationalism to an appreciation of the role of discourse, language, the generation of new meanings in the emergence of nationalism. Rather than a return to the immanentist or essential views of nationality that often underlay earlier historians' conceptions of nationalism or the ideological constructions of nationalists themselves, one might suggest a half-turn toward a discursive analysis that appreciates both the social and cultural construction of nationality and nationalism. To social history's contribution of an enhanced context beyond a narrowly conceived political realm may be reintroduced the additional context of the discursive sphere in which experience is interpreted and given meaning.

For East Europeans and Caucasians the earlier successes in nation-state building in Western Europe provided a model for an anticipated future. Their own condition as minorities within multinational dynastic empires could now be challenged by reference both to the experience of other "advanced" European peoples and to the doctrine emanating from the French Revolution that linked political legitimacy to popular sovereignty and ethnic claims. Nationalism, then, in this view is the product of a broad social and economic transformation, but one that is mediated through the interpretations provided by a nationalist intelligentsia. It is to be understood as part of intellectual history as well as social history. In this way an analyst can avoid the temptation to segregate economic changes from intellectual and political changes and see the social and ideological formation first of patriotic intellectuals and then of newly conscious nationalities as the result of the complex totality of these changes.

The "creative political action" that turned a disparate people into a nationality was, at least in its first stages, usually the work of a small and increasingly coherent urban intelligentsia. These early patriots have been intensely studied by Miroslav Hroch, who in distilling the experiences of more than a half-dozen small nationalities in Europe has set out three phases in the development of nationalism. Phase A is the initial period of primarily scholarly activity when small groups of intellectuals elaborated the idea of nationhood and fostered a "scholarly concern for the nation."[4] In Phase B, a growing number of patriots engaged in "conscious national agitation directed towards the broad masses in an attempt to win them for the programme of national, cultural (and eventually even political) emancipation."[5] Finally Phase C marks the advent of "mass nationalist activity." Hroch's own research on national movements among the smaller nationalities of Europe has been well-grounded in an empirical sociology and quantitative methodology and has conclusively shown that the patriotic intelligentsia for these peoples was overwhelmingly urban, the products of areas with dense educational networks and economic transition toward industrialization. The peoples he has studied—Czechs, Slovaks, Lithuanians, Estonians, Finns, Norwegians, and the Flemish—developed in a context in which they lacked a native aristocracy and were unable to rely on the local bourgeoisie for cultural-political leadership. The national intelligentsia turned in a democratic direction and sought its allies and supporters among the lower middle class and the peasantry. Nationalism, which in Western Europe more closely fits the familiar characterization as a "bourgeois" phenomenon, was in the East far less the result of activity by the owners of the means of production and much more the active concern of teachers, journalists, priests, petty officials, and writers—particularly in the intermediate Phase B.

The Hrochian framework provides a useful program for research into the early history of Armenian national consciousness, but it requires an attempt to gather the sociological data on the whole first and second generations of Armenian patriots that is impossible without using archival material in various European and Soviet collections. Such an effort would enable us to move beyond an investigation of leaders to an analysis of the social and intellectual characteristics of those they influenced. In the absence of names of members of patriotic organizations or lists of subscribers to nationalist newspapers one can only attempt at this time a more modest task—to outline the process of self-creation of a sense of Armenianness, a task that can provide an agenda for more fundamental research in the future.

The long history of the Armenians falls into two sharply distinguished blocs—that of the classical and medieval periods (sixth century B.C.–fourteenth century A.D.) and that of the modern national reemergence from the eighteenth century to the present. It is tragically divided by the catastrophic intermediate period (fourteenth to eighteenth centuries), the lost centuries when Muslim invaders destroyed the last Armenian polities and initiated the slow but relentless process of de-Armenizing the historic homeland of the Armenians. The modern period is separated not only by time but also by place from the earlier period, for a geographical shift in the centers of Armenian life from eastern Anatolia to dispersed colonies occurred during the long hiatus of early modern times. The making of a modern Armenian nation, then, took place largely outside the Armenian heartland in the Armenian communities of western Turkey, Russia, India, and Europe. It was here, away from the "fatherland," that the first generation of patriotic intellectuals emerged and provided a new definition for a vision of Armenian nationhood.

The notion that Armenians were not always (and consistently) aware that they made up a distinct and historically distinguished nation, that they were part of a coherent linguistic and religious community with a unique culture, is difficult for many Armenians today to accept. Their very experience at home, in church, and in school has been the affirmation and reaffirmation of a legacy that stretches back at least to Tigran the Great, if not Urartu, certainly to Grigor Lusavorich ("Armenia was the first Christian nation"), to Saint Vardan and the defense of religion and nation against those who attempted to destroy Christianity and thereby eliminate the essence of Armenianness. It is precisely this age-old legacy that conscious and patriotic Armenians in the diaspora are dedicated to preserving in the face of the acculturationist and assimilationist attractions of Western society. Yet when one takes a closer look at the early modern history of Armenians, one finds that all but a rudimentary sense of being Armenian had been lost for many (if not most) Armenians, particularly in Armenia proper, in the years before the nineteenth-century revival. Language and religion (and these in adulterated forms) were almost all that was left of Armenian culture and consciousness as Armenians entered their third millenium. As an illustration, let us remember the story of the adventurer Joseph Emin, who traveled into Anatolia in the mid-eighteenth century and confronted the Armenians of the most backward regions of the Ottoman Empire with their own past.

Emin, an Armenian who had grown up in British India, took upon himself a lifelong mission to liberate the Armenians from Muslim rule. Inspired by the advances of European civilization, he was appalled by the contrast between the life of the West and that of his own people: "I grieved with myself, for my religion and my country, that we were in slavery and ignorance like Jews vagabonds upon the Earth."[6] In 1759 he started out for eastern Turkey, "into the mountains of Upper Armenia," disguised as a scientist intent on collecting flowers, roots, and birds. When he reached his first Armenian village, Emin narrowly escaped a beating at the hands of the villagers who were startled to hear a mounted horseman speak Armenian. In order to save himself Emin pretended to be what the peasant had thought him to be, a Turk. Later in a private meeting with the village head Emin asked why the Armenians opposed his riding alone: were they against Armenians being warriors or acting freely? The headman answered: "Sir, our liberty is in the next world; our king is Jesus Christ." Emin asked: "How come that about? Who told you?" They answered: "The Holy Fathers of the Church, who say, the Armenian nation has been subject to the Mahometans from the creation of the world, and must remain so till the day of resurrection; otherwise we could soon drive the Othmans out of our country."[7] Surprised by this novel reading of history,

Emin pulled out his copy of Movses Khorenatsi and asked the priest to read from it. Here was proof that Armenians had been independent long before the Ottomans had come to Anatolia.

This peculiar story told by Joseph Emin illustrates the abysmal lack of awareness of the Armenian peasants of eastern Anatolia. The story would be repeated by other travelers and agitators through the nineteenth century. These accounts reveal two interesting aspects of the Armenian condition:

1. Part of the effectiveness of Muslim rule over Armenians stemmed from Armenian conviction that this subjugation was in some sense justified, was ordained by God, and that liberation would come either in heaven or only after 666 years (according to ancient prophecy).
2. The passivity of the Armenians was in many ways a rational response to their relative weakness vis-à-vis the Muslims. Yet at the same time it was encouraged by the leading authorities among the Armenians, particularly the clerics.

By the eighteenth century many Armenians had very little left of their national culture, except for a language reduced to mutually incomprehensible dialects and mixed with vocabulary borrowed from the dominant nationality. Their religion was mixed with superstition and borrowings from pagan practice, and their church was notoriously corrupt. Their ancient nobility, the *nakhararner,* had almost entirely been eliminated, and only a few centers of precarious autonomy continued to exist in Karabagh, Sasun, and Zeytun. Knowledge of Armenian history had been effectively wiped out, except among a small group of monks who copied and recopied the ancient texts.

Against this background of social backwardness, cultural annihilation, and political impotency, the first modern generation of Armenian patriots undertook a revival of Armenian letters. The most extraordinary effort in this regard was made by the Armenian Catholic congregation at San Lazaro in Venice, founded by Mekhitar Sebastatsi (1676–1749) in 1717. Here a dedicated group of teachers and scholars began to issue a series of publications that continue to the present time but that in the mid-eighteenth century were quite unique in their number and quality. In 1749–1769 the two volumes of the *Haykazian Bararan,* a dictionary of the Armenian language, were published, making Armenian the sixth world language (after Latin, Greek, French, Italian, and Spanish) to have such a complete dictionary. (The first English dictionary appeared only in 1755, the first German in 1774–1786).[8]

These energetic monks organized schools, both at the monastery and in Armenian communities (the first was in Transylvania in 1747); they were the initiators of the first modern Armenian theatrical performances as an extension of their educational project; and they developed the nascent art and craft of Armenian printing. From Venice and Vienna the Mekhitarists began issuing new editions of the ancient Armenian historians in multiple copies, as well as more strictly religious texts. They translated Western classics into Armenian and supported and published the first modern history of Armenia by the Mekhitarist monk Mikayel Chamchian.[9] Though the Mekhitarists were not alone in this effort at recovery of the Armenian past, their work was key to the reconstruction of Armenian history, and the selection of particular aspects of that history that would function for coming generations as the operative tradition.

The scholarly endeavors of the Mekhitarists, as well as the publicist activities of diaspora Armenians like Shmavon Shmavonian in India (who published the first Armenian newspaper in Madras in 1794) and the cultural and educational efforts of Patriarch Hovhannes Kolot of Constantinople (1715–1741), were all acts of courage and faith, given the enormity of the task of national resurrection. At the beginning of the nineteenth century Armenians were still a people fragmented by geography, by social class, even by language and religious affiliation. The majority of Armenians lived in the Ottoman Empire and were peasants in the mountains of eastern Anatolia, but many had lost their language or spoke corrupted dialects. The turn toward a renewed patriotism came not from the uneducated in the villages of Armenia but from the towns and cities of western Anatolia—Istanbul and Izmir—and in the Armenian colonies of the Russian Empire—Tiflis, Baku, Nor Nakhichevan, Moscow, and the Crimea. I would like to look at these settlements in order to sketch out the contours of the next generation of patriotic intellectuals—the activists, journalists, and writers who moved beyond scholarship to patriotic propaganda—the men and women of Hroch's Phase B.

The transition from a primarily clerical group of scholars to a predominantly secular and political intelligentsia that characterizes Hroch's Phase B was for the Armenians in Russia a gradual process that began in the fourth decade of the nineteenth century and accelerated only in the second third of the century.[10] The shift occurred while the relationship of Armenians to the Russian Empire underwent a fundamental change. Originally the Armenians who had settled in Russia had been people of commerce involved in the transit trade from Persia through Russia to Europe. Armenians had gathered in the Crimea, in Moscow, Saint Petersburg, and Astrakhan; after an invitation by Catherine the Great in 1779, they founded the colony of Nor Nakhichevan at the mouth of the Don (present-day Rostov). The annexation of the Crimea in 1783, of eastern Georgia in 1800–1801, and most significantly of the khanate of Erevan in 1828 brought tens of thousands of Armenians under Russian rule and transformed this people-in-exile into an ethnoreligious community under a single ruler, a community—though scattered—whose future now was intimately intertwined with tsarist political and economic development.[11]

Russian military occupation of the *Armianskaia oblast'* and the subsequent demographic shifts brought some 90,000 Armenians from Persia and Turkey into the Caucasus; it began an intensive process of social change that contributed to the increase in "social communication" among Russian Armenians of which Deutsch has spoken. Not only did the newly found security provide the preconditions for economic growth and the expansion of an Armenian urban bourgeoisie (particularly in Tiflis), but Russian state policy aided the accumulation of wealth and political power by Armenian traders and merchants to the detriment of competing social elites, such as the Georgian nobility. The Russian government granted Armenians tax exemptions and significant degrees of self-rule in their communities and treated the Armenian church with special care. Armenians were placed under the religious authority of Etchmiadzin; the Catholicos was given powers to censor Armenian books throughout the empire, to open and run religious schools, and to call upon the state to enforce its will on recalcitrant parishioners. A delicate and often difficult partnership between the tsarist state and Etchmiadzin was established by the *Polozhenie* (Decree) of 1836, which regularized the government's role in church affairs while sanctioning church authority over religious schools. By the 1840s Armenians throughout Russia, distant though they were one from another geographically and linguistically, were now for the first time subject to similar laws, the same church authorities, and to the vicissitudes faced by their ethnic brethren.[12]

Perhaps the single most formative experience of the embryonic intelligentsia in early nineteenth-century Russia was the slow but steady expansion of a school system. Caucasian Armenians had no schools before the Russian annexation, and the first schools established by the government—a noble *uchilishche* (1802) and an orthodox seminary (1816) in Tiflis—were alien to most Armenians. Armenians had founded schools in Astrakhan (the Agababov school, 1810), in Nor Nakhichevan (1811), and in Moscow (the famous Lazarev Institute, 1815), but not until 1813 did the energetic Nerses Ashtaraketsi manage to open the *Zharangavorats* in Etchmiadzin. Ten years later he opened the premier school for Armenians in Transcaucasia, the Nersesian *Jemaran* in Tiflis. These schools were the nuclei of a small network of schools in churches and homes, usually involving a single dedicated teacher. By the end of 1836 Caucasian Armenians had twenty-one Armenian church schools (and 824 churches).[13]

As education expanded, the church hierarchy attempted to keep learning within a strictly prescribed religious framework, but young priests and university-educated lay instructors, like the writer Khachatur Abovian (1805–1848), worked to stretch the peripheries of education and introduce Western literature, science, and a demythologized history. Students were pulled in one direction by the rigid traditional instruction of most of the priests and in another by younger *kahanas* and lay teachers. One of the new generation of teachers and an important transitional figure in the history of the Russian Armenian intelligentsia was Gabriel *kahana* Patkanian (1802–1889), the father of the patriotic poet Rafayel Patkanian (Gamar-Katipa, 1830–1892) and the teacher of the radical journalist and political activist, Mikayel Nalbandian (1829–1866).

Gabriel Patkanian was the son of Serovbe Patkanian (1770–1836), a poet and teacher who had been educated by the Mekhitarists in Venice.[14] Gabriel moved from Tiflis to Astrakhan in 1807 when his father became director of the new elementary school for Armenians in that Caspian port. He studied Russian and French, as well as classical literature, in the local Russian school. In 1817 he was appointed secretary of the Armenian assembly by the Astrakhan primate and given a teaching post in the diocesan school. Like his father he was at first a scholar, publishing in 1820 (at the age of eighteen) a study of the doctrine of orthodoxy (*Vardapetutiun ughaparutian*). Seven years later he translated the history of Alexander the Great by Dioderus Siculus into classical Armenian. He followed his father to Nor Nakhichevan in 1827 where they began a new school. But a powerful local political figure, Harutiun Khalibov, who favored an exclusively religious form of education, had Gabriel Patkanian dismissed from the school. Patkanian soon was ordained as a priest in Grigoropol' in the Crimea and then sent by the influential Nerses Ashtaraketsi back to Nakhichevan to open a boarding school (1832). The principal avenue for an intellectual still lay through the church, but Patkanian already had a much broader notion of Armenian education than his superiors, and before long he was again singled out for punishment. In 1845 his former patron, now Catholicos Nerses V, ordered Patkanian exiled to the Norashen monastery in Georgia and turned his school over to a narrow-minded pedagogue.

In 1846 Patkanian was reinstated as a teacher at the Nersesian Jemaran in Tiflis. There he worked with a group of clerics to publish *Kovkas* (Caucasus), a newspaper written in classical Armenian. *Kovkas* discussed theological issues and Armenian history, published biographies of prominent Armenians like the Lazarevs, and translated the verses of the popular French writer Eugene Sue. The newspaper lasted only a year before being closed down by the censors. Three years later, Patkanian issued a second periodical, *Ararat,* which was the first newspaper in the Russian Empire printed in modern Armenian. Patkanian, like his friend Abovian and other modernizers, had become an advocate of writing in the vernacular Armenian (*ashkharhabar*) instead of the classical Armenian of the church (*grabar*), and the use of the spoken, dialectical Armenian was quickly identified with the cause of cultural innovation and educational reform. *Ararat* was, for its small audience, a forum for secular ideas. Its language was an affront to the church establishment, a brazen opting for change and progress over custom and tradition. Church and government joined in an effort to suppress the newspaper, and in 1851 it was closed by the censor for a trivial breach of decorum. Patkanian retired to Nor Nakhichevan and the Surp Lusavorich church in which he had taught in the 1830s.

The priest-teacher-journalist Patkanian stood between his Mekhitarist-trained father and the more secular generation that was growing up around him, a generation that included his friend Abovian, his son Rafayel, and his pupil Nalbandian. The son of a blacksmith, Mikayel Nalbandian was perhaps the most radical, certainly the most contentious and openly anticlerical, of the mid-century Armenian patriots. He spent eight years in Patkanian's school, where he learned Russian and French and was exposed to Western literature and science. When his teacher was exiled from Nakhichevan, Nalbandian took up his cause and wrote unsigned attacks on Patkanian's successors. He incurred the enmity of the church authorities and eventually was forced to flee to Moscow where he studied at the Lazarev Institute and Moscow University. There he met Stepanos Nazariants (1812–1879) and, in the more permissive atmosphere that followed the death of the Emperor Nicholas I, the two young Armenians collaborated on an avowedly secular, even anticlerical newspaper—*Hiusisapayl* (Northern Light, 1858–1864).[15]

Nalbandian has been used and misused by Soviet historians as the Armenian equivalent to the Russian "enlighteners" of the late 1850s and early 1860s—Herzen, Ogarev, Chernyshevskii, and Dobroliubov. But though he was influenced by many of the same intellectual currents as the Russian radicals, Nalbandian's interests were almost exclusively contained within the world of the Armenians. He began his career as a servant of the church, and he remained concerned with the overwhelming power of the Armenian church hierarchy, its continuing efforts to stifle Western learning in Armenian schools, and the alliance of the church conservatives with obscurantist community leaders. Nalbandian frequently attacked the influences of Catholicism in the Armenian community and church. His struggle against his own Armenian church establishment was connected to his attack on Catholicism, for Nalbandian had a genuine hatred for the conservatism of the Catholic church and its anti-Enlightenment, anti-liberal attitudes. In 1857 he published his translation into modern Armenian of the first half of Eugene Sue's *The Wandering Jew*, a novel that contained a savage portrait of Jesuits. As if to make clear his intention, he added a long introduction denouncing the Catholic order. The ferocity of his attacks on Catholics should be understood as part of Nalbandian's struggle to liberate Armenian literature from its medieval, religious roots, which he felt had been revived and nourished by the Mekhitarist fathers. He felt that the lack of life and vitality in Armenian writing and its failure to command a wide audience among Armenians were the result of the monopoly of writing in the hands of clerics. He called for removal "of the glasses of medieval religion" and observed:

> The transformation of the world has been amazing, yet what is even more amazing is that there are still so many people who do not believe that this transformation has taken place.[16]

While in one sense Nalbandian was the heir of the Mekhitarists, the pupil of a teacher taught by a father trained in Venice, he and his generation turned their backs on the Catholic fathers and their revivalist tradition and looked more directly toward the West of the French Enlightenment and European revolutions. In the same year that he published Sue's novel, Nalbandian wrote to a friend about the dubious influences of the Mekhitarists on Armenian letters:

> Enough! Let us remove this shame from ourselves, that the enlightenment of our nation must proceed from the hands of execrable papist monks! Their "light" is far more pernicious than darkness—therefore let them keep it for themselves. There are figures in the Armenian nation right now who are able to write a thousand times more lucidly, truthfully, and purely than any Venetian monk.[17]

Nalbandian and his associates were the first generation to speak clearly of an Armenian nationality distinct from the Armenian religious community. Indeed this secular nation had emerged, and would continue to form itself, in confrontation with the outworn clerical leadership that had maintained the traditions of the Armenian people through the long dark intermission between medieval and modern times. For Nalbandian the foundation of the modern Armenian nation was the common people:

> Whoever loves his nation, whoever has dedicated his person to the moral service of the nation must not serve the nation's idols—rather, the advantage of the common people. The common people constitute the machine of the nation.[18]

But for Armenians that machine had been shattered and had to be regenerated through the implantation of consciousness. "And consciousness," Nalbandian reminded his readers, "emerges from enlightenment." For Armenians to be reconstituted as a nation, genuine national schools had to be founded—"schools in which the Armenian language will be heard, in which various enlightened ideas will be presented to students by means of the Armenian language."[19]

This new sense of Armenian nationality that was being defined by Russian Armenian writers and journalists in the mid-nineteenth century was at one and the same time the product of the intellectual revival that the Mekhitarist and Armenian church fathers had begun, as well as a westernized reaction to the traditional view of Armenians as a primarily religious community dominated by the church. Beginning with the *kahanas* of Gabriel Patkanian's generation and proceeding with the university-trained scholars and writers like Abovian and Nazariants, a secular intelligentsia emerged that found its most outspoken representative in the bold, somewhat reckless, and ultimately victimized Nalbandian. By 1858 a secular and secularizing generation of Armenian intellectuals may be said to have appeared. That was the year of *Hiusisapayl* and Abovian's *Verk Hayastani,* the first novel in modern eastern Armenian. Two hundred subscribers signed up in advance to receive the Moscow-based newspaper of Nalbandian and Nazariants. Clearly there was a growing interest in Western ideas, for a concerted challenge to the traditional leadership of church and community, and for a clearer identification of Armenians as a nationality. But the invention of that modern nation was only just beginning. In the years ahead new writers would appear to take up the cause, and a determined clerical reaction would attempt to divert the new national consciousness back into traditional concerns. Ultimately the formation of the Armenian nation would require further social and political shaping. The Armenian nation would fully emerge only after official repression and events far beyond the control of Armenians would force all classes of the Armenian population to examine their past and their precarious future.

4 Populism, Nationalism, and Marxism among Russia's Armenians

The river Arax in its course through the Ararat plain has for over a century not only divided Russia from Turkey and Persia but, by the arbitrary decision of some cartographers, it has been the boundary between Europe and Asia. For the Armenians living on either side of the river, the Arax has meant a passage from intermittent violence to relative security, from backwardness and poverty to potential material well-being, and from ignorance and darkness to easier access to the benefits of European civilization. In time, the peoples to the north of the river developed quite differently from their compatriots to the south until by the second half of the nineteenth century one can speak of at least two distinct political cultures among the Armenians: the Caucasian or Russian-Armenian, increasingly secular and evolving under a more direct impact of capitalism and the influence of the Russian intelligentsia; and the Western or Turkish-Armenian, still heavily indebted to the church but responding to Western European ideas through the Constantinople intelligentsia. As a historian of the Armenian revolutionary movement, Anahide Ter Minassian, explains, the intelligentsia in the two Armenias matured under different influences: "The Armenian intelligentsia in Turkey studied in Italy and France: it was aroused by the French revolutions, the liberation of Greece, the unification of Italy, and pre-Marxian socialism. The Armenian intelligentsia in Russia studied in Moscow, Saint Petersburg, Dorpat, Leipzig, Berlin. It went through the same phases as the Russian intelligentsia and discovered Marxism."[1]

Scholars have clearly demonstrated the important role that the Caucasian-Armenian intelligentsia played in the formation and development of the Armenian revolutionary movement both in Russia and in Turkey. The Hnchak and Dashnak parties were both formed by Russian Armenian intellectuals, and the ideological complexions of these and other Armenian parties were colored by the polemics and disputes that divided the Russian revolutionary movement. Two principal issues affected the Armenian revolutionary movement: the nature of the relationship of the Armenian liberation struggle with those of other peoples of the Russian Empire, particularly the Russian revolutionary movement; and the question of the appropriateness of socialism as a programmatic goal for the Armenian political parties. These two questions provided a constant source of tension within the Armenian revolutionary camp and prevented any effective unity. The disagreements were serious, went far beyond personal clashes, and determined the ultimate separation of the Armenian revolutionary movement from the populist and later Marxist parties that developed among the Georgians and Russians.

Too often the history of small nations like the Armenians has been treated in isolation from the history of their neighbors. To understand the evolution of the Armenian revolutionary movement, it is necessary to trace and analyze the relationship of Armenians to Russian populism and Marxism, as well as to the development of socialism and nationalism among the Georgians. As Russians and Georgians moved from populism to Marxism, there was a coincident shift among Armenian activists from the multinational populist movement to nationalism. Only a small minority of young radicals adopted the theories of Marxism. In this chapter I will deal in some detail with the formation of the two major Armenian revolutionary parties—the Hnchak party and the Dashnaktsutiun—and the conflict between socialism and nationalism that prevented both unification among the Armenians and joint action with other nationalities in Transcaucasia.

The Armenians of the Caucasus had been cut off from the Armenians of Persia and the Ottoman Empire since the annexation of Eastern Armenia into the Russian Empire in the late 1820s. At the end of the Russo-Turkish War of 1877 still more Armenians came under Russian rule as a result either of emigration or the incorporation of Kars and other territory into the Romanov Empire, so that by the last decade of the last century over one million Armenians lived in the Caucasus. The overwhelming majority were peasants (upwards of 80 percent), and the rest were urban dwellers—merchants, businessmen, workers, shopkeepers, professional people. There was no Armenian nobility to speak of, and Armenian urban culture was preeminently bourgeois. Armenians historically had been tradesmen in the ancient Georgian kingdom, and by the second half of the nineteenth century, they had an extraordinary hold on the nascent industry of Transcaucasia as well as the municipal governments of Baku and Tiflis.

Transcaucasian society, particularly in the cities, underwent a significant transformation in the 1870s and 1880s. With the emancipation of peasant serfs in the late 1860s and early 1870s and the opening of the railroad connection from Tiflis to the Black Sea port of Poti, the first signs of a breakdown of the traditional, patriarchial way of life became apparent. The preeminent position of the Georgian nobility in Transcaucasian society began to give way as the vigorous Armenian middle class emerged as the principal entrepreneurs in the newly established industries. Local newspapers wrote with enthusiasm and pride about the new textile mill opened by Mirzoev brothers that by 1872 provided employment for eight hundred workers, most of them Armenian.[2] The modernization and development of the oil industry in Baku and the building of refineries in Batumi further promoted the penetration of capital into Transcaucasia and the growth of a working class. Although the economy of the Caucasus remained largely agricultural, the pockets of industry and the railroad links produced a steady disintegration of the natural economy of the isolated villages of Armenia, Georgia, and Azerbaijan and the establishment over time of production for market. These developments stood out in stark contrast to the economic stagnation, physical insecurity, and social disorder evident in Turkish Armenia.

The central facts of Armenian life one hundred years ago, thus, were the division of the nation among the Russian, Persian, and Turkish empires and the relatively privileged status of a small part of the nation—the Armenian bourgeoisie of Transcaucasia and Constantinople. For many, the disparity between the peasantry of eastern Anatolia and the urban elite of Tiflis, Baku, and Constantinople was acceptable as a natural, indeed inevitable, development of modern life, perhaps the first stage of a slow evolution toward a more prosperous European social order. But to a small minority of young and sensitive Armenians, this disparity was intolerable and was justified neither by nature nor history. It was instead the product of repressive policies of the Ottoman state and the Russian autocracy and could be corrected only by revolutionary activity. Precisely what activities should be undertaken, however, and to what end were among the key issues that divided the first generation of Armenian revolutionaries.

A revolutionary intelligentsia among the Caucasian Armenians began to appear only at the beginning of the 1880s. Earlier a few isolated intellectuals, like the journalist and poet Mikhail Nalbandian (1829–1866) or Stepan Vosgan (1825–1901), a participant in the events of 1848 in Paris, had associated with radicals in Russia and Western Europe, and in Transcaucasia itself the first group of enthusiasts for Armenian liberation was formed in April 1869 in Aleksandropol—the so-called "Society with a Noble Aim" *(Barenapatak unkerutiun).*[3] In the 1870s the liberal westernizing tendency, represented by the supporters of the Tiflis-based newspaper *Mshak* (Cultivator), began to influence many educated Armenians. For twenty years, from 1872 until his death in 1892, the editor of the paper, Grigor Artsruni (1845–1892), was a popular and influential leader of the Armenian community in Tiflis. His advice and help were sought by politically active Armenians from Turkey, and his view that for Armenians Russia represented the "lesser evil" prevailed until the mid-1880s.[4] The Russophilia of Artsruni and the *Mshakakanner* filtered into the schools where it steadily displaced the more conservative views associated with Petros Simonian, editor of *Meghu haiastani* (The Bee of Armenia) and the rector of the Nersessian Jemaran.[5] From the memoirs of the period, it is evident that a new interest in literature and politics gripped young Caucasian Armenians, as they took their education into their own hands, read the novels of Raffi and the poems of Patkanian, and formed study circles to discuss the important political and philosophical issues of the time. The currency of the Armenian Question and the excitement fed by the Russian victory over the Turks in 1877–1878 stirred concern for the plight of the Armenians in the Ottoman Empire and the possibility of a resolution of their problem through foreign intervention.[6]

While the leading diplomats of Europe gathered in Berlin to restrain Russia's role in the Turkish Empire, Armenian students in Tiflis were meeting illegally in groups of ten to fifteen persons to read the works of liberal and radical Russian writers from Belinskii and Turgenev to Dobroliubov, Chernyshevskii, Shchedrin, and Pisarev.[7] Teachers opposed the meetings, but the students found them a source of inspiration. Although poorly organized, these circles, modeled on the *kruzhki* of Russian students, provided the participants with a feeling of comradeliness, shaped their social consciousness, and aroused their desire to serve their own people. But unlike their Russian classmates emerging from such circles north of the Caucasus, the Armenian students of Tiflis did not, on the whole, become revolutionaries but remained followers of Artsruni's *Mshak,* essentially reformists, though now, as a result of membership in the circles, with somewhat broader political and social interests. Only a few turned to more revolutionary approaches.

In the classical period of Russian *narodnichestvo,* which can be dated roughly from 1866 to 1881, Armenians did not become involved with this movement for peasant socialism in any significant numbers. According to the tsarist police, of fifty-four members of populist organizations in the Caucasus in 1876, thirty-seven were Georgians, five Russians, four Azerbaijanis, and only three Armenians.[8] The *Mshakakan* brand of liberal nationalism was far more attractive to Armenian students in the Russian Empire than the revolutionary populism of the radical Russian intelligentsia. The earliest liberation circles among Russian Armenians, far from populist in the Russian sense, did not aim at bringing down the autocracy; they were nationalist rather than socialist in inspiration and were primarily directed toward Turkish Armenia. In the 1880s the international ramifications of the Armenian Question remained central to the concerns of Caucasian Armenian intellectuals, and hope existed that Russia would come to the aid of Turkish Armenians. But increasingly, exposure to Russian radical thought had a profound effect on the conception of the special role Caucasian Armenians might play in the liberation of the Armenians in Turkey. From Khanazatian's memoirs it is clear that the Caucasian Armenians were struck by the inactivity of the Armenian intelligentsia in Constantinople and Smyrna, their lack of interest in the fate of those living in the Armenian Vilayets of eastern Anatolia. Armenians in western Turkey apparently were more interested in the parliamentary politics of republican France than in the conditions of the peasants of Armenia.[9] Thus the only avenue for Western civilizing influence and the only source of revolutionary leadership was the intelligentsia of the Caucasus. Tiflis and Erevan were, in fact, closer to Erzerum and Van than were Constantinople and Smyrna, and from their reading of Russian literature and political tracts, the Caucasian Armenians were influenced by the radical Russian feelings of guilt and responsibility before those less privileged.

The young Armenians of the 1880s–1890s did not adopt the specific aims of the Russian populists, namely the development of socialism based on the peasant commune, for there were no communes among Armenian peasants. Rather, the Armenian radicals imbibed the same sense of mission, of service to the people, that gripped the radical Russian intelligentsia. Young Armenians, gaining a sense of what it meant to be an Armenian as they were simultaneously being sensitized and politicized by Russian radical thought, reacted most strongly to the plight of their ethnic compatriots of whom they had almost no firsthand knowledge. For the Armenians the Russian *khozhdenie v narod* (going to the people) became transformed into *depi erkire* (toward the homeland). Their moral and political commitment was the same, but emphasis on Turkey led to the Armenians separating themselves organizationally from the revolutionary movements of the Russians and Georgians. The peculiar position of the Armenians as a people divided between two empires imposed a stark political choice on radical Armenians: as radical opponents of political oppression they might join with their comrades of other nationalities and work toward the elimination of the Russian autocracy, or they might go their own way, organize autonomously, and work against the Ottoman oppressors of the Armenian peasants in Anatolia. Paradoxically, the Armenians' contact with Russian populism helped to form their consciousness of the conditions in which their brethren in Turkey lived and, therefore, impelled Caucasian Armenians to turn from the struggle against Russian autocracy toward the national struggle in Turkey.

Briefly in the early 1880s, Armenian students impressed by the populist assassination of the Tsar Alexander II became interested in the activities of the terrorist wing of the populist movement *Narodnaia volia* (The People's Will).[10] But though they were inspired by the spirit of self-sacrifice of the *narodnovoltsy*, few Armenian students actually joined them. In the age of the repressive Alexander III, Russian autocracy appeared too strong to be seriously affected by a small revolutionary party of intellectuals, while the tottering Ottoman regime seemed a much more vulnerable target. Somewhat unrealistically people spoke of a few hundred soldiers taking Van in a few days. Unreasonable hopes were placed on Great Britain even as it entered into a diplomatic arrangement with the Porte.[11] The Armenian revolution was born in a romantic haze, inspired by Russian populism, the Bulgarian revolution, and the nationalist poets and novelists.

In 1880 a committee of the terrorist party *Narodnaia volia* was formed in Tiflis, and three Armenians—Grigor Ter Grigorian, Abraham Dastakian, and Tamara Adamian—were members along with three Georgians—Vasili Sulkhanov, Vasili Rukhiladze, and Anna Sulkhanova. But the Armenians under Dastakian's leadership split from the Georgians in 1882 and formed their own circle, having lost interest in the multinational revolutionary struggle and preferring to dedicate themselves—in their words—to the "undefended claims of the unfortunate Armenian people."[12]

Soon the former *narodnovoltsy* led by Dastakian managed to attract other members—Simeon and Srapion Ter Grigorian, Aleksandr Petrosian ("Sandal"), David Nersessian, Aresdages Tokhmakhian, and Tigran Pirumian—and the 1883 were recognized as the leading collective by other informal groups in Tiflis. To get their message out the circle published an underground newspaper, *Munetik* (The Crier), edited by Simon Zavarian, Grigor Aghababian, and Aleksandr Movsesian (Shirvanzade), which called for armed resistance. Another paper, *Hairenaser dzain* (Patriotic Voice), edited by Simeon and Srapion Ter Grigorian, also occasionally appeared, taking a more moderate line advocating passive resistance. Patriotic works by Raffi, Gamar-Katiba, and Nalbandian were also published.[13] Whatever its populist roots, the Dastakian group had clearly become a patriotic conspiracy aimed at the liberation of Turkish Armenia. They sent their members, Pirumian and "Sandal," to Turkey to survey conditions and report back on revolutionary possibilities. Like so many other groups of that time, the Dastakian circle had no formal organization and no clear ideological content. Not surprisingly, when Dastakian, Nersessian, Adamian, and the Grigorian brothers left Tiflis to continue their education in Russia, the group fell apart (fall 1883).[14] In the mid-1880s a group of Armenian students in Tiflis made contact with the poorest stratum of Armenian workers, porters who had emigrated from Mush in Turkey after the war of 1877–1878, in order to create educated cadres that could then be sent back into Turkey to agitate among the Armenian peasants. Like the activity of Russian populists among the urban workers, this work was seen, not as a means to create conscious proletarians, but rather as a convenient means to link up with an inaccessible peasantry.[15] Within a year a serious tactical disagreement divided the student agitators in this group. A majority wished to continue to concentrate on the liberation of Armenians in Turkey, but a minority argued in favor of working on problems facing Caucasian Armenians as well and formed their own group in Tiflis in 1882–1883. This proto-populist circle, led by Kristapor Mikayelian (1859–1905), a member of *Narodnaia volia,* managed to hold together for four years, agitating among the poor in the towns and trying to interest friends in other cities to work among workers and peasants. In that time it reprinted Nalbandian's pamphlet on agriculture on a hectograph (1884) and put out a leaflet protesting the government's forcible closing of nearly 600 Armenian schools in February 1885.[16] But within a few years of its founding, the Mikayelian circle had responded to new political developments and turned toward nationalism.

The Russophilia of the Caucasian Armenian intelligentsia was tested severely after 1881 when the Emperor Alexander III (1881–1894) reversed the tolerant policies of his father toward the non-Russian nationalities and engaged in a policy of Russification and persecution of nationalists. Although the *Polozhenie* of 1836 had guaranteed the Armenian clergy and community the authority to operate primary schools, the tsarist government summarily shut down the hundreds of Armenian schools attended by about 20,000 students.[17] In response to this provocative act by the government, the Armenian revolutionary circle in Tiflis opened a number of secret Armenian schools and distributed an inflammatory leaflet written by their leader, Kristapor Mikayelian, in which the depth of national feeling of the group's members is evident. Addressing himself to his "Brother and Sister Armenians," Mikayelian wrote: "Our schools are for us as sacred as the holy temple; from our glorious past we have been left two holy things—the national church and the national schools. These two holy things, having preserved our language, have preserved us as a nation." "Our schools are being closed with the help of bayonets. Let each Armenian family become its own separate Armenian school. Victory will be ours." "As for the Armenian language, let that Armenian who meets another Armenian and does not speak to him in Armenian be cursed."[18]

The closing of the schools acclerated the development of Armenian nationalism and weaned the Armenian revolutionaries away from working together with Russian Socialists. The Mikayelian group did not survive the school crisis very long. In the fall of 1885 two of its members, Gevork Gharajian and Aleksandr Petrosian, traveled through the Armenian villages of Transcaucasia to investigate peasant life and assess their revolutionary potential. Returning to Tiflis they read rather pessimistic reports to their comrades. Already the group's rather amorphous ideology—a combination of Russian peasant socialism with nationalism, liberalism, and even anarchism—was proving inadequate as a cement to keep the six members in a single organization. By 1886 the group was dissolved, and its members went their separate ways.[19] Interestingly enough, out of this group came some of the most influential of the future leaders of both the Dashnaktsutiun and its rival, the Hnchak party, men intellectually and emotionally indebted to the philosophy of the populist circles.

Having shown the limited legacy of this brief flirtation with populism, it must also be noted that in one important aspect the influence of populism on the further development of the Armenian intelligentsia has been greater than previously imagined. From the 1880s, a significant number of Caucasian Armenian revolutionaries abandoned much of the *Mshakakan* liberalism along with its admiration of Western capitalism and committed themselves to social-

ism in one form or another as a programmatic goal. This ideological development separated the young radicals of Transcaucasia somewhat from the
Turkish Armenian intelligentsia that remained basically liberal in its outlook.[20]
Even more immediately, the influence of socialism created new strains within
the Caucasian Armenian community. Armenian life in Tiflis, Baku, and Erevan
had long been dominated by the wealthy and politically influential bourgeoisie, but insofar as these worldly men had political interests they were pro-
Russian. The relative security provided by the autocracy and the close relations between business and the state linked the Armenian oil men of Baku
and the *mokalake* of Tiflis with the tsarist authority. The most progressive
attitudes among the propertied class in the cities were articulated by Artsruni
and his liberal newspaper, *Mshak*. In general, then, the Armenian merchants
and industrialists, with their international connections, fit their stereotype as
cosmopolitan businessmen with extra-national loyalties, and the politics of
many of them were alien to the radical intellectuals emerging in their midst.
As the young radicals moved from liberalism to socialism, and from a pro-
Russian orientation to a more narrow concern for the national struggle in
Turkey, they drew away from the Armenian national bourgeoisie. It should be
emphasized that nationalism among the Caucasian Armenians was most
clearly not a "bourgeois" creation but rather an ideology evolved and spread
by a Russian-educated intelligentsia. In time, the Armenian middle class would
have to be forced by terror to become part of the national struggle.

In the history of nineteenth-century socialism, the period after the death
of Marx in 1883 is remarkable for the vigor of the challenge presented by the
theories of Marx, Engels, and their followers to the variety of other socialist
tendencies—anarchism, syndicalism, Blancism, and Russian populism. By the
end of the century an international socialist organization had been formed,
and national parties in most European states openly proclaimed their acceptance of the Marxist theory of history and its prediction of capitalist collapse
and proletarian hegemony. As preached in the final decade of the century, the
Marxism of the Second International appears now as more dogmatic than
scientific, more an economic determinism than a dialectical historicism, but
the power of the theory lay precisely in its confidence that the history of the
industrial West would culminate in socialist revolution, and for Plekhanov
and the Russian Marxists, this confidence extended to a conviction that Russia—indeed the rest of the world—must inevitably follow the path already
broken by the West.

Such a theory proposing that societies must move from feudal agrarianism
through capitalism to socialism, one might reasonably expect, would have
little appeal for young Armenians whose impatience precluded waiting
through a lengthy capitalist development, then just beginning in the cities
of Transcaucasia and Turkey. The theories of the Russian populists, which
compressed the political overthrow of autocracy and the socialist revolution
into one continuous process, were much more congenial. Populism permitted

reliance on the peasantry rather than waiting for the development of an urban proletariat. Populism approved the use of terrorism as a weapon in the revolutionary arsenal. The romantic urges of young Armenians were much more consistent with populism than with the drier theories of Marxism, and only a small number of Armenian radicals adopted the general philosophical outlook of West European Social Democrats in the late 1880s. The majority of the Armenian revolutionary movement developed primarily as a sister to the Russian peasantist parties and a vigorous opponent of the Marxists. Crucial to the avoidance of Marxism of the majority of Armenian revolutionaries was the consistent emphasis in Armenian political thinking on the unity of the Armenian nation, of the solidarity of goals of all Armenians, and the danger of class division among this small people. This remained a key tenet among many Armenian radicals even as tensions developed in the 1890s between radical intellectuals and the bourgeoisie, not to mention the increased antagonism between the middle and working classes. Central to the Marxist theory was the notion that the driving force in history is the struggle between classes, that members of the same class have the same interest no matter what their nationality. For the Marxists nationality and nationalism were transitory, the products of the bourgeois stage of history to be superseded after the proletarian revolution by internationalism. For most Armenian revolutionaries, nationality was the touchstone of their worldview.

The second half of the 1880s was for the history of the Russian revolutionary intelligentsia the hiatus between the period of populist hegemony of the 1870s and the victory of Marxism in the late 1890s. Except in the minds of Georgii Plekhanov and some of his closest followers, the distinctions between Marxism and other forms of socialism were not yet very clear. Marx was admired as one of the great theoreticians of socialism, but he was also known as the rather cranky leader of the First International and an uncompromising critic of the anarchist Mikhail Bakunin. In his first political pamphlets written from a Marxist point of view—*Socialism and the Political Struggle* (1883) and *Our Differences* (1885)—the former populist Plekhanov set out to distinguish his brand of Marxism from the dominant school of populist thought, arguing that the peasant commune on which the populists had hoped to build their socialism was in the process of disintegration and that socialism could come to Russia, as in the West, only as the result of the development and consequent overthrow of capitalism. The instrument of revolution was not the peasantry, which had so often disappointed the populists, but the urban working class. Such ideas represented a break with decades of Russian revolutionary thinking and were resisted by most young intellectuals. Among Armenians only a few, like Gevork Gharajian in Geneva and I. Kh. Lalaiants in Kazan, found them to be compelling.

Gevork Gharajian, who had left the Caucasus in the summer of 1886 to study at the Ecole d'agriculture in Montpellier, was soon encouraged to move to Geneva where an active colony of students from Russia and the Caucasus was engaged in revolutionary politics. The emigres, still very sympathetic to the moribund *Narodnaia volia,* avidly read its exile journal—*Vestnik narodnoi voli*—and greatly respected the exiled populists Petr Lavrov, Lev Tikhomirov, Polonskaia, Rusanov, Stepniak-Kravchinskii, etc. Plekhanov, however, who had already turned from populism to Marxism, was despised by most of the students for rejecting terrorism and taking a passive, scholarly approach to the revolutionary struggle.[21]

Gharajian met Plekhanov in Geneva in late 1886, after having read *Capital,* Vol. I, in French. They discussed the Armenian Question, and Gharajian explained that Armenian revolutionaries planned partisan warfare and terrorism against the Turks with the hope that such incidents would instigate European diplomatic intervention as they had earlier in the Balkans. Plekhanov put little hope in diplomatic pressure and indicated his belief that Russian Armenians should concentrate on the liberation of Russia, which in turn would aid the Armenians in Turkey.[22] Gharajian was deeply impressed with Plekhanov's erudition, and in 1887 he began work on a translation of the *Communist Manifesto,* the first into Armenian.[23]

The heady political atmosphere in Geneva attracted two more Caucasian rebels in the summer of 1886—the young Avetis Nazarbekian and his fiancée, Maro Vardanian. Charismatic personalities extremely well-read in Russian and German revolutionary material, the Nazarbeks were soon known to the Russian emigres as "the Emperor and Empress of Armenia."[24] The handsome Avetis Nazarbekian had written for the liberal journal *Armenia,* published in Marseilles by Mkrtich Portugalian, but, like other young activists, was disturbed by Portugalian's hesitation in forming a revolutionary party. Together with Gevork Gharajian, Kristapor Ohanian, Ruben Khanazatian, and Gabriel Kafian, the Nazarbeks put out Avetis Nazarbekian's pamphlet entitled *Haiaker Kamelion* (The Armenian-eating Chamelion).[25] This marked the definitive break with Portugalian and the liberal Armenakans whom the Geneva revolutionaries considered to be too moderate. The Geneva revolutionaries decided to publish a newspaper to rival *Armenia,* and money was raised by holding a Caucasian evening of drama, dance, and dinner.

Late in 1886 Nazarbekian, Maro Vardanian, and Gevork Gharajian wrote a draft program for a new party. While the immediate goal of the party was independence for Turkish Armenia, the eventual goal was a socialist republic. And socialism could be achieved only by revolutionary means. In August 1887 the six young Armenian revolutionaries in Geneva formally established a new Armenian revolutionary party, a party without a name and with no social base within the country they hoped to liberate.[26] Their principal means of recruiting support was through their newspaper *Hnchak* (The Bell)—so named to honor the first Russian revolutionary newspaper published abroad, Alexander Herzen's *Kolokol*—the first issue of which appeared in November 1887.[27]

The party was socialist but not specifically Marxist, although the group had quite good relations with Plekhanov and his comrade, Vera Zasulich. As Khanazatian remembers, the group was much closer to *Narodnaia volia* and even the "purest nationalists."[28] The Hnchak program contained elements both of Marxism and populism[29] and noted that mankind was divided into two parts—the *shahagortsogh* (the exploiters) and the *shahagortsvogh* (the exploited), which were the vast majority. However, socialism was *"voch anmijakan ail heravor npatak"* (not an immediate but a distant goal).[30] Although the Hnchaks referred to themselves in their program as *sotsialist-ramkavarakan* (Social Democrat) and used Marxist language, their debt to the Russian populists became quite clear in the fourth section of the program in which revolutionary means—propaganda, agitation, and terror—were discussed. The end toward which their efforts were to be directed was the liberation and unification of Persian, Russian, and Turkish Armenia into an independent state.[31]

In Transcaucasia itself the influence of Marxism, as one might expect, was almost completely absent in the late 1880s, and even the former interest in populism had abated. When the populist Kristapor Mikayelian returned to Tiflis from Moscow in the summer of 1887, he found few signs of the circles that had once been so popular among Caucasian students. The leading activists had left for either Russia or Western Europe to further their studies. Mikayelian attempted to put out an illegal journal in Tiflis with the aid of his close friend Simon Zavarian, but the necessary funds could not be found. The Armenian revolutionaries in Tiflis at this time were isolated and disunited but firm enough in their commitment to the national struggle in Turkey to reject the offers of Georgian radicals to work together in a common effort against the autocracy. Instead, Mikayelian and a small group who met at a boarding house called the *Iuzhnye nomera* (Southern Pension) formed a new patriotic organization in the winter of 1889—*Eritasart Haiastan* (Young Armenia).[32] Their purpose was to send men to Turkey to attack the Kurds who preyed on Armenian villages; their hope was to attract the attention and sympathetic support of the Western powers. Although *Eritasart Haiastan* existed as a separate organization for only a year, its twenty members were very active in setting up other circles in the Caucasus, Persia, and Turkey and in the effort to organize all Armenian revolutionaries everywhere into a single federation—the *Hai Heghapokhakanneri Dashnaktsutiun* (Federation of Armenian Revolutionaries). Once again Armenian revolutionaries had chosen not to engage in a multinational struggle against autocracy but to carry their fight alone into Turkey itself. The adoption of an ostensibly socialist ideology did not alter that determination.

The socialist nationalism forged in the late 1880s and early 1890s in the Caucasus and in Geneva by young Armenians gave birth to two revolutionary organizations. The history of the Armenian revolutionary movement from 1890 through the next century was a story of conflict and rivalry between the Hnchak party and the Dashnaktsutiun. For this reason, perhaps, the close relations of these organizations at their inception has been unnecessarily obscured. The soil from which both Hnchaks and Dashnaks sprang had been fertilized by the contradictory influences of the Russian populism and Armenian nationalism of the 1880s. What ultimately divided them appeared in 1890 to be a mere difference of emphasis on the relative weight to be given to the socialist program of the Geneva revolutionaries and the nationalist sentiments of the Armenians in the Caucasus and in Turkey. Yet such nuances betrayed deeper differences in their understanding of the nature of the anticipated revolution and the relationship of the radical intelligentsia to the upper strata of Armenian society.

The peculiar combination of socialism and nationalism adopted by Armenian radicals defined them as separate from the conservative and liberal bourgeoisie, which was content to maintain peace with the Russian autocracy, preserve their privileged position in the capitalist economy, and avoid involvement in Turkey. Yet many Armenian radicals desired an all-nation movement against the Turks and were prepared, not only to deemphasize the anti-Russian aspects of their efforts, but even to abandon socialism in order to secure liberal and bourgeois support. Furthermore, as the nationalist revolutionaries turned toward their anticipated constituents both in Turkey and Transcaucasia, they were struck by the lack of interest in socialism and the persistence of hope in European intervention. While socialism might have appealed to egalitarian intellectuals, it was certain to provoke the antagonism of Armenian businessmen and European statesmen and, therefore, seemed to the more moderate of the young nationalists to be a great liability.

On his journey back to the Caucasus in 1889, the Hnchak organizer Ruben Khanazatian traveled through Constantinople, hoping to set up secret cells to aid the new movement. He was able to arrange for monthly deliveries of *Hnchak,* but in his search for cadres, he spent long hours trying to explain the difference between Hnchak socialism and "nihilism." Local youths remained convinced that socialism was alien to Armenians, and only a few recruits were found to form a Hnchak circle.[33] His modest success with young Armenians can be compared with the greater doubts expressed by the foremost veteran of the older generation's struggle for Armenian liberation, the aging "Eagle of Vaspurakan," the former Patriarch of Constantinople, Khrimian-Hairik. Khanazatian visited Khrimian to discuss the new party, but when he explained Hnchak's socialist program, the patriarch became concerned about the opinion of foreign powers: "What will England or your tsar's government say?" The younger man answered that until the Armenians acted and shed their blood, Europeans would not free them.[34] Self-reliance was the confident stance of the younger generation, though many others were wary of this new path.

After a short visit with his parents in Vladikavkaz, Khanazatian traveled south to Tiflis to recruit young Armenians into the Hnchak party. As in Constantinople, so in Tiflis, he met resistance and indifference to his ideas among many of his contemporaries, some of whom were more interested in the latest fads, like hypnotism, or in their own careers than in politics. But he soon made contact with about twenty young radicals, some of whom were associated with *Eritasart Haiastan*. They responded to his patriotic plea to found a revolutionary socialist organization, although they, too, had doubts about the efficacy of publically proclaiming their socialism in view of the help hoped for from the Great Powers.[35]

At a second meeting the group adopted the socialist program of *Hnchak* and agreed to work in coordination with that Geneva-based group. But the question of socialism was far from settled. The students invited Aleksandr Kalantar, a man they esteemed highly, to participate in the political debate, and at a third meeting Kalantar spoke against a socialist program and called for a *zut azgayin tsragir* (a purely national program).[36] Kalantar's view prevailed, and the meeting decided that the new revolutionary party would have a nationalist rather than socialist program. Khanazatian, disappointed at the results of the meeting, nevertheless was content that a political core for the revolutionary party had been established.[37]

Besides programmatic differences, the Armenian radicals were divided along tactical lines. The Hnchak leadership had decided that revolutionary cadres should be sent into Turkey to propagandize and organize the Armenian peasantry of Anatolia, but when this question was raised in Tiflis, the university graduates and advanced students spoke in favor of having some members stay behind and work as leaders in the Caucasus. The teachers, like Hovsep Arghutian and Harutiun Iusufian, were joined by the younger university students in a spirited defense of the move into Turkey.[38] Debates similar to this had raged among urban Russian populists before their "going to the people" in 1873–1874, and like their Russian counterparts, the Armenian revolutionaries of 1889–1890 soon coalesced around the tactic of going to their people. Early in January 1890, Khanazatian provided an example by leaving for Trebizond where he established a Hnchak group. Almost overnight, he reported, political life among the local Armenians quickened.[39] Throughout the Caucasus young, somewhat romantic Armenians prepared to launch a military expedition against the Turks, a plan that in the fall of 1890 led to a tragic and unnecessary loss for the revolutionary movement.[40]

The debate over a socialist program not only concerned the degree of development of Turkish Armenia and the appropriateness of such an economic structure for the Armenian peasantry; it also revealed an ambivalence among the younger generation of educated Armenians toward the West as a model of social evolution. For some, industrial capitalism and parliamentary liberalism were so great an advance for the backward and despotic agrarian society in Anatolia that realism dictated working toward a liberal, political revolution and autonomy for Armenia as the only accessible goal. But for others, particularly those with experience among the Russian populists and Marxists in the West, the inequities, class conflicts and political corruption that they observed

in Western Europe propelled them to consider a program of transcending or
foreshortening the bourgeois stage of historical development and establishing
a collectivist order in which the means of production were controlled socially.
Their realism was reflected in the adoption of their minimum program and
the postponement of socialism to a later date.

The meetings of Armenian revolutionaries continued in Tiflis from the
fall of 1889 into the summer of 1890. The entire spectrum of Armenian radical
and liberal opinion, as well as the different social classes, were represented
in these meetings. The veterans of *Narodnaia volia*—Dastakian, Mikayelian,
Zavarian—held discussions with the middle-class nationalists who met at the
Severnye nomera (Northern Pension), men like the wealthy Konstantin Khatisian and Gabo Mirzoian. But the majority of the participants in these gatherings were followers of Artsruni, national liberals dedicated to the liberation of
Turkish Armenia, the most prominent of whom was the journalist Khachatur
Malumian (Aknuni). Thus, the socialists were in a distinct minority.[41]

As the final outlines of a unified revolutionary party took shape, the
Tiflis radicals sent Arshak Ter Gregorian to Batumi to invite Khanazatian, as
representative of the Hnchaks, to participate in the discussions once again.[42]
In the summer of 1890 Khanazatian, Mikayelian, Zavarian, Dastakian, Malumian, Mirzoian, Khatisian, Ter Gregorian, and Dr. Hovhannes Loris-Melikian met to found the revolutionary union.[43] The meeting was marked by
moderation and compromise in an effort to create an umbrella organization
under which various tendencies in the liberation movement could operate.
The men from Tiflis opposed establishing the party center in Geneva where
it might fall under the influence of the dynamic Nazarbeks. Khanazatian suggested Trebizond as a compromise, and though Tiflis was probably the favored
choice, it was agreed to move the central committee to Turkey. The party was
to have two official newspapers. *Hnchak* would remain the theoretical organ,
edited by Nazarbekian and Mikayelian in Geneva, while *Droshak* (Banner)
was to be published in Tiflis with a more popular format. Hnchak groups
were to become sections of the new Armenian Federation of Revolutionaries,
the Dashnaktsutiun.[44]

On the all-important question of the party's aims Khanazatian was willing, once again, to compromise on its explicit socialism. As he wrote later in
his memoirs: "My work in Trebizond and Constantinople had demonstrated
to me clearly that there is no base for Marxist activity in that country. In the
Turkish environment, Marxism had no business."[45] The majority of the Tiflis
delegates feared that a socialist program would frighten away potential adherents to the cause.[46] Although Khanazatian feared concessions to the non-
socialists, he accepted the assurances of the Tiflis socialists that the new federation would be socialist without calling itself socialist. Indeed, its first *Manifesto*
proclaimed the "political and economic freedom of Turkish Armenia" as the
party's goal.

As with the other Armenian circles, the Dashnaktsutiun, too, subordinated the social question to the national question. The young socialists who wrote the *Manifesto* were angered by Europe's failure to recognize Armenia's national suffering. Their first public declaration rang with such phrases as "patience also has its limits" and "the people have understood that their strength is within themselves; the formerly slavish, patient Armenian has today become revolutionary." Ending with the phrase "this is not the time to wait," the Dashnak founders called on the whole nation—young people, the aged, the rich, women, even the clergy—to unite in the struggle for national liberation.[47] The Dashnaks did not see themselves as the representatives of any single group or class among Armenians but rather as the revolutionary vanguard of the whole nation. As a coalition of socialists and nonsocialist nationalists, they considered it necessary to create a national movement with an ostensible socialist ideology. Of course, Dashnak socialism had much more in common with Russian populism, with its principles of association and cooperation, than with the ideas of Russian Marxism, a socialism that emphasized class divisions and struggles and denied the primacy of nationality.

Thus, both Hnchak and the Dashnaktsutiun were socialist and nationalist at their origins, and their goals and tactics seemed to many to be congenial enough for the Hnchaks to enter the Armenian Revolutionaries' Federation. But when Khanazatian arrived in Geneva early in 1891, he found that his fellow Hnchaks were much less willing to compromise on the question of socialism than he had been in order to form a broad revolutionary coalition. The Geneva Hnchaks had received complaints from party members that Dashnaks treated them poorly and were convinced that the Dashnaktsutiun was in the hands, not of the socialists Mikayelian and Zavarian, but of the nonsocialist nationalists.[48] Nazarbekian also disapproved of the first circular of the new federation, the *Droshake Trutsik Tert,* no. 1 (the contents of which are unknown to us, for this document has not survived). After lengthy deliberations, the Hnchaks decided to end their agreement with the Dashnaks and communicated their intentions in the issues of *Hnchak* for May 18 and June 5, 1891. The Geneva party claimed officially that no union of the two Armenian parties had ever taken place.[49]

In their initial phases, both Armenian revolutionary parties, while stimulated by events in Turkey and Europe, were in large part products of the intellectual and political history of the revolutionary movement within Russia. Their debt to *narodnichestvo* is undeniable, and even the Hnchak adoption of Marxist language affected only very slightly the party's basic sympathy toward the populists. Between the parties the differences would grow, but in the early 1890s they centered on the relative commitment to socialism, on the one hand, and the importance given, on the other, to an all-nation struggle in alliance with non-socialist elements. The major difference between the Russian and Georgian populists and the majority of Armenian revolutionaries in the Caucasus was the overwhelming dedication to the cause of national liberation by the Armenians, which diverted them from the struggle against Russian autocracy. Both the populist effort to unite revolutionaries of different nationalities into a common struggle against autocracy and the implicit internationalism of the Marxists found little more than rhetorical support among Armenian revolutionaries. For radical Armenians the nation, which existed at that time only in historical memory, had to be re-created through their efforts. The means was revolution, the end was a new Armenia, autonomous or independent; but in determining the form of the struggle and the nature of future Armenia, the Caucasian revolutionaries fought with each other even as they carried the war across the Arax into Turkey.

5 Labor and Socialism among Armenians in Transcaucasia

For all its intensity the discussions over socialism and nationalism, indeed political activity in general, among Caucasian Armenians before the 1890s was entirely contained within the ranks of the urban intelligentsia. In only isolated instances were the radical or liberal intellectuals able to make contact with people outside student circles or the readership of the middle-class press. Thus, a sense of irreality often accompanied the discussions in Tiflis or Geneva, and the newly formed Armenian Revolutionary Federation (Dashnaktsutiun), in the absence of a mass following, was only as strong, only as unified, as the personal commitments and idiosyncracies of a handful of men permitted. Within months of the founding of the Dashnaktsutiun the conservative "fraktsia" split with the party, and its leader, Konstantin Khatisian, left for Bulgaria to make bombs.[1] A month later other nationalists left the party, and after the fiasco of the Gugunian Expedition the tsarist government exiled Mikayelian, Zavarian, and Arghutian to Bessarabia.[2] But the most severe blow to the hopes for a unified revolutionary movement came in 1891 when the Hnchak leadership in Geneva decided to dissolve their union with the Dashnaktsutiun.[3]

As two separate parties, both claiming to be socialist and dedicated to the liberation of Turkish Armenia, the Hnchaks and the Dashnaks now stood as rivals in a common cause. Their activity, occasionally jointly but usually separately, was carried on largely in Turkey, at least until 1903. At first the Hnchak party played an unchallenged leading role in the revolutionary movement in Turkey, capturing the attention of the public and the diplomatic community with their demonstrations at Kum Kapa in Constantinople (July 15,

1890), their leadership in the Sassun insurrection in the spring of 1894, the armed demonstration at Bab Ali in Constantinople (September 18, 1895), and the revolt at Zeitun (October 12, 1895-February 1, 1896).[4] These Hnchak activities have been credited for the Armenian Reform Program signed by Sultan Abdul Hamid under European pressure in October 1895 and blamed for the Hamidian massacres of Armenians in 1895–1896.[5]

Demonstrations, rebellion, and retaliatory massacres led to the revival in interest in the Armenian Question and aroused the fears, not only of the Ottoman government, but of the Romanov regime as well.[6] Hnchak's program clearly spelled out its opposition to the autocracy and the revolutionaries' intent to unite all of Armenia into one independent state. As William Langer points out, Russia "from the outset opposed all far-reaching reform" in the Anatolian provinces and was backed in her efforts by her ally, France.[7] While the Turkish army dealt with revolutionary manifestations in Sassun and Zeitun by wiping out whole villages, on their side of the border the Russian police pursued and arrested intellectuals known to sympathize with the Armenian cause. To the Russian authorities Armenian nationalism was felt to be an immediate threat to the internal order of the empire. On July 4, 1895, the Department of Police reported that "a party of agitators, not content with strictly national questions, pursues international and revolutionary ends. This is why it is absolutely essential to interdict all collections of money among the Armenians of Russia, to interdict all transports of arms and munitions toward Turkey by way of Persia, to place the activities of the Armenian Workers' Revolutionary Association under surveillance, and to bring its adherents to account."[8]

Two months later, on September 6, the Hnchak leader Ruben Khanazatian and the writers Alexander Shirvanzade, Ghazaros Aghaian, and Avetik Isahakian were arrested along with 108 others. Despite Hnchak pleas that they were guilty of no crime against Russia for their fight was confined to Turkey, the police held to the view that the Armenian revolution would have dire consequences for Russian authority in the Caucasus.[9] Their fears were justified, for the Hnchaks "were the first to denounce the autocracy as the essential obstacle to the solution of the Armenian problem. The Dashnaks hesitated longer to fight on two fronts, at once and the same time against the Ottoman Empire and against the Russian Empire."[10]

As Russian policy abroad became clearly opposed to Armenian interests and domestic state policy turned against the Armenians, the Armenian intellectuals and bourgeoisie were forced to abandon what was left of their traditional Russophilia. Although radicals had since the early 1880s allied themselves with anti-tsarist forces and students had been mobilized during the school crisis of 1885, the historic hopes laid on Russia by more moderate elements began to crumble only in the 1890s. In December 1892 the funeral procession for Grigor Artsruni turned into a political demonstration when it was halted by the police on Golovinskii Prospekt, the central street in Tiflis. The crowd of sixty thousand surged past the police barricades to continue their march. That evening the police rounded up politically suspect intellectuals.[11] Through the following year Russian Armenian society was disturbed by the long trial of the participants of the Gugunian expedition, and in January 1896 the government closed most of the Armenian clerical schools.

At the same time anti-Armenian feeling was developing noticeably in the Caucasus.[12] Long-suppressed resentments by displaced Georgian nobles and nationalist intellectuals who saw the Armenian bourgeoisie in control of municipal institutions in Tiflis, Baku, and Erevan and much of the industrial economy of Transcaucasia were now expressed openly in the press and in Duma elections. Georgian elites were themselves undergoing rapid social changes and were pressured by economic dislocations. The Georgian nobility, dependent as it had been on serf labor, steadily declined economically after 1870, while the commercial and industrial middle class among the Armenians rose to dominate the textile, tobacco, and other local businesses. Transcaucasia was being transformed by capitalist production methods and industrialization. The oil boom in Baku and the completion of the Tiflis-Baku rail line in 1883 linked all of Transcaucasia into a single market economy, ending the isolation of many villages and small towns and introducing new horizons for peasant producers and those who wished to break with agrarian life. Capitalism and industry affected each nationality differently, and conflicts that arose from antagonistic social interests quickly took on national overtones.[13]

The violent upsurge of Russian chauvinism and Armenophobia in the Caucasus was in part stimulated by the editor of the official newspaper, *Kavkaz* (Caucasus), V. L. Velichko, a poet known as the "Katkov of the Caucasus" for his broadly conservative views and his advocacy of Russian national pride. His attacks on Armenians were republished in Ilya Chavchavadze's *iveria* and in Topchibashev's *Kaspii* in Baku. Liberals, like Niko Nikoladze, Khristafor Vermishev, and Georgii Tumanov, tried through their newspaper, *Novoe obozrenie* (New Review), to deflect the growing hostilities between the Caucasian peoples and to preach peace and cooperation but, in November 1899, the paper was closed down by the government for nearly a year for allegedly expressing "separatist ideas" and antigovernment opinions.[14] The Tiflis Duma election of 1897 occurred in an atmosphere poisoned by the nationalist press, but the Armenians won the greatest number of seats as usual given the high property qualification *(tsenz)* required for each candidate. A year later the governor-general, Prince Golitsyn, dismissed and indicted most of the city board, and a Georgian was ultimately elected mayor.[15]

The escalation of national rivalries, the heating up of the Armenian Question, and the activities of radical nationalists encouraged outward expression of Armenian nationalism by social groups other than the intelligentsia. The Russified middle class among the Caucasian Armenians began changing the Russian endings to their names back to Armenian. Thus Mirzoev became

Mirzoian and Melikov became Melikian. Tutors were hired to teach Armenian to Armenians who spoke only Russian. Priests refused to preach in Russian as they had done on official occasions, and the schools advocated ending instruction in Russian.[16]

While nationalism became the form in which discontents were expressed by the upper and middle classes, it had less effect on the lower classes.[17] The growing number of workers in the cities either remained indifferent to politics in the 1890s, concerning themselves primarily with the difficulties involved in making a living, or turned at first toward a socialism tinged with nationalism and later toward Marxism. In the 1890s the Armenian workers of Transcaucasia were a varied group of artisans, day laborers *(kintos)*, factory workers, and peasants employed in towns seasonally, a class still in the process of formation. According to the Russian census of 1897 there were 1,243,000 Armenians in the Caucasus; almost half of them—506,000—lived in the backward, nonindustrial province of Erevan where there were only about 8,000 workers. The bulk of the approximately 30,000 Armenian workers in Transcaucasia were employed in the oil industry of Baku, the refineries of Batumi, or in the factories and workshops of Tiflis.[18]

The Armenian workers of Transcaucasia were almost completely unprotected by the law, by trade unions (which were nonexistent), or by other forms of organization. It is difficult to speak of a "labor movement" in the 1890s when there was little continuity in organization, little development in the forms of struggle, and few lasting gains until the last years of the decade. There were, however, sporadic and violent strikes to improve the degrading working conditions or raise wages and shorten hours. As early as 1872 Armenian workers at Mirzoev's textile works in Tiflis went on strike when the owners lowered their wages. The manager demanded that workers return at the new wage or face being replaced. Although a few skilled workers *(mastera)* left the mill, most workers returned.[19] In the early 1880s strikes were reported among tobacco workers in Baku, 90 percent of whom were Armenians, and among Armenian workers in Batumi.[20] But not until the mid-1890s were strikes numerous enough to draw the attention of radical intellectuals to their political potential. In 1894 Armenian tobacco workers at the Bozarjian factory in Tiflis walked off the job when they discovered that their sick fund had been confiscated by the owners. Workers demonstrated in the streets until the police arrived and arrested their leaders. The factory was closed and workers laid off. Later when the owners reopened the factory they hired only women workers whom they considered more "obedient and neat."[21]

The most impressive strikes in the 1890s were those of railroad workers. In April 1896 400 workers struck near Akhtala because of irregular payment of wages. They broke into the office of the administration and were fired on by gendarmes. The workers quickly disarmed the gendarmes, and additional police had to be called to quell the protesters. Eight of the leaders of the strike, Georgian and Armenian villagers hired to build the rail links south of Tiflis, were arrested and tried. Additional clashes involving Armenian construction workers occurred on the railroads in December 1896 and in October 1897.[22] As far as is known these strikes, indeed all strikes up to the great railroad strike of December 1898, were spontaneous expressions of labor dissatisfaction and were carried on without the participation of socialist workers or intellectuals. As a Social Democratic historian of the period puts it, the period up to 1900 was "the period of the spontaneous-unconscious movement" as distinct from the years 1900 to 1905, which he sees as "the period of the conscious political-economic movement."[23]

Workers made contact with the nationalist and socialist intellectuals throughout the 1890s, though not on a sustained basis, and in time some of them formed study groups and political organizations. At age 14 the son of a Tiflis artisan, Ashot Khumarian, briefly spent some time in the Nersesian Seminary where he and his classmates absorbed the nationalism of their teachers and discussed current issues in their self-educational circles. Khumarian, however, soon left the seminary to take up, first, metalwork and later the printing trade. He maintained contact with his friends in the seminary and together they became acquainted with Avetis Araskhanian, the liberal editor of *Murj* (Hammer), a newspaper that often printed articles on the "workers' question." Araskhanian advised the young workers and students to subscribe to *Hnchak*. About the same time the worker-student circle met the *narodnovolets* Stepan Ter Stepanian, who agreed to lecture them and discuss the populist literature that he had brought from Russia.[24] In this way these teenage radicals became acquainted both with the Armenian and Russian revolutionary movements and decided to set up their own secret organization.

Sometime in 1892 Khumarian and his friend, the artisan Arshalius Khazhakian, organized the *Hai Banvor Heghapokhakanneri Asotsiatsia* (Armenian Worker Revolutionaries' Association) and began to publish a patriotic newspaper, *Azat Haiastan* (Free Armenia). Most noteworthy about the group was the fact that its membership included not only the usual complement of seminary students but artisans and workers as well. The distance between poorer students like Khumarian and the artisans was not very great. They were often members of the same family and enrolled, according to their material exigencies, either in school or as apprentices to a master craftsman.[25] As might be expected for a Caucasian Armenian political organization in 1892, the association's program, largely inspired by *Narodnaia Volia* and *Hnchak,* was a mixture of patriotism and the vaguest notions of socialism and called for the liberation of western Armenia by revolutionary means and the establishment there of a democratic order.[26]

The first two issues of *Azat Haiastan* appeared in 1893. Although only sixty copies of the first number were distributed, the second carried words and music to a workers' hymn that proved to be quite popular among students and workers. Through the energetic activity of the association's members other worker-student circles were set up outside of Tiflis, in Aleksandropol,

Kars, Sarikamish, and Kaghzvan. The next year sixty people gathered in Khumarian's apartment to celebrate May Day. The room was decorated with red flags and pictures of Marx and Lassalle, and the participants sang the new workers' hymn.[27] Clearly some members of the association identified with the growing Social Democratic movement in Western and Central Europe and were reinforced by the iconography of socialism. But apparently these sentiments were not shared by all and, later in 1894, one wing of the association seized the organization's press and paper in an effort to turn the group in a more nationalist direction. Khumarian and his close associates set up a second press and in January 1895 issued a socialist newspaper, *Kriv* (Struggle). Nine months later the Russian police arrested Khumarian and dispersed his group. Neither wing of the association had much success in its ostensible purpose of fomenting rebellion in Turkish Armenia, but this first Armenian workers' organization was, in the words of V. Nevskii, "a typical socialist organization of the transitional type, in many ways like organizations in Russia, moving from populism to Marxism."[28]

The uneasy cohabitation of socialism and nationalism within Armenian political organizations did not survive the heating up of the Armenian Question in the mid-1890s. Shortly after the schism and subsequent collapse of the Armenian Worker Revolutionaries' Association, the leading Armenian political party at the time was torn apart by tactical and programmatic disagreements. The Hnchak party had in its first seven years become a widespread network of cells and circles stretching from Turkey and Transcaucasia to Egypt and the United States, but its center remained the small group around the Nazarbeks, the editors of *Hnchak,* who moved from Geneva to Athens and then to London. The distance between the socialist leadership of the party and the non-socialist elements, particularly in Turkey, Egypt, and America, grew greater after the Hnchak demonstrations in Constantinople drew only ambivalent responses from the Great Powers and bloody reprisals from the Turks. The anti-Nazarbek wing blamed the center for the massacres, for the decline in support from Europe, and for the unnecessary burden of the socialist program. In August 1896 the anti-socialist Hnchaks met in London, eliminated socialism from their program, and called for new elections to the party's central committee.

The Nazarbek faction rejected the demands of their opponents and in September opened the Second Congress of the Hnchak party. The congress agreed to eliminate public demonstrations as a tactic, but no concession was made on socialism. The split could not be repaired. From October 26, 1896, to January 13, 1897, the Nazarbek wing of the party met to reconstitute what was left of their organization. The anti-Nazarbeks met separately and in 1898, under the initiative of Arpiar Arpiarian and Levon Pachalian, held a congress in Alexandria to form the *Verakazmial* (Reformed) Hnchak party.

The reasons for the demise of the party stemmed from their initial rapid series of successes. Their constituency had grown diverse and scattered with conflicting interests and visions of Armenia's future. Anahide Ter Minassian suggests that the political differences were grounded in social conflicts: "The Hnchaks of Turkey and the Hnchaks of Egypt, where a rich bourgeoisie of bankers, high functionaries, great landed property owners existed, reproached the Caucasian Hnchaks for tying the Armenian question in Turkey to the fate of the Russian workers. In putting the accent on class struggle the Caucasian Hnchaks had frightened not only conservative Muslim society but the Armenian bourgeoisie which was disassociating itself from the national problem, just as was Western capitalism, which no longer intended to support the Armenian movement."[29]

The Hnchak party never recovered its former vigor after the schisms of the late 1890s. Not only did the anti-socialists break off to form a separate party, but the Nazarbeks themselves resigned from the central committee, and from the Left a prominent Hnchak-Marxist, Ervand Palian, also quit the central committee to issue his own journal, *Handes* (Review), in 1900. Palian believed that even the old Hnchak party was overly committed to patriotism and national independence and that a clean break with the center was necessary in order to create a genuine Armenian Social Democratic party. He never found much support in Transcaucasia, but his thinking along Marxist lines was consonant with trends in the Caucasian intelligentsia.[30]

With the swift decline of the Hnchak party the Dashnaktsutiun emerged as the leading force in the Armenian revolutionary movement. At a time when the Armenian Question ceased to interest the leading politicians of Europe, the Armenian Revolutionary Federation engaged in a variety of activities within Turkey to promote revolutionary consciousness and organize self-defense. Their most spectacular demonstration took place on August 24, 1896, when a band of twenty-six Dashnaks, led by 17-year-old Papken Siuni, seized the Imperial Ottoman Bank in Constantinople, held its occupants as hostages, and threatened to blow it up before being given safe passage out of the country.[31] The Turks replied to this public insult with a massacre of about 6,000 Armenians in the city. Once again Armenian revolutionary activity, aimed at directing attention toward the plight of Ottoman Armenians, had instead stimulated the most brutal response from the Turks.

The Dashnaktsutiun, more so than the Hnchaks, avoided becoming involved in Caucasian politics. Almost no effort was made to organize urban workers in the 1890s or engage in the electoral campaigns for the city dumas. Their interventions into Caucasian life were restricted to recruiting cadres and raising money for the revolution in Turkey. Both the Hnchaks and the Dashnaks followed the example of the *narodnovoltsy* and adopted terrorism as a means to defend themselves and their people from "officials, spies, traitors, extortionists, and all exploiters."[32] "Propaganda by the deed" was a means of educating the people in their own self-worth and power and of demonstrating the vulnerability of the enemy. But in the Caucasus itself the principal victims of the Armenian terrorists were Armenians themselves. First the

Hnchaks in 1895, desperately in need of funds, turned their weapons on rich Armenians and demanded that they contribute financially to the national revolution. In December of that year two merchants of Tiflis, Zakar Abovian and Petros Makarian, were wounded by Hnchaks, and the less fortunate Stepan Gevorkian was killed on the busiest street in the city.[33] The Dashnaks soon adopted this form of "taxation," and terrorism, though condemned by the Marxists, became a permanent feature of the Armenian revolution both in Transcaucasia and Turkey. The Armenian revolutionaries were prepared to "execute" members of their own bourgeoisie whose indifference to their struggle, in their view, made them accomplices of the national enemy.

The adoption of terrorism as a tactic not only indicates the militant dedication of Hnchak and Dashnak activists to their cause but betrays an attitude about the relationship of revolutionary cadres to the masses. Whereas the Marxists in the 1890s rejected terrorism as a tactic in favor of less dramatic agitation within the working-class milieu, the Hnchaks and Dashnaks were impressed by the populists' exemplary behavior and discipline and by the necessity of heroic inspiration for creating sympathy and support among the Anatolian peasantry. On October 7, 1895, the Dashnak leader Simon Zavarian wrote to his comrades in Geneva: "I am not in agreement with the socialists that the masses influence the individual. On the contrary, individuals, heroes, inspire the masses psychologically. Carlyle, Mikhailovskii, it seems are more correct."[34] To the Dashnaks the Marxists seemed to be overly patient in their anticipation of the preconditions for revolutionary consciousness; to the Marxists the Dashnaks and Hnchaks seemed overanxious in their attempt to generate revolutionary fervor in the absence of social preconditions.

With the attention of Armenian revolutionaries focused almost exclusively on Turkish Armenia, the consequent hegemony of nationalist aims over social issues established in the Dashnasktsutiun, and the schisms in the Hnchak party, the question of the relevance of socialism to the Armenians seemed to have been decided in the negative by the last years of the nineteenth century. But precisely in these years a revival of interest in socialism, and specifically Marxism, began in the Caucasus. The sources for this new trend were varied. Russian Marxists had come to Tiflis early in the 1890s, founding the Afanasev circle in 1891. Others followed, and by the end of the decade a significant number of Russians interested in Marxism were working in Transcaucasia.[35] These men and women worked in the railroad yards and factories and set up propaganda circles to educate workers. These circles, not unlike those formed earlier by the populists, were dedicated to broadening the mental horizons of workers through the teaching of literacy, political economy, and eventually socialism. The workers were interested in self-improvement and only incidentally became involved in political matters.

A second source of Marxism came from Armenians, like Gevork Gharajian, who had studied abroad, had adopted a Marxist perspective, and returned to the Caucasus with literature. There seems, however, to have been few direct ties between the handful of Armenian Marxists studying in Europe, like the Berlin-based *Materialist* group led by Hakop Ioannisian and Sarkis Kasian, and Armenian students and workers in the Caucasus. Yet the early translations of Marx, Engels, Plekhanov, and Paul Lafargue into Armenian did reach the secret circles that grew to number as many as twenty in 1896 in Tiflis alone. A third source of Transcaucasian Marxism was the group of Georgian intellectuals and workers who turned to the left largely under the influence of two students, Noe Zhordania and Pilipe Makharadze, who had been introduced to Marxism while studying in Warsaw. The Georgian press noted the arrival in 1894 of this so-called "third generation" *(mesame dasi)* of young Marxists who sought to combat the growing nationalist mood among Georgians. Within a year one of the leading Georgian periodicals, *kvali* (Trace), was in their hands, and the Marxists were able to spread their ideas through the legal press. Both in Russia and the Caucasus the legal liberal and radical press carried the salvos of an intense debate between neo-populists and Marxists on the possibility of capitalist development in Russia. Armenians read in *Murj* and *Taraz* (Fashions) about the labor movement and social issues, and not surprisingly the historical prescriptions of the "scientific socialist" theories began to impress the intelligentsia.[36]

The development of large-scale industry in Russia, the building of the Trans-Siberian Railroad, and the visible collapse of the rural communes appeared to many to confirm the Marxist notion of the inevitability and necessity of capitalism in Russia and belie the populist hope of preserving the collectivist qualities of the agrarian order. Not surprisingly with the appearance of significant numbers of urban workers and the first signs of a militant labor movement in the late 1890s, the Marxist prescription of proletarian revolution took on a new validity. Although Transcaucasian development lagged behind central Russian, to many intellectuals in the Caucasus history seemed clearly to be on the side of the Marxists. For here was a theory that not only explained what was happening but did not regret the advance of capitalism in backward Russia. Here was a theory that simultaneously provided a transcendence beyond capitalism that liberalism did not promise. Marxism for Caucasian intellectuals was a westernizing theory that linked their homeland with European evolution, indeed with the most advanced nations, and with the growing Social Democratic labor movement. For those Armenians and Georgians frustrated by the inactivity of their peasants or uninspired by nationalist ambitions abroad, Marxist socialism provided an analysis and a political practice based on the workers in the cities of Transcaucasia itself. For the first time since the early 1880s Armenian radicals again conceived of working together with other nationalities in a common revolutionary movement against the Romanov monarchy.

In the years 1896-1897 Russian Social Democracy underwent a profound change, shifting its energies from the propaganda circles designed to educate leading workers to a strategy of economic agitation among workers based on their "everyday needs and demands."[37] The new tactics proved their value in the textile strikes in St. Petersburg in those years and within a short time they were being applied by socialists throughout the empire.[38] In Transcaucasia Social Democratic workers organized a strike of several thousand railroad workers in Tiflis in December 1898. More than a simple struggle over wages, this strike was fought over the loss of rights and privileges, such as the use of complaint books to express grievances, which the workers had enjoyed a decade earlier but had steadily been eroded away. When a delegation from the workers appeared before the administrators they were asked if they had been incited by the Armenian workers. A Russian delegate answered that Armenians played no special role, that all workers—Russian, Georgian, and Armenian—were disturbed by conditions. As reported in *Rabochee delo,* "The workers, in general, conducted themselves peacefully; they only beat up the director of the railroad."[39] Troops were called to put down the strike, but on the third day the Ministry of Communications capitulated and wired that the workers' demands be granted. The victory was marred by the arrest and exile of some workers, but this only helped to solidify the rest of the workers around their leaders. "The local intelligentsia soon after organized an evening party and subscriptions to help those arrested and their families."[40] Attempts to divide the workers along national lines had failed, and the workers had learned that in collective action their will could be made palpable. Although these perceptions were not shared by all workers, more and more of them recognized that the source of their discontents lay not with individual managers but with an alien class of owners backed by the police and the autocratic state. Social Democrats shaped and developed precisely such views.

In the evolution of Social Democracy in Transcaucasia the distance between intellectuals and workers was, at least in the initial stages, not very great. The Georgian Marxists around *kvali* or the Armenians close to the Hnchaks provided a theoretical and literary nourishment to workers even as genuine leaders emerged from the workers' milieu itself. In 1897 a Social Democratic "Tiflis Committee" was formed, almost exclusively of Georgian workers. Armenian workers remained somewhat aloof from the Georgians, and in 1898 former members of the Hnchak party and workers from several socialist circles joined to form the Union of Tiflis Workers.[41] These Armenian worker-socialists maintained ties through Gevork Gharajian, Melik Melikian, and Haik Pilosian with local Georgian and Russian Social Democrats and distinguished themselves from both the Hnchaks and Dashnaks whom they considered nationalists. According to a police report this "Armenian revolutionary party no longer considers patriotic propaganda a means sufficiently powerful to win over to the revolution the lower classes of the Armenian population, especially the workers who in order to live must work out other problems. This is why it introduced into its program the propagating among the workers of Social Democratic ideas leaning toward anarchism. It denigrates all governments and all laws which subjugate the Armenians, wherever they live, and collaborates therefore with Russian revolutionaries with whom it has concluded agreements long ago."[42] The police believed that the group had many supporters among the small number of Armenian workers and noted that these workers "are very often much more daring and headstrong than their Russian and Georgian comrades who nevertheless were involved earlier in the movement and have a more violent national temperament."[43]

In 1900 the Armenian worker-socialists began issuing an illegal journal, *Banvor* (Worker), which carried on its masthead the slogan: "Proletarians of All Countries, Unite!" By this time the close identification of this small group of workers and intellectuals with international Social Democracy was a point of pride and presumably considered not to be a political liability among their constituents. The paper was handwritten and distributed in a few dozen copies in worker districts. *Banvor* made it clear that its position was internationalist, opposed to the Dashnaks, and even the Hnchaks, whose nationalism had isolated Armenian workers from their class brothers and sisters of other nationalities. Like the Armenian populists of a decade and a half earlier the Armenian revolutionary organization linked the liberation of the Armenian working people to that of the lower classes in Russia and Transcaucasia. Twenty-three issues of *Banvor* appeared before the police in February 1901 arrested Pilosian, Kozikian, Kakhoian, their Georgian associate Bajashvili, and others, thus decimating the organization.[44]

Several developments in Russian and European political life at the turn of the century influenced Armenian political formations. After 1897 there was a general decline of interest in Europe in the Armenian Question, and the Ottoman Empire enjoyed a brief respite from the intense pressures of the Great Powers to reform its internal order. Within Russia student demonstrations in 1900–1901, followed by political protests by workers, brought to an end the "agitational" period in the labor movement and led to a reassertion of the political aims of Social Democracy.[45] The revitalization of political life was accompanied by police repression of Armenian institutions and organizations. In 1899 all the charitable societies in the Caucasus were dissolved with the understanding that they would be permitted to reestablish themselves only when they conformed to new state regulations that prohibited aid to schools, poor students, libraries, and other cultural institutions.[46] The next year the Armenian Printing Society was closed down. The governor-general and his police subordinates conceived the Armenians to be a subversive element and sought to eliminate the educational infrastructure from which their radical intelligentsia sprang. Their policies culminated in the seizure of the Armenian church's properties on June 12, 1903.

By the first years of the twentieth century the multinational labor movement, influenced by Social Democratic theorists and activists, had become a palpable force on the Transcaucasian political scene. The great majority of Social Democratic workers were Georgians, railroad workers, or artisans who had formed their own circles in close contact with students and the men around *kvali*. In 1898 about thirty-five workers and intellectuals gathered in Nadzaladevi to mark May Day; all but two were Georgians. When early in 1899 an official Tiflis Committee of the Russian Social Democratic Workers' Party (RSDRP) was set up, its membership was entirely made up of self-selected Georgian workers. A few months later the committee arranged a public celebration of May Day, and Armenians and Russians joined with the Georgians to make up the crowd of about seventy-five who gathered for a "picnic" in Avchaly outside Tiflis.[47] But it was not until the celebration a year later that banners were unfurled with slogans in three languages and that speakers of all nationalities were heard. While committed to an internationalist ideal of organization, the Social Democracy of Transcaucasia was basically a Georgian movement in which Armenians particularly felt as outsiders.[48] Only in the years before the first Russian Revolution did a multinational movement develop in Baku, first established by Georgian workers from Tiflis but soon taken over by Armenians and Russians and somewhat later joined by Azerbaijanis.[49]

In the first three years of the new century the Social Democratic movement in Transcaucasia grew rapidly. Whereas approximately 400 workers had marched the four *versts* outside of Tiflis to celebrate May Day 1900, a year later 3,000 gathered in the center of the city for an open demonstration. *Iskra* (Spark) proclaimed, "the open revolutionary movement in the Caucasus had begun."[50] A demonstration of that size was not only impressive statistically but had a powerful psychological effect on Caucasian workers; their collective power was now manifest. By 1902–1903 peasants in western Georgia, stimulated and organized by workers from Batumi, joined the revolutionary movement led by Social Democrats, refusing to pay rents and taxes and substituting their own elected authorities for tsarist appointees. With this influx of thousands of new recruits from another social class, Social Democracy emerged as the *de facto* national liberation movement of the greater part of the Georgian people. In time nationalist sentiments filtered into the self-conception of many Georgian Social Democrats, and this progressive concentration on specifically Georgian issues, along with the broadening of the social base within the Georgian masses, only served to alienate further potential recruits from among the Russians and Armenians.

For Armenians the enormous initial success of the socialist labor movement was problematic. For the commercial and industrial bourgeoisie Social Democracy was a dual threat, as a militant movement of their employees and as a national-class expression specifically of Georgians. For the Armenian nationalist intelligentsia Social Democracy remained a rival in the battle for the loyalties of Armenian intellectuals and workers. And for Armenian workers and their Marxist champions Social Democracy was a movement that claimed to express proletarian class interests but in its present manifestation seemed more concerned with their Georgian confreres than with Armenian workers. The power of organized workers was not apparent to all, and for those Armenians impressed with Marxism the time had clearly arrived to form their own national organization of Social Democrats.[51]

In the summer of 1902, just a little over a year after the arrests of the *Banvor* group and a few months after the police had rounded up the Tiflis committee, a number of Armenian Marxists formed the *Hai Sotsial-Demokratneri Miutiun* (Union of Armenian Social Democrats) in Tiflis.[52] Like most Social Democratic groups in Russia at this time the union considered itself a local chapter of the RSDRP and adhered to the more political tendency among Marxists, then coalescing around the newspaper *Iskra*. In October the union issued the first number of its newspaper *Proletariat*, in which its party manifesto was published. Probably written by Stepan Shahumian, the manifesto was a succinct Marxist analysis of recent Transcaucasian developments—the penetration of capitalist relations of production, the decline of the villages economically and culturally, the rise of the large industrial centers, Baku, Tiflis, and Batumi, and the creation of a landless proletriat forced to migrate to the towns. The only solution to the chaos created by capitalism was social revolution and the establishment of a society based on the principle of social ownership of landed property and the means of production.[53] There was no mention in the program of a united struggle of the Armenian nation, but instead a joint struggle of workers of all nations against the tsarist autocracy. The only concession to the national question was made at the end of the manifesto: "Taking into consideration that within the Russian state there are many different nationalities at various levels of cultural development, and proposing that only broad development of local self-government can secure the interests of these different elements, we consider essential in the future free Russia the establishment of a federative republic."[54] The union stopped short of advocating political autonomy for the Caucasian nationalities, given that they were not separated geographically one from another, but did call for cultural autonomy—freedom of language, for national schools, etc.[55] Organizationally the union stood firmly on the principle of joint action with socialists of other nationalities and pledged "to struggle together with [the RSDRP] for the interests of the all-Russian proletariat in general and for the Armenian in particular."[56] With this group Armenian radicals had come full circle back to merging themselves with Georgian and Russian revolutionaries. Within six months the logic of this position compelled them to dissolve the Union and enter the Tiflis Social Democratic organization. Armenian Marxists, equipped now with an internationalist analysis based on class struggle, turned their back on the Arax and their face to the workers of Transcaucasia.

The points at which historians begin and end short studies like the present one are by nature somewhat arbitrary. The beginnings of the Armenian revolutionary movement can be traced back long before 1880, at least into the eighteenth century, and the consequences of the nationalist-socialist conflict exist to the present day. But with that caveat the year 1903 seems an appropriate as well as convenient point at which to conclude this discussion of the development of the nationalist intelligentsia and the emergence of a Social Democratic labor movement among Caucasian Armenians. In March 1903, the first Caucasian Conference of Social Democratic Organizations was held in Tiflis and, though accurately reflecting the Georgian hegemony within the movement, the conference, in a spirit of internationalism, selected two Armenians, Arshak Zurabian and Bogdan Knuniants, along with the Georgian Dmitri Toporidze, to represent the Caucasus at the forthcoming Second Congress of the RSDRP. The high point of Social Democratic unity, both ethnically and politically, had been reached by early 1903. The Second Congress, instead of completing the unification of the party, gave birth to the Bolshevik-Menshevik schism. The great majority of the Georgians, with the notable exception of the young Stalin, sided with the Mensheviks, while the leading Armenian Social Democrats, with the exception of Zurabian, leaned toward the Bolsheviks.[57]

On the nationalist side 1903 is even more significant as a turning point. On June 12 the tsarist government ordered that the estates of the Armenian Church be turned over to the Ministry of Agriculture and the Department of State Properties. Henceforth the Armenian clergy were to be paid employees of the state. The *Polozhenie* of 1836 governing Armenian church relations with the Russian state thus was abolished. Catholicos Khrimian asked the tsar for a postponement of the edict, and when he was refused he instructed his bishops and priests not to obey the government's order. The Dashnaktsutiun encouraged the Catholicos in his actions and organized a Central Committee of Self-Defense in the Caucasus. Demonstrations broke out in July and August in Alexandropol and Erevan, culminating in a march by about 7,000 Armenians in Gandzak. Troops fired into the marchers, killing ten and wounding seventy. Other protests followed in Tiflis, Kars, Baku, and Shusha with even more casualties. Dashnaks retaliated by assassinating prominent tsarist officials, and the governor-general himself, Prince Golitsyn, was wounded. In the years 1903 through 1905, between the organized terrorism of the Armenian revolutionaries, the increase in strike activity of workers, and the armed resistance of Georgian peasants, Transcaucasia was rapidly becoming ungovernable and previewed for the whole of Russia the revolutionary situation that developed in 1905.

Through the nineteenth century and well into the twentieth the Armenians were a people in the process of forming a nation. Divided by frontiers and scattered by historical misfortunes, Armenians had neither a common history nor a common culture. The nationalist writers provided a heroic image for young Armenians and a cause around which they might unite, although at the same time the notion of a single national interest for all Armenians was compromised by the divisions within the nation, divisions of class, culture, and vision. Nationalist revolutionaries failed to unify all in a common struggle and were forced to intimidate the reluctant to follow their leadership. At the other end of the political spectrum the Marxists found a narrow base among workers and some radical intellectuals but never proved to be a serious threat to the nationalists until the revolution of 1917. The only hope for a Social Democratic challenge to Armenian nationalism was in a unified, multinational labor movement. To some extent such a movement developed in the early twentieth century in Baku, but in Georgia the movement was nearly exclusively Georgian.

Armenians in the Caucasus were divided at the beginning of the twentieth century between the many who still held hope for a revolutionary overthrow of Ottoman rule and those few who had turned toward the struggle against autocracy and capitalism within the Russian Empire. The tension between socialism and nationalism that had plagued Armenian political life for two decades could not be resolved. The Social Democrats among the Armenians found themselves isolated between the nationalists among their own people and their fellow socialists among the Georgians and Russians who neglected the Armenian workers. The intensification of national ill-will worked in favor of national identification by workers and against a multinational Social Democratic labor movement. The result was a steady growth in the influence of the Dashnaktsutiun among all levels of Caucasian Armenian society especially in the years 1903 to 1917, when it turned its attention to Caucasian affairs, led the campaign to regain church lands, became more overtly socialist, and even began to organize among workers within the Russian Empire.

The power of nationalism for Caucasian Armenians of various classes stemmed from their ambivalent position within the Russian Empire. Their nation was divided by an international border, and the privileged position that many Armenians had achieved within the Russian Empire was seriously challenged by the tsarist government in the last decade of the nineteenth century and the first years of the twentieth. Nowhere was their weight in economic affairs or their cultural pride matched by a share in real political power. The Armenian bourgeoisie may have controlled municipal institutions in Tiflis, Baku, and Erevan, but above them stood the Russian bureaucracy. The largely disenfranchised Georgians among whom they lived now challenged them as well. In an age of nationalism and nation-building it was understandable that educated Armenians desired the unification of their people and the formation of an autonomous political unit. Although the realization of this ideal may have been much more important for the national bourgeoisie, the intelligentsia, and the peasants of Anatolia than for the workers of the Caucasian cities, the workers were on the whole swept along by the ethnic appeals of the leading strata of their society. Thus, as Georgian workers joined the Social Democratic intelligentsia in a broad-based socialist movement, the Armenians in large part coalesced around national parties and organizations. Socialism remained a rhetorical cover behind which the national struggle was fought.

6 Rethinking the Unthinkable: Toward an Understanding of the Armenian Genocide

Ideology or Social Ecology?

Historians generally have explained (or excused) the Turkish deportations and massacres of the Armenians during the First World War as the result of conflicting ideologies, either religious or nationalist, or as the unique political response of the Young Turk triumvirate to a perceived danger to the Ottoman state. Such ideological or political explanations necessarily focus on the leadership of the two peoples in conflict—on the Ottoman government and the Armenian revolutionaries—as if by understanding the attitudes and behavior of these key actors the deep causes and broad dimensions of the genocide might be revealed. While such a focus on the political and intellectual elites is essential to explain the instigating events of early 1915 that precipitated the Armenian tragedy, the scope of the killing, the degree of popular violence on the part of both Turks and Kurds, and the wide participation in the genocide of people of various social classes requires a different kind of explanation— one that examines the social environment in which Kurds, Turks, and Armenians lived in the late Ottoman Empire. On the Armenian side such a broader investigation is needed to explain both the passivity of the overwhelming majority of the Armenian victims as they met their death and the armed resistance of a small minority. On the Turkish side the principal question to be asked is: How did the relatively benign symbiosis of several centuries, during which the ruling Ottomans referred to the Armenians as the "loyal millet" *(millet i-sadika),* break down into the genocidal violence of 1915? It is the contention of this essay that an answer to that question can only be reached, however partially, when the historian looks beyond the world of politics and ideas into the social life, the social tensions and conflicts, experienced by ordinary as well as powerful people.

Both Turkish and Armenian historians have usually examined their respective people from rather ethnocentric points of view, largely ignoring the multinational context in which Armenians, Kurds, and Turks lived in Anatolia. While Armenian historians write as if Armenians continued for unbroken centuries to maintain their traditional national consciousness and aspirations for freedom and independence, Turkish historians and their allied Western analysts write the story of the Ottoman Empire almost exclusively from the point of view of the dominant people in the empire, the Turks. Ottoman historiography, according to Professor Bernard Lewis of Princeton University, looked first at the rise of Islam, then at the Seljuk invasions and sultanates, and finally at the rise of the house of Osman. "These events form the main theme of Ottoman historiography. The histories of the subject millets are treated only in so far as they affect Ottoman history."[1] There was no interest in the history of the Turks before their conversion to Islam "or of their country, before it was conquered, for Islam."[2] Ironically, this same approach was adopted by Lewis in his classic study of the emergence of modern Turkey and has found its way into much of the Western writing on Turkey.

Through a less ethnocentric history that broadens the context from the usual political and ideological explanations to the wider society, it may be possible to move the debates between Armenian and Turkish historians beyond the so-called "provocation thesis" that holds that the Armenians themselves caused their own destruction by engaging in revolutionary and subversive activities.[3] Much of the current state-sponsored campaign to deny or distort the history of the Armenian genocide has been built on this idea of provocation of the Turks by subversive, violence-prone Armenians. Beginning with the proposition that Armenians and Turks lived in relative harmony for many centuries, the thesis claims that noxious outside influences—American missionaries, Russian diplomats, Armenian revolutionaries from the Caucasus—worked to undermine this peaceful relationship. Like other conservative views of social discontent and revolution, this argument, put forth by Western historians from William L. Langer to Stanford Shaw and Turkish historians like Salahi Sonyel, neglects to evaluate the social and political conditions out of which resistance and protest grew. As a form of explanation the "provocation thesis" remains on the political-ideological level and makes no effort to probe the negative features of the Ottoman social and political order. Neither Armenian resistance nor acquiescence in that order is explored.

The "provocation thesis" has changed its form over the years. Some writers limit their criticism to denial of the number of victims, claiming that no more than 200,000 lost their lives.[4] Others reject the notion of genocide because the premeditated policy of extermination cannot be linked to the Young Turk leadership. Still others speak of a civil war in Anatolia in which Armenians and Turks alike were killed and in which violence to protect the motherland from usurpers and separatists was justified. This latest form of the argument was succinctly put by no less than Dr. Sukru Elekdag, the ambassador of the Turkish Republic to Washington, in a letter to all members of the House of Representatives designed to prevent passage of a resolution to mark the Armenian genocide (January 10, 1985):

> The Armenian allegations regarding the events of 1915 have been challenged and found by unbiased scholars to be unsustainable. Those events stemmed from an armed uprising by large numbers of Armenians who were Ottoman citizens seeking to impose the establishment of an exclusively Armenian state in an area of Eastern Anatolia that was predominantly non-Armenian. Their uprising was instigated and supported by Tsarist Russia whose armies were invading the Eastern region of the Ottoman Empire.
>
> Authoritative scholars insist that the events of 1915 can not be characterized as a "massacre," let alone a "genocide. . . ." Professor [Justin] McCarthy [of the University of Louisville] concludes, on the basis of exhaustive research in the archives of various European powers, as well as those of the Ottoman Empire, that Ottoman Armenians lost their lives during a tragic civil war as a result of famine, epidemics and intercommunal fighting. Professor McCarthy also demonstrates that large numbers of non-Christian citizens of that region of the Empire also died as a result of the same causes. Multitudes of Turks and other non-Christians died at the hands of self-proclaimed Armenian revolutionary groups.[5]

Ambassador Elekdag is more subdued and more eloquent than some of the other revisers of Ottoman history. For example, the historian Salahi R. Sonyel writes more passionately in defense of the harmony of Ottoman life:

> Despite the so many shortcomings of the Armenian people . . . they had enjoyed the best fruits of Ottoman society until a minority of alien, self-seeking, sanguinary and adventurist terrorist leaders decided to convert them into pawns in the power game, by allowing their wires to be pulled by foreign powers for their own ulterior purposes. . . . Nevertheless to hold all the Turkish nation responsible for the Armenian tragedy, and to overlook the irresponsible actions of these powers, and of certain Armenian leaders, who were the chief culprits, is a travesty of justice.[6]

The first fundamental criticism to be made of the idea that "outside agitators" disrupted the relatively peaceful relationship that had long existed between the *millet i-sadika* and the ruling Turks is that such an imagined past was the cultural construction of the dominant nationality, its ideologists and rulers, and was not shared by the subordinate peoples of the empire that lived in a limbo of legal inferiority. The Armenians, like the other non-Muslim peoples of the empire, were not only an ethnic and religious minority in a country dominated demographically and politically by Muslims, but given an ideology of inherent Muslim superiority and the segregation of minorities, the Armenians were also an underclass. They were subjects who, however high they might rise in trade, commerce, or even governmental service, were never to be considered equal to the ruling Muslims. They would always remain *gavur,* infidels inferior to the Muslims. For centuries Armenians lived in a political and social order in which their testimony was not accepted in Muslim courts, where they were subject to discriminatory laws (for example, they were forced to wear distinctive clothes to identify themselves), where they were not allowed to bear arms when most Muslims were armed, and where their property and person were subject to the arbitrary and unchecked power of Muslim officials.

Active persecution of non-Muslims was relatively rare in the earlier centuries of the Ottoman Empire, but, scholars of the *millet* system tell us, "discrimination was permanent and indeed necessary, inherent in the system and maintained by both Holy Law and common practice."[7] Islam did not recognize social or racial inequalities, such as those between rich and poor or black and white, but it did believe in three basic inequalities: master and slave, man and woman, believer and unbeliever. Whereas the slave could not become free except by will of the master, and a woman could not become a man, the unbeliever was able to join the faithful but chose not to take up the true faith. Thus, the inferiority of the *gavur* was voluntary. Unbelievers were to "stay in their place" and not appear to be equal or better than the Muslims. "Trouble arose when Jews or Christians were seen to be getting too much wealth or too much power and enjoying them too visibly."[8] Yet the decline of the Muslim world outside the empire, and the rise of Christian Europe to unprecedented material and political power, had profound, differential effects on the status relations of the Muslims and non-Muslims within the empire.

Even in the Tanzimat period, when reforming rulers and bureaucrats eliminated some of the most excessive practices against their subjects and attempted to create the basis for a *rechtsstaat* in the empire, the Christians benefited from the movement toward equality under the law only partially. As Roderic Davison, a distinguished historian of the Tanzimat, explains:

> Though by 1860 the condition of the Christians . . . had improved considerably over what it had been only a few years before, they could still complain legitimately about unequal treatment. They still protested the general prohibition of bells on their churches, the frequent rejection of their testimony in Turkish courts, occasional rapes of Christian girls or forced conversions, and other sorts of personal mistreatment. The Armenians of Eastern Anatolia had strong complaints about the marauding habits of armed Kurdish bands. There were occasional fanatical outbursts against Christians by local Muslim groups. There was still no equality in opportunity to hold public office.[9]

Beginning in the late 1870s and through the following decade the Armenians of the provinces began to petition in ever larger numbers to their leaders in Istanbul and to the European consuls stationed in eastern Anatolia. Hundreds of complaints were filed; few were dealt with. Together they make up an extraordinary record of misgovernment, of arbitrary treatment of a defenseless population, and a clear picture of the lack of legal recourse.[10] Though the most brutal treatment of Armenians was at the hands of Kurdish tribesmen, the Armenians found the Ottoman state officials either absent, unreliable, or just one more source of oppression. It was hard to say which was worse—the presence of Turkish authorities or the absence in many areas of any palpable political authority. Corruption was rampant. Turks as well suffered from it, but the Armenians had the added burden of not belonging to the favored Muslim faithful. A few examples of Ottoman justice are suggestive. In May 1872 a 14-year-old girl was kidnapped and raped by a Muslim. Her parents appealed to the Turkish officials, but they declared that she had become a Muslim and therefore her parents no longer had any claim over her. Three petitions to the Porte by the Armenian patriarchate failed to bring any redress.[11] Two hundred instances of Armenian lands being illegally seized by Kurds and Turks were brought to the courts, but judges consistently ruled in favor of the Muslims. When Armenians resisted the extortionary demands of the Kurds, either individually or collectively, the response from the Turkish army was often excessive. Massacres were reported from all parts of eastern Anatolia, particularly after the formation in the early 1890s of the officially sanctioned Kurdish military units known as the Hamidiye. Against this background of growing Kurdish aggressiveness, Western and Russian indifference, and the collapse of the Tanzimat reform movement, a small number of Armenians turned to a revolutionary strategy.

As part of the "provocation thesis," William L. Langer, Stanford and Ezel Kural Shaw, and others have argued that the Armenian revolutionaries were willing to sacrifice their compatriots in order to create a separate, independent Armenian state in eastern Anatolia. Langer argues that the first major Armenian revolutionary party, the Hnchaks, believed that massacre of their peasant constituents was required to interest Europe in the plight of the Armenians and was "the price to be paid for the realization of the phantastic national-socialist state of the fanatics."[12] He and those who have followed him seriously distort the aims and motives of the revolutionaries. The Armenian revolutionary parties arose from a number of self-defense groups within Turkey, a tradition of resistance to state intervention characteristic of some highland Armenians, like those of Zeitun and Sassun, and from the radical intelligentsia of Russian Transcaucasia.

Appalled by the indifference of better-off Armenians in the cities of western Turkey toward the suffering of poorer Armenians in historic Armenia, young Russian Armenians began organizing the self-defense of the Armenians of the provinces while at the same time engaging in a series of spectacular demonstrations in the capital to remind Europe of the desperate plight of the Armenians. The first major manifestations—at Kum Kapa in Istanbul (1890) and Bab Ali (1895)—were organized by the Hnchak party, a semi-Marxist group of Caucasian intellectuals who hoped to resurrect the Armenian Question. The Hnchaks believed that, given the futility of moral appeals to the Great Powers, the only practical solution to the Armenian Question was the organization of self-defense by the Armenian peasantry. When the Hnchak leader Khanazatian told the revered cleric Khrimian *hairik* that his party's goal was socialism, the priest, who remained hopeful that Christian Europe would react to Armenian pain, was convinced that such a radical position would alienate the Europeans. "What will England or your tsar's government say?" Khanazatian answered that until the Armenians shed their blood, Europeans would not act to free them.[13]

From a careful reading of party programs, the revolutionary press, and memoirs, it becomes clear that the Hnchaks believed that no one would take the Armenian cause seriously if Armenians themselves did not act to raise the issue of their political freedom. Their major enemy, besides the Turks and Kurds, was the passivity and inactivity of the Armenians. Instead of relying on European aid as the primary source of support, the Hnchaks held that Armenians must become self-reliant. Here was no cynical plan to have Armenians massacred in order to provoke European intervention, like that in Bulgaria, but rather a pessimism about dependence on European goodwill and a commitment to organizing activity and stimulating national consciousness among Armenians. It would hardly have made sense for the Hnchaks to proclaim openly their allegiance to socialism and to expect at the same time backing from capitalist Europe or tsarist Russia.

The revolutionaries were aware that their activities would result in Turkish reprisals, but they believed that it was no longer possible to remain hostage to those fears. If they did not act soon, it was feared, Armenians as a distinct people would disappear. Undeniably the Hnchaks raised the banner of resistance, but those historians who see their rebellion, isolated and intermittent as it was, as a rationale for the horrendous massacres of 300,000 Armenians in the years 1894 through 1896 excuse the government that carried out those massacres as its preferred method of keeping order in the empire. The extreme view of William L. Langer that the Hnchaks deliberately and cynically carried out provocations in order to call down upon the Armenians the wrath of the offended Turks is based on a misreading of the sources, a disregard for the causes of Armenian resistance, and inadequate consideration of the reasons for the Turkish perceptions of the Armenian threat.[14]

Most Armenians, of course, did not join the revolutionary movement but continued to hope for the best within the Ottoman legal structure. Even after the "Bloody Sultan," Abdul Hamid II (1876–1909), abrogated the Ottoman Constitution, the Armenian religious leaders and the middle class preferred to petition the government or appeal to the Western powers for redress. Given the general passivity of the Armenian peasantry of Anatolia and the hostility of the Armenian community leadership, the revolutionaries remained a vocal and violent irritant for the Turks but no real threat to the continuance of the sultan's power. Resistance attracted only a small minority of Armenians, and the revolutionary movement itself split over issues of tactics and goals. In the aftermath of the massacres of 1894 through 1896 the Hnchak party broke into two factions, one still committed to the original populist-Marxist program, the other considerably more moderate and gravitating toward liberalism. Though it never regained its original prominence among Armenians, the Hnchak party remained notable as the only Armenian revolutionary party that clearly called for Armenian independence in its party program.

The argument that the revolutionaries hoped to provoke massacres in order to excite the Europeans makes even less sense in the period after the decline of Hnchaks. The dominant party after 1896, the Dashnaktsutiun, proposed a program of autonomy within the Russian and the Ottoman empires, a "free Armenia" *(azat Haiastan)*. This vague formulation, carefully chosen to avoid charges of separatism, was refined in 1907 to make even clearer that the Dashnaks favored the formation of autonomous regions within two federative states, one Ottoman, the other Russian. Like the Hnchaks, the Dashnaks worked to stir the lethargic Armenians to action. In alliance with oppositional movements of other Ottoman peoples, most importantly the Young Turks, the Dashnaktsutiun expected European pressure on the Ottoman Empire to combine with the internal revolution to bring down Abdul Hamid's autocracy. Later the party abandoned its hopes of European intervention and became more overtly socialist. Disciplined and dedicated to a revolutionary strategy, the Dashnaks faced the same dilemma as their predecessors, the Hnchaks: both passivity and resistance led to the same result—the progressive destruction of the Armenian people. The only morally courageous choice was revolution.[15]

From Symbiosis to Massacre

If one rejects the easy analysis of the "provocation thesis," and puts aside the notion that the victim can be blamed for his or her own destruction, what are we left with? How can we arrive at a more complete interpretation of the massacres and genocide? A number of comparative models have been suggested in historical and sociological literature, but in this essay explanation will be sought through contextualization of the events.[16] Besides the ideological and political influences that shaped state policy, the social, geographic, and demographic environment must be considered.

First, a few points should be made about developments in the Armenian millet. The Armenians of Anatolia were a conquered people, a nation that had lost both its political and demographic hegemony over its own historical homeland between the fall of the last Armenian kingdom in 1375 and the national "awakening" of the early nineteenth century. Their survival through those five centuries can in part be attributed to the religious and linguistic tenacity of many Armenians (those who did not convert or emigrate), to the continued efforts of clerics and intellectuals to maintain the Armenian literary tradition, but also must be credited to the remarkable system of indirect rule through religious communities (the millet system) that the Ottoman government eventually sanctioned. Whatever discrimination, abuses, and inferiority the Armenians were forced to endure must be weighed alongside the considerable benefits this cultural and political autonomy provided. The church remained at the head of the nation; Armenians with commercial and industrial skills were able to climb to the very pinnacle of the Ottoman economic order; and a variety of educational, charitable, and social institutions were permitted to flourish. Without exaggerating the harmony of Turkish-Armenian relations between 1453 and 1878 or neglecting the considerable burdens imposed on non-Muslims, particularly Anatolian peasants, we can nevertheless safely characterize this long period in which the Armenians came to be known as the "loyal millet" as one of "benign symbiosis."

Armenians and Turks coexisted in an unequal relationship, one of subordination and superordination, with the Muslims on top and the non-Muslims below. The sheer power and confidence of the ruling Muslims worked for centuries to maintain in the Armenians a pattern of personal and social behavior manifested in submissiveness, passivity, deference to authority, and the need to act in calculatedly devious and disguised ways. It was this deferential behavior that earned the Armenians the title "loyal millet" in an age when the Greeks and Slavs of the empire were striving to emancipate themselves through revolutionary action. The Armenians in contrast worked within the Ottoman system and accepted the burdens of Muslim administration without much protest until the second half of the nineteenth century. Many travelers noted the lack of spirit of the provincial Armenians, their renowned cowardliness, character traits that appeared to distinguish them from the Turks and Kurds. The aristocratic British traveler Mark Sykes, who later became an influential diplomat, provides one of the more extreme characterizations of the Armenians.

> Even Jews have their good points, but Armenians have none. His cowardice, his senseless untruthfulness, the depth of his intrigue, even in the most trivial matters, his habit of hoarding, his lack of one manly virtue, his helplessness in danger, his natural and instinctive treachery, together form so vile a character that pity is stifled and judgment unbalanced.[17]

One can certainly agree that Mr. Sykes's judgment was unbalanced, that he failed to reflect on what life might be like for an unarmed, settled, Christian population living among armed, often nomadic Muslims who enjoyed the support of the state.

Blame for bringing an end to centuries of relative peace between Muslims and Armenians in Anatolia need not be exclusively placed either on Armenians who turned to resistance nor on Turks who used armed force to maintain an inequitable, repressive social order. Rather, the social environment of the early modern period began to change radically in the nineteenth century, and influences far beyond Anatolia began to affect the peoples of the Armenian plateau. The fallout from the French Revolution, the rise of European nationalism, the inroads of European capitalism, the expansion of Russia into the Caucasus and British shipping into the Black Sea—all had effects on the internal life of the Ottoman peoples, differentially felt by the various millets. For urban Armenians, who had long had connections with both Europe and Russia through their far-flung diaspora, the impact of the West was much more immediate and direct than on all but a few Muslims. The Armenian merchant and financial families more and more frequently sent their children to be educated abroad or at the new schools set up in Turkey by Catholic and Protestant missionaries. By the 1840s liberal Armenians were working out a constitution for their millet, a document that would serve as a model for other millets and for the Ottoman Constitution itself. And most significantly the Armenians, along with other minorities, adopted the latest European intellectual and artistic fashions and adapted to the new capitalist ways of doing business. Armenian education, publishing, and upward mobility in the urban economy were significantly more developed than that of the Muslims. And as the Turks themselves strove to imitate the ways of the West, it seemed as if the Armenians were already halfway there.

The wealthy, visible Armenians of the Ottoman capital worked to improve their position in the empire both through pushing for internal political reform and by close cooperation with Europeans. Armenians, particularly the commercial class in Galata, sought protection, even citizenship, from the Western embassies and benefited from the capitulations given reluctantly by the Porte. Politically the Ottoman Armenians sought a future within the empire. Reform of the more repressive Ottoman institutions, like tax farming, guarantees of equality under the law, and perhaps autonomy under a Christian governor for the Anatolian provinces made up the program of the Armenian liberals. Given the new aspirations of the Christian minorities and the European orientation of a few reforming Turkish officials, a consensus grew among a number of government figures that the traditional millet system had to be transformed if it was to survive into the age of nationalism and liberalism. An alliance of mutual interest tied progressive bureaucrats and liberal Armenians together in an effort to "modernize" the empire along European lines. The consequence of success would be to undermine the traditional hierarchical, Muslim-dominated political and social order in which Christians were at a legal disadvantage.

The reform movement (Tanzimat) held out hope to the minorities that the Ottoman Empire might be reorganized so that all the sultan's subjects would be equal citizens under the law. This notion of legal protection of non-Muslims was central to the aims of what came to be known as Ottomanism *(osmanlilik)* and was instituted briefly in the constitution proclaimed in December 1876. But the ideological umbrella of Ottomanism was broad enough to include under it those who believed that the unity of the empire could be best guaranteed by having the Ottoman Turks rule over the other nationalities. While some Ottoman reformers were prepared to go as far as the liberal Prince Sabbaheddin and call for a federation of equal nations, others used the guise of Ottomanism to mask their Turkish nationalist or Pan-Turanian preferences.

Unfortunately for the westernizers, when Abdul Hamid abandoned the Ottomanist program he found sentiment in favor of his antireform, anti-Western stance among conservative and religious elements. Ottoman society proved to be resistant to the reform legislation, and for several decades no serious opposition to the sultan's patriarchal rule was generated among the Turkish population. The sultan himself was frank about his strategic choice:

> I made a mistake wishing to content myself with the example of my father, Abdul Mecid, who sought to carry out reforms by persuading the people and creating liberal institutions. From now on, I shall follow the example of my grandfather, Sultan Mahmud. Like him, I understand that it is not possible to move the peoples whom God has placed under my protection by any means other than force.[18]

With the failure of reform—the end of Tanzimat, the withdrawal of the constitution in 1878, the steady replacement of Ottomanism with policies preferential to Muslims—and in the face of European disinterest in the fate of the Armenians through the 1880s, the situation of the Ottoman Armenians began to deteriorate rapidly. At the same time the Armenians had themselves changed dramatically in the four middle decades of the nineteenth century. Influenced by Western ideas, Armenian intellectuals had developed a new interest in the Armenian past, and instead of conceiving themselves solely as part of a religious community, more and more Armenians began to acquire a Western sense of nationality, a feeling of kinship with Christian Europe, and a growing alienation from the Muslim peoples among whom they lived. The depth or spread of this new nationalism should not be exaggerated. Certainly more potent in the larger cities and in localities where Armenian or missionary schools helped to shape new ways of thinking, Armenian nationalist ideas spread slowly into eastern Anatolia. Equally if not more influential in shaping Armenian attitudes in the late nineteenth century than the positive images created by Armenian and foreign intellectuals was the negative experience of poor Armenians at the hands of their Muslim overlords.

The former equilibrium between the millets was rapidly disappearing by the last decades of the century. And nowhere was this more brutally evident than in the Armenian provinces. The rise in tension in eastern Anatolia and the resultant resistance and massacre must be understood, not only as the product of the failure of the traditional Ottoman political structure to adapt to the new requirements of the non-Muslim peoples, but also as the result of fundamental social changes in eastern Anatolia itself. The mountainous plateau of historic Armenia was an area in which the central government had only intermittent authority. An intense four-sided struggle for power, position, and survival pitted the agents of the Ottoman government, the Kurdish nomadic leaders, the semiautonomous Turkish notables of the towns, and the Armenians against one another. Local Turkish officials ran the towns with little regard to central authority, and Kurdish beys held much of the countryside under their sway. Often the only way Istanbul could make its will felt was by sending in the army. Though the Porte saw Armenians by the turn of the century as an unruly and subversive element, earlier in the century it had been the Kurds who had repeatedly revolted against the Ottoman state and collaborated with the invading Russians. Only with the campaigns of 1834, 1843, and 1878 were the troops of the sultan able to put down the major Kurdish insurrections. Still, in many areas the Kurdish beys had carved out a de facto autonomy and remained the most powerful authority, ruling over the local Armenian peasants with little interference from Istanbul. Travelers and diplomats reported that in Van, Bitlis, Diarbakir, and elsewhere the Kurds held the Armenians in a kind of semi-feudal servitude. Not only did Armenian villagers pay taxes in kind and money to the beys, but they were obligated to work a set number of days for the Kurds and to board and feed them in Armenian villages during the winter months. In some area Armenians were even bought and sold like sheep or cattle, and their land and homes were seized by the Kurds. The Russian vice-consul in Van, Tumanskii, wrote in May 1901:

> In Sassun *kaza* there exists an almost feudal dependence of Armenians on the Kurds with all its juridical consequences: each Armenian is assigned to some Kurd and is obligated to labor for him; Kurds sell their serfs when they need money; if a Kurd kills a serf, the lord [of that serf] takes revenge by killing a serf belonging to the murderer. Some beys have even insisted on the "right of the first night" in Armenian villages.[19]

However intolerable this system, Armenians in general bore up under it, except for an occasional revolt such as that at Zeitun in 1862. But in the last third of the nineteenth century, as the population of Muslims and Christians grew, as additional Muslims from the Caucasus and the Balkans settled in the area, and as many Armenians emigrated to Russia, Europe, and America, the competition for the limited agricultural resources of the area intensified. Armenians could not rely on the Ottoman state to defend them from the more powerful Muslim landlords, and pressure grew on those Armenians left in Anatolia to protect their endangered position.

Certainly Armenian intellectuals and revolutionaries played a role in bringing Armenian acquiescence and acceptance of the existing order to an end, but so did foreign travelers, western diplomats, and increased contact with the outside world. One of the most important factors in precipitating the collapse of the harsh equilibrium in eastern Anatolia was Abdul Hamid's decision to align the Ottoman state with the Kurds and back them against the Armenians. Organized into official irregular armed units called Hamidiye, Kurdish villagers were trained by Turkish *yuzbashis* from the regular army and given special uniforms and access to arms.[20] Though the Kurds had been much more a threat to Ottoman unity than the Armenians in years past, the sultan backed these fellow Muslims against Christian Armenians whom he saw as a disruptive element linked to his enemies abroad. In this way Abdul Hamid guaranteed Kurdish loyalty and at the same time created a force to repress the Armenians and contain the independent ambitions of the urban Turkish notables.[21]

Instead of pursuing the programs of reform demanded by the European powers, the Porte committed itself to maintaining a cruel status quo in which its Armenian subjects had the choice of remaining the silent victims of the Kurds and state injustice or of organizing their own self-defense. They did both. Many observers have noted that the urban Armenian elites, particularly the clergy and the wealthy business class, opposed the revolutionary parties, and only with great difficulty did the radicals, always a tiny minority among Armenians, convince some of the more self-reliant of their countrymen, like those of Sassun and Zeitun, to resist Kurdish taxation and impositions. The Ottoman government reacted to instances of Armenian resistance as if they were insurrections against the state, and in putting down these "rebellions" the Turkish army and Kurdish irregulars did not merely fight the armed rebels but massacred women and children and burnt villages.

Diplomatic reports and eyewitness accounts by travelers and missionaries testify to the "great severity" with which the Ottoman government suppressed any effort by Armenians to defend themselves. A series of massacres began with clashes in Sassun. In the summer of 1893 Kurdish tribes entered the *kaza* of Sassun and attacked the Armenian village of Talori. The Turkish *mutessarif* of Guendj arrived with his troops and arrested several Armenians, but no Kurds. The soldiers then plundered the Armenians, and the *mutessarif* told the authorities at Bitlis that the Armenians were in revolt. The villagers re-treated into the mountains for several months, returning only the next spring. They refused to pay taxes because of the state's failure to protect them from the Kurds. This led to a second visit by the army, along with Hamidiye troops.[22] When British consuls in eastern Anatolia complained to the sultan about the excessive force used against the Armenians, Abdul Hamid replied to the British ambassador:

> The Armenians, who for their own purposes invent these stories against the Govt., and finding that they receive encouragement from British officials, are emboldened to proceed to open acts of rebellion, which the Govt. is

perfectly justified in suppressing by every means in its power. . . . His Imperial Majesty treated the Armenians with justice and moderation, and, as long as they behaved properly, all toleration would be shown to them, but he had given orders that when they took to revolt or to brigandage the authorities were to deal with them as they dealt with the authorities.[23]

This policy of massacre, which crescendoed in the killings of 1894 through 1896, was a means of maintaining the decaying status quo as the preferred alternative to reform and concessions to the Armenians.[24] Encouraging the anti-Armenian hostility of the Muslims, the state created an Armenian scapegoat onto which the defeats and failures of the Ottoman government could be blamed. The social system in eastern Anatolia was sanctioned by violence, now state violence, and the claims of the Armenians for a more just relationship were rejected. No right of popular resistance was recognized, and all acts of rebellion were seen as the result of the artificial intervention of outside agitators.[25]

From Massacre to Genocide

Whereas the Hamidian policy had at its base a deep conservatism and opposition to liberal reform along Western lines, the policy of the Young Turk government during the First World War was fundamentally a revolutionary project to alter completely the ethnic and political balance in eastern Anatolia and by so doing to permit the eventual creation of a new ethnically Turkic empire. By eliminating one factor, namely the Armenians, in the four-way power struggle in the region, the Young Turks could with one blow end Western and Russian interference in Ottoman affairs, achieve the long-desired goal of Turkish nationalists to create an undisputed homeland for the Turkish people, and even work toward the Pan-Turanian utopia of a Turkic empire stretching from Istanbul to Central Asia. What has come to be known as "the first genocide of the twentieth century" has its origins in the aspirations of a small group of Turkish politicians associated with the Committee of Union and Progress (Young Turks), but both the radicalization of their intentions and the final implementation of their plans occurred in the context of a deepening social and political crisis and the near destruction of the Ottoman state at the hands of external enemies.

Ottoman Armenians and other minorities joyfully greeted the 1908 revolution that brought the Young Turks to power. They hoped that the restoration of the liberal constitution would provide a political mechanism for peaceful development within the framework of a representative parliamentary system. The leading Armenian political party, the Dashnaktsutiun, had been loosely allied with the Committee of Union and Progress and continued to collaborate with them up through the first years of the Great War. Nevertheless, the deep social hostilities between the peoples of the empire persisted, indeed worsened, in the first two decades of the twentieth century.

Armenians were visible in the business world and as close colleagues of European investors and entrepreneurs. Muslims, who dominated the empire politically, were subordinated economically and socially to non-Muslims in the work world. Non-Muslims, who made up only 17 percent of the population of Anatolia in 1912, were disproportionately represented in towns and cities. Around 1900 non-Muslims made up 55.9 percent of Istanbul's population, 61.5 percent of Izmir's, 42.8 percent of Trabzon, and about one-third of the population of Diarbakir *kaza*, Erzerum, Sivas *kaza,* and Ankara *kaza*.[26] Of the forty-two printing plants in the empire, twenty-six were owned by non-Muslims, only eleven by Muslims; of metalworking plants, twenty were owned by non-Muslims, only one by a Muslim; of the famous Bursa raw silk manufactories, six were owned by Muslims, two by the government, and thirty-three by minorities.[27] Armenians and Greeks, and to a lesser extent Jews, made up a large and influential number of the owners and operators of industrial and commercial enterprises.

Besides industrial ownership, Armenians and Greeks held important positions as managers and salaried employees in Western-financed companies, in mining and especially on the railroads. The Anatolian railroad was largely financed and managed by Germans, but middle-rank positions were held half by Europeans, half by Ottoman Greeks and Armenians. Armenians and Greeks also made up the guards and station personnel, while

> Turks made up most of the people working on the trains, the lines, and the workshops. . . . Although 90 percent of all persons employed by the railroads were Ottoman subjects, Europeans (especially Germans) occupied the highest and most lucrative posts. They held the middle-level positions in about equal numbers with the Ottoman Christians. Mostly Muslim Turks held the lowest categories of work. The Ottoman Turkish, Greek, and Armenian employees expressed numerous grievances against the European administration. They were dissatisfied that they received unequal pay for performing the same functions that the Europeans carried out. . . . An Armenian stationmaster may have earned twice the wage of a Turkish fireman but it was only a fraction of his European supervisor's salary.[28]

This reversal of the traditional Muslim-*dhimmi* hierarchy created resentments toward Christians, Europeans, and the elements of European life filtering into the Ottoman Empire. The social hostility generated by the Muslims' inferior status in the industrial and commercial world targeted Armenians in particular, as those who were Ottoman but suspiciously sympathetic to Europeans. Even at lower social levels tensions grew between Armenians and Muslims. Kurdish and Turkish porters in Istanbul and other port cities competed with Armenians who dominated the handling of goods. At the time of the massacres in Sassun and other eastern districts in 1894 through 1896,

Armenian porters were attacked, with many killed, while others were deported to the east. Most were replaced by Kurds.

Social grievances in towns, along with the population pressure and competition for resources in agriculture, were part of a toxic mix of social and political elements that provided the environment for growing hostility toward the Armenians. Whatever resentments the poor peasant population of eastern Anatolia may have felt toward the people in towns—the places where they received low prices for their produce, where they felt their social inferiority most acutely, where they were alien to and unwanted by the better-dressed people—were easily transferred to the Armenians. The catalyst for killing, however, was not spontaneously generated out of the tinder of social and cultural tensions. It came from the state itself, from officials and conservative clergy who had for decades perceived Armenians as alien to the Turkish empire, dangerous revolutionaries and separatists who threatened the integrity of the state. Armenians were seen as responsible for the troubles of the empire, allies of the anti-Turkish European powers, and the source of politically radical ideas, including trade unionism and socialism, into the empire.

The initially liberal program of the Young Turks met opposition from the leaders of the non-Muslim millets, who were fearful that a civil order without ethnic distinctions would cost them their privileged status. Powerful Greek and Armenian clergy opposed the laws that would have eliminated the separate (and usually superior) educational institutions and the exemption from the draft of non-Muslims. The goal of the Young Turks to restore full sovereignty to the Ottoman state, thus ending the privileges of foreign powers within the empire, also challenged the advantages that the non-Muslims had gained from their association with the European states.

As Europe drifted through the last decade before World War I, the Ottoman government experienced a series of political and military defeats: the annexation of Bosnia-Herzegovina by Austro-Hungary in 1908, the subsequent declaration of independence by Bulgaria, the merger of Crete with Greece, revolts in Albania between 1910 and 1912, losses to Italy in Libya (1911), and in the course of two Balkan wars (1912–1913) the diminution of Ottoman territory in Europe and the forced migration of Turks from Europe into Anatolia. As their liberal strategies failed to unify and strengthen the empire, the Young Turk leaders gradually shifted away from their original Ottomanist views of a multinational empire based on guarantees of civil and minority rights to a more Turkish nationalist ideology that emphasized the dominant role of Turks. In desperation a group of Young Turk officers, led by Enver Pasha, seized the government in a coup d'etat in 1913, and for the next five years, years fateful for all Armenians, a triumvirate of Enver, Jemal, and Talaat ruled the empire. Their regime marked the triumph of Turkish nationalism within the government itself.

Less tolerant of the non-Turks in the empire, the triumvirate scuttled the liberal Ottomanism of earlier years and amalgamated the views of Pan-Islam and Turanist nationalism. "Pan-Turanism, like Pan-Islam," writes Feroz Ahmad, "was an expansionist ideology which suited the mood of the Young Turks, then in full retreat at the opposite front [in Europe]. . . . Turkish nationalism, centered around the Turks in Anatolia, was in the process of development in 1914. It was to emerge out of the defeats in World War I, only after Pan-Turanism and Pan-Islam had proved to be mere dreams."[29]

This shift toward nationalism and Pan-Turanian expansionism left the Armenian political leadership in an impossible position. Torn between continuing to cooperate with the Young Turks in the hope that some gains might be won for the Armenians and breaking with their undependable political allies and going over to the opposition, the Dashnaktsutiun decided to maintain its alliance with the ruling party. Other Armenian cultural and political leaders, however, most notably the Hnchak party and the Armenian patriarchate, opposed further collaboration with the government. As Turkey entered the First World War, even as Armenian soldiers joined the Ottoman army to fight against the enemies of their government, the situation grew extremely ominous for the Armenians. They were dangerously exposed. The bulk of their population lived in the mountainous plateau that lay between the two belligerents, Turkey and Russia. Everywhere in their historic homeland, except for an occasional town or cluster of villages, they were a minority living among hostile Turks and Kurds, and the perception by Muslims as a disloyal, treacherous people, one that favored the Christian government of the tsars to that of the Turks, seemed to be reinforced by the events of the world war.

Anxious to fight the Russians in 1914, the Turkish government instigated the war by attacking Russian ships in the Black Sea. Enver led a huge army against tsarist forces on the eastern front late in the year, and at first he was dramatically victorious. Kars was cut off and Sarikamish surrounded. But the Turkish troops were not prepared for the harsh winter in the Armenian highlands, and early in 1915 the Russians, accompanied by Armenian volunteer units from the Caucasus, pushed the Turkish army back. A disastrous defeat followed in which Enver lost three-quarters of his army, perhaps as many as 78,000 men killed and 12,000 taken prisoner. Ottoman Armenians fled to the areas occupied by the Russians, confirming in Turkish minds the treachery that marked the Christian minorities.

Enver's defeat on the Caucasian front was the prelude to the "final solution" of the Armenian Question. The Russians posed a real danger to the Turks, just at the moment that Allied forces were attacking at Gallipoli in the west. In this moment of defeat and desperation, the triumvirate in Istanbul decided to demobilize the Armenian soldiers in the Ottoman army and to deport Armenians from eastern Anatolia. What might have been rationalized as a military necessity, given the imperial ambitions and distorted perceptions of the Ottoman leaders, quickly became a massive attack on their Armenian subjects, a systematic program of murder and pillage. An act of panic and vengeance metamorphosed monstrously into an opportunity to rid Anatolia once and for all of the one people that stood in the way of the Young Turks' plans for a Pan-Turanian empire.

One of the key questions about the Armenian genocide is the degree of official state involvement in the carrying out of the massacres that accompanied the forced deportations of Armenians. Turkish and Turkophilic historians, like Stanford and Ezel Kural Shaw, have conceded that deportations took place in 1915–1916 but have argued that they were carried out for strictly military security reasons and all precautions were taken to safeguard the Armenians. Moreover, blame for the necessity for deportation is laid on the Armenians, who rose in revolt in April 1915 in the city of Van. Here, for example, is the extraordinary account of the genocide by Stanford and Ezel Kural Shaw in the second volume of their history of the Ottoman Empire:

> Armenian leaders . . . now declared their open support of the enemy, and there seemed to be no other alternative. It would be impossible to determine which of the Armenians would remain loyal and which would follow the appeals of their leaders. As soon as spring came, then, in mid-May 1915 orders were issued to evacuate the entire Armenian population from the provinces of Van, Bitlis, and Erzerum, to get them away from all areas where they might undermine the Ottoman campaigns against Russia or against the British in Egypt, with arrangements made to settle them in towns and camps in the Mosul area of northern Iraq. In addition, Armenians residing in the countryside (but not the cities) of the Cilician districts as well as those of north Syria were to be sent to central Syria for the same reason. Specific instructions were issued for the army to protect the Armenians against nomadic attacks and to provide them with sufficient food and other supplies to meet their needs during the march and after they were settled. Warnings were sent to the Ottoman military commanders to make certain that neither the Kurds nor any other Muslims used the situation to gain vengeance for the long years of Armenian terrorism. The Armenians were to be protected and cared for until they returned to their homes after the war. A supplementary law established a special commission to record the properties of the deportees and to sell them at auction at fair prices, with the revenues being held in trust until their return. Muslims wishing to occupy abandoned buildings could do so only as renters, with the revenues paid to the trust funds, and with the understanding that they would have to leave when the original owners returned. The deportees and their possessions were to be guarded by the army while in transit as well as in Iraq and Syria, and the government would provide for their return once the crisis was over.[30]

Accompanying the argument that the Ottoman government did not initiate a program to annihilate its Armenian population are denials that massive killing actually took place. The Shaws, again, are representative of this approach:

> The Entente propaganda mills and Armenian nationalists claimed that over a million Armenians were massacred during the war. But this is based on the assumption that the prewar Armenian population numbered about 2.5 million. The total number of Armenians in the empire before the war in fact

came to at most 1,300,000, according to the Ottoman census. About half of these were resident in the affected areas, but, with the city dwellers allowed to remain the number actually transported came to no more than 400,000, including some terrorists and agitators from the cities rounded up soon after the war began. In addition, approximately one-half million Armenians subsequently fled into the Caucasus and elsewhere during the remainder of the war. Since about 100,000 Armenians lived in the empire afterward, and about 150,000 to 200,000 immigrated to western Europe and the United States, one can assume that about 200,000 perished as a result not only of the transportation but also of the same conditions of famine, disease, and war action that carried away some 2 million Muslims at the same time. Careful examination of the secret records of the Ottoman cabinet at the time reveals no evidence that any of the Committee of Union and Progress leaders, or anyone else in the central government, ordered massacres. To the contrary, orders were to the provincial forces to prevent all kinds of raids and communal disturbances that might cause loss of life.[31]

On the question of central government and Young Turk involvement, the documentary evidence has been subject to much controversy. In 1919 one of the survivors of the genocide, Aram Andonian, compiled documents and memoirs supplied to him by a lower-level Turkish official in Syria, Naim Bey, who had been appalled by the massacres. But this source was considered doubtful, even a forgery by many scholars, and official Turkish historiography launched a campaign in the 1970s against the book.[32] More recently the sociologist Vahakn N. Dadrian has published a detailed defense of the documents in which he demonstrates their authenticity.[33] Dadrian claims that the documents in Andonian's collection conform to the accusations and documentation found in the 1919 court martials held in Istanbul (under the Kemalists) that found Talaat, Enver, Nazim, Shakir, and others guilty of crimes against the Armenians and sentenced them in absentia to death.

From these documents one not only gains clear evidence of premeditation and intention to eliminate the Armenians from Anatolia but also great insight into the mentality and motivations of the chief actors. On February 18 (March 3), 1915 (corrected dates are taken from Dadrian), the Young Turk official Behaeddin Shakir wrote to the delegate at Adana, Jemal Bey:

> The only force in Turkey that is able to frustrate the political life of the Ittihad ve Terakke [the Committee of Union and Progress] is the Armenians. From news which has frequently been received lately from Cairo, we learn that the Dashnaktsutiun is preparing a decisive attack against the Jemiet [Assembly of the Committee of Union and Progress]. If we examine minutely the historical circumstances of the past we shall find that all the storms which have obstructed the patriotic efforts of the Jemiet are the result of the seeds of discord sown by the Armenians.
>
> It will be forbidden to help or protect any Armenian.
>
> The Jemiet has decided to save the fatherland from the ambition of this cursed race, and to take on its own patriotic shoulders the stain which will blacken Ottoman history.
>
> The Jemiet, unable to forget all old scores and past bitterness, full of

hope for the future, has decided to annihilate all Armenians living in Turkey, without leaving a single one alive, and it has given the Government a wide scope with regard to this. Of course, the Government will give the necessary injunctions about the necessary massacres to the Governors. All the delegates of the Ittihad ve Terakke will do their utmost to push on this matter.

The property left will be temporarily confiscated by any means that the Government thinks fit, with the intention of its being sold afterwards and the money used for reorganizing the Jemiet on a broader basis, and for patriotic purposes. With regards to this, if you deem it necessary, demand an explanation from the Executive Committees which are to be formed. If you see anything in the administration which is not in order, you can apply either to the Governors-General or to us.[34]

In a second letter to Jemal Bey, on March 25 (April 7), 1915, Shakir wrote:

It is the duty of all of us to effect on the broadest lines the realization of the noble project of wiping out of existence the Armenians who have for centuries been constituting a barrier to the Empire's progress in civilization. For this reason, we must take upon ourselves the whole responsibility, saying "come what may," and appreciating how great is the sacrifice which has enabled the Government to enter the world war, we must work so that the means adopted may lead to the desired end.

As announced in our dispatch dated February 8, the Jemiet has decided to uproot and annihilate the various forces which have for centuries been an obstacle in its way, and to this end it is obliged to resort to very bloody methods. Be assured that we ourselves were horrified at the contemplation of these methods, but the Jemiet sees no other way of ensuring the stability of its work.

We are criticized and called upon to be merciful; such simplicity is nothing short of stupidity. For those who will not cooperate with us we will find a place that will wring their delicate heart-strings.

I again recall to your memory the question of the property left. It is very important. Do not let its distribution escape your vigilance; always examine the accounts and the use made of the proceeds.[35]

The operations were to be carried out, as much as possible, in secret, that is, away from the eyes of foreigners. In a telegram of September 3 (16), 1915, Talaat told the governor of Aleppo that the American ambassador was receiving information about the massacres from his consuls:

Be careful that events attracting attention shall not take place in connection with those [Armenians] who are near the cities and other centers. From the point of view of the present policy it is most important that foreigners who are in those parts shall be persuaded that the expulsion of the Armenians is in truth only deportation. For this reason it is important that, to save appearances, a show of gentle dealing shall be made for a time, and the usual measures be taken in suitable places.[36]

Still later, in December, Talaat telegraphed:

We hear that there are numbers of alien officers on the roads who have seen corpses of the above-mentioned people [the Armenians] and are photographing them. It is recommended as very important that those corpses should at once be buried and not left so exposed.[37]

The records in European and American archives on the Genocide present an overwhelming case for the brutality of the forced marches, the massacres, and the eventual starvation of the survivors in the Syrian desert.[38] Yet one of the most revealing accounts linking the Young Turk leadership directly to the massacres and deportations is the diaries and memoirs of the American ambassador to the Ottoman Empire, Henry Morgenthau. Here he tells of his conversations with Enver and Talaat Pasha. As more and more evidence came into the American embassy that Armenians were being deported and murdered, Morgenthau requested a meeting with Enver and encountered the minister of war quite frank about what was happening.

The Armenians had a fair warning . . . of what would happen to them in case they joined our enemies. Three months ago I sent for the Armenian Patriarch and I told him that if the Armenians attempted to start a revolution or to assist the Russians, I would be unable to prevent mischief from happening to them. My warning produced no effect and the Armenians started a revolution and helped the Russians. You know what happened at Van. They obtained control of the city, used bombs against government buildings, and killed a large number of Moslems. We knew that they were planning uprisings in other places. You must understand that we are now fighting for our lives at the Dardanelles and that we are sacrificing thousands of men. While we are engaged in such a struggle as this, we cannot permit people in our own country to attack us in the back. We have got to prevent this no matter what means we have to resort to. It is absolutely true that I am not opposed to the Armenians as a people. I have the greatest admiration for their intelligence and industry, and I would like nothing better than to see them become a real part of our nation. But if they ally themselves with our enemies, as they did in the Van district, they will have to be destroyed.[39]

Enver argued that European sympathy only encouraged the Armenians:

I am sure that if these outside countries did not encourage them, they would give up their efforts to oppose the present government and become law-abiding citizens. We now have this country in our absolute control and we can easily revenge ourselves on any revolutionists. . . . The great trouble with the Armenians is that they are separatists. They are determined to have a kingdom of their own, and they have allowed themselves to be fooled by the Russians. . . . You must remember that when we started this revolution in Turkey there were only two hundred of us. . . . It is our experience with revolutions which makes us fear the Armenians. If two hundred Turks could overturn the Government, then a few hundred bright, educated Armenians could do the same thing. We have therefore deliberately adopted the plan of scattering them so that they can do us no harm.[40]

Morgenthau goes on:

In another talk with Enver I began by suggesting that the Central Government was probably not to blame for the massacres. I thought this would not be displeasing to him.

"Of course. I know that the Cabinet would never order such terrible things as have taken place," I said. "You and Talaat and the rest of the Committee can hardly be held responsible. Undoubtedly your subordinates have gone much further than you have ever intended. I realize that it is not always easy to control your underlings."

Enver straightened up at once. I saw that my remarks, far from smoothing the way to a quiet and friendly discussion, had greatly offended him. I had intimated that things could happen in Turkey for which he and his associates were not responsible.

"You are greatly mistaken," he said. "We have this country absolutely under our control. I have no desire to shift the blame on to our underlings and I am entirely willing to accept the responsibility myself for everything that has taken place. The Cabinet itself has ordered the deportations. I am convinced that we are completely justified in doing this owing to the hostile attitude of the Armenians toward the Ottoman Government, but we are the real rulers of Turkey, and no underling would dare proceed in a matter of this kind without our orders."[41]

Morgenthau's conversations with Talaat Pasha were equally revealing.

"It is no use for you to argue," Talaat answered, "we have already disposed of three quarters of the Armenians; there are none at all left in Bitlis, Van, and Erzeroum. The hatred between the Turks and the Armenians is now so intense that we have got to finish with them. If we don't, they will plan their revenge."

... "I have asked you to come here so as to let you know that our Armenian policy is absolutely fixed and that nothing can change it. We will not have the Armenians anywhere in Anatolia. They can live in the desert but nowhere else."[42]

Estimates of the Armenians killed in the deportations and massacres of 1915–1916 range from a few hundred thousand to 1,500,000. Whatever the actual number of those killed, the result was the physical annihilation of Armenians in the greater part of historic Armenia, the final breaking of a continuous inhabitation of that region by people who called themselves Armenian. By the act of genocide the Young Turks prepared the ground, not for their imperial Turanian dream, but for the Kemalist republic, the Turkish state that now occupies the Anatolian peninsula. Once the Greeks were driven into the sea at Smyrna in 1922 and Cilicia cleared of Armenians, the Turkish nationalists gained a homeland for the Turkish people. Though they would have to share eastern Anatolia with Kurds who in time acquired their own political ambitions, the successive Turkish regimes were successful in gaining international recognition of their rights to the territory that once made up the heartland of Armenian kingdoms and the eastern marchlands of the Byzantine Empire.

The new Turkey was founded on the bloody extinction of other claimants to its territory, and defense of the integrity of the new state came to mean, at various times, support of conservative, discriminatory, and often military and dictatorial regimes. Allied with the greatest power of the Western world, present-day Turkey refuses to acknowledge the historical experience on which its own territorial hegemony is based. Armenians must be purged from memory, not only in Turkey but internationally as well, and Kurds must be forcibly transformed into "Mountain Turks."

Though there is no, and cannot be any, justification for genocide, historians have rationalized the actions of Turkish nationalists. Consider the apparently balanced judgment of one of the most distinguished American scholars of Islam, Bernard Lewis:

> For the Turks, the Armenian movement was the deadliest of all threats. From the conquered lands of the Serbs, Bulgars, Albanians, and Greeks, they could, however reluctantly, withdraw, abandoning distant provinces and bringing the Imperial frontier nearer home. But the Armenians, stretching across Turkey-in-Asia from the Caucasian frontier to the Mediterranean coast, lay in the very heart of the Turkish homeland—and to renounce these lands would have meant not the truncation, but the dissolution of the Turkish state.[43]

Are we to suppose that the national interest of one people justifies the physical extermination of another? Are dual claims to a single territory to be settled by deportation or massacre? Should we not find the moral authority to condemn unequivocally killing so deliberately aimed at political advantage? If Turks and Armenians are to rid themselves of the pathological consequences of the mass murders that bind them together in historical memory, then the crimes must be recognized; their causes must be examined dispassionately; and the courage must be found to rethink the unthinkable.

PART TWO

STATE, NATION, DIASPORA

7 Armenia and the Russian Revolution

On March 1, 1917, the Armenian mayor of Tiflis, Aleksandr Khatisian, was suddenly summoned to the palace of the Caucasian viceroy, the Grand Duke Nikolai Nikolaevich. He was told to come at once, not to bother even to change into his official uniform. The viceroy solemnly informed the mayor that there had been a rebellion in the capital, Petrograd, and that he was sympathetic to the aims of the rebels to change the tsarist government. He called for calm in the city, and allowed Khatisian to make a public announcement about the recent events.[1] What had happened in Petrograd, of course, was the overthrow of the 300-year-old Romanov monarchy and the beginning of the Russian Revolution, which in eight short months would see the country pass from tsarist autocracy through a stilted liberal regime to a militant social-ist dictatorship of the Bolshevik party. The events, reported so portentously by the viceroy, had enormous political, social and international significance. Local in origin, they soon became global in repercussions. As the ripples spread outward from central Russia, they engulfed the Armenian people, those who had managed to survive more than two years of war and systematic massacre at the hands of the Turks.

By 1917 the Armenians had become a politically conscious and mobilized nationality. Not only was the urban bourgeoisie in the cities of Caucasia and the Middle East engaged in Armenian community politics, but even the most backward peasants of eastern Anatolia had been swept into an unavoidable involvement with Armenian national affairs because of the First World War, the Russian invasions of eastern Turkey, and the Ottoman policy of deporta-tion and destruction of the Armenian people. Yet the divisions that had marked the Armenians in the past could not be quickly and completely overcome. As the Russian Revolution progressed, as the struggle between central Russia and its conquered borderlands was transformed from civil to national war, the fate and future of the Armenians in Armenia depended on their ability to accomplish two extraordinarily difficult tasks: (1) to overcome the divisions within their own nationality—divisions of class, of communities, and of party—and (2) to secure some support, material and military, from one or more of the Great Powers in order to preserve an Armenian political entity. These two tasks were tightly intertwined, for support in European capitals required a united front from the Armenians, but it should be emphasized that Armenian unity and persuasiveness were never sufficient conditions for preservation of an Armenian political presence in Armenia. Much more important, indeed ultimately crucial, was the intervention of the Great Powers. Armenia's location between Turkey and Russia, its remoteness from the Western powers, meant that the fate of the Armenians would be determined by decisions and events outside the control of the Armenians themselves. It would depend on the success of the Russians in reestablishing authority over the borderlands, on the ability of the Turks to thwart the designs of acquisitive Westerners, and on the willingness of the Allies to attempt to penetrate deep into Asia Minor in a risky and costly cause.

The February Revolution was greeted with widespread enthusiasm by Armenians. With the tsar removed, traditional Armenian Russophilism lost its ambivalence about the nature of the Russian government and hopes for a Russian military political solution to the Armenian Question were revived. At the time of the February events Russian troops were occupying much of Turkish Armenia. The campaigns of 1916 had led to the capture of Erzerum, Trebizond, Erzinjan, and the whole of the Lake Van region. Even Mush and Bitlis had been taken, though the Turks retained ground in that area in 1917. The first concern of Armenian political leaders was to maintain the Caucasian Front, to keep the Russian Army in place and the Turks from reconquering northeastern Anatolia. With Transcaucasia inundated with hundreds of thousands of refugees from Turkish Armenia, the communities in Baku, Erevan, and Tiflis were anxious to resettle them on the other side of the Arax. The tsarist government had hindered resettlement, but the new revolutionary authorities were expected to be more sympathetic. Armenia's fate was understood to be tied to a Russian victory. Indeed, Armenians of the liberal middle class became outspoken defenders of Russian expansionism. In May 1917, the Armenian liberal Khristofor Vermishev told the Kadet Party Congress:

> The attacks on what is called Russian imperialism are completely beyond understanding. In the Caucasus this imperialism created a legal order and a secure life which Armenians had not known before. Russian imperialism had its dark sides, but in general it was a positive force. . . . Armenia has waited for long years for Russian imperialism to say its mighty word in Turkish Armenia and lead the Armenians from under the Turkish yoke.[2]

The issue of war and peace became a central question for the leaders of the Russian Revolution. Vermishev's praise of "Russian imperialism" was not an eccentric Armenian opinion but was consistent with the views of the leader of the Kadet party, Pavel Miliukov, the first foreign minister of the new Provisional Government. Miliukov advocated carrying the war to "a victorious end" and informed the Allies that Russia's war aims remained the same as they had been before the revolution, i.e., Russia maintained her territorial claims against the Central Powers. The annexation of Turkish Armenia was to be one of the several prizes of victory over Turkey. At the other end of the political spectrum, however, the Left, particularly the Social Democrats centered in the Petrograd soviet, opposed such a policy. They called for a "democratic peace without annexations or contributions."[3] The socialists wanted to bring the war to a close as soon as possible and return to the territorial *status quo ante bellum*. The first major political crisis within the revolution occurred in April precisely over the question of war aims. The soviet, which had the support of workers and soldiers, proved to be much more powerful than the government, and Miliukov was forced to resign as foreign minister as the government formally adopted the war policy of the soviet.

The soviet position left the fate of Turkish Armenia in doubt, yet most Armenian political parties, including the Dashnaktsutiun, supported the notion of a "democratic" peace. Russia was still in physical occupation of Turkish Armenia, and the Provisional Government created its own *ad hoc* policy toward the conquered and depopulated territory. On April 26, just before the fall of Miliukov, an "arrangement about Turkish Armenia" was worked out by the government. Turkish Armenia was placed under the authority of a "general commissar" to be appointed by the government and directly responsible to Petrograd.[4] General Averianov was appointed commissar, and the Dashnak Dr. Zavrian his civil assistant. In the next six months hundreds of Armenian refugees drifted back into their homeland. The cities of Van and Bitlis were governed directly by Armenians, and a new pro-Armenian Russian administration was set up for the whole territory.

The revolution had made it possible for Russian soldiers to express openly and potently their opposition to continuing the war in any but a purely defensive manner. The long years of debilitating fighting had left the army demoralized, weakened by lack of supplies, and anxious to return to their homes. One solution to the problem of maintaining the Caucasian Front was to move Armenian soldiers from other fronts to replace the Russians in Transcaucasia. Just before his government fell in October 1917, Prime Minister Aleksandr Kerensky ordered about 35,000 Armenian soldiers to transfer to the Caucasus, and several thousand made their way as far as Baku.[5] As Russian troops began to "vote with their feet" and leave the front on their own, Armenian rifle battalions were left as the major force standing between an exposed Transcaucasia and the reorganized Turkish armies.

Besides providing elemental security and territorial gains, the Armenians believed that the revolution would realize their Western-inspired political hopes. No major Armenian political party called for a declaration of independence at this point. Rather, they advocated autonomy for Armenians within a democratic Russian federation. The Dashnaktsutiun, by 1917 the indisputable leader of most of the Caucasian Armenians, favored the division of Transcaucasia into cantons that would approximate the ethnic divisions of the region. They supplemented this territorial division with the notion of "extraterritorial cultural autonomy," a principle that would guarantee each citizen national cultural rights no matter where he or she lived. In April the Caucasian Dashnaks put forth their immediate demands to be fulfilled before the calling of the Constituent Assembly. They included both national and social improvements, the amelioration of workers' conditions, the lowering of land rents, nationalization of schools, and the use of local language in judicial and administrative bodies.[6]

Dashnak hopes were pinned on a pro-Armenian policy by the liberal-socialist Provisional Government, but throughout 1917 this government was losing its support in the population. As the war wound on and the government proved unable to satisfy the aroused expectations of soldiers, workers, and peasants, the lower classes became increasingly discontented with the Coalition Government and ever more radical in their demands. Workers in Petrograd and other large cities gravitated toward the Bolsheviks, who advocated the end of the coalition uniting "all the vital forces of the nation" and the establishment of a government of the lower classes based on the soviets. The futile attempt by the Right and the military to seize power in late August only further widened the polarization between the upper and lower classes and increased worker and soldier support for the Bolsheviks. On October 25, Lenin and his followers seized power in the name of the soviets.

The social polarization and labor radicalism evident in Petrograd was considerably more muted in the rest of the country. Although Baku, with its thousands of oil workers, had a large Bolshevik following, less-industrialized Tiflis and Erevan possessed only a smattering of Leninists. Tiflis was dominated by the Georgian Mensheviks, who ruled through the local soviet, and Erevan was largely under the influence of the Dashnaks. The October Revolution changed fundamentally the relationship between Russia, now Bolshevik, and Transcaucasia, which was not prepared to follow the center into an unknown future. Neither the Mensheviks nor the Dashnaks believed that Russia was ready for socialism, and neither party wished to break the alliance with the Entente as the Bolsheviks seemed determined to do.[7] Whereas in the period from February to October, the Armenians had almost unanimously supported the general trend of the revolution toward democracy and the election of a Constituent Assembly, after October, with radical socialists in control of the central government, almost all Armenian political parties (with the notable exception of the small group of Armenian Bolsheviks) opposed the people in power in Petrograd. The entire Russian orientation of the Armenians of Transcaucasia was now seriously called into question.

Though most Armenian political leaders opposed the Bolshevik call for an immediate end to the war and the creation of soviet power, they were less hostile to Lenin's ideas on nationalities. Not only did the Bolshevik program guarantee formally the full civil and social rights of all peoples, but in his writings Lenin specifically called for "self-determination of nations including separation" from Russia if they should so desire. For the Armenians this meant that they would be permitted to decide for themselves whether or not they wanted association with Russia or independence. Should they choose to remain within a Russian state, however, they would have to accept the Bolshevik principle of a centralized state with a certain degree of territorial autonomy but could not choose national cultural autonomy or a federal relationship with the center.

At the same time Lenin rejected out of hand any suggestion that Russian troops could be used to annex Turkish Armenia to Russia. In May 1917 he had declared: "If the soviet seizes power tomorrow . . . we shall say: Germany, out with your armies from Poland; Russia, out with your armies from Armenia—otherwise, it will be a lie."[8] Lenin meant to carry out the program of no annexations or contributions seriously. In early December his government issued the "Appeal to the Muslims of Russia and the East," which nullifed the secret treaty that tsarist Russia and the Western powers had made depriving Turkey of Armenia.[9] In his anxiety to reassure the minorities and other governments that the new Soviet government was not imperialist as previous Russian governments had been, Lenin was prepared to allow the creation of an independent Armenia by the Armenians but not with the help of Russian troops. Such a policy, while ideologically quite principled, was in reality unrealistic, for the withdrawal of Russian troops would have led to the return of the Turkish army to Armenia and made any Armenian decision about the future of Turkish Armenia impossible.

Bolshevik policy toward Armenia was a reflection of Lenin's desire to secure Muslim help in the struggle with British imperialism, but if carried out it would have placed the Armenians in a most dangerous position. On January 11, 1918, the Soviet government modified its original policy in its declaration "About Turkish Armenia." While continuing to call for the withdrawal of Russian troops from Turkish Armenia, the Bolsheviks now called for the "unhindered return to 'Turkish Armenia' of refugee Armenians," the formation of an Armenian militia in the area, and the creation of an elected soviet to govern the region.[10] Unfortunately this imagined scenario could never be put into effect. Within a month of the declaration, Turkish military forces had crossed the old Russo-Turkish frontier and were moving into Transcaucasia. Turkish Armenia would never again be secure under Russia occupation. At the same time the central Soviet government was faced by an equal danger from advancing German troops, and in March 1918, Lenin and Trotsky were forced to sign the humiliating Brest-Litovsk Treaty, ceding to Germany vast territories in western Russia and to Turkey the districts of Kars, Ardahan, and Batumi.

With the seizure of power in Petrograd by the Bolsheviks, followed shortly by the Bolshevik dispersal of the democratically elected Constituent Assembly and the signing of the Brest-Litovsk Treaty, Transcaucasia was cut off politically, and later physically, from central Russia. The Mensheviks and Dashnaks refused allegiance to the Soviet government, and just weeks after the October Revolution, a Transcaucasian commissariat (ZAVKOM) was formed in Tiflis as an autonomous political authority. Three months later, in February 1918, a local parliament (Seim) was established, and finally in April, under pressure from the Turks, Transcaucasia was declared an independent federative republic.[11]

From early 1918 to early 1921 Russia resembled less a single country than a fragmented continent. It was rent apart by a ferocious civil war, attacked by foreign armies, and fractured by nationalist and separatist movements. In this period Russia ceased to be the major power dictating the course of Caucasian history. Not until 1920 would Soviet Russia again be the principal factor in the outcome of the revolution south of the Caucasus. The most immediate and palpable danger to the peoples of Transcaucasia was Turkey. With Russia in turmoil and unable to field an army on far-flung fronts, the Turks were now able to regenerate their Pan-Turkic ambitions. The Turkish offensive began in early February 1918 with the capture of Erzinjan. In March Erzerum was taken, and soon the whole of Turkish Armenia was in the grasp of the army of General Karabekir. No outside powers were able or willing to come to the aid of the Armenians,[12] and Caucasian Armenians were now faced with the same fate that their brethren in Turkey had experienced. The level of fear and hostility toward the local Muslim population rose rapidly, and in Erevan province Armenians and Azerbaijanis attacked one another. Christian villages were besieged by Muslims, and vice versa. The dictator of Erevan, Aram Manukian, did not hesitate to use violence against Muslim peasants. About the same time in Baku, Armenians joined with the Bolsheviks and other soviet parties to put down a Muslim attempt to take over the city. Armenian soldiers used the occasion to take revenge on the Muslims for earlier atrocities.[13] It was clear that force of arms and ruthless repression were to be the means of securing power in Transcaucasia. As political order and any spirit of compromise dissolved in the bloodshed, the final arbiter of politics in Armenia became raw military muscle.

Of the three major nationalities of Transcaucasia, the Armenians were in the greatest danger in the spring of 1918. The Azerbaijanis stood to benefit from a Turkish victory that would eliminate the Armenian threat and restore Baku to the control of the Muslims. The Georgians were willing to deal with the Turks and the Germans for guarantees that Georgian lands would not be annexed by Turkey. But the Armenians were an obstacle to the realization of the Pan-Turkic plans of a Muslim state stretching from Istanbul through Caucasia to Central Asia. The Dashnaktsutiun was in an extremely vulnerable position. The party was opposed to separation from Russia, but Russia was now unable to aid the Armenians against the Turks. Therefore the party leaders in Tiflis reluctantly went along with the Georgian Mensheviks and the Azerbaijanis and gave into Turkish pressure to declare Transcaucasia an independent state on April 22, 1918. About the same time the Dashnaks of Baku, a city then firmly in the hands of a Bolshevik-led soviet, opposed the Seim's declaration of independence and recognized Soviet Russian authority.[14]

The situation went from bad to worse in the months of April and May, 1918. The fortress of Kars, packed with refugees, fell to the Turks on April 25. Thousands of Armenian immigrants and soldiers poured into Erevan province. Armenians in Tiflis stormed into the streets, protesting the policies of the Transcaucasian government that had led to the fall of Kars. The Turks meanwhile invaded Erevan province, the last refuge of the Armenians, on May 15. They moved forward steadily until they had reached Sardarabad, about twenty-five miles from the capital. There the ragged Armenian troops under Silikian, Bek Pirumian, and Dro held off the Turks and on May 24 drove them back. As the Armenians fought to preserve a small foothold in Transcaucasia, the Georgians were responding to German suggestions that they withdraw from the Transcaucasian federation and set up an independent Georgian state to which the Germans would promise support. On May 26, the Menshevik leaders of Georgia declared Georgia an independent state, and they were followed two days later by the Azerbaijanis. The Armenians had been abandoned by the other peoples of the Caucasus. Reluctantly, fatalistically, the Dashnak leaders in Tiflis concluded that there was no alternative to a declaration of Armenian independence. The Armenian National Council took upon itself the task of forming a government for the Armenian provinces.

The chances for the survival of an independent Armenian state in 1918 were remote indeed. Although they had been beaten back from Erevan province for the time being, the Turks still presented a serious threat, and they continued their advance through Azerbaijan toward Baku. Given a choice, the Armenian leadership in Tiflis would not have declared independence, preferring some kind of political relationship with Russia or at least with the other peoples of Transcaucasia. But hostilities between these peoples and the cool calculation by Georgians and Azerbaijanis that they could improve their situation by abandoning the Armenians and allying with the Germans and Turks respectively left the Armenians completely isolated. The decisions of other nations forced the Dashnaks to take upon themselves the role of leaders of a new state, a state that came into existence in an incredibly inhospitable environment.

Two conditions were required for an independent Armenia to become a viable sovereign state: unity among Armenians in support of the state and material and diplomatic support from at least one of the Great Powers. With Russia unable to aid, Armenia's political fortunes rested with the Entente, but in the short term she had to deal with Turkey. On June 4, the representatives of the Armenian National Council signed a peace treaty with the Turks. In the next few weeks the Tiflis Armenians began forming a government for a country that did not yet exist in any real name. Only on July 19 did the government of the Armenian republic arrive in its designated capital, Erevan. There the genteel politicians of Tiflis were faced by tens of thousands of starving and homeless refugees, cholera, typhus, and the nearby threat of the Turkish Army.[15] Essentially the first months of the new republic were simply a holding operation, as the Armenians watched the world war come to a close. The defeat of the Central Powers and the subsequent withdrawal of the Turks from Transcaucasia created an entirely new political universe for the Armenians. With British troops occupying Baku and Batumi, with the Entente about to redraw the maps of Europe and the Middle East, Armenia's chances for survival appeared considerably brighter than they had only a few months earlier.

The period of Armenian independence lasted only two years, from the end of World War I to the coming of the Red Army in the last month of 1920. The failure to establish an independent state might be blamed on the Dashnak leaders of the republic themselves, or on the failure of the Entente to provide necessary aid, or on the imperialist designs of the Soviet and Turkish states. But rather than exercise the function of an ethical arbiter, I would like instead to evaluate the outcome of this experiment in independence in a less moralistic and more dispassionate way. First of all, it should be remembered that independence came about because of the absence of alternatives; it took place in a power vacuum and lasted as long as the two large states that had divided Armenia in the last century and a half were both too weak to establish hegemony over this small country. As soon as either or both of these powers, Russia and Turkey, regained strength, one was likely to reestablish its authority over Armenia. If the two powers were evenly matched or in alliance, Armenia was likely to be divided between them. This outcome was not a new occurrence in Armenian history. For thousands of years, Armenia had lain between great rival empires, and it was almost a law of Armenian history that she could enjoy autonomy or independence only when the great empires on her borders were weak, distracted by more important affairs in other parts of the world, or so evenly balanced one with the other that they were willing to accept a relatively autonomous Armenian buffer state between them. More often than not, Armenia was simply divided between the great imperial states of the area.

As long as Soviet Russia was engaged in a fight for its life against the White armies and foreign interventionists, as long as Turkey was unable to resist the plans of the Allies to divide up her empire and detach Armenia from it, the small nations of the Caucasus had a realistic chance of maintaining their independence. But once the Allies retreated from Russia, and once the Whites were defeated, Soviet troops were able to mass on the borders of Azerbaijan and reassert Russian dominance in Transcaucasia. The revival of Turkish nationalism under the banner of Mustafa Kemal meant that Russia would be unable to regain all her conquests of the war years and that Turkish Armenia would fall to the armies of the Nationalists. By the end of 1920 Russia and Turkey reemerged as the hegemonic powers in Armenia, and Armenia was divided between them. One part continued as an Armenian political entity, the other lost all official designation as Armenian.

In line with the view that ultimately the possibility of independence depended less on the Armenians themselves than on outsiders, I would also argue that the rule of the Dashnaks should not be judged by the failure of independence but rather by their record in the two years in which they managed the political and economic life of the Erevan republic. Were the Dashnaks able to solve some of the life-threatening problems Armenians faced between 1918 and 1920, or were they responsible for exacerbating those problems?[16]

Shortly after taking office, the first prime minister of the Armenian Republic, Hovhannes Kachaznuni, described the problems faced by his government in a land of refugees and famine. The government had no link with the past, no inherited administrative machinery. It had to start from scratch and create everything from ruins and chaos. The prime minister minced no words when he told his colleagues that the new rulers of Armenia had found the country in a condition that could only be characterized as catastrophic.[17] Yet out of this chaos the Dashnaks created an administrative apparatus, with an elected parliament. In the interests of national unity the Dashnaktsutiun organized coalition governments and included representatives of the smaller Armenian People's Party (liberals), an antirevolutionary middle-class party made up of Tiflis businessmen and professionals. The Armenian Left, the Socialist Revolutionaries and the Social Democrats, refused to join any coalition that included representatives of the bourgeoisie. To them, the willingness of the Dashnaks to ally with the liberal middle class simply exposed the nationalist party as a "petty-bourgeois" rather than a true socialist party. But for the Dashnaks the alliance with the middle class was consistent with their foreign policy goal of achieving support and recognition from the victorious Western powers. By late 1918 their earlier Russian orientation had been replaced by a decidedly Western European orientation.

Armenia needed immediate help—material supplies and a pledge of support for her security. Famine was widespread in Erevan, and the underfed population was susceptible to disease. As Richard Hovannisian tells us, "It was verily a land of death."[18] Approximately 200,000 people, almost 20 percent of the republic's population, had died by the middle of 1919. A newspaper account told the following horror story:

> The populace is feeding upon the bodies of dead cats and dogs. There have even been cases when a starving mother has eaten the kidney or the liver

from the corpse of her own child. . . . The skeleton-like women and children rummage in the refuse heaps for moldered shoes and, after cooking them for three days, eat them.[19]

Before the revolution the Erevan area had received one-third of its food supply from Russia. With this source cut off and the number of refugees increasing daily, the Armenian economy was unable to stabilize itself. Inflation soared, and the money issued by the government became worthless. At the same time the Armenians faced hostile governments in Georgia and Azerbaijan and the embryonic nationalist movement headed by Mustafa Kemal in Anatolia. Armed clashes with the Georgians in Lori and Borchalu and with the Azerbaijanis in Karabagh and Zangezur only added to the new government's problems. With the support of the British, the Armenians were able to retake Kars. Flushed by their survival, the government celebrated the first anniversary of the republic on May 28, 1919, by audaciously proclaiming the annexation of Turkish Armenia. This rhetorical gesture could not be enforced since the Dashnaks did not have adequate military force. Indeed, the declaration not only angered middle-class Armenians in Tiflis and emigrants from Turkish Armenia but infuriated the Turkish nationalists.

When the Paris Peace Conference opened in January 1919, the Armenians were represented, not by one, but by two delegations. The two separate missions reflected the division between eastern and western Armenians and the traditional conflict between the liberal middle-class Armenians and the Dashnaktsutiun. The delegation from the Republic of Armenia was headed by Avetis Aharonian, a writer and Dashnak activist. The rival delegation, the so-called "Armenian National Delegation," was led by a wealthy Egyptian Armenian, Boghos Nubar Pasha, one of the founders of the Armenian General Benevolent Union in 1906. Nubar and his associates were hostile to the Dashnaktsutiun, which they regarded as a revolutionary and a socialist organization, and opposed the new Armenian republic on the Ararat plain, which had failed to include Cilicia in its territorial demands. Nubar claimed to represent the Armenians of Turkey, regardless of class or religious affiliation, while Aharonian justified himself as the official representative of an established, though as yet unrecognized, government and the spokesman for the Armenians of Russia. Rather than fight one another, the two leaders decided to work together in a single joint delegation and present a single list of demands to the peace conference.[20]

Given the Armenophile atmosphere in Paris and the pledges of support from various Allied leaders, particularly President Woodrow Wilson, the Armenians set out grand and lavish demands for territory. They envisioned an Armenian state stretching from the Black Sea to the Mediterranean, including Trebizond and Cilicia, Van, Bitlis, Diarbakir, Kharput, Sivas, Erzerum, Marash, Adana, Kars, Karabagh, Zangezur, and Erevan province. Much of this territory, like Trebizond, had never belonged to the Armenians but was justified for security or commercial reasons. Almost nowhere in this vast territory, except in Erevan province, did the Armenians constitute a majority of the population, but as was pointed out, considerations of current demographic patterns would require turning a blind eye to the recent massacres of Armenians and the forced migrations and deportations. Several Allied delegations were disturbed by the Armenian territorial claims, particularly the French, who had their own designs on Cilicia, and a French newspaper scorned the grandiose plans of the Armenians as "l'Empire arménien."

One by one the various Allied powers refused to take on the principal responsibility for the Armenians. It was finally decided by the leaders gathered in Paris that the United States should become the mandatory power protecting the Armenians. President Wilson was prepared to shoulder this burden but, as is well known, he was unable to convince the Senate to take on the mandate. After a national campaign and a bitter debate in the Senate, the architect of Armenia's defeat in Congress, Senator Henry Cabot Lodge, wrote to a friend: "Do not think I do not feel badly about Armenia. I do, but I think there is a limit to what they have a right to put off on us."[21] Even though the Allied powers granted *de facto* recognition to Armenia in January 1920, no real military assistance was forthcoming. America sent food, money, and other supplies that were crucial to Armenia's survival, but as the Russian Civil War wound down, there was to be no further aid.

Without Western support Armenia survived as an independent state only so long as her two most powerful neighbors, Russia and Turkey, could not physically threaten her. But by 1920 Anatolia had become the heartland of a new Turkey for the Turks, and the Nationalists were determined to rid the area of foreigners—the British, the French, the Greeks, and the Armenians. In February 1920 the Kemalists attacked Marash, the city in southeastern Anatolia held by the French and occupied by the Armenians. After fierce fighting it appeared as if the Turks would be forced to withdraw, but at the crucial moment the French decided to abandon the city and the Armenians to their fate. As many as 11,000 Armenians may have perished in the fighting in the "white massacre" by the Kemalists that followed the fall of the city.[22] All of Cilicia was soon lost to the Turks.

Since Kemal and the Nationalists were at war with the Western powers, Soviet Russia viewed the mobilized Turks as a powerful ally in the "anti-imperialist" struggle. By the spring of 1920, Bolshevik troops had reached the North Caucasus, and on April 28 the Red Army marched into Baku, establishing the Soviet Republic of Azerbaijan. The Russians were once again the chief arbiters of the fate of Transcaucasia. Kemal agreed to recognize Azerbaijan as part of the Soviet sphere in exchange for weapons, food, and monetary aid. The Turks told Foreign Commissar Chicherin that their government was prepared to "take upon itself military operations against the imperialist Armenian government."[23] Suddenly, with the appearance on Armenia's frontiers of Soviet troops and Turkish Nationalist forces, the Armenians' political affiliation

with the Western Allies had become an enormous liability. The Dashnaktsutiun was viewed by the Soviets and the Kemalists as an agent of Western
imperialism and could expect little mercy from either the Russians or the
Turks. Armenian Communists used the proximity of the Red Army to instigate
revolts within Armenia, but until the last days of the republic the Dashnaks
managed to repulse these insurrections. Bolshevism had little support within
Armenia, and could hope to come to power only through direct Soviet intervention.

The final act in the drama of independence was largely a matter of inexo-
rable international forces eliminating alternatives for the Armenians and dictating the collapse of a pro-Western state between Soviet Russia and
Nationalist Turkey. In the late spring of 1920, the Republic of Armenia sent
a delegation to Moscow, headed by the writer Levon Shant, to seek Soviet
support for Armenian independence and claims to Turkish Armenia. Chicherin
made it clear that Soviet Russia would not back Armenian claims to Anatolia
and was more interested in solidifying an alliance with the Turkish Nationalists than in shoring up an Armenian state. Armenia was now caught between
the Soviet anvil and the Turkish hammer. The signing of the stillborn Treaty
of Sèvres by the Allies on August 10, 1920, giving Armenia in principle a large
part of northeastern Anatolia (the boundary was to be drawn later by President Wilson), was small consolation. The Dashnak leaders apparently decided
to take matters into their own hands. Underestimating actual Turkish military
strength in the area, the Armenians seized the coal mines at Olti. This act
was the provocation that the Turks required for launching a war against the
Armenians. In late September, the army under Karabekir Pasha moved against
the Armenian republic, advancing up to Sarikamish. Kars fell to the Turks at
the end of October, and Alexandropol (later Leninakan, now Gyumri) was
occupied on November 7. Within Armenia Communists organized a Revolutionary Committee and, on November 29, declared Soviet control. The Red
Army then crossed the border into Armenian territory.[24]

The Dashnaks faced annihilation and reluctantly sent a delegation, headed
by Aleksandr Khatisian, to Alexandropol to negotiate with the Turks in order
to keep them out of Erevan. At the same time they continued negotiations
with the representatives of Soviet Russia. In its last days the government of
independent Armenia signed treaties with both the Soviets and the Kemalists.
Anxious for the best deal for the Armenians, Khatisian in Alexandropol signed
away Armenian claims to Turkish Armenia and denounced the Treaty of Sèvres. On the same day (December 2, 1920), in Erevan the government of
General Dro signed an agreement with Silin, the representative of the Soviet
Russian Republic, proclaiming the new state of Soviet Armenia.

The failure of independent Armenia was the fault neither of the leaders
of the republic nor of their adversaries within the Armenian community. It
was not the result of Dashnak incompetency or aggressiveness, though the
ruling party was not entirely blameless. Giving up their Russian orientation

for a European orientation in 1918 had been a reasonable enough move in view of the impossibility at the time of Russian aid to Armenia, but it had been a gamble. Indeed, it had been quite a long shot. Once the Soviets moved into the Caucasus in 1920, the Dashnaks were faced with a new peril. Soviet Russia would not unconditionally support a republic linked to the Western powers and ruled by a party with a long history of antagonism to the Bolsheviks. The Dashnaks might have acted more quickly to attract Soviet support; they might also have been less provocative toward the Turkish Nationalists. But ultimately they were the victims of the requirements of larger powers.

Soviet Russia had no interest in supporting Armenia as an independent state when it could end its diplomatic isolation by linking up with Armenia's enemy, the Nationalist Turks, and identify the Soviet cause with the national liberation struggles of Muslim peoples. Armenia was expendable to the Soviets and always subordinate to Russia's revolutionary goals. Faced by invasions on two frontiers, the Dashnaks had no choice but to capitulate and hope for the best. Fortunately for the Armenians, a small portion of historic Armenia was preserved by the Dashnak-Soviet agreement and the Russo-Turkish Treaty of 1921. Kars and Ardahan were lost; Ararat and Turkish Armenia were gone; but Erevan, Alexandropol, and Russian Armenia in its pre-1878 boundaries remained in the new Soviet republic. Armenia's future lay in that small corner of its devastated homeland.

One's first impression of this period, so marred by disease, starvation, and demographic disaster, is that it was a time of destruction rather than nation-building and does not belong in our general scheme. But in fact, several important occurrences in this period irrevocably shaped the process of Armenian nation-building in our century. First of all, the center of Armenian population shifted to the Caucasus as a result of the 1915 massacres and deportations, the emigration of Turkish Armenians to the north, and the reconquest of eastern Anatolia by the nationalist Turks. Second, without military aid from the Allies, the Armenians could not hope to reestablish an Armenian population in eastern Anatolia. That aid was not forthcoming and therefore recovery of Turkish Armenia became impossible. Third, the Dashnak republic preserved a small portion of Armenia for Armenians and set up an embryonic state structure in Erevan. Finally, one great power was prepared to aid the Armenians in a limited way if they restricted their territory to Caucasia. The Russians, for their own ideological and political reasons, came to the rescue of the Armenians and made possible the continued existence of an Armenian political entity, albeit no longer sovereign and independent.

The Armenians have constituted a *people* all over the world, in hundreds of communities and for many centuries, but for the first time in modern history they constituted a *nationality*, in the sense of a conscious and mobilized ethnic group, by the end of the nineteenth century. Armenians continue to constitute a *nationality* in the twentieth century in various parts of the world where their communities organize for cultural and political preservation and advancement—for example, in Lebanon, France, Argentina, and the United States. But the Armenians constitute a *nation* in only one part of the world, in Haiastan itself, in the various incarnations of the Republic of Armenia—independent, Soviet, and independent again. What kind of nation that is, how it was formed and transformed in the last seventy-odd years, and what its prospects might be will be the subject of the remaining chapters.

8 Building a Socialist Nation

In the period following World War II American social scientists developed a number of interpretive concepts that soon became pervasive in academic circles. Such descriptive and analytic terms as "totalitarianism," "modernization," "nationalism," "nation-building," and "political integration" proved to be useful devices for understanding a world dominated by two major rival social systems into which new nations were emerging. Yet in the context of the cold war and European decolonization, it was not surprising that supposedly value-free and "scientific" terms contained within them little-explored moral and political assumptions. Understandably, ideas like "modernization" and "totalitarianism" were securely based on Western political preferences and tended to judge all societies in terms of an idealized version of capitalist democracy. The ideological biases implicit in these concepts have been pointed out by a variety of critics, particularly in the 1960s as the consensus about America as a political ideal was compromised by the new awareness of social and racial injustice within the country and by the ill-conceived adventure in Southeast Asia. Alternative theoretical approaches were sought by historians, political scientists, and sociologists, but the utility of the old terms, despite their imprecision and covert moral tone, led to their continued, though modified, employment.

The idea of "modernization" has spawned numerous theoretical and empirical works in the several decades of its existence, but it remains a vague and variously defined term. Modernization has had too many meanings for a quick review, but in general it has referred to the process of development in which backward societies become increasingly like the advanced industrial countries of the West. Following Max Weber, some theorists have seen modernization as the expansion of human control over the physical and social environment. More concretely, the process is explained in terms of industrial-ization, urbanization, the spread of literacy, and the increase of social mobility and political participation. For many the process was thought to be natural, organic, and perhaps inevitable if a society were to survive in today's world as a stable and prosperous system.

Implicit in the theory of modernization was a belief that very different societies around the world were fated to become more like one another, that national and ethnic differences would be gradually reduced if not eliminated, and that there would be a convergence between the states of the "socialist" and capitalist blocs. There was little disagreement on the part of most theorists that becoming more like advanced industrial societies was a good thing and worthy of encouragement and support. The coincidence of modernization theory and the growth of American imperial ambitions in the decolonized world in the 1960s—modernization through armed encouragement of "de-mocracy" and "free enterprise"—may not have been wholly accidental. As one critic noted:

> The idea of modernization has proven congenial to American policymak-ers, so much so in fact that "development" and "modernization" came to be viewed as long-range solutions to the threats of instability and Communism in the Third World. Certainly, by virtue of its overriding concern with political stability, its often explicit anti-Communism, and its indifference to the entire issue of economic and political imperialism, there is little in the modernization literature that would seriously disturb White House, Pentagon, or State De-partment policymakers.[1]

Another problem with the theory of modernization, besides its ideological bias, is that despite its apparent historical dimension, it is often presented in a basically ahistorical form. Modernization theories, working backward from an idea of modernity, interpret "premodern" societies as distinctly different and draw a sharp dichotomy between traditional and modern societies, the latter being much more responsive to social change and technological innova-tion. Critical historians and anthropologists have pointed out that the diversity of non-modern societies is so great that it is inaccurate to lump them together in a single category and label them "traditional." Many of them are not as static and unchanging as some Western observers have thought. Also, the very term "society" might not be proper for premodern social and political communities because, as Clifford Geertz has pointed out, they are not highly integrated, homogeneous social and cultural entities but quite heterogeneous and contain a variety of traditions.[2]

The critics of modernization theory today are as abundant as the propo-nents, if not even more numerous. Still, any observer can perceive that a process of social change is taking place around the world, in various social systems at various levels of development, which is breaking down old ways of doing things and introducing new ways associated with and often borrowed from advanced industrial societies. That process was observed and analyzed in the nineteenth century by Marx and linked to the power of the new capitalist mode of production that first emerged in England. But in the twentieth century development from agrarian to industrial society has occurred not only under capitalist conditions but also, with the establishment of Soviet power in Russia, under a state-directed noncapitalist system. Perhaps the remaining power of the idea of modernization lies not so much in its accuracy and precision as in its imprecision, in its general suggestiveness, and in its usefulness for describing similar processes under way in different modes of production.

For our purposes, I would like to use the term "modernization" in a general way to refer to two distinct processes, one social or socioeconomic and the other political. Socially, I will define modernization as the process in which (1) the economy of a country is transformed from subsistence peasant agriculture based on the household to an industrial system based on the factory and its appropriate technology, on wage labor, and on production for exchange; (2) the village is increasingly displaced as the center of social life by the city (urbanization); and (3) in this general increase in social change and social mobility, the dominant ideology shifts from religious to secular. Politically, I will use modernization to refer to the process of increasing participation of the population in decision making, the spread of notions of equality, and recourse to law rather than arbitrary power. As a society becomes more modern, people cease to be subjects and become citizens. It must be emphasized, however, that the social process of industrial and urban development does not depend on—nor necessarily lead to—the political process of greater participation in decision making, equality, and legality. They are separable developments, though certain aspects of modernization, such as the rise of literacy, the spread of popular education, and the social insecurity caused by the new mobility, may contribute to linking these two processes.

As I mentioned above, modernization can take place under various socioeconomic systems, and indeed much of the Soviet-American struggle over the Third World was directed at guaranteeing the system under which modernization will take place, market capitalism or state-directed planning. Just as Americans sought to spread the benefits of the so-called free world to underdeveloped countries, so the Soviets tried to export their own version of modernization through revolution, often, as in Eastern Europe, "revolution from above." Both of the superpowers seemed determined to transform agrarian societies into "modern" ones in their own image. Modernization theory, whether in its capitalist or Soviet version, clearly played a role far beyond the academy and operated as a rationalization for the preferred forms of social development advocated by the two world giants.

Modernization theory and its little brother, convergence theory, have tended to emphasize the similarities in development that take place in very different societies. Technology is often the key factor that determines that industrial societies will have basic similarities to one another. But without denying these symmetries between capitalist and noncapitalist industrialization and urbanization, the differences between a market economy and a planned economy, between parliamentary systems and one-party dictatorships, between cosmopolitan, denationalized societies and a multinational republic that preserves through a pseudo-federal structure ethnic differences, are great enough to warrant a careful look at modernization in a noncapitalist context. I would like to explore here the process of social and political modernization in Soviet Armenia to see how this small country was transformed from agrarian to industrial, from a disparate and dispersed people into a nation. As we shall see, modernization in Armenia evolved step by step with the building of an Armenian nation, and so far it has passed through three distinct periods: (1) the initial Soviet period (1921–1928) characterized by a mixed economic system (NEP) and fairly tolerant political practices; (2) the Stalinist period (1928–1953) of "revolution from above," radical socioeconomic transformation, and political "totalitarianism" complete with terror; and (3) the post-Stalin period (1953 to the early 1990s), which has been marked by a relaxation of total state control and a more moderate pattern of social change. The revolution set off by the Gorbachev reforms will be discussed in the final chapters.

Before Soviet Power

It is difficult, at the outset, to speak of a "traditional" society in Armenia at a particular point in time. As I have mentioned elsewhere, Armenians in the nineteenth century were divided between the large urban centers of Constantinople, Izmir, Tiflis, and Baku and the backward villages of eastern Anatolia and Erevan province. The division between traditional and modern was less chronological for Armenians than along class lines, with the peasants living in a traditional, pre-capitalist social order while the urban Armenians were already experiencing the effects of modern Western life.

The first phase of modernization for Armenians took place, then, in the nineteenth century in various urban communities under the influence of the capitalist and industrial revolutions that were revolutionizing European society. That modernization affected only a minority of Armenians, however, and the dislocations and trauma of the First World War, the massacres of 1915, and the Russian Revolution and Civil War (1917–1921) left the Armenians who had come under Soviet power with only remnants and traces of a century of development. The second phase of modernization for Armenians began in 1920, a modernization outside the capitalist world, a modernization aided by and limited by the Armenians' political connection with Soviet Russia.

By the end of 1920 the Armenians who had survived the most destructive and traumatic period of their history were in a desperate situation. The world looked with pity and sympathy at the people they invariably referred to as "starving Armenians," and the wealthier nations of the West, which had promised so much and done so little to preserve an independent Armenia, now extended charity to the thousands of refugees in the Middle East and the Caucasus. The Armenians had lost the lands in Turkey that they had inhabited since antiquity, and the only part of their ancient homeland still under some kind of Armenian political control was centered around Erevan. The population of Russian Armenia had fallen precipitately in the years since the outbreak of World War I. Whereas the last Russian census before the war had revealed a population slightly over a million in the areas that later became Soviet Armenia, by 1920 that figure had dropped to 720,000, a decline of 30 percent. Almost half the population were refugees.[3]

The progress that Armenians in Turkey and Russia had made in the century preceding World War I toward the formation of a conscious and mobilized nationality had been almost entirely annihilated by the years of war and revolution. Not only were territory and human lives lost, but the political institutions in which Armenians had worked, the cultural gains, and even the social structure of the Armenians had been shattered. There was no more Tiflis duma for the *mokalakebi* of Sololaki to exercise their dominance over the city's political and economic life. With the establishment of Menshevik Georgia and Musavat Azerbaijan, the Armenians of Tiflis and Baku lost the privileged position that they had built up during a century of Russian rule. With the establishment of Soviet republics in the Caucasus, there was no place for the Armenian bourgeoisie, and this deracinated class had no choice but to give up any claims to their old way of life or to emigrate abroad. A few of them migrated to Armenia to make careers in the new bureaucracy and economy of the Soviet republic.

Just as severely shattered as the Armenian merchant class was the Armenian intelligentsia. Many had been murdered by the Turks, and others were forced to leave Armenia forever because of their connections with the enemies of Bolshevism. The great majority of the prerevolutionary generation of Armenian political leaders were no longer welcome in Armenia. Only a few intellectuals remained in Transcaucasia to aid in the building of the new Armenian state. The old Bolshevik writer Hakop Hakopian, considered by the Communists to be the first Armenian proletarian writer, was adopted by the new regime, and those giants of prewar Armenian culture who were not openly hostile to the Soviets were encouraged to return to Armenia. The poet Hovhannes Tumanian, the historian Leo, the writers Nardos, Demirchian, Mirakian, Shushanik Kurginian, the actors Siranush, Alikhanian, Ter-Davtian, the artist Martiros Saryan, and others were assisted by the government in relocating in Erevan. While links with the culture of the past were being maintained, a new revolutionary intelligentsia for the Soviet future was also being prepared. Conflict within this intelligentsia between more traditional nationalists and the younger enthusiasts of socialism was intense throughout the 1920s and, although at times quite vicious in tone, the dialogues among intellectuals were among the most vital in the history of Armenian literature and art.

The Armenians had never been a people who shared to a very large degree a national consensus about the shape of the society in which they would like to live. Bourgeois liberals and nationalist socialists had disagreed quite violently about the utility of capitalism for developing the backward Armenian masses, and among the Armenian socialists there had been little agreement about the political structure of a future Armenia. The Dashnaks before 1918 had been prepared to live in a federated Russia that would guarantee national cultural autonomy for Armenians, but the Bolsheviks had urged the complete subordination of Armenian national aspirations to the overall historic mission of proletarian liberation. Within Armenia itself the Dashnaks had managed to achieve an enviable level of support or at least acquiescence to their rule. From 1905 to 1920 they had been the principal protectors of the Armenians against the dual threat from Russian autocracy and Turkish expansionism. They had maintained an Armenian presence in Caucasia despite the invasions from all sides, and their terrorization of local Muslims, reprehensible as it was from a moral point of view, nevertheless shifted the demographic balance in the area around Erevan in favor of the Armenians. But the economic difficulties of the years of independence had eroded some of that support, and small groups began to search for an alternative solution to Armenia's problems through an ideological, political, and military alliance with Soviet Russia. The various rebellions in 1920, most notably in Aleksandropol in May, undercut Dashnak authority and signaled the adoption by a small minority of Armenians of the old Russian orientation, this time with a new revolutionary twist.

The Establishment of Soviet Power

The imaginative claims of Soviet historians notwithstanding, the creation of a Soviet republic in Armenia came about not through a popular uprising or the enthusiastic demand of the people but rather as a measure of last resort by the defeated, discouraged, and disintegrating Dashnak government of independent Armenia. On December 2, 1920, the last Dashnak Council of Ministers signed away its powers to General Dro, making him temporary dictator of Erevan. Within the next few hours Dro met with the representative of Soviet Russia, Silin, and the two issued an order proclaiming Armenia an "independent socialist republic." All power was to be placed in the hands of a revolutionary committee (Revkom), made up of five Communists and two Left Dashnaks, the latter to be approved by the Communists. It was further agreed that no repressive measures were to be carried out against the Dashnaks or other non-Communists. An eyewitness in Erevan, British adventurer Oliver Baldwin, reports that "people were amazed, incredulous, but for the most part apathetic. Anyhow, they thought, it would be better to have the Russians back and to lose their independence than to be massacred by the Turks."[4] Three days later, the Red Army marched into the city. There was no resistance; crowds stood in silence. The city was bedecked with red flags and rosettes, and hanging from the old parliament building were pictures of Marx, Lenin, and Trotsky. Speeches were made, the Internationale was sung; and the Revolutionary Committee took power. The revolution that was to change Armenia fundamentally was just beginning. It was to be a revolution imported from outside and directed from above.

The first government of Soviet Armenia, the *Heghkom* (Revkom), was headed by Sarkis Kasian and included young and militant Bolsheviks: Askenaz Mravian, Avis Nurijanian, S. Ter-Gabrielian, I. Davlatian, and A. Bekzadian (foreign commissar). These were men marked by the years of fierce underground and military struggles during the Civil War, deeply hostile to the Dashnaks, who had, after all, suppressed the revolts by Armenian Bolsheviks and executed many of them. They were men in a hurry, almost completely inexperienced as administrators, and brutally insensitive to the weariness and desperation of the country they now governed. As soon as the *Heghkom* arrived in Erevan, a secret police organization, the infamous Cheka, was set up (December 6), and all governmental institutions of the old republic were abolished. The agreement with the Dashnaks establishing a coalition government was disregarded, and many officials associated with the former government were arrested. The Russian policy associated with "war communism" was applied to Armenia completely unsystematically and with great cruelty. Banks and major industries (the preserves factory of Esapov, for example) were nationalized, and the old Russian imperial law code was replaced by the legal statutes of the Soviet Russian Republic. But most onerous of all the new measures of this first Bolshevik regime was the policy of confiscating food stuffs and grain from the peasants and townspeople who they believed had surpluses.[5] Red Army men moved into villages and took whatever they thought necessary from peasants who themselves were living close to subsistence. In the minds of many, the new government became identified with requisitioning and confiscation. In addition, the Soviet leaders did nothing to expel the Turks from those parts of Armenia that they continued to occupy. The shortages of food and fuel, caused in part by the Menshevik Georgian blockade of Armenia, combined with general resentment toward the precipitate actions of the young Bolsheviks to produce an active opposition. When the Red Army marched out of Armenia in February 1921 to overthrow the Mensheviks in Georgia, the Dashnaks under the command of Simon Vratsian began an armed rebellion against the new Soviet government in Armenia. Within days the Dashnaks had taken Erevan and Zangezur. They desperately tried to secure assistance from Europe and even entered into negotiations with the Turks, but to no avail. Vratsian's forces held out in Erevan for a month and a half, but once the Red Army had conquered Georgia, it turned back to Armenia and drove the Dashnaks into the mountains of Zangezur and eventually across the border into Persia.[6]

The first experiment with Soviet rule in Armenia had been an unmitigated disaster. Without taking account of the backward and difficult state in which the Armenians found themselves, the Bolsheviks had tried to implement a primitive idea of communism with little plan or preparation. Once the Red Army returned to Erevan, the policy of "war communism," now discredited throughout the Soviet world, was replaced by the considerably more moderate policy known as the New Economic Policy (NEP), and the old *Heghkom* was replaced by a new government headed by Alexander Miasnikian. No less a figure than Lenin himself urged the Caucasian Communists to deal cautiously and sensitively with the largely peasant population of Transcaucasia.

In his letter to his Caucasian comrades, Lenin outlined how the Soviet republics in the south differed from central Russia and therefore required different treatment. Caucasia was more backward, "more peasant than Russia," but at the same time was at an advantage because it might be able to establish trade more easily and faster with the capitalist West. He called on the Caucasian Communists to exercise "greater gentleness, caution, concessions in dealing with the petty bourgeoisie, the intelligentsia, and especially the peasantry."[7] A degree of autonomy was being offered to Transcaucaia by Lenin, who feared overemphasis on the importance of centralizing power in the Soviet republics. But at the same time many Communists favored great standardization of policy and practice, more power in the hands of the central party leadership, and fewer concessions to the minority nationalities. Marxists, it was argued, were internationalists and should discourage national peculiarities. When local Communists advocated local solutions to problems dealing with minorities, the centralizers fumed about "local nationalism." But the standard solutions to local problems that emanated from Moscow, though delivered in appropriate internationalist rhetoric, were in fact Russian solutions. As Lenin put it so graphically: "Scratch many a communist, and you will find a Great Russian chauvinist!" Ironically, among those whom Lenin suspected of such Russian chauvinism were non-Russian Caucasian comrades, among them Sergo Orjonikidze and Joseph Stalin.

The nature of the ties between the half-dozen Soviet republics and Moscow was determined piecemeal over time, by practice. There was no clear plan imposed by the center. Yet steadily the rights and autonomous privileges of the separate republics were whittled away, and more and more prerogatives fell to the central leaders. Each Soviet republic signed a treaty of alliance with Soviet Russia defining their relationship. On September 30, 1921, Armenia signed such a treaty but limited its ties to financial cooperation. Nevertheless, a few months later, in December 1921, Armenian delegates attended the All-Russian Congress of Soviets, thus linking their republic closer to the Russians. In March 1921 the RSFSR signed a treaty with Kemalist Turkey that established the frontier between Transcaucasia and Turkey. Only later that year did Armenia, Azerbaijan, and Georgia meet with Turkish representatives (with a Russian representative present) to ratify the treaty. By the end of 1922 the Soviet republics had surrendered their autonomous role in foreign affairs, which thenceforth became the prerogative of the central Russian authority.

Given the weakness of Soviet Armenia—the dismal state of the economy, the lack of dependable support for the new government from the population, and the peculiar demographic situation in which more Armenians were living in Georgia and Azerbaijan than in Armenia itself—the Armenian Communists were among the most energetic supporters of a political and economic union of the three Transcaucasian republics.[8] The Armenians needed as much aid as possible from Russia and her immediate neighbors, Georgia and Azerbaijan, but the Georgians, who were stronger economically, were much less enthusiastic about uniting with the other republics. Some Georgian Bolsheviks even protested the integration of Georgian railroads with those of the other republics. Georgian resistance to unification was ultimately overcome with the aid of centralizers like Orjonikidze, and on March 12, 1922, the Federative Union of Soviet Socialist Republics of Transcaucasia (FSSSRZ) was created by treaty. In the next few months the tendency toward centralization was accelerated, and on December 13, 1922, the federation of republics was changed into a single federated republic (ZSFSR), a more unified political and economic unit. Lenin himself had grave reservations about the centralization imposed on Transcaucasia and expressed his opposition vehemently,[9] but by early 1923 he was seriously ill and the centralizers, led by Stalin, were able to achieve their constitutional goals. The final stage in political unification took place in 1923–1924 as the various Soviet republics formed the Union of Soviet Socialist Republics (USSR), centralizing foreign policy, defense, foreign trade, communications, and most domestic economic policy at the all-union level. Thus by early 1924, Armenia was a republic within the Transcaucasian republic, which in turn was a member of the union of Soviet republics.

Essentially, Soviet Armenia existed within a pseudo-federal system in which the final decision-making power lay outside the republic. The all-important matter of who should decide the budget was resolved in favor of the center, and Armenia's budget became part of the budget of the ZSFSR, which in turn was part of the budget of the whole USSR. The ruling party of Armenia was not a separate and independent Communist party but a constituent part of the All-Russian Communist Party [RKP(b)], a local branch of a highly centralized political instrument directed by a small group of men in Moscow.

Internally, the structure of the Armenian republic was made to conform to norms then under construction in the Russian republic. In 1922, the RSFSR adopted a series of law codes—criminal, civil, agrarian, labor and judicial—and in the following years the Armenian SSR, together with the other Soviet republics, adopted the same codes, sometimes with minor revisions. The law, along with complementary systems of soviets, smoothed away many differences between the legal and institutional orders of the minority nationalities. In January 1922, the first Congress of Soviets of Armenia adopted a constitution modeled on that of the RSFSR. Everywhere the stress was on standardization and uniformity in the interest of binding the periphery closer to the center, and most efforts by local leaders to preserve national peculiarities in law went down to defeat. At the same time the organs of the Communist party gained an unquestioned superiority over governmental institutions, over elected soviets, until the soviets became instruments of the party and the congresses of soviets largely ceremonial affairs. All other political parties were eventually eliminated—in November 1923 Dashnaks in Erevan formally abolished their party within Armenia—and the Communist party achieved a complete monopoly of political power.

Thus the framework had been created by 1924 for such close ties between center and periphery that only a very limited area of competence remained to the Armenian republic. Armenia could not be considered in any real sense to be a sovereign state, though officially in Soviet law it was so designated. The most important political and economic decisions affecting Armenians were made outside of Erevan, in Tbilisi and in Moscow, though a whole host of cultural and local issues were left to the Armenian Communists.

Modernization and Renationalization in the 1920s

In the first decade of Soviet power the government of Armenia embarked on a program of economic restoration and cultural revival. Its policies, directed at expanding the agricultural base of peasant life, building new canals and industries, and establishing schools and cultural institutions, were the first tentative steps toward the modernization of Armenia through state initiative. At the same time as this social and economic development was beginning, the Soviet leadership was also engaged in a program of revitalizing the national culture of the Armenians and stimulating the use of their national language. Modernization in the Soviet context of the 1920s went hand in hand with nation-building. Economic development was seen as consistent with cultural and political renationalization. Whereas modernization had led elsewhere to the weakening of national culture and gave rise to assimilationist tendencies, in the Armenian republic state policy was aimed at encouraging the simultaneous processes of modernization and renationalization. The expectation in the short run seemed to be that Armenians could change their traditional ways into modern ways, yet remain Armenian; indeed through education and state promotion of culture, they would become even more Armenian. The implicit conflict between modernization and renationalization, between a people becoming more like other "advanced peoples of the world," on the one hand, or remaining unique and ethnically distinct, on the other, was not clearly faced.

Let us look first at the process of economic and social modernization as conceived and carried out by the Armenian Communists in the 1920s.

Economically, the Soviet government had first to reestablish a viable agrarian economy in Armenia before it could seriously consider its transformation into an industrial one. The Communist party found itself in a very paradoxical situation. Dedicated to building a socialist society based on industry, the Communists had come to power in an overwhelmingly peasant country. For Marx and Marxists, socialism presumed the prior existence of a highly developed industrial economy and a politically conscious working class ready to take power. Socialism, after all, was envisioned by Marx as the extension of full democracy both in the political and the economic spheres. But the reality of the 1920s in Russia and Armenia was that of an agricultural rather than an industrial country in which workers and peasants did not rule themselves but were ruled by a small group of party members who held power in the name of a nearly nonexistent working class.

The Communists were not content to preserve the *status quo*. They were militant modernizers, convinced that a noncapitalist, state-directed program of development would prove superior to the bourgeois capitalist method of industrialization. In a capital-poor country, cut off from Western aid, the peasants would have to be the major source of wealth; they would have to be taxed to pay for the new industries; they would have to supply the grain to the growing towns and cities and provide the foreign exchange needed to acquire technology and machinery abroad. Lenin's New Economic Policy, a strategic retreat from the crude communism of the Civil War, established a mixed economy in which the state controlled the "commanding heights" of industry and trade, while the peasants and much of the rest of the nation worked in a largely private, semi-capitalist market economy. NEP was seen by Lenin as a form of "state capitalism," a necessary first step for a backward nation to build the basis for socialism.

In the early 1920s, about 90 percent of Armenians were living on the land. The country had too little land to support so many people in agriculture, yet few ambitious industrial projects were undertaken in this period. The first major development projects in Armenia were the building of canals (for example, the Shirak Canal, constructed between 1922 and 1925), irrigation of desert areas (particularly the Sardarabad desert), and the electrification of the country. By 1928 Armenians could boast twenty hydroelectric plants. Clearly, peasant life was being improved. By 1926, agricultural production had reached 71.5 percent of its prewar level.[10] The peasants did not own their own land but were free to use it after paying a tax to the state. The state in turn purchased the peasants' produce at fixed prices, and the peasants were permitted to sell surpluses on the open market. Some peasants did well enough to hire extra hands to work their lands; others who could not succeed in agriculture drifted into the towns looking for jobs in the new industries.

Industrial production in Armenia also recovered to just under three-quarters of the prewar level by 1926. Progress was slow but steady, although as late as 1927 there was still a sizable unemployment problem. Between one-third and one-half of workers in Erevan were out of work in the fall of 1927.[11] The cities grew steadily, siphoning the surplus population from the villages. The census of 1926 revealed that the number of town and city dwellers had almost doubled since the previous census in 1897. However, over 80 percent of Armenians were still living in the countryside.[12] Less than 13 percent of Soviet Armenians could be considered "proletarians," even by the most gener-ous use of that term. Nevertheless, it is clear that along with agrarian restora-tion and capital construction, Soviet modernization in Armenia involved urbanization. The government assigned the architect Alexander Tumanian to draw up a master plan for the reconstruction and transformation of Erevan from a provincial center into a national capital.

Besides economic development, industrialization, and urbanization, Soviet modernization also involved the shift of values from traditional and religious to secular and socialist. The Soviet government actively worked to wean Arme-nians away from their loyalty to the national church and replace that faith with a commitment to building a socialist Armenia. A better life in this world was to be preferred to delayed gratification in the next. The church was forbid-den to engage in religious propaganda, while antireligious propaganda was encouraged by the state. In the uneven contest between church and state, churches were closed, priests were persecuted, and the Catholicos Kevork V (1911–1930) retaliated by refusing until 1927 to recognize the atheist Soviet regime.

The new Soviet order attacked the traditional attitudes of Armenian men toward their women. The Communists urged the liberation of women from housework and family life and brought them into the labor force. The *Ginbaz-hin* or "women's section" was organized to struggle for women's equality, but resistance from the patriarchal leaders of Armenian villages was great.[13]

Language and literacy were important in the reconstitution of the Armeni-ans as a nation, but they were also instruments through which the new Soviet political leadership could integrate the Armenians into the new political order. From 1930 all Soviet children were required to attend elementary school, an essential step toward the socialization of young people into the new society. In Armenia the language of instruction was Armenian, but the content was Soviet. Children, as in any stable society, were taught the dominant values of the ruling elite; in Armenia they were taught to defend the October Revolution and to hate its enemies, including the former leaders of Armenian national life, the Dashnaktsutiun. They were taught to be suspicious of the capitalist West and to support revolutionary struggles throughout the world. Children were encouraged to develop a collective spirit and reject personal egotism. At the same time they were inculcated with the secular internationalist values of the Communist party as well as with a fresh appreciation of the history and literature of the Armenians. It is not surprising that internationalism competed with a revived nationalism in many young minds or that the newly formed Erevan University was a hotbed of nationalism. Already in the 1920s a conflict was growing between the effects of Communist modernization and Armenian renationalization.

As must be apparent by now, Soviet modernization constituted an attack on many traditional Armenian mores and institutions—on the patriarchal family and the subordinate role of women, on the authority of religion and the national church, on village life and its former authorities. But at the same time, Soviet policy was also directed toward preserving, indeed nourishing, many aspects of Armenian national life, at renationalizing Armenia. Let us look now at the processes that were making Armenia more Armenian.

Despite the political limitations placed on the Armenians, the Soviet government operated in the 1920s according to certain principles that were very attractive to Armenians. State policy aimed to redress the economic imbalance between more developed central Russia and the less developed borderlands. This meant that economic aid in the form of capital would have to be given to the nationalities. Furthermore, the Communists sincerely intended to eliminate civil, legal, and social distinctions between minorities and to achieve "national equality." Discrimination as it had been known under tsarism was to be eliminated. Finally, colonial aspects of imperial Russian rule were to be consciously avoided, and a policy of encouraging members of local nationalities to run their own areas was actively promoted. This new policy, known eventually as *korenizatsiia* (rooting) or "nativization," was outlined first in a resolution of the Tenth Party Congress in March 1921. The party was to develop administrative and economic organs that would operate in the local languages and with people from the local nationality. Schools, theaters, and newspapers in national languages were to be established as well. For convenience, we shall examine the initial phase of renationalization as it affected four distinct areas: territory, demography, culture, and politics.

Territorially, Armenians were guaranteed a physical space of their own to which those who had been scattered around the globe could return. Frontiers were settled in treaties with foreign states and other Soviet republics. Though Armenia lost much territory, including mountainous Karabagh in which Armenians constituted a majority, there were to be no more armed struggles with Armenia's neighbors over borders. Russia had entered as final arbiter, and there was little opportunity for protest. With the establishment of a close tie with Soviet Russia, the threat from Turkey was eliminated. In the minds of many Armenians the ultimate justification for the dominance of Russia over Armenia continued, even after the revolution, to be the conclusion that without Russian protection, Armenia simply could not exist.

Demographically, Armenia now became the haven of Armenians displaced by the wars and political changes in the rest of the world. Armenians from other parts of the Soviet Union migrated to Armenia, either for nationalist reasons or to better their prospects in life. Tiflis and Baku Armenians, displaced by the nativization of Georgia and Azerbaijan, went to Armenia to find opportunities no longer available in their former homes. Like the Jews, the Armenians had been a cosmopolitan people without a territorial base; they had flourished as middle-class members of mixed urban populations. But as the policy of *korenizatsiia* developed local cadres of local nationalities, the Armenians were pushed out of political and economic positions in other republics and migrated to Armenia.

As the first caravans of Armenian refugees arrived from Greece, France, Iran, and elsewhere in the mid-twenties, they were joined in Erevan by the immigrant intellectuals and middle-class elements. To these new settlers in the towns of Armenia were added poor peasants looking for work. A new urban population was being formed in Armenia from very disparate elements. Speaking different dialects, bringing varied customs, foods, and historical experiences, these immigrants melded together to form the first generation of the new Soviet Armenian nation. In a real physical sense, this represented the renationalization of Armenia.

Culturally, the Soviet policy of nativization meant the spread of the use of the Armenian language into all aspects of Armenian life. Armenian became the official language of the Soviet republic, to be used in all government institutions, in the courts, in the schools. At first it was difficult to implement this policy, for many Communists were Russified Armenians who did not know Armenian well, but in time Russian was largely replaced in official circles by Armenian.

At the same time all the institutions that any self-respecting nation-state required were established in Armenia—an opera, a film studio, national radio, an academy of sciences, museums, and a state university. For the first time since the Middle Ages, Armenian became a language of science. A new literary language based on the eastern Armenian dialect was developed, along with a new orthography. Established artists, like Saryan, Shirvanzade, Isahakian, Tumanian, and Spendiarov, were able to pursue their art under the auspices of official support from an Armenian government. New artists in new art forms appeared, most notably Bek-Nazarov, the gifted film director who translated Sundukian's stage comedy *Pepo* into fresh cinematic images. The 1920s was a period of cultural renaissance for Armenian artists and scientists. It would later be looked back upon fondly as a period of relative freedom and great creativity.

Along with the revitalization of high culture, the government campaigned for the spread of education and the liquidation of illiteracy. As part of the "cultural revolution," hundreds of groups were set up in 1928–1929 to teach reading. By 1931 Erevan could claim to be a city that had eliminated illiteracy. A new audience had been created for the publications and periodicals that poured out of the state publishing houses.

Politically, renationalization meant that the government of Armenia would be in the hands of Armenians. From the very beginning of Soviet rule in

Armenia, the Communist elite was almost entirely Armenian. Ninety percent of the members of the party were Armenian; the head of the party and the government were always Armenians, though Armenians of proven loyalty to Moscow. After Kasian and Miasnikian (who was killed in a plane crash in 1925), the party was headed by Ashot Hovhannisian until 1927, by Haik Hovsepian in 1927, by Haigaz Kostanian from 1928 to 1930, and by the vigorous and popular Aghasi Khanjian from 1930 to 1936. Within the limits of the Soviet framework, Armenians ran their own affairs, and in the 1920s those limits were fairly broad and flexible.

In the late 1920s the Armenian Communist party was pressed to put an end to the tolerance of non-Communist intellectuals in influential positions. Most notable was the independent Marxist ("Specifist") David Ananoun, who in 1927 lost his job as part of a campaign against "counterrevolutionary nationalists." Other former Dashnaks and Mensheviks were purged from institutes and party cells, along with those accused of being Trotskyists. One hundred and twenty members of the Trotskyist opposition were arrested in April 1927, and in the turmoil of these purges, the head of the Communist party of Armenia, Ashot Hovhannisian, was dismissed for his underestimation of the dangers of Trotskyism and Specifism. The real significance of these purges was to end the period of relative intellectual freedom and discussion in Armenian political circles. Many old Bolsheviks, men who had joined the party before the revolution, lost their posts as a stronger line was taken against any manifestation of opposition to the ruling Stalinist clique.

As the 1920s came to a close, Lenin's NEP faded as Stalin and his associates adopted an ambitious Five Year Plan for development. Peasant agriculture was to be collectivized, all private industry eliminated, and the entire country mobilized to convert the Soviet Union from an agrarian to an industrial economy. Another revolution was being planned, this time a "revolution from above," to complete the modernization of the country.

The political, economic, and cultural changes that took place in Armenia in the first decade of Soviet power represented a restoration of a devastated nationality and the foundation of a new nation. The new Soviet government, with little active support from the population, nevertheless managed to achieve a degree of acquiescence in its rule, as it brought peace and security to a ravaged land and began the tentative revival of economic and cultural life. There was opposition—the Dashnaktsutiun remained active clandestinely within Armenia, and the prerevolutionary intelligentsia was never wholly comfortable with the brash young Communists who, thanks to the Red Army, now held power in Armenia. But the successes of the Soviets in turning a land of refugees into a stable, growing society increased the popularity of the regime. Particularly welcome was the policy of nativization, the Armenizing of Armenia, which elevated the language of Abovian and Raffi to an official state language, spread education from the towns into the villages, created science in Armenian, and subsidized an Armenian cultural establishment. The limits on the expression of nationalism tightened at the end of the twenties, but the renationalization of the country continued into the thirties. In contrast to what many critics of the Soviet policy toward the nationalities say, in the 1920s, at least, there was no deliberate effort at Russifying non-Russian peoples. On the contrary, great attention was given to fighting Great Russian chauvinism and promoting nativization. The denationalizing that took place was due to the general policy of development (modernization, in our terms), not to purposeful Russification.

Implicit in this period was a tension between the effort at modernization and the policy of nativization. Modernization meant the breakdown of many traditional and customary national forms, the end of isolated village life, the emancipation of women, the secularization of education, the attack on the church. It meant making Armenians more like other peoples, eliminating certain national distinctions. Modernization contained within it the threat of assimilation. Yet at the same time, the policy of *korenizatsiia* was pulling in the opposite direction, making Armenia more Armenian and making Armenians more aware of their history, culture, and language. The tension between the two was real, but the political system established in the 1920s prevented any real resolution of the conflict. The tension would grow, but so would the political repression that would make impossible any discussion of the anxieties of the nationalities in a modernizing state. Not until fifty years had passed would the Stalinist lid come off and a new expression of nationalism be heard throughout the Soviet Union.

By the end of the 1920s Armenians had stepped back from the brink of extinction. It was now clear that they would survive, even thrive, in this new nation being built in their ancient homeland. Visiting Armenia in the late twenties, the Nobel Peace Prize laureate Dr. Fridtjof Nansen was deeply moved by the spirit of this people as heard in their music:

> The notes of the Armenian folk-songs echo long in the soul. I could not help thinking of what my friend Kurgenian said after hearing one of the melodies sung that evening: "Wouldn't you say that a people whose soul goes out in songs and music like that can never die?" And I felt that he was right.[14]

9 Stalin and the Armenians

For a quarter of a century, from the late 1920s to the early 1950s, the government of the largest country in the world was dominated by a single man, Joseph Stalin. The enormous power of this enigmatic person has led many to attempt an understanding of Soviet history in that period through an investigation of the leader's biography. The sources and the contours of his tyranny have been sought in his Georgian origins, his unhappy childhood, his intense respect for and rivalry with his mentor Lenin, his experience in the Bolshevik underground, his commitment to Marxism and Leninism, his personal insecurity, and his single-minded drive for power. Even his most formidable opponent within the Communist party, Leon Trotsky, could not restrain himself at times from explaining Stalin's political success in terms of Stalin's psychology:

> Such attributes of character as slyness, faithlessness, the ability to exploit the lowest instincts of human nature are developed to an extraordinary degree in Stalin and, considering his strong character, represent mighty weapons in a struggle. . . . In selecting men for privileged positions, in welding them together in the spirit of the caste, in weakening and disciplining the masses, Stalin's attributes were truly invaluable and rightly make him the leader of the bureaucratic reaction. [Nevertheless] Stalin remains a mediocrity.[1]

In recent years scholars have broadened their vision from the individual Stalin to look at the social-historical context in which he exercised his extraordinary power. The history of Russia and the revolution became the primary focus of attention, though notable analysts still seek to expose the psychological wellsprings of Stalin's ruthless dictatorship.

The overwhelming majority of Western writers on the Soviet Union have looked at the rise of Stalin and the system over which he ruled as the logical, perhaps even inevitable, outcome of the Bolshevik movement and ideology.

Terror and dictatorship were implicit in Lenin's elitist view of the revolutionary party, it is argued by many. Still others hold that the seizure of power by the Bolsheviks in October 1917, usually interpreted as a *coup d'etat* by a small conspiratorial party, sounded the death knell for democratic alternatives and set in motion the trends that led to Stalinism. Whatever the sources, the dominant view is of an "unbroken continuity between Bolshevism and Stalinism."[2] While supporters of Leninism, like Trotsky, argued that Stalin had betrayed the original revolution, most Western observers argued that Stalin simply fulfilled the intentions of the revolution, that Stalinism is the reality of the promised socialism. This view has been put forth by many eminent scholars, among them Robert V. Daniels, Adam Ulam, Arthur P. Mendel, Zbigniew Brzezinski, and such writers as Aleksandr Solzhenitsyn. Their arguments generally emphasize the similarities between the various periods of Soviet history—War Communism, NEP, the Stalinist years, and the post-Stalin period. The 1920s are seen as a prelude to the full-blown totalitarianism of the 1930s and 1940s, and the period after Stalin's death in 1953 is viewed as essentially the same political and social order with some of the more noxious aspects, such as mass terror, removed or modified. Not surprisingly, those who argue for continuity in Soviet history cling to the totalitarian model as an explanatory device and tend to be the harshest critics of the USSR and most fearful of its global ambitions. On the other hand, the handful of Western analysts who see the Stalin period as a distinctive episode in Soviet history and not as the inevitable outcome of Bolshevism generally saw the USSR as a state capable of adjustment and change and therefore a potentially less belligerent international competitor. Paradoxically, many Western opponents of socialism equated socialism with Stalinism—in this way they found themselves in agreement with the Stalinists—while many Western socialists consider Stalinism to be the most perverted form of a once-revolutionary, nominally "socialist" state.

As we look at the Stalin years in relation to the Armenian republic, we should keep in mind several general questions. Was Stalinism a distinct sociopolitical formation essentially different from what existed in the USSR before 1928, or was it simply a more intense, more vicious form of the same dictatorial regime? For Armenians, did Stalinism represent a continuity with the policies of modernization and renationalization of the NEP years (1921–1928) or a fundamental break? And finally, how can we evaluate the effects of the Stalinist period in terms of our general theme in these chapters, the building of a modern Armenian nation in the Soviet Union?

The first decade of Soviet rule in Armenia had established an Armenian political framework within which the economy could be restored and the society embark on a gradual but steady modernization. Armenians were required to accomplish the most elemental tasks involved in human survival, the feeding, housing, and organization of a starving and diseased population, half of whom were homeless refugees. From this nadir of Armenian existence, the newly formed nation-state then began the construction of capital projects as a basis for further economic development: the building of hydroelectric plants, canals, and irrigation projects and the rebuilding of the city of Erevan. At the same time Armenia began a significant renationalization, gaining a secure territorial base that became the haven for Armenians dispersed around the world. A government of Armenians created the political, cultural, educational, and scientific infrastructure of a new nation, and the Armenian language was elevated to the level of an official state language.

The achievements of the 1920s, impressive as they were, were almost totally eclipsed by the radical social and economic transformations of the country introduced at the end of the decade. The first and most intense phase of the so-called Stalin Revolution occurred with the implementation of the First Five-Year Plan (1928–1932). All moderation in economic planning was abandoned when in April 1929 the Sixteenth Party Congress of the CPSU adopted the version of the Five-Year Plan that had the most ambitious targets. The policy of supporting independent peasant agriculture, which had worked so well in the 1920s to restore the countryside, was terminated, and a drive for the formation of collective farms began in earnest. Since voluntary collectivization had little effect on the peasants—only 3.7 percent of the peasant households in Armenia had been collectivized by the end of 1929—the Communists began the new year, 1930, with an intensive drive to collectivize. Militants from the cities and Russian troops moved into the villages. Those Armenian peasants who resisted were deported from their homes (perhaps as many as 25,000 in 1929–1930) or arrested.[3] Those peasants who had the largest farms or the greatest number of animals fell under suspicion as rural capitalists, *kulaks,* and were expelled from the villages. Thus the most productive producers were eliminated. By February 1930 the party announced that 63 percent of all peasant households in Armenia had been collectivized.[4]

The assault on the villages by the party and the army in 1929–1930 was a return to the crude and violent methods of the earliest days of Soviet power in Armenia and gave rise to fierce resistance. Communists were murdered in several villages; army units were attacked; Armenian villagers joined with Muslim peasants to fight against the collectivizers. Everywhere peasants slaughtered their own livestock rather than give it up to the collectives. The number of cattle in Armenia fell by nearly 300,000 head between 1928 and 1933.[5] Such occurrences took place in every part of the Soviet Union, and on March 4, 1930, Stalin called a halt to this aggressive policy in his famous article, "Dizzy from Success." Facing a widespread rebellion against its agrarian policy, the government now reversed itself temporarily and allowed the peasants to decide themselves if they wanted to join the collectives. In Armenia as elsewhere, the decision was overwhelmingly against collectivization. By the fall of 1930, the number of Armenian peasant households in the collectives had fallen to 8.9 percent.[6]

The turn toward moderation proved to be shortlived, however, and a second campaign of forced collectivization began in the fall of 1930. In Armenia the opposition grew, and even some party cells sided with the peasants. The party organization in Daralagiaz, for example, called for the end of collectivization and the policy of discrimination against *kulaks*.[7] Many parts of Armenia fell into the hands of anti-collectivization rebels. Dashnaks appeared in some areas, and only with the intervention of the army were the main uprisings crushed in early 1932. Some rebel bands held out in mountainous Zangezur until 1934. Collectivization was finally imposed on Armenians with the help of Russian troops. By the end of 1933 nearly two-fifths of the peasantry had been collectivized.[8] By 1936 that figure had reached four-fifths, and on the eve of World War II all but 1.7 percent of Armenia's peasants lived and worked on the collective farms.[9]

The campaign for collectivization was the single most important offensive launched against traditional Armenian society by the Soviet government. The Communists, primarily located in the cities, had been quite weak in the countryside, and until the early 1930s Armenia's villages had remained largely immune from Communist influence. Many villages were still governed by the old families who for centuries had held the office of *tanuter* or headman. In the spring of 1933 these families were purged from the new collectives, so that their traditional authority could be replaced by the new Soviet officials. It seems clear in retrospect that the collectives were much more a political device in Armenia than an economic one. They aided in the destruction of the old village governance system and made it easier to rule the countryside through the collective units. It would be a long time before the economic benefits of collectivized agriculture would be at all apparent. Armenia had entered collectivization with a total of 166 tractors in the whole country, hardly enough to effect the mechanization of large-scale agriculture, which was one of the rationales for collectivized agriculture.[10] Agricultural output fell as a result of collectivization and only surpassed the 1928 level at the end of the 1930s.[11] There were economic benefits to be sure, but the political advantages to the Soviet state far outweighed them. As a result of collectivization, the peasantry disappeared as an independent force in the economy or a political threat to the Communists in the cities.

Besides the independent peasantry, a second class was destroyed in Armenia by the Stalin Revolution—the commercial bourgeoisie. Armenians, long known as merchant people, had lost many of their commercial and industrial enterprises as a result of the revolution of 1917 and the sovietization of Transcaucasia. Nevertheless, this traditional activity continued to flourish on a somewhat reduced scale in the early Soviet period. In the mid-1920s, nearly half (46.4 percent) of all commerce was handled by private traders. By 1935 this private trade had been completely eliminated and only state and cooperative institutions engaged in trade.[12] Private industries were also abolished, and the entire economy was put under the guidance of a state plan. The market system had been eliminated, though in this land of chronic shortages a sort of "free market" remained in the flourishing black markets.

At the same time as some classes disappeared or were changed significantly, a new class was taking shape—the industrial working class. The Five-Year Plans invested heavily in industry, increasing production by 1935 to 650 percent of the value of the gross product of 1928. Armenia was being changed into an industrial country. Whereas industry had accounted for a mere 21.7 percent of economic production in 1928, in early 1935 it measured 62.1 percent.[13] The percentage of industrial and white-collar workers in Armenia grew steadily until it reached 23.3 percent of the population in 1935 and 31.2 percent in 1939.[14] Industrial, construction, and railroad workers alone numbered over 53,000 in 1939, an increase of more than two and a half times since 1928.[15] Unemployment was eliminated; indeed, with all the construction in Armenia there was a labor shortage. All workers were forced to join the official unions, which were primarily organizations to discipline workers rather than to protect them against management. Working conditions were difficult, and pay was low. Absenteeism was high, and many workers simply left the factories and construction sites for their villages. At the same time, the tempo of growth in the country was noticeable to all and inspired in many a faith in a better future. Many poor peasants rose rapidly through work and education to become skilled workers, engineers, and even to enter the political hierarchy. A new Soviet-trained intelligentsia was emerging to compete with the prerevolutionary intellectuals and specialists.

The forced modernization of the Stalinist period brought fundamental changes to Armenian society. More urban, more industrial, Armenians were also more literate, more mobile, and Armenian women were considerably freer than they had been. Among women literacy rose from 19 percent in 1926 to 62 percent in 1939.[16] But whereas in the 1920s modernization has been accompanied by a vigorous policy of "nativization," in the 1930s Soviet nationality policy underwent a significant shift. In the first phase of the Stalin Revolution, the so-called cultural revolution of the 1928–1931 period, the Leninist policy of *korenizatsiia* (nativization) was not only continued, but intensified. Greater emphasis than ever was placed on the teaching and use of native languages. Extra efforts were made to recruit local cadres. Russians and other non-natives were encouraged to learn the local languages. In their public pronouncements, Stalin and the other party leaders repeated the theme that the greater danger to the Soviet Union was Great Russian chauvinism, not the local nationalism of the minority nationalities.

Official enthusiasm for *korenizatsiia* began to ebb perceptibly, however, in 1933–1934. Greater emphasis was placed on employing experts rather than natives when choosing cadres. The value of the Russian language as *lingua franca* was reasserted. In 1934 Stalin told the Seventeenth Party Congress that local nationalism was as great a danger to socialist unity as Great Russian chauvinism. In subsequent years articles touting *korenizatsiia* disappeared from the press, and Russian was recognized as the "international language" of the Soviet peoples, the most "progressive" language in the USSR, the "language of the socialist revolution." Whereas earlier non-natives had been urged to learn local languages, after 1933 minorities were encouraged more forcefully to learn Russian. In 1938 the learning of the Russian language was made compulsory for all Soviet students. At that point most Armenians in school were still receiving instruction only in Armenian (77.7 percent), and only a tiny fraction (2.8 percent) were studying in Russian.[17] In years to come the percentage learning Russian and studying entirely in Russian would steadily climb.

These policy changes downgraded the local nationalities to a secondary level and elevated Russians to the level of a superior people. Increasingly expressions of Russian nationalism could be heard in music and opera, seen in theaters and movie houses. While Raffi, Patkanian, and even certain Soviet Armenian writers were condemned as "nationalists," films lauding the achievements of Peter the Great, Suvorov, Ivan the Terrible, and Aleksandr Nevskii were produced. Nationalism was condemned, but Soviet patriotism was praised; *azgaserutiun* was prohibited while *hairenaserutiun* was permitted. In July 1934 the Russian word *rodina* (motherland), previously prohibited, appeared in a Pravda editorial. More and more, writers wrote about a new people, the "Soviet people." This resurgence of official pro-Russian Soviet nationalism culminated in Stalin's famous toast at the end of World War II (May 24, 1945) when he drank to the health of the Russian people, "the leading nation of all the nations belonging to the Soviet Union." Marxist internationalism had been distorted into national subordination to the Russian people. As one observer put it: "In the late thirties and even more so during World War II, state policy on the national question underwent a sudden shift towards Russification."[18]

Strict limits were placed on the expression of artists and writers as the Stalin Revolution marked the end of the relative intellectual freedom that Soviet writers and artists had enjoyed in the first decade of Soviet power. The "cultural revolution" of 1928–1931 launched an offensive against those writers, artists, architects, and educators who were not prepared to join the experiment in forging a new proletarian art. But this brief swing to the cultural Left was abandoned quickly, and by 1932 a more conservative policy was adopted in the arts. In each branch of the arts creative experimentation and modernism were attacked, and artists were urged to return to classicism. Writing was to be realistic in style; architecture was to employ classical and national motifs. In all areas the international modernism of the period was to be shunned: no Bauhaus, no Joyce or Kafka. A policy of mobilizing all artists into a single union for each artistic field was implemented. On May 9, 1932, the Armenian Communist party adopted a resolution echoing that of the central party that dissolved all existing organizations of writers, musicians, architects, and painters. In August 1932, a single union of Armenian writers was established in Erevan to which every writer was required to belong. The various unions of artists became instruments of state policy, the means to discipline and reward artists and to set the limits of expression. The Armenian architect Karo Alabian became a major arbiter of Soviet tastes in architecture as he ascended to head the all-USSR Union of Architects.[19] Not only were the artists forbidden to deal with certain topics, not only was the content of their work prescribed, but even the form, the style in which they worked, was strictly limited. Art was to be "national in form, socialist in content." This meant that though the language and motifs of artists in Armenia should have Armenian qualities, the content should conform to the general themes dictated by the party in its struggle to build socialism. Positive heroes were to be drawn as models for emulation. Negative aspects of Soviet life were to be played down or eliminated altogether. In other words, though the style was supposed to be realistic, it was in fact highly romanticized.

This new policy of intellectual restriction was followed by an attack on intellectuals as ferocious as the earlier attack on the peasantry. Those unable to conform to the new artistic order fell under suspicion. Many were arrested and perished in prison. In Armenia the writer Aksel Bakunts was arrested for "bourgeois nationalism" because he had written a story in which an old man complained about the lack of land in Armenia, sadly pointing toward Turkey and noting, "But there is a lot of land there." The poet Eghishe Charents, who earlier had been one of the most fervent supporters of Soviet power in Armenia, was accused of "right deviationism" and nationalism for his poem "Message." On the surface the poem appeared to be standard verses in praise of Stalin, but when one read the second letter in each line vertically, a secret message read: "Oh Armenian people, your only salvation lies in your collective powers." Both Bakunts and Charents died in prison. Other writers were also arrested and exiled, among them Alazan, Grigor Mahari, Vahan Totovents, Vanantetsi, and Ter Simonian.

The Stalin Revolution with its attendant political repression created immense dislocations in Soviet society that became the source of great discontent. Many parts of the population were forced to underconsume in the aftermath of collectivization. The movement from villages to cities, from farms to factories, was traumatic for many of those forced to move. The old intelligentsia, squeezed out by the restrictive cultural policies of the Stalin years and by the rising Soviet-trained intelligentsia, had a variety of complaints, not the least of which was directed against the party's invasion of the fields of art and science, which had previously remained autonomous. Old Bolsheviks loyal to the revolutionary and internationalist views of Lenin were appalled by the social conservatism, Russian nationalism, and crudity of the Stalinist clique. Many Communists and non-Communists among the minorities were unhappy with the increased centralization of the state and the attacks on local nationalism, which were associated with Stalin's rule. The promises of socialism, that the workers themselves would take power, that social and economic equality would replace the old class hierarchy, seemed to wither away as a new bureaucratic elite secured its hold on every aspect of life. It was against this background of deep-seated and potentially violent discontent that the central party leadership decided to take extreme measures to rid the party of suspected oppositionists and to centralize power even more in the hands of the Stalinist faction.

The "Great Purges" of 1936–1938 hit various segments of Armenian society, but none more than the membership of the Armenian Communist party. In a real sense, the purges were the destruction of one ruling elite in Armenia and its replacement by another more tightly controlled by the central party leadership. The ruling party that directed Armenian affairs at the end of the 1930s was significantly different from the one that had begun the decade. In May 1930 Aghasi Khanjian, a 29-year-old party veteran, was appointed first secretary of the Communist party of Armenia. Born in Van, Khanjian had been a Marxist since his teenage years and had proven his loyalty to the Stalin faction while working in Leningrad from 1922 to 1928. He was transferred to Erevan in 1928 and rose rapidly in the party ranks because of Stalin's patronage. Opposed by the old Armenian Bolsheviks who had ruled Armenia since the early twenties, Khanjian was able to remove them from office one by one and emerge as the dominant political force in Armenia, though he had been considered an outsider at the outset of his rule. Khanjian oversaw the Stalin Revolution in Armenia, while managing to establish a personal political following. By the end of the First Five-Year Plan, he appeared to be a defender of the Armenian language, literature, and history, condemning "Great Russian chauvinism" in an important speech in January 1932. But two years later he spoke vehemently against Armenian nationalism, which, he claimed, was rampant in the old Armenian intelligentsia. Khanjian was right in line with the recent shift in Stalin's nationality policy toward condemnation of local nationalism and away from emphasis on the danger of Great Russian chauvinism.

By 1936 Khanjian had weathered many political storms and to all appearances seemed secure in his position. He had gained a certain degree of popularity in Armenia and seemed to have the support of Stalin. But the young leader of Armenia's Communists did have one formidable opponent, Lavrenti Beria, the first secretary of the Georgian party and until 1936 the first secretary of the Transcaucasian party committee. Beria, a former secret police officer, was very close to Stalin and in 1935 had rewritten the history of Bolshevism in Transcaucasia to elevate his boss to the pivotal role in the revolutionary movement. He was well on his way to turning the whole of Transcaucasia into his personal political fiefdom, and Khanjian with his local base of support in Armenia stood in his way. Early in June 1936 it was suddenly and unexpectedly announced that Khanjian had committed suicide. The circumstances of his death are murky, but it is clear that a serious threat to Beria's monopoly of power had been removed.

The next three years witnessed the most violent measures against Armenian Communists. One after another the men who had ruled Armenia in the first fifteen years of Soviet power were arrested and shot: Aramais Erznkian (1879–1937), commissar of agriculture from 1921 to 1930; Sarkis Kasian (1876–1937), head of the first Soviet government in Armenia; Avis Nurijanian (1896–1937), a member of that first government; Sahak Ter-Gabrielian (1886–1937), Armenia's representative in Moscow from 1921 to 1928 and chairman of the Council of People's Commissars from 1928 to 1935; and even A. Amatuni, who had headed the Armenian party in the years after Khanjian's death.

The purges not only hit the top party leaders but the lower ranks as well. Thousands perished in the last years of the 1930s until the bloodletting was finally called off by Moscow. Russians were brought to fill places formerly held by Armenians. In 1939, for example, the Russian Aleksei Korotkov became the head of Armenia's secret police. Most positions continued to be held by Armenians, but now they were younger men and women, trained in Soviet institutions and loyal to the Stalin-Beria leadership. The old Armenian ruling party had been eliminated by the eve of World War II and replaced by a new elite that owed everything to their patrons, Stalin and Beria. In September 1937 one of Beria's proteges, Grigor Arutiunov, was named first secretary of the Communist party of Armenia; he continued to hold that position until 1953 when Stalin died and Beria was removed, arrested, and shot. As a result of the purges, any vestige of Armenian autonomy disappeared. Even the party members realized that above the party stood that fearful instrument of Stalin's direct rule, the secret police. In 1938 Beria was summoned to Moscow by Stalin and appointed to head the Ministry of Internal Affairs, the agency in charge of police and prisons.

By the outbreak of the Second World War, the essential features of Stalinism had been established. The Soviet Union had become a new kind of political and social order in which an all-powerful state had eliminated all centers of autonomy and resistance to its monopoly of power, in which civil society and the economy had been swallowed up by the state. Political decision making was tightly centralized in the hands of Stalin himself and his closest associates, Beria, Molotov, Malenkov, and Zhdanov. The remnants of the autonomous prerogatives of the national republics or local administrations had been entirely eliminated as the secret police rose to dominate all sections of the party itself. Terror was the instrument that guaranteed political conformity and passivity; the slightest deviations from the prescriptions of the central leadership were punished with imprisonment or death.

Stalinism represented a distinct sociopolitical formation essentially different from what existed in the USSR before 1928. Leninism in practice certainly meant the establishment of a single-party dictatorship. Politically, both NEP and the

Stalinist years were marked by the Communist monopoly of power. But in the first period the degree of dissension, even factionalism, within the party permitted a real political dialogue to continue even as rival parties were eliminated. In society as well, various associations were formed that maintained a relatively free discussion on art, economics, nationality policy, and other vital issues. The party permitted a significant degree of autonomy in intellectual life that corresponded to the limited autonomy granted to nationalities and economic life.

All this ended with Stalinism, which was a calculated assault on all semi-independent centers of potential power and influence. Economic autonomy, the remnants of intellectual freedom, and the remaining prerogatives of national minorities were eliminated as the Stalinist police-party-state expanded to envelop all of society and bring it under its direct control. Stalinism, thus, was something new, something unique. Though it grew out of Leninism, just as it grew out of the Russian past and Stalin's personal requirements to maintain his own power, it also represented a new sociopolitical system, one effected finally by the mass use of police terror.

The effect of the Stalin Revolution was to break the back of peasant resistance to the rapid and forced industrialization of the country. Collectivization permitted the exploitation of the peasantry to build cities, to create a new working class made up of displaced persons from the countryside, and to transform the USSR from a backward and vulnerable agrarian country into an industrial giant that would successfully resist the invasion of Nazi Germany. Defenders of Stalin rationalize his harsh policies as essential for the victory over Hitler. But this *ex post facto* justification is inadequate to explain the excesses of Stalinism, the irrationality of the purges that weakened the army and the state bureaucracy, the unnecessary burdens endured by the Soviet people because of the rapidity of the economic changes demanded by the leadership. The human costs were truly staggering.

Stalinism was an excessively violent, excessively repressive, excessively cruel form of modernization. A more gradual pace of economic and social development would have produced better results without the great costs; and certainly the superfluous political repression of the period, besides being morally reprehensible, stifled and wasted energies and talents of thousands of able people who became innocent victims of the purges. For a small nation like Armenia the loss of a poet or a political leader is an especially heavy sacrifice, not easily made up. Stalin and his agents wantonly condemned Armenian intellectuals and leaders to ruined lives. From 1920 to 1940 Armenia lost two generations of its intellectual and political elite, first the prerevolutionary elite that was identified with the anti-Bolshevik forces that had ruled Armenia during that brief independence, and then the revolutionary elite, who had led Armenia up to the mid-1930s. It would take a long time for Armenians to recover from these losses.

The Second World War marked a distinct period in the history of Soviet nationality policy. Every resource of the country had to be mobilized to repel the invasion of Nazi Germany, and one of these resources was the revival of nationalism, both Russian and minority. In Armenia the persecution of the church ceased as the clergy was invited to join with the state in the struggle against fascism. Church leaders took the initiative in raising funds for Armenian military forces that the government now reconstituted. Editorials sang the praises of the Armenian people, who

> not only have preserved their national existence and have created their wonderful culture, but together with all leading peoples, headed by the Great Russian people, are conducting a most righteous struggle against the most reactionary force in the world—bloody German imperialism.[20]

Armenia, along with other national republics, was given its own ministries of defense and foreign affairs in 1944, thus restoring the image if not the reality of full state sovereignty. Armenians fought and died in the Soviet war against the Germans. Erevan feared that the Turks might attack Armenia while the Soviet army was fighting for its life on the Western Front, but the Turks wisely maintained their official neutrality. When the war ended with an Allied victory, the Soviet government included in its territorial demands the districts of Kars and Ardahan, Armenian irredenta, but as the warm feelings of alliance between the USSR and the Western powers cooled into the cold war, the Soviet demands were rejected by the West, which soon took Turkey under its protection.

Armenia emerged from the war poor and hungry, like the rest of the Soviet Union, but she was better off than the western parts of the country that had been devastated by the Germans. Despite the widespread impoverishment of the time, the government decided to invite Armenians in the diaspora to return to the homeland, and tens of thousands of *hairenadartsner* (repatriates) made the journey to Armenia. There they found less than they had dreamed of. Many were immediately rounded up on suspicion of being Western agents and exiled from Armenia to Siberia or Central Asia. Others were given homes and a new start in life, but they were bitterly resented by the local Armenians who ridiculed the returnees as *aghber* (brother). The economic resources of the country had been stretched to and beyond the breaking point by the war, and with the coming of the cold war much aid from the West was cut off and hopes for liberalization quickly faded. The policy of encouraging immigrants at a time of shortages was certainly shortsighted, however noble its inspiration may have been. The postwar immigrants never became completely integrated into Soviet society, as had the immigrants of the 1920s, and twenty years after their migration to Armenia many of them took the first opportunity to leave.[21]

The international tensions that marked the cold war created fears within the Soviet Union of a new danger of war with the West. In the late 1940s, as the wartime alliance with the United States was transformed into a bitter and potentially deadly conflict over the fate of Eastern Europe and East Asia, Stalin reinstituted the policy of tighter control over his own society that had characterized the late 1930s. A new campaign was launched against nationalism, bringing the all-too-brief flowering of wartime cultural life to an end. In November 1948 the Congress of the Armenian Communist party condemned scholars and writers for "idealizing the historical past of Armenia," for "ignoring the class struggle" in the history of Armenia, and for being too attracted by the "reactionary culture of the bourgeois West."[22] Whereas the authorities had permitted the republication of Raffi's classic novel *Kaitser* in 1947, four years later the book was castigated as an example of "bourgeois nationalism" and a wrong-headed idealization of Armenia. The publication was considered a "crude political error."[23] The next year, 1952, the historian M. Nersesian was attacked for praising nineteenth-century figures like Raffi, Patkanian, and Artsruni, and his colleague V. Parsamian was criticized for not recognizing that the Russian annexation of Armenia in the 1820s had had "progressive significance" for the Armenians and was no longer to be considered simply the lesser of two evils. Most notably, the composer Aram Khachaturian, a figure of international reputation, fell into disfavor with the party arbiters of music policy and was forced to apologize for writing "bourgeois" music.[24]

The last years of the Stalin era were harsh and dark in cultural policy, though they were also years of restoration and rebuilding after the war years. Any slight expression of Armenian pride was condemned as nationalism, and while some material progress was being made, a deep national frustration was building on the part of people who were forbidden to express feelings and views contrary to official policy. The Armenians of the early 1950s were a much different people than those who had lived through the first stages of the Stalin Revolution. Twenty years of experience, of living in cities, of living through the war, of education and work experience, had created a much more sophisticated and westernized people, a more modern people. Yet limits, very strict limits, were placed on this people's freedom of expression. The political system in the USSR had simply not changed sufficiently to accommodate the newly educated people that it had created. In Armenia and other national republics a tension was building between the demands of Soviet-style modernization and the nationalist aspirations to which the renationalization of the republics had given rise. Armenians in Armenia were more conscious of their language, history, and culture than ever before in their history, yet outlets for real expression of their national pride and interests simply did not exist in the Stalinist political world.

By the early 1950s the Soviet economy was also showing clear signs of stagnation. Forced modernization was reaching its limits. The command economy was no longer responding to commands. As confusion developed about what to do next, the news arrived that Stalin was dead. What was not immediately apparent to those who grieved over his passing was that not only had the Soviet Union lost its leader of the last twenty-five years but a whole historical epoch had also come to an end.

Though the years of Stalin's rule had transformed Armenia more fundamentally than the previous half century, this modernization from above was a mixed blessing. Economically Armenia grew into a more industrial and urban society, but politically the last vestiges of self-rule and self-definition had been eliminated. Any expression of national pride or unique Armenian achievement was strictly prohibited. The leading role of the Russian people had to be recognized. Passive acceptance of Russian direction was now required. Seething below the surface, the national passions and tensions produced by the forces of modern life came up against the repressive apparatus of the Stalinist state. An explosion was always possible, but people had been effectively intimidated into silence. When Stalin died in March 1953, those passions and tensions bubbled slowly to the surface, and a new expression of nationalism was heard in Armenia. The quarter-century of Stalinism that had propelled Armenia forward in material terms but had held her back politically and spiritually was ending. Armenians now had to learn once again how to express openly their own national interests, their despair at the past they had endured, and the lasting hope of what the future could be.

10 Return to Ararat: Armenia in the Cold War

In the intense historiographical debate that has continued for more than a quarter of a century, the cold war has provided both a legitimation for the now-dissolving division of Europe as well as a broadly accepted view of the enemy. The orthodox, liberal interpretation of a besieged West responding to Communist aggression from an expansionist Soviet Union was most effectively challenged in the 1960s by "revisionists" who claimed that blame for the breakup of the Grand Alliance must be shared by East and West equally. Though Soviet archives remain closed, access to American and British primary materials has permitted a "post-revisionist" synthesis, much more nuanced than the earlier understandings of the intentions of the principal players, but one that has made significant concessions to the revisionist critique of cold war orthodoxy. Models of Soviet behavior based on *a priori* theories of totalitarianism or the nature of Communist regimes or deductive readings of Stalin's paranoid psychology have been modified by appreciations of Soviet strategic interests and their postwar weakness. Rather than an expansionist world conqueror the Soviet Union is now understood by many historians to have been a significantly more vulnerable power than was popularly believed at the time, with considerably more modest goals at the end of World War II. And the division of Europe appears to be less the consequence of a frustrated Soviet expansionism than an eventual commitment on both sides to a conventional spheres-of-influence policy.

Orthodox Western interpreters incorporated the conflict over Iran, Turkey, and Greece—and the Soviet attempt to resurrect the Armenian Question—into their general picture of Soviet expansionism and a necessary Western response. Here was a particularly egregious example of Soviet imperialism and the cynical use of nationalism for expansionist purposes. The fate of small nations was of no real interest to the Soviets, it was generally agreed among non-Soviet writers, while for the Americans the preservation of Greek, Iranian, and Turkish independence was paramount. Yet that conflict can also be seen as a struggle between two imperialisms—Eastern and Western—for influence in the eastern Mediterranean and northern Middle East, a sphere of influence up for grabs. Whereas the USSR held on to Eastern Europe—at the cost of breaking up the Grand Alliance and launching a long and sterile cold war—it lost its privileged position in Iran and made no inroads into Turkey.

In a major study of the origins of the cold war in the Middle East, Bruce R. Kuniholm makes a useful distinction between the traditional Great Power rivalry between Britain and Russia in the years before World War II and the ideological struggle between the Soviet Union and the United States flowing from mutually exclusive worldviews. National interests were confused with the self-images of proselytizing states proposing alternate destinies for the small states of the region. "The policy of containment in the Near East," writes Kuniholm, "was a realistic and a pragmatic policy. The trouble with it was not its conception . . . [but] in its rationalization, in the legacy of that rationalization, and in analogies engendered by the policy's success in the Near East."[1]

For the Great Powers Armenia has often been used as a pretext for inter-vention—into either the Ottoman Empire or the Russian Civil War. At the end of the Second World War the festering Armenian Question was once again raised, this time by the Soviet government supported both by Soviet and diaspora Armenians, and this time the proposed solution was to increase the territory of Soviet Armenia by absorbing a small part of the Armenian irre-denta in the Turkish republic and by inviting hundreds of thousands of Arme-nians outside historic Armenia to return to the motherland. Armenia and Georgia provided the Soviet Union with an argument for territorial conces-sions from Turkey, just as Azerbaijan and Kurdish claims justified similar advances against Iran. The ultimate failure of the Soviet plan, itself part of the postwar defeat and isolation of the USSR, left the Armenian Question at least for the next four decades, orphaned in the cold war divide between East and West. Diaspora Armenians briefly hoped that the victorious Allies would redress the losses Armenians had suffered during and after the First World War, but they were to be bitterly disappointed. In the end the interests of this small nation were not taken seriously by any of the Great Powers.

Soviet foreign policy at the end of the Second World War was directed at two goals at once: maintenance of the Grand Alliance and the establishment of a sphere of influence in the countries along its most vulnerable borders— in Eastern Europe and the so-called Northern Tier (Turkey, Iran, Afghanistan). The Soviet government was determined to parlay its costly victory against the Nazis into a new balance of power in Europe and the Middle East. The *cordon sanitaire* of unfriendly states established along the USSR's western borders was to be broken, and the Soviet Union would use what power and pressure it could to maintain paramount influence in the countries immediately to its west and south. Though for a time, particularly at the Yalta Conference, these two goals seemed compatible, they proved to be mutually exclusive once the West resisted Soviet dominance in these areas. When a choice had to be made between the Grand Alliance with its potential material support for Soviet recovery and the "bird in the hand" of East Central Europe, Stalin opted for the latter.

Stalin had long been interested in extending Soviet influence in Turkey. During the brief period of the Nazi-Soviet Pact he attempted to convince the Germans to permit establishment of a Soviet base for land and naval forces near the straits and to recognize that the USSR's center of aspirations is "the area south of Batum and Baku in the general direction of the Persian Gulf." Turkey's independence and territorial integrity would be guaranteed only if it joined the pact. The Germans, however, refused to agree to these Soviet suggestions. The USSR then declared its strict neutrality in case of a Turkish-Axis war, and the Turks reciprocated, confirming the 1925 treaty.

For the Soviet Union a unique opportunity arose in the last years of the war. It had gained enormous influence and prestige among its Allies because of its extraordinary and heroic resistance to Nazism. Three-quarters of Hitler's forces had been thrown against the USSR, and with unheard-of losses (7 million Soviet soldiers, 13 million civilians dead) the Soviets had defeated Germany. At the same time Turkey had sat out the war, adopting a policy of armed neutrality. Formally an ally of Britain and France since 1939, Turkey signed treaties of friendship and nonaggression with Germany and Bulgaria in 1941. Turkey also continued to observe the Treaty of Friendship and Neutrality with the Soviet Union, signed on December 17, 1925.

As long as Britain and the USSR were on the defensive in the war (up to 1943), Turkish policy proved to be advantageous to the Allies. Germany did not invade Turkey and threaten the USSR from Anatolia. Even as they prepared to occupy Iran in August 1941, Britain and the USSR attempted to allay Turkish fears by declaring their intentions to respect the Montreux Convention and the territorial integrity of Turkey.[2] But after 1943, with British forces in the Mediterranean and Soviet forces in central Russia on the offensive, Turkish neutrality lost its value for the Allies. Yet the Turks persisted in their policy and refused to declare war on the Germans. As an Office of Strategic Services report on Turkey concluded, Turkey's policy was basically opportunistic.[3] Indeed they continued to send supplies to the Axis powers, and it was even suspected that the Turkish foreign minister provided Berlin with Allied war plans. The Turkish government avoided provoking the Allies, and in order to placate the Western powers the Turks repealed the *Varlik Vergisi,* the heavy tax on wealth that was directed against non-Turkish minorities, on March 15, 1944.

With the war coming to an end and Germany no longer a viable alternative, Turkey had only three diplomatic options: continuation of its alliance with Britain; the formation of a bloc of Balkan or Middle Eastern states to stand between East and West; or the adoption of a Russian orientation. The Soviets attempted to promote the last option and prevent the middle one. As in Iran, so in Turkey, Stalin was prepared to flex his muscles to replace British influence with Soviet. As long as the Allies were united, the Turks could do little but maneuver among them. The best scenario for Turkey would be the collapse of the Grand Alliance, which would then permit a Turkish alliance with the West against Russia. Because it had sat out the war as a neutral, Turkey needed either to accommodate Soviet interests in the postwar world or find powerful allies in the West to defend the republic.

All through the war the suppressed hostilities between the Allies repeatedly surfaced. Yet the shared goal of winning the war almost invariably encouraged papering over differences and finding a common policy. The United States, at least in the person of President Roosevelt, was not as actively interested in Middle Eastern affairs as either Churchill or Stalin. In 1944 tensions developed between Britain and the USSR over Turkey's relationship with Germany. Britain was content to have Turkey break economic and diplomatic ties with Germany, but Stalin apparently began to suspect British interest in the Turkish entry into the war. A Balkan campaign by Turks and the Allies would lessen the effort at Normandy and also potentially threaten postwar Soviet hegemony in the Balkans. On July 15, 1944, Stalin wrote to Churchill: "In view of the evasive and vague attitude with regard to Germany adopted by the Turkish Government, it is better to leave Turkey in peace and to her own free will and not to exert fresh pressure on Turkey. This of course means that the claims of Turkey, who has evaded war with Germany, to special rights in post-war matters also lapse. . . ."[4]

At the Yalta Conference, as expected, Stalin brought up the subject of the Montreux Convention, claiming that the convention was outmoded. He was disturbed that the Turks had the right to close the straits in time of war or perceived threat. The Soviet Union could not accept a situation in which Turkey had a hand on Russia's throat. The Big Three agreed that Turkey should be invited to join the United Nations only if it declared war on the Axis by the end of February. No love was lost on Turkey by any of the Allies, and the Soviets were invited to make proposals to the upcoming meeting of the Allied foreign ministers. Turkey finally complied with the demands of the Allies, and on February 23, 1945, declared war on Germany and Japan and thus became a member of the United Nations.

Stalin was determined to enhance the Soviet position in the Northern Tier, and on March 19, 1945, the USSR denounced its treaty of neutrality and nonaggression with Turkey as out of date and called for a new political treaty. Turkey informed the Soviet Union that it was prepared to examine any proposals it might make for a new pact.[5] On May 20 the Soviets abrogated the Soviet-Turkish Treaty of Neutrality and Friendship. On June 7, Foreign Minister Molotov met with Ambassador Selim Sarper in Moscow and informed him that the USSR wanted a revision of the Soviet-Turkish border in the region of Kars and Ardahan and a revision of the Montreux Convention to give "real" guarantees to the USSR, namely bases on Turkish territory and joint control of the straits in time of war. He hinted that if Turkish policy were reoriented away from Britain toward the Soviet Union the other demands might prove unnecessary. Sarper rejected the demands for territory or bases.[6] Molotov told Sarper on June 18 that Turkey and the USSR should conclude a treaty of "collaboration and alliance" on the basis of the points made on June 7, and added that the Armenian Soviet Socialist Republic needed territory. Once again the Turkish government replied that Turkey's sovereignty and territorial integrity would be violated by such concessions to the USSR and that consequently the Soviet points offered no basis for discussion.[7]

The Soviet initiative against Turkey began in the post-Yalta euphoria, when relations between the Big Three were relatively warm. The USSR was energetically pursuing a policy of securing "friendly" governments on its borders and increasing its political influence in the countries of Eastern Europe and the Middle East. Rather than primarily an effort to satisfy aspirations of the Armenian (or Georgian) people, or to promote the fortunes of the international Left, Stalin's policy toward Turkey, like that in Eastern Europe, was based on a rather traditional notion of developing spheres of influence. Turkey's vulnerability, combined with the enormous prestige of the Soviet Union, should have been sufficient, Stalin might have thought, to force them to make concessions. But in fact the Turkish government never backed down from its initial position of rejecting Soviet demands. Indeed, Soviet pressure worked only to unify the Turks and drive them into the Western alliance.

The death of President Roosevelt and the succession of Harry S. Truman significantly altered the personal dynamics among the Big Three. The new president was much more suspicious of Stalin than Roosevelt had been, and he was willing to use much tougher language and take a harder line with the Soviets in order to force them to accede to American positions. Truman was quickly briefed on Turkey and the Balkans by the new Turkish ambassador to Washington, Huseyin Baydur, and by the secretary of the navy, James Forrestal. Of high-ranking American officials, Forrestal was one of the most wary of Soviet intentions, and he told the president that if the Russians were going to hold a rigid attitude, it was better to have a showdown with them now than later. When he met with his new ambassador to Turkey, Edwin Wilson, Truman expressed his view that the United States should support Turkey against Soviet pressure.[8]

In the thinking of the West, particularly of high officials in the Truman Administration, the Munich analogy was uppermost: totalitarian regimes, like those of Nazi Germany and the Soviet Union, were not to be appeased. The recent experience in Poland where the Soviets had pressured the West to concede a dominant role to their supporters fortified resistance to granting any more such concessions to the Soviets. "If Eastern Europe served the Truman administration as an example of how not to deal with the Soviet Union, the countries of the Northern Tier provided a different kind of example, and verified the viability of a firm and determined response to Soviet pressures. In short, the traditional buffer zone between the Russian and British empires came to play the same role between the Soviet Union and the United States, and served as a forge for the latter's policy of containment of the Soviet Union."[9] The United States and Britain never considered Armenian national aspirations in their policy deliberations. It was quickly learned that there were few Armenians left in the disputed territories in Turkey. An argument based on demographics could not be made, given the effective deportation and massacres of Armenians in this region thirty years earlier, and the historic claims to the territories appeared muddled to the uninitiated.

Once the issue of Armenian irredenta in Turkey was raised, political organizations in the Armenian diaspora mobilized in support of the Soviet demands. The Armenian National Council of the United States addressed an appeal to the San Francisco Conference for the unification of the lands of Turkish and Soviet Armenia and the return of Armenians to their motherland. Armenian clerical and lay delegates from around the world met in Echmiadzin to elect a new Catholicos on June 16–25, 1945. The new head of the church, the unanimously elected Gevorg VI, sent a letter to Stalin calling for repatriation of Armenians and the return of Armenian lands in Turkey.[10] With the support of the conclave that had elected him, the Catholicos wrote: "The Armenian people are firmly convinced that the Great Russian people will aid them in realizing their patriotic and humane aspirations of recovering their national patrimony."

Armenians combined two goals in one campaign: to repatriate the diaspora Armenians to Soviet Armenia and to have Armenian lands in Turkey returned to the only existing Armenian state. They also asked for reparations from Turkey to the Armenian people. After decades of hostility between large numbers of diaspora Armenians and the Soviet republic of Armenia, a new relationship between diaspora Armenians and Soviet Armenia was being forged at the end of the war—a joint effort to raise and solve the Armenian Question in a coordinated way. Repatriation by definition was linked to the need for territory to settle the immigrants. The two major issues (one might say fears) that determined the consciousness of politically minded Armenians—the problem of the lost homeland and the evident process of de-Armenization of diaspora Armenians—could be solved by the return of Armenians to Armenia. Even the major Armenian political party in the diaspora, the Armenian Revolutionary Federation *(Hai Heghapokhakan Dashnaktsutiun)*, long opposed to the Soviet domination of Armenia, reconciled itself after 1944 to the necessity of working with Soviet Armenia to restore and rebuild the homeland.

Despite alarm at the Soviet pressure on Turkey, the Americans deferred to the British on this matter through 1945. During the Potsdam Conference

Churchill met with Stalin for dinner (July 18) and brought up the question of the Straits. The prime minister expressed sympathy with Russia, "a giant with his nostrils pinched by the narrow exits from the Baltic and the Black Sea," and agreed to a revision of the Montreux Convention that would give Russia access to the Mediterranean. At the plenary session on July 22, Churchill agreed with Stalin that Montreux had to be revised but said that the Turks must not be alarmed. When Molotov mentioned the territories in eastern Turkey, Truman intervened and asked for postponement of discussions, for he was not prepared to discuss this issue. Nevertheless, the Big Three agreed that Montreux had to be revised. Having failed to convince his Allies of the Soviet position on Turkey, Stalin opposed any mention of the straits issue in the final communiqué. Apparently he had become convinced that bilateral discussions directly with Turkey were the best way from the Soviet point of view to deal with this problem. The moderate proposal offered by the United States in November, which opened the straits to all commercial vessels at all times, to warships of riparian powers at all times, but only very limited access to warships of non-riparian powers, was unsatisfactory to Stalin.

In mid-December Stalin told Foreign Minister Bevin that the Soviet Union wanted bases at the straits and the Georgian and Armenian portions of Turkey's eastern provinces. When Bevin replied that Turkey would continue to mobilize for fear of Soviet intentions, Stalin said there was no need for such fears. Bevin concluded by telling Stalin that the defense of Turkey was of vital interest to the United Kingdom.[11]

While the Great Powers pondered the fate of the straits and the eastern territories, Armenians and Turks mobilized around the territorial issues. On November 27, Gevorg VI sent a note to all three Great Powers calling for them to support the return of Armenian lands guaranteed by the Treaty of Sèvres. This was a significantly greater demand than the original Soviet demand for Kars and Ardahan, the considerably smaller regions gained by tsarist Russia in 1878 and lost after World War I. On December 2, *Pravda, Izvestiia,* and *Sovetakan Haiastan* (Soviet Armenia) published the November 21 decree of the Soviet government authorizing the repatriation of Armenians. In early December Turkish students demonstrated in Istanbul. Protesting a Soviet radio broadcast, they attacked two Communist printing houses in the city. General Kiazim Karabekir proclaimed that the Turks would fight for every inch of their territory: "The world must know that the Straits form the throat of the Turkish nation and the Kars Plateau its backbone." By the end of the month the National Assembly in Ankara voted to increase funding for the army.[12]

Soviet claims to Turkey became somewhat muddled late in 1945 when Georgian claims were added to the Armenian. On December 20 *Pravda, Izvestiia,* and *Krasnaya zvezda* (Red Star) reprinted an article from the Georgian party's newspaper, *kommunisti,* by S. R. Janashia and N. Berdzenishvili of the Georgian Academy of Sciences that demanded a strip of territory in Turkey 180 by 70 miles. At about the same time the Soviet consulate began enlisting

Turkish Armenians for repatriation. In his memoirs, Nikita Khrushchev provides some insight into what may have led Stalin to amplify Soviet claims to eastern Turkey.

> Stalin jealously guarded foreign policy as his own special province. The one person able to advise Stalin on foreign policy was Beria, who used his influence for all it was worth. At one of those interminable "suppers" at Stalin's, Beria started harping on how certain territories, now part of Turkey, used to belong to Georgia and how the Soviet Union ought to demand their return. Beria was probably right, but you had to go pretty far back in history to the time when the Turks seized those lands from Georgia. Beria kept bringing this subject up, teasing Stalin with it, goading him into doing something. He convinced Stalin that now was the time to get those territories back. He argued that Turkey was weakened by World War II and wouldn't be able to resist. Stalin gave in and sent an official memorandum to the Turkish government pressing our territorial claims.[13]

Even as Soviet pressure was applied to Turkey in favor of the Armenians and Georgians, the USSR was also supporting the national movements of Kurds and Azerbaijanis to Iran. On December 12, the pro-Soviet Tudeh party declared the establishment of the Autonomous Republic of Azerbaijan in Iran. Three days later, the Kurdish republic of Mahabad was proclaimed. These actions, as well as Soviet support for Zionism and the eventual establishment of Israel, were consistent with the general thrust of Soviet policy directed at weakening British influence in the Middle East. To the West, however, which was growing increasingly suspicious of Soviet actions in Eastern Europe, as well as the Middle East, Stalin's drive to replace British with Soviet influence was interpreted as an expansionist drive by a Communist empire, akin to the aggressive policies of the defeated totalitarian enemy, Nazi Germany. *Time* speculated on the Soviet Union's reasons for its new policy toward Turkey and concluded that it hoped for new political concessions that might lead to a "Moscow-influenced Turkish government." The cession of territory would give Russia an improved strategic position on the Black Sea. Russia disliked having Turkey "right next to her great oil city of Batum [*sic*] and her new oil-rich satellite, Azerbaijan."[14] Both the American ambassador to Turkey, Wilson, and the State Department's Office of Near East and African Affairs (NEA) agreed that Soviet tactics were like those of the Nazis and that the Soviets sought domination of Turkey. NEA wrote that the demands for Kars and Ardahan were "a clear piece of press-war effrontery reminiscent of Hitler's press attacks on Czechoslovakia."[15]

By the end of 1945 Turkish resistance and American resolve to contain Stalin's influence began to coalesce into a coherent policy. The Turkish government was most impressed by the assurance of the United States that "general questions involved in present Turco-Soviet relations extend beyond Turk territory into sphere of world peace and security in which US has deepest interest."[16] Angry at having been kept in the dark by Secretary of State Byrnes during the Moscow Foreign Ministers' Conference, Truman read him a long letter expressing the president's own views on foreign policy (January 5, 1946). Taking a much tougher line toward the Soviets than Byrnes, he said: "There isn't a doubt in my mind that Russia intends an invasion of Turkey and the seizure of the Black Sea Straits to the Mediterranean. Unless Russia is faced with an iron fist and strong language another war is in the making. Only one language do they understand—'how many divisions have you?' . . . I'm tired of babying the Soviets."[17] Truman was upset by the losses suffered in Eastern Europe, where Soviet influence at the end of 1945 was very great. Increasingly he and the State Department were coming to believe that Soviet influence must now be stopped in the Northern Tier. Since Britain could no longer maintain its former hold on the Middle East, the Americans would either have to accept Soviet dominance or move in themselves.

On January 2, 1946, Feridun Cemal Erkin, secretary general of the Turkish Foreign Office, told Ambassador Wilson "that while patience is beginning to wear out in Turkey as result of continuous pressure to which they have been subjected by [the] USSR since last March, Turkish authorities are firmly resolved to prevent any incident or manifestation of aggressive character in Turkey." He said that further Soviet pressure would encourage strong articles in reply in the Turkish press and patriotic demonstrations throughout the republic. Wilson warned that there should be "no manifestation against Armenians," and Erkin agreed.[18] The next day Radio Ankara broadcast a refutation of the claims of Soviet Georgia to Turkish territory: "Facts remain that country known as Georgia has never counted within its borders even small part of territories which lie behind frontiers of Turkey today."[19] Prime Minister Sukru Saracoglu told Wilson that the USSR had been misled by its agents in Turkey into thinking the country was "ripe for softening up and that external pressure by press and radio from Moscow, drumming up Armenian and Georgian claims, etc., plus pressure from . . . [within] through setting up new Communist newspapers and spreading Communist propaganda, would result in disintegrating regime and preparing way for 'friendly' Govt." Exactly the opposite had occurred. The result of Soviet activities has been that the Turks have become completely united against Soviet demands.[20]

At the same time the Turkish government was careful not to provoke the Soviets. The prime minister sent word to the Turkish press asking them to avoid offending the USSR, but articles headlined "Machiavellism now Molotovism" and "Stalin is doing what Hitler did" appeared nevertheless. The Soviet ambassador in Ankara, Sergei Aleksandrovich Vinogradov, made a formal protest, and the Turkish government expressed its regret for the offensive articles, noting that the government had interceded and hoping that the Soviets would prevent articles offensive to Turkey from appearing in the Soviet press. The tone of the Turkish press changed markedly in the weeks following this exchange.[21]

With little to show for their efforts in the name of Armenia and Georgia, the Soviet government adopted a new tactic in early 1946. They began to hedge on the question of Armenian and Georgian territories in Turkey. The Bulgarian minister, Antonov, who apparently was acting as an agent of the Soviets, told a high Turkish diplomat that "he believed [the] cause of difficulties was Soviet lack of confidence in [the] present Turkish Government and expressed [the] opinion that if Saracoglu were replaced as head of Government there would be no further difficulties."[22] In late January Antonov met again with Acting Foreign Minister Sumer, who told him that Turkey would like to settle its differences with the Soviets but that would require abandonment by the USSR of claims for the eastern territories and bases on the straits. Antonov said: "[Y]ou can forget about Kars and Ardahan." What was important from the Soviet point of view was "agreement with Turkey regarding Straits."[23]

On the first day of February, Ambassador Wilson met with Ambassador Vinogradov of the USSR and expressed the opinion that the only question between Turkey and the USSR was the straits. Vinogradov disagreed, saying that the issue of Kars and Ardahan remained "very important to [the] USSR" and was a prerequisite for a Soviet-Turkish treaty of alliance. Vinogradov was also upset at the coming of an Iraqi delegation to negotiate a mutual assistance pact with Turkey. He believed this was a British-backed move aimed against the USSR. Three days later Sumer met with Vinogradov, who asked him: "Why don't you make a little effort to improve our relations?" Sumer inquired about the territorial demands in the east and the request for bases. Vinogradov replied that while the territorial question was important, it was not as important as that of the straits, which was "vital." Sumer rejected the idea of bases and asked that the USSR withdraw its request for the eastern provinces. "Vinogradov replied [that the] Soviet Government was obligated by [its] constitution to defend interests of various Soviet Republics, that [a] request for [the] eastern provinces had been made on behalf of [the] Armenian representative and [the] Soviet Government, therefore, could not withdraw [the] request." At the end of the conversation Vinogradov remarked, "We waited [a] long time regarding [the] arrangement we wanted with Poland and finally got it; we can wait regarding Turkey." Sumer went away believing that nothing had changed with the Antonov feelers: "the USSR stands pat on demands for territories and bases and believes that time works in its favor."[24]

The unyielding position of Turkey, Britain, and the United States began to take its toll on the Soviets. On February 21, 1946, Bevin spoke to the House of Commons, mentioning that the current frontier between Turkey and Russia had been drawn by Stalin himself. The Turks were reassured by Bevin's speech and considered it an event of great international significance.[25] Vinogradov was upset at Bevin's speech and told Sumer that Molotov had set down preconditions for a treaty of alliance. Sumer said that Turkey wanted only a treaty of friendship, not of alliance. Vinogradov made one more attempt to win on the territorial issue. He spoke of Molotov's request for eastern provinces and said Armenia needed these. If Turkey would grant the Soviet request, she would be more than compensated elsewhere. Sumer replied, "Turkey will neither cede territories nor annex territories."[26]

The first week of March 1946 marked a major turning point in East-West relations. The Soviet Union refused on March 2 to withdraw its troops from Iran, and fears grew that Stalin intended military action against Tehran. The Turks were worried by the events in Iran and anxiously awaited the outcome of that standoff. On March 5, Winston Churchill made his famous "Iron Curtain" speech in Fulton, Missouri. Of the Middle East, he said: "Turkey and Persia are both profoundly alarmed and disturbed at the claims which are being made upon them and at the pressure being exerted by the Moscow Government." Ambassador Wilson informed the secretary of state that the

> USSR may shortly be in position to strike at Turkey if and when this should appear advisable from viewpoint Soviet interests. Soviet objective regarding Turkey . . . is to break present Turkish Government, install "friendly" government, resulting in closing Turkish gap in Soviet security belt from Baltic to Black Sea, giving USSR physical control of Straits and putting end to Western influence in Turkey. In short, domination of Turkey. Present Soviet military dispositions raise question whether they have decided to use force to achieve this objective. I have held belief that USSR would use indirect methods of aggression against Turkey, such as employment Armenian and Kurdish "fronts" in Eastern provinces, rather than take risks involved in open war. . . . To embark on war against Turkey would mean that Soviet rulers have taken fundamental decision to break with policy of cooperation with Western democracies. This would be very grave decision fraught with heavy risks.[27]

By early April the crisis in Iran was over, and Stalin had publicly agreed to remove Soviet troops. When General Walter Bedell Smith, the new American ambassador to Moscow, met with Stalin on April 4, he asked him bluntly: "How far is Russia going to go?" Stalin answered: "We're not going to go much further." "You say 'not much further,'" Smith went on, "but does that 'much' have any reference to Turkey?" Stalin explained that Turkey was weak, not strong enough to protect the straits, but the Soviets have no intention of attacking Turkey. The Turkish government was unfriendly and that is why the Soviets had demanded a base on the Dardanelles.[28]

Each of Stalin's maneuvers in Turkey had ended in failure. The Armenian and Georgian claims had little resonance in the West, except among diaspora Armenians and Communist parties. The demands for a revision of the Montreux Convention were unheeded. Attempts to destabilize the Turkish government or secure a more friendly government were equally unsuccessful. On April 6, the Americans made a display of their commitment to Turkey by sending the U.S. battleship *Missouri* to Istanbul, where it was enthusiastically received by the Turks. To reconsider its policy the Soviet government recalled Ambassador Vinogradov to Moscow for consultations.

American intelligence officers made their own assessment of the Armenian claims during the March crisis and concluded that strategic and political considerations regarding the Middle and Near East in general weigh infinitely more than championship of Armenian irredentism in the Soviet claims regarding the Armenian (or Georgian) provinces of Turkey. As a by-product, however, the Armenian question is played up both as a good pretext for the Soviet claims and as an effective means of enlisting the sympathy and/or support of Armenians throughout the world.[29]

In the course of the review the report dealt with a number of arguments that might have compromised Armenian rights to territory held by Turkey—the Turkish rationalizations for the deportations of Armenians, the relations of Armenian political leaders with Nazi agents, and alleged Armenian sympathy for Communism. The report acknowledged the losses suffered by Ottoman Armenians thirty years earlier and refuted charges that "Armenians as a body—or even substantial sections of the Armenian population—were subversive elements threatening the security of the Ottoman Empire." This was seen as

a mere pretext invoked to justify the extermination of over a million Armenians, uprooted mostly from regions remote from the war fronts—and whose able-bodied men who might have caused trouble had been drafted into labor battalions. The argument is compatible to Nazi accusations of Jewish subversive activities, and is equally invalid. Assertions have been made that Armenians also have massacred Turks. But the sporadic raids of terrorist groups, or acts of savage vengeance of individual Armenian volunteers with the Russian armies in the east or with the French Legion Armenienne in Cilicia, cannot be equated with the systematic, organized, and prolonged massacres of a whole minority by the Ottoman Government.[30]

On relations of various Armenian political figures with the Nazis, the report stated:

In the first years of World War II, there were contacts between German agents and some Tashnag [Dashnak] leaders. Efforts were made to enlist the support of the Tashnag Party for the Nazis, and there are reports of promises of the reestablishment of a Tashnag Armenian republic after the defeat of the USSR. Although some Armenian leaders, notably those in Nazi-dominated areas, were won over, official central and regional bureaus as well as the overwhelming majority of the Tashnags refused to enter into such an alliance. Even at the height of the Nazi successes before Stalingrad, and at a time when the Soviets were actively persecuting Tashnags in Iran, the notorious German agent Franz Mayer failed in his efforts to win general Tashnag support. Nevertheless, the outright "collaboration" of individual Tashnags and the broadcast appeals of one prominent leader over the Berlin radio for a crusade against the common Bolshevik foe cast the stigma of pro-Nazism on the party as a whole.

In July 1944 the Tashnag Party decided to reverse the anti-Soviet policy it had followed since 1920, when the Soviets annexed the Armenian Republic founded by the Tashnags. The change was officially explained as a determination to help the USSR in its efforts to rebuild Armenia; but it does not imply Tashnag reconciliation to Soviet overlordship. The Tashnags have not given up their long-range goal of a "United and Independent Armenia," but hold that under present conditions, when Soviet might and the Soviet hold on Armenia are unshakable, it would be unpatriotic to block the efforts that are being made for the progress and territorial aggrandizement of Armenia. They believe that their ideal will have to be achieved in two stages: union of Turkish and Russian Armenia now; and independence whenever they can attain it. Although the diehards are unhappy about this compromise, the party as a whole seems determined to contribute its support to the Soviet policy of rebuilding a United Armenia, with the reservation that once the task is accomplished they will turn against the Soviet regime.[31]

On diaspora Armenian attitudes toward the Soviet Union, the report argued that they were more influenced by nationalism than commitment to communism.

> On the whole . . . Armenians have no use for communism either as an economic ideal or as a system of government. Their present orientation toward the USSR derives not from sympathy for the Soviet regime but from a realization that the fate of their homeland depends on the USSR, that there is no other power likely to uphold Armenian aspirations, and that Soviet support of the Armenian cause can contribute not only to the rebuilding and aggrandizement of Armenia but also to the protection of Armenians in insecure areas.

> For these reasons sympathy for Soviet policy and desire to migrate to the Armenian SSR are lowest among Armenians in the US, Great Britain, and South America, and progressively increase in France and Italy, Cyprus, Palestine, Ethiopia, Egypt, Lebanon, Syria, Iraq, Turkey, and Iran (especially in Azerbaijan), approximately in the order named.[32]

Yet at the end the intelligence report rejected the Soviet claims to Armenian irredenta in Turkey.

> From the strictly legal point of view, it is doubtful whether the present Soviet claims have any solid basis since, by the Treaty of Kars in 1921, the Communist Government of Armenia, under Soviet sponsorship, confirmed the final cession of Kars and Ardahan to Turkey. However, the USSR's unofficial spokesmen have indicated that their claim is based on what they assert to be the essentially Armenian character of the provinces under dispute; that although the Armenian population of the area is negligible at the present time, it was depopulated of Armenians only as a result of the Turkish massacres and deportations; and, finally, that the Treaty of Kars was signed at a time of internal and international emergency when the USSR could not defend its borders, and consequently is not valid. . . .

> Soviet leaders wish to regain all the territory held by Russia before World War I. With the exception of a compromise settlement in Finland, the provinces of Kars and Ardahan are the only important remaining objects of this *irredenta*. Therefore, as a matter of overall prestige as well as of their standing among dissatisfied minorities in the neighboring area—Kurds, Armenians, Assyrians, etc.—the possession of Kars and Ardahan appears important to the Soviet authorities.[33]

Of greatest concern to the State Department's analysts were the strategic implications of a Soviet annexation of the Kars region.

> Strategically, however, the plateau of Kars still has considerable importance for the Russians, despite the substantially reduced role of strategic defense positions of modern warfare. Although long-range and atomic bombing of the Baku fields and the Batum pipeline terminal cannot be seriously hampered by any degree of positional advantage in the Kars plateau, the latter still remains the key position for preventing ground warfare from reaching Soviet territory. The Soviet concern for surrounding the USSR with "shock-absorbing" areas shows that the Russians still attach considerable significance to this last consideration. . . . This line of defense may not be essential for the USSR but it is vital to Turkey. The substitution of Soviet for Turkish defense positions on these heights would carry with it the threat of a lightning invasion of Turkey at the very beginning of a war without giving time to a stronger ally to come to the rescue. At the same time, the establishment of the USSR in a commanding position within easy reach of the mountains of Kurdistan and the valleys leading to Iraq and its oil fields, to the Near East and the Mediterranean, and to the Persian Gulf and the Iranian and Arabian oil fields, offers immediate strategic advantages. Among other things, the expansion of Soviet ideological and economic penetration of the Near and Middle East would be greatly facilitated and reinforced.[34]

In an appendix to the report a brief history of American interests in and commitments to Armenia was outlined, with special mention of President Wilson's support for an independent Armenian state. But the final paragraph noted:

> In 1934, an inquiry into the status of Armenia brought the following elucidation of the US attitude: ". . . The recognition which the United States accorded in 1920 to the 'de facto government of the Armenian Republic' is no longer effective since the Armenian Republic has ceased to exist as an independent State."[35]

Both powers were distancing themselves from Armenia. On August 7, a Soviet note to the Turkish government called for a revision of the Montreux Convention: free passage of all merchant ships and warships of Black Sea powers, but restrictions on other warships; joint defense of the straits by Turkey and the Soviet Union. No mention was made in the note of the eastern territories![36] A clear retreat on the issue of Kars and Ardahan had taken place.

The State Department advised Truman to oppose Soviet demands for bases and to support Turkey's resolve. Truman agreed. The American military concluded that Turkey should be equipped militarily. "Strategically Turkey is the most important military factor in the Eastern Mediterranean and Middle East. She is one of the few national entities and the only nation now possessing . . . a firm resolution to oppose the apparent Soviet policy of expansion in the area."[37]

The Turks consulted with Britain and the United States, and all three sent negative replies to Moscow. By the end of October 1946 the crisis over the straits was over. The new American policy of refusing to make concessions to the Soviets seemed to be successful. Moreover, a de facto alliance of Turkey, Britain, and the United States had been forged from the crisis over Kars and Ardahan and the straits. On October 21, the State Department's Loy W. Henderson drafted a memorandum expressing American policy toward Turkey: "It is . . . the policy of the United States Government to give positive support to Turkey." This meant moral, diplomatic, economic, and military aid.[38]

By the end of 1946 American diplomacy and preparations for even stronger responses had effectively kept the USSR out of the Middle East. The Soviet-backed republics of the Azerbaijanis and Kurds were defeated by Iranian troops and a cruel repression. A major shift in the balance of power and influence in the northern Middle East had taken place. The Soviet Union had realized few of its ambitions after the war, and the United States was replacing Britain as the major power in the region. Early in 1947 Britain began to disengage itself from many of its imperial obligations: Burma was to be given self-government; the United Nations was to deal with Palestine; Britain would soon quit India; and notification was given to the United States that for economic reasons Britain would soon pull out of the eastern Mediterranean. The State Department responded by recommending to the president that the United States take over the protection of Greece and Turkey.

The full implications of the American acceptance of this burden were spelled out by Truman in his speech to Congress announcing the "Truman Doctrine." On March 12, 1947, the president placed the conflict over influence in the Middle East into the broader ideological context of the struggle between democracy and totalitarianism.

> The future of Turkey as an independent and economically sound state is clearly no less important to the freedom-loving peoples of the world than the future of Greece. . . . At the present moment in world history nearly every nation must choose between alternative ways of life. The choice is too often not a free one. One way of life is based upon the will of the majority, and is distinguished by free institutions, representative government, free elections, guarantees of individual liberty, freedom of speech and religion, and freedom from political oppression. The second way of life is based upon the will of a minority forcibly imposed upon the majority. It relies upon terror and oppression, a controlled press and radio, fixed elections, and the suppression of personal freedoms. I believe that it must be the policy of the United States to support free peoples who are resisting attempted subjugation by armed minorities or by outside pressures.[39]

Though Soviet claims to Turkey spoke in the name of both national security and the historic claims of Soviet peoples, its goals in Turkey and the rest of the Near East were certainly directed primarily to the former rather than the latter. Stalin was probably unsure how far he was willing to go in Turkey and probed as deeply as he was able before being stopped by the Americans. The Middle East was simply not as important to his strategic considerations as was Poland, where he was more willing to risk American discontent in order to promote Soviet interests. Given Soviet material weakness at the end of the war and the extension of its power into East Central Europe, it is extremely probable that Stalin would have been quite content with territorial adjustments in eastern Turkey and a revision of the Montreux Conventions. He would have been very pleased to have a more friendly government in Ankara, but he was not attempting to make Turkey a full satellite of the Soviet Union as imagined by American policymakers.

Turkey played on American fears that Stalin wanted to make Turkey and Iran satellites of the Soviet empire and secured a powerful ally against Soviet demands for territory. The United States came to see that "Turkey constitutes the stopper in the neck of the bottle through which Soviet political and military influence could most effectively flow into the eastern Mediterranean and Middle East" and brought Turkey into its sphere of influence, which in the Northern Tier extended right up to the borders of the Soviet Union.[40] In their understanding any concessions to Stalin would have led to Turkey becoming a Soviet satellite.

In subsequent years Turkey became a member of NATO, and American bases were established on its territory. Millions of dollars of American aid and hundreds of advisors poured into Turkey to help create a stable economy and a democratic polity. For decades, however, both proved to be elusive, and the military alliance with the United States bolstered conservative regimes dependent on the military. For Armenians their quest for a return of a small part of their lost patrimony in Turkey was denied. Their petitions and appeals went unheard by the Western powers. One delegation of Armenians visited Dean Acheson just after President Truman's speech, apparently unaware of the full implications of the turn in American policy.[41] Hundreds of thousands of diaspora Armenians "returned" to Soviet Armenia, many of them to suffer from the material shortages and political oppression that marked the last years of Stalin's dictatorship. The Armenian Question was laid to rest, a victim of a divided world that in part was created in the postwar crisis over Soviet claims to Armenian irredenta.[42]

11 The New Nationalism in Armenia

Western writers and analysts of the Soviet nationalities have generally emphasized that the USSR, like the Marquis de Custine's description of tsarist Russia, was a "prisonhouse of nations." In histories and commentaries the view has been put forward that the minorities of the periphery suffered an imperial conquest by the Russian government (disguised in socialist garb), were oppressed and kept from free expression of their national aspirations, and were made the victims of a consistent campaign of Russification. The recent explosion of nationalism in the former USSR is explained as the inevitable reaction to the government's policy of assimilation and Russification. The picture drawn by such writers as Robert Conquest, Richard Pipes, Walter Kolarz, and others is bleak indeed and stands in stark contrast to the rosy and romanticized image one gets from Soviet writers and their apologists, who emphasized the creation of a united Soviet people distinguished by the absence of interethnic tensions. On the one hand, we are presented with a vision of an *"empire éclaté"* (Hélène Carrère d'Encausse); on the other, with the benign utopia overflowing with *druzhba narodov* (friendship of the peoples). As with so many other aspects of the historiography and political analysis of the Soviet Union, the problem of the minority nationalities became a victim of the intellectual cold war that separated Western and Soviet scholars and often led to oversimplification of the peculiar and complex experience of the Soviet peoples.

While a study of developments in the Soviet Republic of Armenia cannot inform us completely of the experiences of other Soviet nationalities, it may serve as a useful corrective to the facile generalizations previously offered by both the extreme supporters of the Soviet Union and their adversaries. No overview of Soviet reality is possible without taking into account the diverse histories of the constituent peoples of the USSR and without an appreciation of the shifts and even reversals in the policies of the central government toward the minorities. The Soviet peoples have lived through revolution, civil war, the period of restoration under "state capitalism" known as the New Economic Policy, the vicissitudes of the "Stalin Revolution," the Second World War, a second period of restoration, this time under the constraints of an established Stalinist police-state, a period of reform that saw the revival of a repressed civil society, and finally the rapid collapse of the Soviet system. The years since the death of Stalin have produced a society and a state of much greater diversity and tolerance than that which existed in the 1930s and 1940s, a society with increased opportunities, legal and illegal, for self- and group expression, a society in which the tensions generated by a rapid and forced modernization and a policy of national cultural development within strict limits erupted in new manifestations of nationalism.

While Stalin had initiated and overseen a genuine *social* revolution that had changed both the class structure and political leadership of the country, his successors were much more restrained in their reshaping of the Soviet system. Their dilemma lay in deciding how much of the Stalinist order to preserve while trying to rid the country of the more vicious aspects of police rule and intellectual repression. Both the great reformer Khrushchev and the great defender of the post-Stalin *status quo,* Brezhnev, tampered little with the Soviet social structure. Instead, their reforms were *political* in nature—the reduction of independent police power and the subordination of the police to the party, greater power for the Central Committee and local party leaders, a certain degree of decentralization in decision making that increased the prerogatives of the national republics, greater tolerance of intellectual diversity though with repeated efforts to keep artists and writers in line, more contact with the West, and greater attention to bettering the material life of Soviet consumers. Terror was significantly reduced in Soviet life. The bloody purges of the 1930s were replaced by more mundane kinds of punishment, such as demotion or transfer to another post. Instead of being shot or exiled to Siberia, many dissidents were issued a one-way ticket abroad.

The political advances of the last forty years have made it possible for the underlying tensions in Soviet society to come to the surface. Economic hardships are no longer tolerated in silence and have given rise to persistent complaints about shortages, lack of adequate housing, limited job opportunities, and unsatisfactory work conditions. Likewise, the frustration of ethnic interests and the resulting sense that national minorities are threatened in a modernizing, multinational, Russian-dominated state led to open expression of nationalism. It should not be assumed that there was more discontent after 1953 than there had been under Stalin. Rather, in Khrushchev's and Brezhnev's USSR discontent could be more openly articulated. In post-Stalin society the public constantly tested the limits of expression and occasionally moved beyond those set by the state.

The pull toward modernization from one end and the pressure for renationalization from the other gave rise to a vital and bold nationalism among
Armenians in the relatively permissive atmosphere of the post-Stalin quarter-
century. Let us consider first the political changes that took place since 1953
that created the framework within which this nationalist expression emerged.
Then we will look at the underlying social dynamics in Armenia that led
not to the assimilation or Russification of the Armenians but rather to their
consolidation as a nation and to the increased cohesion of the Armenians as
an ethnic entity. Finally we will discuss Armenian nationalism as it appeared
in the years before Gorbachev came to power.

Political Change

Stalin's agonized passing left the Soviet leadership with a crucial decision
to make—whether to continue his repressive policies and centrally directed
political and economic machine or to strike out in a new direction. Political
realities and the economic and social paralysis into which Stalinism had led
the country persuaded Khrushchev and his allies to break gradually but steadily with the more repressive aspects of the past. One key consideration was
the danger that one of the most feared of the Kremlin leaders, Lavrenti Beria,
might use his command of the police to make himself all-powerful. Within
days of Stalin's death, Khrushchev engineered an elaborate plot to have Beria
arrested, and a so-called collective leadership replaced what would later be
referred to as "the cult of personality." An intellectual "thaw" that opened
up discussion of political and artistic matters was quickly perceptible. Within
months, Beria's lieutenants were also removed from positions of power, both
in the center and in Transcaucasia. In Armenia Grigor Arutiunov was replaced
in November 1953 by Suren Tovmasian, a member of the generation of Soviet
politicians that came to power when the purges removed the older generations
of leaders. When the Seventeenth Congress of the Armenian Communist party
met in February 1954, a general housecleaning was carried out. All members
of the Bureau of the Central Committee, the highest governing body in the
country, were removed from office except one (Anton Kochinian), and half of
the Central Committee was dismissed. The Beria machine was gone and a
new leadership came to power in Armenia, a leadership that would display
an extraordinary staying power.

The political shifts were reflected in the new policy toward culture. Anastas Mikoyan, a close associate of the new party leader Khrushchev, came to
Erevan in March 1954 to announce that the great figures of the Armenian
past who had been condemned as "nationalists" were now to be rehabilitated.
Writers like Raffi and Patkanian, who only a few years before could not be
published, now were considered giants of national culture. Mikoyan even
defended the poet Charents, who had perished in the purges of the thirties,

and a short time later a school was named for him.[1] Writers who had survived the repression of the Stalin years—men like Gurgen Mahari, Vagharshak Norents, and Vhram Alazan—now appeared in Erevan. The works of Aksel Bakunts, who was rehabilitated but could not be resurrected, were reissued. A Russian critic, writing in 1956, bemoaned his untimely and tragic death at the hands of Stalin's police:

> Bakounts' last unfinished novel was devoted to Khachatur Abovian's youth. Abovian had a tragic and mysterious end. He left his house one night never to return and vanished completely. Bakounts' fate was one of the episodes of another tragedy. The enemies of our culture took him away from his house in 1937, and he never returned; he met his death as a communist.[2]

Destalinization reached its high point in the years between 1956 and 1962. Khrushchev's famous "secret speech" at the Twentieth Party Congress in February 1956 was a critical turning point in Soviet history, for the party leader revealed officially the enormity of Stalin's crimes. In Armenia the discussion of the issues raised spread through the intelligentsia. Meetings of the party organizations were held in the Union of Writers, at Erevan State University, and at other educational institutions.[3] Apparently the criticism of past policies went much further than party leaders were comfortable with, and the press condemned "anti-party manifestations." The secretary of the Erevan City Committee of the Komsomol, K. Uzumian, warned young people of the dangers of succumbing to anti-Marxist views. His strongest attacks were leveled against teachers who "commented incorrectly and in an un-Marxist way on the personality cult."[4] Armenians apparently took the criticisms of Stalin too seriously, and the authorities curtailed discussion in the next year and renewed the attack on Armenian nationalist tendencies among intellectuals. The campaign against Stalin revived in the early 1960s, culminating in the removal of Erevan's monument to the late dictator. Under cover of darkness the largest statue of Stalin in the Soviet Union was pulled down by soldiers, and when Erevan awoke the next morning, a huge empty pedestal stood on the hill overlooking Lenin Prospekt. It was unclear what would replace Stalin. Only years later was another statue raised on that pedestal, appropriately a gigantic figure of "Mother Armenia."

Destalinization entailed much more than shifts in leadership or greater cultural freedom. It also meant a reduction in the control of the periphery by the center. More competence in local affairs was granted to local officials, so that it was no longer necessary to clear every economic decision in advance with Moscow. Industrial enterprises in Armenia were placed under the local ministry of industry, and local agriculture under the local ministry of agriculture. Decentralization of decision making was a welcome change from Stalinist practice, which had inhibited any initiative from local officials who feared taking responsibility on themselves because of the obvious risks. While limits on local autonomy were maintained by the Khrushchev leadership, the local

Armenian party and state apparatus increased its power significantly and, to a degree, its independence from Moscow. The period of "indirect rule" had begun, and over the next two decades the Armenian elite, like the national elites in many other republics, used this opportunity to solidify its position within the republic, to increase its popular support by making concessions to local nationalism, and to make itself ever more invulnerable to interference from the central government. One Western observer of Soviet nationality policy sums up this development as follows:

> With industrialization, urbanization and the educational explosion, *new national elites* have been emerging since the 50s in numbers which exceed by far those of the old elites. Many have in the meantime moved up into key positions in the economy, the Party and the education system and have become custodians of a new national awareness which attempts to combine fundamental acceptance of the Soviet order with loyalty towards their own nationhood.[5]

The leadership of the Armenian Soviet Republic has been remarkably stable since 1953. Four men have led the party as first secretary—Suren Tovmasian (1953–1960), Zakov Zarobian (1960–1966), Anton Kochinian (1966–1974), and Karen Demirchian (1974–1988). All of them were men who made their careers in the party apparatus within Armenia. Tovmasian and Kochinian came up through the Arutiunov machine, and Kochinian had an unusually long tenure in positions of power. He was first elevated to the Bureau of the Armenian Communist party in 1946, at the age of 33, and remained a member of the highest ruling body in Armenia for twenty-eight years. For fourteen of those years he headed the government of Armenia (1952–1966) as chairman of the Council of Ministers before he became first secretary of the party. Zarobian worked outside Armenia early in his career, but from 1949 he made the steady climb through the ranks within the republic to the top post. Demirchian, the current leader, is of a later political generation. Born in 1932, he began his career as an engineer and party worker only in the post-Stalin period. He was elected to the Central Committee of Armenia's Communist party in 1966, to the bureau in 1972, and finally as first secretary in 1974. Under these top officials the party leadership changed little over the years, and nothing like the massive purges of leaders that took place in Georgia after 1972 occurred in Armenia. This was a tightly woven network of friends and colleagues, even relatives, who managed through their loyalty to Moscow and their protection of one another within Armenia to maintain their positions of authority.

As might be expected, any group of people who have remained in power, largely unchecked from outside, for long periods of time are subject to the temptation to misuse their power. Armenia was, like Georgia, a republic notorious for the use of official position to acquire material wealth. Many publicized cases of corruption, bribery, misuse of state funds and materials, and other instances of the wheeling and dealing that is commonly referred to as "the second economy" helped forge the reputation of the country as somewhat less "Soviet" than Russia proper. It was well known that to live in Armenia it was necessary to have connections in high places, or what is called in Armenian "Kh-ts-b," and to be prepared to use *papakh* (bribery).[6] When Kochinian was removed as first secretary in 1974, rumors were rampant about his great riches, the fabulous furnishings in his home, and his lavish and generous treatment of his friends and relatives. Such rumors, widely believed, were illustrative of the deepening sense in Armenia that corruption was rampant within the political elite. A growing cynicism about the official rhetoric that promised an egalitarian and just society in the near future eroded whatever support the Communists had secured in earlier years.

Social Dynamics: Modernization and National Consolidation

Kremlinology, the study of the rise and fall and relative position of Soviet leaders, reveals only a small part of Soviet reality. Armenia, like the rest of the Soviet Union, continued the process of economic and social modernization, though after 1953 under much less repressive and forced conditions than under Stalin. The republic maintained a respectable rate of industrial and agricultural development; indeed Armenia grew at a somewhat faster rate after 1950 than the USSR as a whole. Whereas in the Soviet Union as a whole per capita income increased 149 percent between 1960 and 1978, in Armenia it rose 162 percent.[7] Per capita industrial production in Armenia did not keep pace with the Soviet average, however: whereas it increased 688 percent in the entire USSR between 1950 and 1978, Armenia managed an increase of only 538 percent.[8] Still, this was a comparatively high rate of growth and contributed to the increasingly industrial character of Soviet Armenia.

One general indicator of socioeconomic modernization is the shift of labor and production from agriculture to industry to services. In the Soviet Union as a whole the percentage of the labor force working in agriculture and forestry dropped from 46 percent in 1950 to 39 percent in 1960 and to 22 percent in 1975. The percentage of workers in industry rose from 27 percent in 1950 to 34 percent in 1960 and 38 percent in 1975.[9] The Armenians started below the Soviet averages in 1950. Fifty percent of Armenian labor worked in agriculture and forestry in the last years of Stalin, but that figure rapidly dropped to 35 percent in 1960 and to 20 percent in 1975.[10] As for industry, Armenian workers made up only 24 percent of the labor force in 1950, grew to 32 percent in 1960, and to 38 percent in 1975, thus reaching the all-Union level and surpassing the levels of Azerbaijan (28 percent) and Georgia (27 percent).[11] By 1975 the number of Armenian workers employed in services had reached 42 percent of the labor force, the same as the other Transcaucasian republics and above the all-Union level (40 percent).[12] When we remember that over 80 percent of Armenians had been peasants in the early 1920s and that by the 1980s peasants make up only 20 percent of the population, we have a clear picture of the movement in Armenia from an agrarian society to an industrial-service one so familiar in advanced Western countries. In 1979 the great majority of Armenians in Armenia (66 percent) lived in cities and towns, while only a third (34 percent) lived in the countryside.[13]

Sixty years of Soviet-style modernization, with all its vicissitudes, turned Armenia into an urban and industrialized country. The provincial towns, which a half century earlier resembled Persian or Turkish provincial towns, now had a modern Western look about them. Nearly three-quarters of the Armenian population (71.3 percent) in 1980 had secondary or higher education.[14] Over 900,000 of them spoke Russian as a second language.[15] Women in Armenia, who made up only 15 percent of the nonagricultural work force in 1928, now constituted 46 percent of the workers and employees in the republic.[16] Well over two-thirds of the doctors and more than half of the teachers in Armenia were women. The patriarchal attitudes of traditional Armenian men were constantly being challenged, though they were far from being overcome. Few women reached the highest political posts in the republic, and the "cultural revolution" did not reach into the household, where men still dominated and women worked the infamous "double shift."

The expectations of many analysts, both Soviet and Western, that modernization would lead to a reduction of ethnic cohesiveness and national consciousness, that the years of cultural and economic offensive against traditional society would accelerate the process of assimilation, have not been borne out by the evidence. Part of the explanation for the tenacity of national awareness, indeed for the recent explosion of overt nationalism, requires a consideration of the process of renationalization that accompanied the process of modernization in the Soviet context. The policy of *korenizatsiia* (nativization) of the 1920s and 1930s, the renewal of nationalism at various points in Soviet history (most notably during the Second World War), and the underlying socioethnic developments led to a reconsolidation of the Armenian nation, to a re-Armenization of the territory of Soviet Armenia.

Within Armenia 89.7 percent of the population was Armenian in 1979. This was the highest concentration of Armenians anywhere in the world, and the highest level that Armenization had reached in the region around Erevan. Armenians in Armenia were increasing faster (23.4 percent) than non-Armenians (9.9 percent).[17] Thus the trend toward Armenization continued. Among the Armenians in Armenia there was a fierce loyalty to the Armenian language: 99.4 percent of Armenians in the republic considered Armenian to be their native language.[18] So strong was the pull of the Armenian language within the republic that ethnic minorities were motivated to learn it. Of the 50,000 Kurds in Armenia, 28,000 used Armenian as their second language, while only 2,800 used Russian. Among the 160,000 Azeris in Armenia, slightly more spoke Armenian (16,164) as their second language than spoke Russian (15,879).[19]

Over a quarter of the Russians living in Armenia were able to use Armenian as their second language.[20]

This is not to say that there were no real threats to the process of national consolidation. Armenia had the lowest percentage of any major Soviet nationality of its native sons and daughters living within its republic's borders. The total number of Armenians in the USSR in 1979 was 4,151,000, but only 2,725,000, or 65.5 percent, of them lived in Soviet Armenia.[21] Armenians were a much more dispersed people than any other in the USSR, except perhaps the Jews, standing at the opposite pole from the Georgians, the most sedentary people in the USSR, 96.1 percent of whom lived in the Georgian republic. Armenians maintained large communities in Georgia (448,000) and in Azerbaijan (475,000),[22] though these communities were declining as more and more Armenians migrated to Armenia. The number of Armenians in the Russian republic, however, was on the rise, as educated young people sought to broaden their career horizons in the central cities of the Soviet Union. Armenians outside Armenia tended to lose their language and to intermarry with members of other nationalities, and the dispersal of Armenians meant that a significant number would lose their ethnicity within a few generations. Yet on the positive side, it should be noted that twenty years earlier, in the census of 1959, the Armenians in Soviet Armenia represented only 55.7 percent of all Armenians in the USSR. In 1979 Armenia's Armenians made up two-thirds of all Soviet Armenians. In-migration and a fairly strong birthrate—Armenia had a higher birthrate than the Slavic and western Soviet nationalities, higher than Georgia's, though not as high as that of the Muslim peoples—meant that there was reason to remain confident that Armenia would continue to consolidate demographically in the coming decades. The very last Soviet census in 1989 revealed that of the 3,304,776 inhabitants of the Armenian Republic, 93.3 percent were Armenians.

The New Nationalism

By the 1960s a volatile mix of political changes, social processes, and intellectual developments gave rise to a phenomenon that had not been seen for a quarter-century in the Soviet Union—dissident nationalism. Instead of promoting assimilation, Soviet development had led to the consolidation of nations. Instead of Russification, there was greater awareness of national cultures and devotion to national languages. Instead of brutal and unalloyed repression of nationalism, in the post-Stalin period there were not only concessions made to nationalism, but often subtle encouragement of it.

It is useful to distinguish between two kinds of nationalism within the Soviet Union: orthodox or official nationalism and unorthodox or dissident nationalism. The former was characteristic of the post Stalinist decades in which the national elites of the Union republics fostered a base of support within the population by making concessions to the ethnic sensitivities of the ethnic majority. Within limits the government permitted the expression of national pride, patriotic sentiments, even a certain amount of glorification of the past. But once nationalist expression transcended the official limits, once it took the form of public protests or political organization, it becomes dissident or unorthodox nationalism. The line between these two kinds of nationalism was not hard and fixed, and it steadily shifted back and forth, from the 1960s through the 1980s.

In Armenia there was a complex interplay of official and dissident nationalism, a sparring between the government and the demands of the most vocal and activist nationalists in the population. Concessions were possible because of the peculiar nature of Armenian nationalism. Compared to Georgian, Estonian, or Ukrainian nationalism, the Armenian equivalent was not nearly as vociferous in its Russophobia. Instead, Armenians directed their hostility toward their traditional enemy, the Turks. Thus Armenian nationalism was less threatening to the Soviet state, especially since it is the Soviet army that stood between Armenia and the ever-present potential threat from Turkey. Indeed, Armenian nationalists repeatedly appealed to the Soviet leadership for redress of the wrongs they believed that Armenians had suffered at the hands of the Turks. Therefore, Armenian nationalism until 1988 was consistent with the long tradition of Russophilia that marked it in the past. Armenians were still a "loyal millet" within the Soviet Socialist world.

The first major outbreak of dissident nationalism within Soviet Armenia occurred on April 24, 1965, when thousands of Armenians in Erevan demonstrated on the fiftieth anniversary of the 1915 massacres. Crowds gathered at the Spendiarian Opera House as a quiet official commemoration was being held inside. The demonstration soon became disorderly; rocks were thrown, and the protesters demanded loudly that the Turks return the Armenian lands to Armenia. The Russians were called on to aid the Armenians in retrieving their irredenta. Government officials were unable to calm the crowd, and even the Catholicos Vazgen I, a man regarded by many as the true head of the nation, had difficulty in restoring some semblance of order. Every year since then, April 24 has been commemorated in Armenia, but now an official, peaceful march is sanctioned. A few years after the demonstration, the Armenian government ordered the construction of an impressive monument to the victims of the genocide. Visitors to Erevan can now climb the hill called Tsitsernakaberd to view the pylon and the eternal flame of the Egherni ensemble; they can pause and listen to the mournful hymns that are played in memoriam. Fifty years after the genocide, a proper memorial to those Armenians lost in 1915 was raised in a resurrected nation of Armenians.

The Soviet government also built other monuments to Armenia's national heroes. Not only was there an equestrian statue of Vartan Mamikonian, the fifth-century defender of Armenian Christianity, but a modest bust of General Antranik, the defender and avenger of Armenians against the Turks. Tolerance of Armenian nationalism increased to the point that at public concerts or poetry readings artists fearlessly proclaimed their national pride and praised without restraint *mer hairenik* (our fatherland), and audiences in turn transformed such evenings into public demonstrations of their patriotism.

Official nationalism extended beyond the government's concessions to Armenian national culture. Within the Armenian republic Armenians were a privileged people, and the Armenian government proved to be host to Armenians from other parts of the Soviet Union and the rest of the world. Armenians unable to receive higher education or good positions in Georgia or Azerbaijan found welcome in Erevan, and occasionally there was even low-level protest from Armenia against mistreatment of Armenians outside the republic. While such protests that affected other Soviet republics were not made public, there was a loud campaign in the press and other media in 1978 against the attacks on Armenians in Lebanon. TASS, Erevan's party paper *Kommunist,* the writer Marietta Shahinian, and even the Catholicos were mobilized to express concern about right-wing Christian and Israeli activities.[23]

The revival of national expression in Armenia and other Soviet republics could not be contained within official bounds, and in the 1970s in particular there were frequent displays of semi-legal and extralegal dissident nationalism. On January 20, 1974, a young woman of twenty-five, Razmik Zograbian, set fire to a portrait of Lenin in Erevan's central square. She announced that she was protesting "the anti-Armenian internal and foreign policy [of the Soviet government] and the repression of Armenian patriots and dissidents."[24] Investigations revealed that the young protester was a member of a secret underground Armenian nationalist party, the National Unity party, a small group of young Armenians who demanded the return of Nakhichevan, Artsakh (Karabagh), and Western Armenia to the Armenians and the formation of a united independent state. This separatist movement had been formed in 1967 by Stepan Zatikian and others, who managed to put out one issue of the illegal journal *Paros* before they were rounded up, tried, and imprisoned in 1974. In prison Zatikian broke with the more moderate members of his party and began to advocate terrorism. On January 8, 1977, a bomb exploded in the Moscow Metro, killing seven and injuring thirty-seven. Two years later TASS announced that Zatikian, along with Hakop Stepanian and Zaven Baghdasarian, had been secretly tried, found guilty of the bombing, and summarily executed.

The separatists of the National Unity party were the most extreme and violent of the dissidents who emerged in Armenia in the late 1960s and 1970s. A human rights group, much more moderate and concerned with broader civil rights issues, was set up in Erevan in April 1977 to monitor Soviet compliance with the Helsinki Agreement of 1975. The five members of this small group made contact with similar groups in Russia, the Ukraine, and Georgia, but by December of that year they had all been arrested.

The two principal issues that agitated Armenians in the Soviet Union in the 1970s and 1980s were the questions of the future of the Armenian language and the concern over Karabagh. Armenia, Georgia, and Azerbaijan were the only three Union republics that had the language of their titular nationality recognized in their constitutions as the official state language. When in the spring of 1978 new constitutions were being approved for the Transcaucasian republics, an attempt was made to eliminate the clause that affirmed that the language of the majority people was the official language. In Tbilisi an estimated 5,000 people marched in the streets in protest, and the government capitulated almost immediately. Similar demonstrations followed in Erevan, and the provision for an official language was preserved in the new constitution. Any attempt to erode the position of the Armenian language was carefully watched by Armenian intellectuals, and the struggle between those who wanted to expand the role of Russian in the national republic and those who wished to preserve Armenian language dominance continued up to the end of the 1980s.

The single most volatile issue among Armenians was without doubt the question of Karabagh, the autonomous region heavily populated by Armenians but lying within Soviet Azerbaijan. Mountainous Karabagh (*Lernaiyin Gharabagh* in Armenian, *Nagorno-Karabakh* in Russian) had been contested between the independent republics of Armenia and Azerbaijan and was formed as an autonomous region within Soviet Azerbaijan shortly after the establishment of Soviet power. At the time, 94.4 percent of the 131,500 people in the district were Armenian (124,000) and only 5.6 percent (7,400) were Azerbaijani. By 1979 Armenians made up just under 76 percent (123,000), a net decline of 1,000 people, and Azerbaijanis had increased five times to nearly 24 percent (37,000).[25] Armenians were fearful that their demographic decline would replicate the fate of another historically Armenian region, Nakhichevan, which had been placed under Azerbaijani administration as an autonomous republic. There Armenians, a significant minority in the 1920s, had declined from 15 percent (15,600) in 1926 to 1.4 percent (3,400) in 1979, while Azerbaijanis, with in-migration and a higher birthrate, had increased from 85 percent (85,400) to nearly 96 percent (230,000).[26] Besides fears of losing their demographic dominance in Karabagh, Armenians were resentful about restrictions on the development of the Armenian language and culture in the region. Though they lived better than Azerbaijanis in neighboring districts, the Armenians saw that their standard of living was not as high as Armenians in the Armenian republic.[27]

Hostile to the Azerbaijanis whom they blamed for their social and cultural discontents, the Karabagh Armenians preferred to learn Russian rather than Azeri in a ratio of eight to one.[28] Beginning in the 1960s, open friction and clashes between the Karabagh Armenians and the Azerbaijanis were reported by dissidents. On March 23, 1975, a Komsomol secretary in Karabagh, Iasha Bablian, read a poem in public in which he said,

Menk arten desank lusni mius eresuh.
hapa ararati mius eresuh yerp guh desnenk?

We have already seen the other side of the moon.
But when will we see the other side of Ararat?

This clear reference to the lost Armenian lands in Turkey was considered an affront to the Karabagh party secretary, Boris Kevorkov, who was in the audience, and Bablian was soon fired from his job and forced to leave Karabagh. Soon after, purges of Armenian intellectuals were carried out in the region. From Armenia the prominent Soviet writer and high Communist official Sero Khanzadian was sent to Karabagh to investigate local conditions. Officially, the press announced that the manifestations of nationalism and "liberalism" in Karabagh should be condemned and that the question of which republic Karabagh should belong to had been settled once and for all.

But the matter did not end there. Khanzadian, who is well known throughout the Soviet Union as the author of the popular historical novel *Mkhitar Sparapet,* decided to write a letter of protest to Leonid Brezhnev. He was incensed by an article in the international Communist journal *Problems of Peace and Socialism* that had attempted to justify the inclusion of Karabagh in Azerbaijan. Khanzadian stated boldly that "the Armenian population of Karabagh has never voluntarily accepted its present status," that indeed they are "detached and separated from their mother country," and that this condition "is in itself an instance of injustice which calls for liquidation." He called on Brezhnev to right this wrong:

> The purely Armenian region of Karabagh, which is part of the frontiers of our mighty state, with its 80% Armenian schools, with its claim for Armenian as the national language, must be incorporated within Soviet Socialist Armenia. The just solution of this problem is bound to be appreciated by other nations as a new accomplishment of the Leninist nationality policy.[29]

No action was taken on the Karabagh question by the Soviet government, evidently for fear of arousing the ire of Muslim peoples.

The rise of nationalism in Armenia cannot be explained simply as a response to a repressive Russification policy by the Soviet state. The emergence of nationalism was the understandable response to the complex, and at times contradictory, processes of modernization and renationalization. Soviet modernization, whatever its considerable benefits to the Armenians, was initially imposed on the people of the smallest Union republic. The revolution came from above and from outside, uprooted the peasantry, eliminated the traditional political and religious authorities, punished all opponents, and forged a new society much like that in developed Western countries—more industrial, more urban, better educated, more mobile. More possibilities existed in life for Armenians than ever before, yet with these new choices also came new dangers of assimilation and of Russification, particularly if one left the republic.

Closely linked with Soviet modernization was the process of national consolidation, the creation of a new Armenian nation in Transcaucasia. After seventy years of Soviet power, more Armenians spoke, read, wrote, argued, and invented in Armenian than ever before. From the "starving Armenians" of half a century ago, from immigrants from around the world, a new nation had been formed, and with that nation had come a new national consciousness and sense of national interest.

However, this new, modern, renationalized Armenia encountered the limits of Soviet reality, for the social and economic modernization and the consolidation of the Armenian nation had not been accompanied by a corresponding political shift toward fuller democracy. The reforms of Khrushchev that ended the terror regime of the Stalin years stopped short of establishing free discussion of vital political, cultural, and economic issues; they stopped short of establishing free trade unions or of permitting real elections of political authorities. In other words, the political power structure had not modernized in a democratic direction, and the same bureaucratic class that rose to power in the Stalin period maintained itself intact. The Soviet Union remained socialist in name only, for without real power in the hands of the producers, without democracy, there could not be the kind of socialism envisioned by Marx and Engels.

Social and economic modernization and renationalization produced a vital, educated people whose expectations about how they wished to live and be governed in the future increasingly clashed with the restrictions imposed by an undemocratic regime. Nationalism was the expression by Armenians of their fears and hopes for that future—fears that in the modern world, in a multi-ethnic state in which they represented only 2 percent of the population, they might be swallowed up by larger nations and lose what is uniquely theirs, and hopes that in the future Armenia would not only preserve the best of its past and culture but regain what has been lost.

If one emphasized the political limits placed on the Armenians, the future for national development might have appeared to be quite dim by the early 1980s; but if one looked at the social vitality of the Armenians in the Soviet Union, a different picture emerged. For all the complaints about economic stagnation and political restrictions, the Armenians had managed, as so often in their past, to develop a degree of autonomy and self-expression that distinguished them from their imperial rulers. The nation had moved from agrarianism and diaspora to industrialization and reunification. While full political control eluded it, this was not an insurmountable obstacle to cultural and material development. One was reminded of the golden age of classical Armenian literature and culture, the fifth century, when Armenia was divided between two great empires, Byzantium and the Sassanians in Iran, and fragmented into more than a dozen little principalities, and yet at precisely that time the Armenians managed to create a new written language and a distinctly national Christian church and lay the groundwork for a durable national tradition.

If history were kinder, the choices for Armenians might have been easier, but, as in the past, the survivors had no choice but to live the life they had been given. Armenians might have preferred another Armenia, another social system, another time or place, but this appeared a utopian dream. There was no Armenia but Soviet Armenia, no Armenian nation but the one that dreamed at the base of Ararat. Its fate in the twentieth century seemed inexorably, unavoidably tied to the Soviet empire. But as that empire itself began to tremble, Armenians acted among the first to accelerate its fall and to construct a new national democracy.

12 Nationalism and Democracy: The Case of Karabagh

On a clear night in the spring of 1988, 20,000 people quietly marched through the streets of Erevan, capital of Soviet Armenia. For six hours they made their way reverently through the dark town, in disciplined columns, quietly chanting "Karabagh, Karabagh." United by an intense feeling of national purpose and encouraged by the new atmosphere of *glasnost,* the Armenian demonstrators calculated that peaceful protests in support of *perestroika* might reunite with its homeland a small piece of Armenian territory separated from their republic. All hopes were placed on Gorbachev and the new reformist leadership in Moscow, which had repeatedly called for redress of the crimes of the Stalin era and greater sensitivity to the problem of nationalities. In the beginning the demonstrators in Erevan flew, not the provocative tricolor of the shortlived independent republic (1918–1920), but the red flag with blue stripe of Soviet Armenia. They carried portraits of Gorbachev, and their defiant yet loyalist placards warned the Moscow leadership that "Karabagh is a test of *perestroika.*" Their mood was buoyant and optimistic, at least for the first weeks of the movement. Only with repeated disappointments at the decision taken in Moscow and Baku (the capital of Azerbaijan), the distorted reporting of the events in the central media, and the consistent refusal to grant the basic demand of the Armenians did the mood in Stepanakert (the capital of Karabagh) and Erevan turn bitter. The enthusiasm for *perestroika* evaporated and was replaced by cynicism and depression. Within months of the first demonstrations, hopes had been dashed, and the Armenian loyalists turned bitterly against Gorbachev. By year's end when the Soviet leader flew to Armenia to comfort the victims of the devastating earthquake of December 7, the hostility directed at him personally completed the estrangement between one of the most consistently pro-Russian peoples of the USSR and the leaders in the Kremlin. In a year marked by stunning international triumphs, his skillful direction of the Nineteenth Party Conference, and the isolation of his principal foe within the Politburo, the crisis over Karabagh—and the subsequent nationalist stirrings in other parts of the USSR—represented the most frustrating political failure for Gorbachev.

Unlike the national struggles in the Soviet Baltic, which have been largely constitutional and free from popular violence, the Armenian-Azerbaijani conflict over the autonomous region of Nagorno-Karabagh (Mountainous Karabagh) has been far more volatile, less manipulable by political authorities, and more subject to rapid and unpredictable escalation. At first seen in the Western press as one more example of nationalist protest against the policies of the Soviet government, and then as the latest expression of an "ancient enmity" between neighboring Muslims and Christians, the Karabagh conflict was in fact from the beginning a layered problem—in part structured by quite separate religious and cultural allegiances, in part based on the uneven social and political development of Armenians and Azerbaijanis. Rather rapidly the more perceptive reporters noted that the demonstrators in Erevan and Stepanakert were not particularly hostile to the central Soviet authorities or anti-Russian in their expression but were acting in the spirit of *glasnost,* in support of Gorbachev's policies of *perestroika* and *demokratizatsiia,* and directing their particular grievance against the neighboring republic of Azerbaijan. A nationalist struggle for recovery of ethnic irredenta was combined with a broader movement for political reform and ecological survival.

Like most conflicts in the Caucasus, the Karabagh problem has a long historical pedigree. A mountainous region at the easternmost edge of the great Armenian mountain-plateau stretching through eastern Anatolia, Karabagh had been in ancient and medieval times part of the kingdom of the Caucasian Albanians. This distinct ethno-religious group, now long extinct, had converted to Christianity in the fourth century and drew close to the Armenian church. Over time its upper classes were effectively Armenized. When the Seljuks invaded Transcaucasia in the eleventh century, a process of Islamization began that resulted in the conversion of the peoples of the plain to the east of Karabagh to Islam. These people, the direct ancestors of present-day Azerbaijanis, spoke a Turkic language and adopted the Shi'i brand of Islam dominant in neighboring Iran. The mountains remained largely Christian, and in time the Karabagh Albanians merged with the Armenians. The central seat of the Albanian church at Gandzasar became one of the bishoprics of the Armenian church, and the memory of the once-independent national religion was preserved in the stature of the local primate, who was called Catholicos.

Semi-independent Armenian princes governed Karabagh, called Artsakh by the Armenians, until the early nineteenth century when the Russian empire annexed the region from Iran. Through the century of tsarist rule Karabagh was linked administratively to the richer areas to the east, to the agricultural plains and to Baku with its oil fields. With the revolution the Karabagh Armenians expressed their interest in joining independent Armenia, but the Azerbaijanis, supported by the Turks, forced the Karabaghtsis to remain in the new state of Azerbaijan. With the defeat of the Ottoman Empire in late 1918 and the establishment of British hegemony over eastern Transcaucasia, the solution to the Karabagh question was again delayed when the British prevented an Armenian annexation of the region.

When the Communists took over Baku and established the Soviet republic of Azerbaijan in 1920, the new government promised that Karabagh would be ceded to Soviet Armenia. Once again, however, expediency overruled ethnic self-determination when the key decisions were taken by the Caucasian Bureau of the Russian Communist party (Kavbiuro) in July 1921. On the third of July the Kavbiuro resolved to attach Mountainous Karabagh to Soviet Armenia. Mysteriously, two days later, the bureau reversed itself "considering the necessity of national harmony between Muslims and Armenians, the economic linkage between upper and lower Karabagh, and its permanent ties to Azerbaijan."[1] The region was to be given broad autonomy with its administrative capital at Shusha. Recently Soviet Armenian historians have insisted that Stalin and the Azerbaijani party leader Nariman Narimanov pressured the Kavbiuro to pass the new resolution. Narimanov, a contemporary Armenian version claims, threatened that if Karabagh did not remain in Azerbaijan, the Azerbaijani Council of Ministers would resign. The Armenian Central Committee protested (July 16, 1921) against the decision, but to no avail. Armenian party leader Aleksander Miasnikov told the First Congress of the Armenian Communist party six months later that "the last session of the Kavbiuro can be characterized as if Aharonian [an Armenian nationalist leader], Topchibashev [a Muslim nationalist], and Chkhenkeli [a nationalist Georgian Social Democrat] were sitting there. Azerbaijan declared that if Armenia demanded Karabagh, then we will not give them kerosene."[2]

For sixty years Karabagh remained an enclave within Azerbaijan, an anomaly in the Soviet system—the only autonomous national region with a majority that was of the same ethnicity as a neighboring Soviet republic yet was not permitted to join that republic. Discontent with Azerbaijani rule grew, as discrimination against Armenian language, culture, and contacts with Soviet Armenia became a persistent practice. Armenians believed that Azerbaijan preferred to invest economically in regions where its own nationality were a majority rather than in Karabagh where 75 to 80 percent of the population was Armenian. Confident that they were culturally superior to the Muslims, the Armenians generally kept themselves separate from Azerbaijani society. Intermarriage between the two peoples was extremely rare. Yet the repressive and dictatorial state during the Stalinist years precluded growing resentments and tensions from leading to open protests. Armenians moved out of Karabagh over the years or migrated to the new capital of the region, Stepanakert. The city of Shusha, once an Armenian cultural center, became almost entirely Azerbaijani. In 1959 Armenians made up 84.4 percent of Karabagh's population. Twenty years later they were just under 76 percent. Azerbaijanis were almost a quarter of the region's population, yet relations between the two communities were hostile. Karabagh Armenians indicated to the census takers that they overwhelmingly preferred Russian as their second language to Azeri.

With the end of the worst excesses of Stalinism and the establishment of a more tolerant regime under Khrushchev, political expression often took the form of ethnic nationalism. Through the 1960s Armenian discontent coalesced around key ethnopolitical issues: the genocide of 1915 at the hands of the Ottoman Turks, the recovery of national cultural themes in literature and art, and the question of Karabagh. The limits of permissible expression were continuously tested through the 1960s and 1970s. In Karabagh itself intellectuals, even prominent members of the Communist party, and ordinary citizens began to petition and write letters to officials. In 1960 rumors spread that Karabagh would be ceded to Armenia, but the Soviet government responded by stating that only Azerbaijan could make such a concession. In 1963, 2,500 representatives of Karabagh signed a petition to Party Secretary Khrushchev complaining of cultural oppression and economic discrimination. Krushchev refused to deal with the issue. Violence broke out in Karabagh, and it was reported that eighteen Armenians were killed and protesters at Erevan State University arrested.

With the fall of Khrushchev in October 1964 and the coming to power of the more conservative Leonid Brezhnev, dissent from orthodox political views crossed more frequently into semi-legal and illegal activities. In April 1965 the first massive demonstrations took place in Erevan to mark the 1915 genocide. The crowds called for "our lands," in Azerbaijan as well as Turkey, to be returned. The following year a small underground dissident group, the National Unity party, called for the unification of Karabagh and Nakhichevan, another historically Armenian region now in Azerbaijan, with Armenia. Unlike Karabagh, Nakhichevan was very largely Azerbaijani in population, and while claims were raised on historic and cultural grounds, the demographic argument could not be made as it could be for Karabagh. In 1977 Sero Khanzatian, a leading novelist and a prominent member of the Armenian Communist party, wrote a strong letter of protest to Brezhnev calling for the incorporation of Karabagh into Armenia. There was no reply. In December of that year demonstrations once again took place in Karabagh.

When Mikhail Gorbachev came to power in March 1985, the gradual expansion of political expression provided an opening for the pent-up political frustrations of Armenians. Three major issues overlapped in a series of rapidly-developing events:

1. the growing concern over the environmental pollution of the Armenian republic and the danger facing the Armenians from the nuclear plant at Metsamor, near Erevan;
2. the perennial issue of Karabagh;
3. the pervasive corruption and stagnation in the republic connected with the long reign of Party Chief Karen Demirchian.

Throughout the Soviet Union concern over the environment has been tied to the growing ethno-nationalist anxiety over the developmental policies of the Soviet government. Since Stalin's First Five-Year Plan the central planners in Moscow have been able to override regional and republic concerns about the cultural or environmental impact of large-scale, rapid industrialization. In some republics, such as Latvia and Estonia, demographic imbalances have resulted from the in-migration of Russian workers to work in the new plants located in their republics. In Armenia the threat of another Chernobyl was matched by the poisoning of the air by a mammoth chemical industry located in the Erevan bowl and the damage done to Lake Sevan by ill-considered engineering projects. In March 1986, 350 Armenian intellectuals urged Gorbachev to close the nuclear plant in Armenia. Those demands were raised again in two demonstrations held in Erevan in October 1987. This time environmental issues were closely connected, as in the Russian and other republics, with patriotic sentiments about the homeland and the defense of Armenian national rights. The environmental movement gave the Armenians a popular, broad-based issue that mobilized significant numbers of people but that did not yet appear to threaten political authority.[3]

At the same time the political leadership in Armenia was being undermined both from within and from above. From the time that Gorbachev came to power—with his campaigns against corruption and stagnation—the days of the Armenian Communist party leadership, unchanged at the highest level since 1974, seemed to be numbered. Central party press reports were highly critical of Armenia, and at the July 1987 plenum of the Central Committee of the Armenian party the party organization was criticized for corruption and favoritism. The first secretary of the Hrazdan district committee, Haik Kotanjian, spoke of the growth of a "shadow economy," of falsification of reports, of bribery, and called for the resignation of First Secretary Karen Demirchian.

Inexplicably Demirchian clung to power, and the Moscow leaders did not decisively intervene. In December 1987 Demirchian gave a perfunctory report to the Central Committee that *Pravda* reported as "somewhat critical, mostly placid; in any event the speaker constantly radiated confidence that everything is going as it should."[4] Just as the meeting was ending, with the party elite rallying around Demirchian, a high party official, S. M. Khachatrian (chairman of the Party Control Commission), insisted on being allowed to speak. Through shouts from the floor and cries of slander, Khachatrian told of bribe-taking in the police apparatus and the punishment of lower-level cadres while high party bosses went unscathed. The police and the courts were working with illegal, underground businesses, and all of this was overlooked by the party. Khachatrian argued that "a tightly knit group of people who owe their posts to the Party" were "opponents of restructuring" and were responsible for these problems. He was followed by Kotanjian, who repeated his charges of July and claimed that the situation had gotten worse in the meantime. *Glasnost* and *perestroika* were making little headway in Armenia. "Just try to figure out from the local newspapers what is going on in Armenia," Kotanjian challenged. "You can't do it. The most urgent, acute problems are hushed up. People are forced to content themselves with rumors. In Erevan, for example, spontaneous demonstrations were held in defense of the environment. There was not a word about them in the press. Irreconcilable disputes flared up at a plenary session of the republic Writers' Union, but the official report distributed to the newspapers was laconically worded."[5] When he requested that Moscow look into the situation, Kotanjian was denounced by the meeting—accused of careerism, pseudopatriotism, political adventurism, and schizophrenia. Twenty-four speakers attacked him, and only the representative from Moscow tried to turn the discussion away from Kotanjian.[6]

Unified around Demirchian the Armenian Communist elite managed for another five months to thwart the exponents of *perestroika* who wanted to reform the party and replace Demirchian with a leader more in the Gorbachev mold. At this moment, with Moscow alienated from the local Communist leaders and a growing discontent with "business as usual" within Armenia, the Armenians of Karabagh took their fate into their own hands. A year earlier, in October 1987, there had been reports of violence against Armenians in Karabagh. Armenian and Muslim villagers in Chardaklu had clashed at about the same time that Heidar Aliev, the highest-ranking Muslim in the USSR and a former party chief of Azerbaijan, was removed from his seat on the Politburo in Moscow. About 1,000 Armenians had responded in Erevan with a public demonstration, just a day after 2,000 to 4,000 had marched to protest pollution. The situation seemed more fluid, the potential for change more palpable.

In January 1988 a petition with tens of thousands of names was sent by the Karabagh Armenians to Moscow, asking for a referendum to be held in Karabagh on the future of the region. Rumors began to spread that Karabagh's status would be changed. While traveling in the United States, several prominent Soviet visitors—including Sergo Mikoyan, son of the late president of the USSR Anastas Mikoyan, and Zori Balayan, correspondent for the prestigious *Literaturnaia gazeta*—indicated that conditions were favorable for a solution to the Karabagh question. It was reported that Gorbachev had appointed a special commission, with thirteen delegates from Karabagh and four from Moscow, to look into the question. On February 13, 1988, the Karabagh Armenians began demonstrations in Stepanakert. Six days later they were joined by mass marches in Erevan. On February 20, the Soviet of People's Deputies in Karabagh voted 110–17 to request the transfer of Karabagh to Armenia. This unprecedented action by a regional soviet (usually nothing more than a rubber stamp "parliament") directly contradicted official party policy.

Through the following week tens of thousands of demonstrators marched in Erevan, bringing the city to a halt. Estimates of the crowds went as high as 1,000,000. Along with the portraits of Gorbachev and Soviet Armenian flags, banners included appeals to Moscow for justice, calls for Armenian unity, and votes of no confidence in the Armenian government. The demonstrations were orderly and well organized, but tensions escalated rapidly in Karabagh. Rumors spread that thousands of Azerbaijanis were marching toward Stepanakert, burning buildings on their way.

The central Soviet government was slow to react and seemed always to be two steps behind the accelerating events. On February 18 Gorbachev offered to hold a special Central Committee meeting to discuss Soviet policy toward the nationalities in general. The Politburo decided against allowing Karabagh to join Armenia, and representatives of the Central Committee, Georgii Razumovskii and Petr Demichev, were sent to Stepanakert to state the official opposition to any attempt to remove Karabagh from Azerbaijan. On February 25 Soviet army troops arrived in Erevan, and that same day four Armenian deaths were reported in Karabagh. The only concession made to the Karabaghtsis was the replacement of longtime party boss Boris Kevorkov, who had been compromised by his subordination to the Azerbaijanis, by Henrik Poghosian, a man who would soon prove to be a popular spokesman for the aspirations of Karabagh Armenians.

As the crisis escalated, Gorbachev intervened personally, calling for calm and reaffirming the proverbial "friendship between the peoples." He met with Zori Balayan and Silva Kaputikian, a well-known poet, and requested that they carry his message to Armenia that a moratorium on demonstrations be declared for one month while the party considered the issue. Balayan later reported that "Gorbachev did not suggest any repressions or the use of force." "He told us to return to Erevan and that he will do everything to put out the fire." Leaving with the impression that "we had reached our goals," Balayan spoke to the crowds in Erevan, the next day, February 27, and the protesters agreed to suspend the demonstrations for one month.[7] Demonstrations, however, continued in Stepanakert.

Obliquely Gorbachev had remarked to Balayan and Kaputikian that they should consider the tens of thousands of Armenians living in Baku. Oblivious to any apparent danger to his countrymen, Balayan had answered "So what?" Suddenly and ferociously, on February 28, riots broke out in Sumgait, an Azerbaijani industrial town of 220,000 on the Caspian. For two days mobs roamed the streets attacking, beating, and killing Armenians. By the time military forces were called in to quell the riots, at least thirty-one people, most of them Armenian, had been killed.

The reasons for the Sumgait riots remain unclear. They appear to have been triggered by a radio report from Baku in which a Moscow prosecutor had stated that two Azerbaijanis, one 16, the other 23, had been killed and others wounded in clashes with Armenians in Agdam earlier in the month. Armenians strongly suspect that local officials allowed the killings to go on for several days with little real effort to stop them. There are even suspicions of premeditation and prior organization. Whatever the reality behind the rumors, the dimensions of the hatred had only been vaguely sensed before Sumgait.

Though the hostilities between the two peoples are colored by their religious differences, they have deeper cultural and social origins. Muslims ruled in eastern Transcaucasia since the Middle Ages, and Christians lived as subject peoples until the coming of the Russians in the early nineteenth century. The great majority of the Azerbaijanis, however, lived in villages, poor, ruled by their khans and beks, subject to the religious instruction of their mullahs. The Armenians of eastern Transcaucasia, on the other hand, living in town, making up what little working class and middle class existed, benefited disproportionately from the economic advances during the century of tsarist rule. The former social dominance of the Muslims ended, and by 1900 Armenians held the key economic and political positions in Baku, Tiflis, and other cities.

Among the Muslims a sense of social inferiority in the changing environment of autocratic capitalism coalesced into anti-Armenian feelings. The Azerbaijanis remember the clashes in 1905 and the "March Days" in Baku, 1918, when Bolsheviks allied with Armenian nationalists brutally put down a Muslim revolt. They fear Armenian claims to what they hold to be Azerbaijani territory (Karabagh and Nakhichevan) and harbor deep-seated resentments toward Armenians whom they consider to have had unfair advantages over Azerbaijanis. The Azerbaijanis' perception that Armenians are a powerful, influential people close to the centers of Soviet power who have imperial designs on Azerbaijani territory were reinforced by the open demands for Karabagh. Velayat M. Kuiev, Azerbaijani writer and deputy director of the Azerbaijan Literary Institute in Baku, told a Western journalist that the Armenians "have better connections," citing Zori Balayan and Abel Aganbegyan, the economist-advisor to Gorbachev. "Lately the Armenian nationalists, including some quite influential people, have started talking again about 'Greater Armenia.'" "It's not just Azerbaijan," he went on. "They want to annex parts of Georgia, Iran, and Turkey." Azerbaijanis have their own claims to Karabagh, said Kuiev: "There is a town there called Shusha which is the native land of many Azerbaijani writers and composers. Practically all of the Baku intelligentsia come from Karabagh." The violence, he concluded, should be blamed on "inflammatory statements" by Armenians. "The Armenians have always been the first to start conflicts."[8]

Armenians had a different historical and social experience. Displaced from their former positions of dominance in Baku during the years of Soviet rule, Armenians either migrated to their own Soviet republic or contented themselves with a subordinate role in the economic and political life of the Azerbaijani republic. Yet they maintained positions of influence based on their skills and education and developed attitudes of superiority to the Muslims. Many Armenians hold that Azerbaijanis are a primitive and savage people, barely civilized by the Soviet experience, and the bloody days in Sumgait only confirmed these views. As a people that suffered genocide at the hands of the Ottoman Turks and the loss of three-quarters of historic Armenia to the Turkish republic, the Armenians were desperate to prevent the loss of "orphaned" Karabagh. Besides the memory of genocide, they remember the clashes with Azerbajanis in 1905, the massacre of 20,000 Baku Armenians in September 1918 by Azerbaijanis, and the perennial grievances over Karabagh.

With Sumgait the first phase of the Karabagh crisis came to an end. The situation in Transcaucasia had been radically altered. The possibility of a peaceful transfer of Karabagh to Armenia now became remote, and attitudes on both sides hardened. The idea that a mediated settlement satisfactory to both parties might be reached was now utopian. Yet for the next few months the Soviet government, as well as the Armenians, sought some kind of "constitutional" solution. With the palpable danger of further violence, many in Erevan urged caution. But the crude attacks in the press on the Armenian demonstrators as "anti-socialist" and the failure to condemn strongly the Sumgait pogrom fueled emotions in Karabagh and Armenia.[9] The party leader and mayor of Sumgait were dismissed, and trials of the leading participants began, but Armenians were angered by official efforts to picture the Armenian and Azerbaijani actions as equivalent. The movement in Erevan split between those who wished to continue the demonstrations and those, like the writers Balayan and Kaputikian, who spoke out against continuation. To many, continuing the protests appeared to challenge Gorbachev and to endanger his policies of reform. The protest leaders decided to cancel a planned demonstration for Saturday, March 26. A peaceful general strike was called instead, but there was little response to it. When Soviet authorities arrested Paruir Hairikian, a longtime dissident who headed the Union for National Self-Determination and advocated an independent Armenia, several demonstrations were held to protest his arrest.

Tensions rose in May when news of the trials of those who had participated in the Sumgait riots reached Armenia. Talekh Izmailov, an Azerbaijani, was sentenced to fifteen years for beating Shahen Sarkisian, an Armenian, to death. Armenians and Azerbaijanis fought one another in the Armenian town of Ararat. Crowds gathered in Baku and Erevan. This time Moscow reacted immediately, sending troops and dismissing the first secretaries of Armenia and Azerbaijan. Demirchian was replaced by Suren Harutiunian, a party functionary who had worked for six years in Moscow and presumably could distance himself to a degree from the political "mafia" that ran Armenia. Kiamran Bagirov was succeeded by Abdul-Rahman Vezirov, a diplomat who had been out of the country for over a decade and therefore was untainted by the corruption in Azerbaijan.

The crisis simmered through the spring while Gorbachev consolidated his personal position within the Kremlin leadership. In March and April he fended off a challenge from more conservative forces who had instigated a letter from a Leningrad woman criticizing the anti-Stalinist campaign. In June he chaired the Nineteenth Party Conference, which endorsed much of his reform program but made little headway on the question of nationalities. On June 15, the Supreme Soviet of Armenia consented to the entry of Karabagh into the Armenian republic, but two days later the Supreme Soviet of Azerbaijan rejected the transfer of Karabagh. Since the Soviet constitution requires the approval of both republics' parliaments in order to change the boundaries of republics, the constitutional solution had reached an impasse.

Demonstrators and a general strike continued in Stepanakert, even after Soviet troops were brought into the city in June, and the local leadership of the movement, the *Krunk* (Crane) Committee, continued to operate. The Karabagh Communist organization voted to raise the issue of Karabagh's transfer to Armenia. The provincial soviet of Karabagh decided to secede from Azerbaijan and noted that the most acceptable action would be to implement the June 15, 1988, decision of the Armenian Supreme Soviet that consented to the entry of Karabagh into the Armenian republic. The Soviet Executive Committee was instructed to take up the question of renaming the region the Artsakh Autonomous Province. That same evening the Azerbaijan Supreme Soviet called this decision unconstitutional and declared that resolution of Karabagh's status was the prerogative of the Azerbaijani republic.[10]

In Erevan as well hunger strikes and round-the-clock demonstrations kept the pressure on the Armenian Supreme Soviet to declare its support for Karabagh's entry into the republic. The Armenian Communist party, largely discredited in the eyes of much of the population, was losing authority to the growing movement in the streets, which while focusing on Karabagh also raised the issue of greater democracy in Armenia. Harutiunian's time was limited, and the difficulty of reforming the corrupt party apparatus seemed insurmountable. When Armenian delegates returned to Erevan from the Nineteenth Party Conference, they first appeared on Erevan TV and then went directly to a rally on the square in front of the opera. Thousands were present, and a stormy debate ensued. The crowd was dissatisfied with Harutiunian and the other delegates for not raising the Karabagh issue in Moscow. The "Strike Committee" called for a general strike and demanded the immediate resolution of the Karabagh question, transfer of the trials in Sumgait to the USSR Supreme Court, and full information about the reported poisoning of female workers in a garment factory in Masis.[11] The crowd discussed closing down the railroad station and the Zvartnots airport. Demonstrators marched to the airport and occupied the buildings. Airplanes landed but could not take off. With the airport effectively in the hands of the demonstrators, soldiers and police moved into the airport (July 5) and began beating people until the airport was cleared. The marchers moved back toward Erevan and were caught between the airport and another column of soldiers. More beatings ensued, and one young man was shot when he tried to take a picture. Troops closed off the opera square. Thirty-six people were hospitalized.

The break between the crowds and the officials was complete. Rallies were held wherever possible. On July 9 troops again closed off the opera square, and the police suggested that the square near the Hrazdan Stadium be used for rallies. The organizers refused, and two days later a massive rally was held before the Matenedaran, the manuscript library at the foot of Lenin Street. Speakers urged the people not to go back to work, at least not until after July 18, the date set for the session of the USSR Supreme Soviet on the Karabagh question. The Armenian delegation to the Nineteenth Party Conference was sharply attacked for not standing up for national interests.[12]

The Armenian Communist party faced the most serious challenge to its authority since 1921, a challenge from its own mobilized people and their chosen leadership, the Karabagh Committee. Made up of nationalist intellectuals, many of them members of the Communist party, the Karabagh Committee tried to guide the mass movement in peaceful and disciplined actions. Ashot Manucharian, an assistant principal of a secondary school, soon emerged as a leading figure.[13] He and his colleagues were deeply critical of the existing state/party regime in Armenia. At a rally in mid-July, committee member Vano Siradeghian asked the crowd rhetorically, "To what state can the top-official gangsterism that has been ruling this country for seventy years now, and Great Russian stupidity, bring us? This is not just a tragedy for our country, it's a tragedy for the whole world."[14]

The Karabagh Committee called for democratization, social justice, economic reform, and national sovereignty. Referring to itself as the "Popular Armenian Movement," the committee announced its objective as "a sovereign Armenian republic, in the framework of a Soviet confederation, and based on *de facto* autonomy and respect for equality between the republics." On the eve of the Supreme Soviet meeting the committee called for the reelection of party and trade union committees.[15]

With no solution possible on the Caucasian level, all attention focused on the meeting of the presidium of the USSR Supreme Soviet on July 18. Much of the session was broadcast on television, and the whole country had the opportunity to watch the first open discussion of the nationality question. G. M. Voskanian, vice-chairman of the presidium of the USSR Supreme Soviet and chairman of the presidium of the Armenian Supreme Soviet, spoke on the history of Karabagh, mentioning that it was Stalin who changed the original intent of the Kavbiuro to have Karabagh and Nakhichevan in Armenia. He noted that if the resolution to prevent Karabagh's entry into Armenia is adopted, "it will cause both pain and disappointment among the Armenian people, since the entire Armenian people had expected that, in examining this question, we would be guided by the directives in the party conferences' resolutions." He called for a compromise.

Gorbachev, who was presiding, challenged Voskanian: "What do you see as a compromise? I think we must find a decision that does not infringe on either the Armenian or the Azerbaijani people and does not put them in a situation in which it can be said that one side won while the other side was defeated."

The chairman of the Azerbaijan presidium, S. B. Tatliev, noted that 200,000 Armenians in Baku had signed a petition expressing alarm over recent events. "The idea of detaching the Nagorno-Karabagh Province from the Azerbaijan republic is not justified politically, economically or juridically," he went on. "The separation of Nagorno-Karabagh from the remaining part of the entire Karabagh zone and from our entire republic would mean the deliberate destruction of a historically evolved single complex." He requested that "all necessary measures be taken to put an end to the disturbances and other unlawful actions in the Nagorno-Karabagh Autonomous Province and that the full range of powers be used to introduce order there."

The new party chief of Karabagh, Poghosian, dissented from the views of his party superiors: "The past 65 years have been years of oppression of the province's Armenian population." Karabagh is seven times closer to the Armenian border than Nakhichevan is to the Azerbaijan border. There are no close economic ties between mountainous and lowland Karabagh, though Karabagh is in general dependent on Azerbaijan. Poghosian's appeal was echoed by academician Viktor Hambartsumian, who attacked the leadership of Azerbaijan for not taking any serious steps toward improvement.

For the Armenians the hero of the day was Sergei Hambartsumian, the rector of Erevan State University, who boldly stated that a historical injustice had been committed, and that part of the Armenian people, against their will, found themselves in an autonomous formation that was created outside Soviet Armenia. He praised the mass movement of the Armenians and their faith in the victory of reason and justice, though he condemned the events at Zvartnots airport, work stoppages, and hunger strikes. Gorbachev attacked Hambartsumian for not having "a hint of compromise" in his speech. Hambartsumian replied: "We fear another Zvartnots airport incident. We fear exploding bombs, weapons and the like. We have to fear all this." Gorbachev warned against escalation: "There are just as many Azerbaijanis living in Armenia as there are Armenians in Nagorno-Karabagh. Well, are we going to create an autonomous province there, too?" When V. A. Petrosian, head of the Armenian Writers' Union, called Sumgait an attempt at genocide, Gorbachev bristled: "You know what that word implies, the weight it carries. You are making accusations that you will regret for the rest of your life."

More moderate was the position of Harutiunian, the first secretary of Armenia, who called for compromise solutions: "Such options might take the form of placing Nagorno-Karabagh under the temporary jurisdiction of central Union agencies or the Russian republic, transforming the province into an autonomous republic, or sending to Nagorno-Karabagh special authorized representatives of the Central Committee of the Communist Party of the

USSR, the USSR Council of Ministers and the Presidium of the USSR Supreme Soviet."

Gorbachev sided with the hardliners, like Politburo veteran Shcherbitskii, who declared that the situation was becoming "anti-Soviet" and giving comfort to foreigners. Coming down hard on the Armenians, Gorbachev said that the events around Karabagh are "a cunning maneuver on the part of those who want to impede restructuring, a maneuver designed to distract people from the problems that in fact must be solved in these republics: personnel questions and the struggle against negative phenomena, the shadow economy and favoritism." He opposed territorial changes, though he acknowledged that mistakes had been made sixty-five years ago when the state was formed. He praised Vezirov and said "we are hearing more self-criticism from the representatives of Azerbaijan and less from the representatives of Armenia." But his constant theme was the danger presented by nationalist conflicts to *perestroika* and democratization:

> In general, to put it bluntly, we are going through a time of trials. Will restructuring hold up in this situation? Restructuring demands the utmost solidarity of people, but we are being offered discord and national distrust. Restructuring demands democratization and openness, but here we see, under the banner of democratization, shameless pressure on labor collectives and on the population of the republics by irresponsible individuals, and even pressure on bodies of power, including the Presidium of the USSR Supreme Soviet. . . . Victory in this question can only be a common victory. . . . We regard any isolation of the Armenian population of Azerbaijan from Armenia in the sphere of culture, education, science, information and spiritual life as a whole to be inconceivable. Azerbaijanis living in Armenia should be surrounded with the same kind of attention, in exactly the same way and in equal measure.

The resolution of the presidium passed: Armenia's request that Karabagh be joined to Armenia was rejected on constitutional grounds. It was acknowledged that the rights of the Karabagh people had been violated, and the Supreme Soviet was to send representatives to Karabagh to work with the representatives of Azerbaijan and Armenia.[16]

The "constitutionalist phase" of the struggle was over. The party's position was cool and pragmatic, intended at calming the situation in the short run more than arriving at a permanent or a "just" solution. The first imperative was to prevent a repetition of Sumgait, and certainly the effect of any resolution on Soviet Muslims was considered. But for Armenians such "even-handed" treatment was grossly insensitive to the injustices they had suffered from the Azerbaijanis. Both in Stepanakert and Erevan Armenians greeted the Moscow resolutions with hostility and depression. Much of their anger was focused at Gorbachev and his failure to assess the Sumgait events morally and politically. Rallies were held around the clock, and the Karabagh Committee declared the Moscow resolution to be unacceptable.

Many Soviet intellectuals sympathized with the Armenian position, and though they so stated in public addresses (e.g., Iurii Afanas'ev on his visit to Ann Arbor in October 1988) they were unable to express their support in print. When asked why he had not reported on the Karabagh events, the activist editor of the popular Moscow magazine *Ogonek,* Vitalii Korotich, told a Spanish interviewer:

> In my twin capacity as an honest journalist and a responsible politician, I find myself in a professional quandary. . . . On three occasions I sent correspondents there and they all brought me material that made it obvious that one side was right and the other was not. . . . Whatever I do, I prompt a reaction by the Armenians against the Azerbaijanis, or vice versa. . . . You see, I could repeat what other newspapers write in articles calling for internationalist friendship, but such calls will not be heeded. . . .

Later in the interview he made it clear that he had been appalled by the events in Sumgait and said that "the struggle for democracy is a struggle against Sumgait."[17]

After the July session of the Supreme Soviet Moscow began to implement its solution to the Karabagh crisis along two lines: the "restructuring" of Karabagh itself and the containment of the growing nationalist opposition in Armenia. On July 20, the outspoken dissident Paruir Hairikian was stripped of his citizenship and expelled from the Soviet Union. The most fervent advocate of Armenian separatism, Hairikian had, in fact, not been a primary force in the Karabagh movement but had been marginalized by the leaders who rejected his call for independence. Two days later a long article in *Izvestiia* attacked the Karabagh Committee as a subversive organization:

> Their primary aim was to seize power through destabilizing the economy and public life of Armenia. Taking advantage of the fact that the previous leadership of the Armenian Communist Party Central Committee had let the initiative slip from its hands and had yielded its positions step by step, the members of the "committee" created ramified organizational and political structures. "Karabagh sections" are operating at virtually every enterprise, institution and educational establishment, and in a number of cases they have crushed Party organizations, councils of labor collectives, and management. Local police are collaborating with the Committee.[18]

The bureau of the Armenian party noted that the danger of the Karabagh Committee to primary party committees had not been perceived and ordered the activity of the committee to be investigated, especially the behavior of Communists who were drawn into it.[19]

While the Armenians had not achieved all of their goals in Karabagh, the actual policy of the Soviet state benefited them far more than the Azerbaijanis. It was widely conceded that Azerbaijan had discriminated culturally and economically against the Armenians in the region. Following the July decision, the central government sent Arkadii Volskii to Karabagh as its representative with extraordinary powers. Azerbaijani officials lost their authority in the region, and from July until a more radical decision was taken in January 1989 a gradual but steady separation of the region from Azerbaijani control was implemented. *De facto* Azerbaijani sovereignty over Karabagh ended, even as the enclave remained within the Republic of Azerbaijan. Both Volskii and First Secretary Harutiunian met with members of the Karabagh Committee to appeal for calm and time to find a more permanent solution to the Karabagh conflict.

Yet, with the most fundamental decisions about the eventual disposition of Karabagh postponed, the hostilities between Armenians and Azerbaijanis intensified. Azerbaijani refugees from Armenia drifted into Karabagh, and local Armenians feared that an attempt was being made to increase the Muslim population in the area.[20] In mid-September, a busload of Armenian students taking food supplies to Stepanakert was surrounded in the village of Khodzh-aly by Azerbaijanis who attacked them with rocks and gunfire. Armed Armenians from Stepanakert then went to Khodzhaly, and the ensuing battle could only be halted by the intervention of police and internal security (MVD) troops. Demonstrations started up again, and a state of emergency *(osoboe polozhenie)* was declared in Karabagh. Curfews were imposed, and all public gatherings banned. MVD troops cleared the streets.

In Erevan sympathy strikes were organized, and 1 million people gathered to hear Hrant Voskanian, the president of the Armenian republic, promise that officials would consider calling another meeting of the Armenian Supreme Soviet to discuss annexation of Karabagh.[21] The crowd decided to hold a general strike until the meeting was held. On September 22, troops and armed vehicles were deployed in the center of the city, even as the demonstrations continued. In an extraordinarily frank broadcast, a television correspondent reported that the local Communist authorities had lost control in Armenia and that the initiative was with the Karabagh Committee.[22]

Soviet news reports, usually hostile to the Karabagh movement, revealed a growing militance among its leaders. Siradeghian told the crowds: "The chief mistake made on February 26 was to end the strike from a position of strength. . . . We are not a whining nation but a fighting, belligerent one. . . . We must stop holding explanatory talks and speak only from the position of strength given us by our unity." Another committee member, Levon Ter Petrosian, called for Armenian military units in the republic. And Samvel Georgisian dramatically announced that Armenia stands "on the brink of destiny, and from now on let us not hear the word 'comrade'. . . . Moscow's stooges cannot rule Armenia, they are the enemy's local staff. . . . It has long been known that Moscow's interests are at variance with our interests. This means that we must openly declare war. . . ." Manucharian condemned the deployment of troops in Erevan: "Those who are sending the Army here again should know that the Armenian people regard that army as a colonial force."[23]

For another two months the Karabagh movement and the Soviet authorities coexisted uneasily. Demonstrations and strikes occurred under the eyes of the troops. At the same time soldiers were called upon to protect refugees and to supply food to isolated villages.[24] Agdam, an Azerbaijani provincial center near Karabagh, received 177 Azerbaijani refugee families, about 1,000 people, from Stepanakert. It was reported that Azerbaijani villages in Karabagh were not being supplied with food, and food convoys under military guard had to be organized from Azerbaijan proper. At the same time Armenian refugees from Shusha fled to Stepanakert.[25]

In late November the situation began to deteriorate rapidly. Rallies were held in Baku when it was reported that a cooperative formed at the Kanaker Aluminum Plant in Armenia had begun the construction of a workshop in the health resort of Topkhana in Karabagh without the knowledge of the Azerbaijani republic agencies. On November 22, at about 5 p.m., crowds in the large Azerbaijani city of Kirovabad surrounded the city's party committee (Gorkom) building. The Gorkom called for help, and soldiers arrived. They cordoned off the building, but were insulted and threatened. Stones were thrown. A grenade exploded, and three soldiers were killed, others wounded. That evening more than seventy attempts were made to set houses and cars on fire or to "stage pogroms" in Armenian houses or apartments. The local police did nothing; the local party had lost control; and the army was forced to intervene, confiscating firearms and arresting 150 people.[26] A state of emergency was declared in Baku, Kirovabad, and Nakhichevan.

Nearly a year of Armenian protests and demands for Karabagh had, by the fall of 1988, mobilized Azerbaijanis to defend what they considered the territorial integrity of their republic. Protests were sporadic and violent until late November when they took on a more organized, mass form in Baku. Resentment about the silence of the central newspapers in reporting Azerbaijani viewpoints led the Baku printers on November 25 to refuse to print that day's *Izvestiia* and other Soviet papers.[27] Crowds gathered outside Government House, 20,000 during the night, 500,000 during the day. Suddenly, as if on cue, the crowd would chant "Karabagh." In Lenin Square bonfires burned. Though the square was completely surrounded by soldiers carrying submachine guns, the rally organizers and hunger strikers maintained a vigil through the night. The hunger strikers demanded transfer of the Sumgait case to Sumgait, arrest of the nationalist committee in Karabagh (Krunk), and the end of the construction in Topkhana.[28] The demonstrators called for the implementation of the decision of July 18, 1988—retention of Karabagh within Azerbaijan (but not in the *pro forma* way it had been retained) and protection for Azerbaijanis in Armenia. In the square people wore red headbands with "Karabagh" written on them, others wore labels from "Karabakh" cigarette packs on their lapels. Green banners of Islam and even portraits of Ayatollah Khomeini were occasionally raised.[29] An unofficial organization, Varlyg, raised issues of ecology and the inattention to questions of the native language and history. Another organization called Ana (Mother) was formed by women to support the demands of the Azerbaijani young people, but to counsel patience and return to work.[30]

In general the Azerbaijani movement was led by workers, rather than intellectuals, and expressions of hostility toward the privileged could be heard. One of its most influential leaders was the lathe operator Neimat Panakhov, a principal spokesman on Lenin Square. In Azerbaijan as in Armenia, Karabagh was the initial point around which other social and cultural issues swirled. Among the complaints in Baku were claims that Azerbaijani workers, even those with families, were not given apartments when they came into towns from the countryside and were forced to live in dormitories. The targets of these resentments were the relatively privileged Armenians. As one newspaper reported, "It used to be that men coming from outlying areas to work at the plant would live in dormitories and their wives and children couldn't even get residence permits to join them. . . . Gradually, other problems snowballed as well. There was a demand that those responsible for this situation be found. And found they were—in the person of representatives of the Armenian nationality, who were said to be undeservedly using things that there weren't enough of for the Azerbaijanis themselves. . . . In that situation, a spark was enough to set off an explosion." Panakhov managed to have an audience with the new party chief Vezirov and to convince him to release more than eighty apartments to workers.[31]

An article in *Pioner Azerbaidzhana* applauded the school children who left school to join the rallies: "Classes have been canceled in most Baku schools. Groups of youngsters run to the square, not wanting to fall behind their parents or their older brothers and sisters. These wonderful children-patriots' anger, anxiety and resolve and the innocent and serene looks on their faces—all of which seem not in keeping with their ages—touch the heart, and we say with pride: 'Well done!'. . . . When the homeland is in trouble, when encroachments are made on its land, the descendants of Babek, Kyor-ogly, Dzhevanshir, Nabi and Khadzhar are prepared for struggle and exploits in the name of the people."[32]

With news of disturbances in Azerbaijan, the Armenian Supreme Soviet broke off its session. A round-the-clock rally was taking place in the opera square. People demanded that the deputies resume their session. On November 24, some deputies of the Armenian Supreme Soviet gathered at the opera and took up matters that remained on the abrogated session's agenda, including amendments to the USSR Constitution. The Presidium of the Supreme Soviet called the opera meeting unlawful and announced that the session would be resumed after the situation was normalized. The new violence in the countryside and the militance of nationalist leaders on both sides stimulated a new flood of refugees at the end of November and the beginning of December.[33] Armenians began to move from Azerbaijan to Armenia, many of them settling in Leninakan, Kirovakan, and other towns of northern Armenia.

On the eve of his leaving for his first visit to the United States, Gorbachev warned publicly that nationalist conflicts threaten *perestroika*. "We are one family, we have a common home," he said, "and we have accomplished much thanks to concerted effort."[34] He appealed for an end to confrontation: "The principle of a solution is: There should be neither 'victors' nor 'vanquished,' and neither side should bear a grudge. . . . [Redrawing the boundaries] is impermissible in current conditions. . . . At the same time, one cannot justify the position of Azerbaijan's former leadership, which committed numerous deviations from the Leninist principles of nationalities policy with respect to the Nagorno-Karabagh Autonomous Region."[35] At the same gathering in Moscow, Arkadii Volskii, the representative of the Central Committee and the presidium in Karabagh, reported to the deputies that the economy of the region was in

> an extremely neglected state, especially in the social area, with respect to the satisfaction of people's priority needs for housing, water and power supply, medicine and food. There is no excuse for the individuals who brought this mountainous area, where good, hard-working people live, to such a state. . . . A start has been made on overcoming the estrangement and artificial alienation of the Armenian part of the population from Armenia in the sphere of language, culture and education. . . .

Volskii was disturbed that the economic and social improvements had not lessened ethnic tensions:

> Before leaving for this session, we watched a television broadcast of an essentially anti-Armenian rally that has been going on in Baku in recent days. To say that it made a painful impression tells less than half the truth! It is a horrible spectacle that insults our world view. . . . I cannot fail to mention the openly irresponsible behavior of the mass news media—in both Azerbaijan and Armenia. For example, Armenian television offered the following assessment of events in Baku. I quote: "These rallies show the whole gist, the whole psychology of the Azerbaijanis. There is nothing in their hearts but atrocities and killing." Is it really possible to speak of an entire people in this way? The activity of Baku television also cannot be called anything but political blindness, if not worse. In recent days, it has taken the same path. A steady stream of threats and insults addressed to the Armenians pours from the screen. They balk at nothing.[36]

Neither appeals to reason nor piecemeal reforms were adequate to stop the escalating violence in Transcaucasia. Incidents broke out daily. Near the railroad station in Baku, a crowd of 1,500 people tried to beat up an Armenian. Troops intervened in incidents in various parts of the city; 417 people and sixty-three vehicles were detained.[37] The army was used to remove Azerbaijanis from Armenia for their safety. Some had fled into the mountains. A government commission for the refugees in the Caucasus, to be headed by V. E. Shcherbin, began operation in early December. And then nature intervened.

On December 7, at 11:41 a.m., an earthquake of the magnitude of 6.9 on the Richter scale hit northwestern Armenia, destroying large parts of Leninakan, Kirovakan, and almost the entire towns of Spitak and Stepanavan. A shallow earthquake with several heavy aftershocks of 5.8 and 5.2, it was particularly devastating to newly built, prefab, and concrete-slab buildings. At first it was thought that 50,000 had perished, then the toll estimate rose to 100,000, until it settled at about 25,000. Hundreds of thousands were homeless. With Gorbachev in New York and the international press spotlight on him, his decision to return home immediately carried the world's attention toward Armenia. Offers for aid poured in. A commission of the Politburo in Moscow, headed by Prime Minister Nikolai Ryzhkov, traveled to Armenia to coordinate rescue operations. The Karabagh Committee organized its own efforts at aid from headquarters in the Writers' Union in Erevan. A fierce competition between the official and unofficial rescue efforts began, and in the chaos of the first days the Karabagh Committee made its own appeals to prominent Armenians, like Charles Aznavour and Governor George Deukmejian of California, to organize relief efforts in Europe and America. In reality the Karabagh Committee had become a second government in Armenia, one with more popular support and credibility than the Communist party and the Soviet government. If one accepts Lenin's definition, a revolutionary situation existed in Armenia: the old rulers could no longer rule in the old way, and the ruled were no longer willing to be ruled in the old way.

On December 10, the official day of mourning for the victims of the Armenian earthquake, Gorbachev arrived in Erevan. That same day hundreds of women, reacting to broadcasts calling for adoption of Armenian orphans by people in other parts of the Soviet Union, gathered before the Writers' Union. However well-meaning the appeals, they had failed to take into account a deep-seated fear among Armenians about the loss of their orphans, a fear located in memories of the loss of children to Turks, Kurds, and Arabs during the genocidal marches of 1915. With the agreement of the military commandant of Erevan, Manucharian spoke to the women and announced an agreement with the Soviet authorities not to remove any orphans from the republic. That evening a new military commander was appointed in Erevan, and the leading members of the Karabagh Committee were arrested.[38] The government had evidently decided to use the crisis as an opportunity to end the operations of the Karabagh movement and to restore authority to the ruling party.

While still in Erevan Gorbachev gave an interview, castigating the Karabagh movement:

Residents of Armenia were standing on the street. I stopped, and we had a good conversation. The people were all worried, very worried. They were taking it hard. I shared with them the fact that I had been simply astounded by what I had seen, by the magnitude of the disaster that had befallen people. And suddenly, right here in Erevan, I was asked: What kind of relations are we going to have, what kind of dialogue are we going to establish with the unofficial organizations? Again, the subject was Karabagh. You know, I told them just what I thought, in rather sharp language, perhaps. First of all, I said to them: Stop. Look at the calamity that has befallen both the Azerbaijanis and the Armenians, look where they are being pushed and at the point they have already reached—blood is being spilled. Now so great a disaster has struck that the whole country, the whole world, is stunned by what happened in Armenia, by what has befallen the Armenian people. And here is a person in the capital of Armenia asking me what kind of dialogue we are going to set up with unofficial organizations. Only a person devoid of all morality could do such a thing. . . .

I think that there is such a thing as a Karabagh problem. The problem has roots, and it has become exacerbated because at a certain stage the former Azerbaijani leadership took an incorrect attitude toward the Karabagh population, an attitude that was not in the spirit of Leninist traditions and sometimes was simply inhuman. This offended people. We condemn this.[39]

A new stage had been reached in the Karabagh crisis. The leadership in Moscow had decided that repression was necessary, ironically, to preserve the movement toward democratic reforms. As Gorbachev told a group in Erevan, "We are at the brink of a precipice. Any further, one more step, and we plunge into the abyss. . . . We agreed to let both sides think about how to calm Nagorno-Karabagh for a while." The use of martial law ended the worst outbreaks of violence temporarily and gave the regime time to rebuild its support. Prominent leaders, like the head of the Armenian Chruch, Vazgen I, were recruited as spokesmen supporting the government. When Ryzhkov met with Vazgen I, the Catholicos reported that "everywhere in Armenia people are expressing feelings of great respect for M. S. Gorbachev, who, putting off all other matters, came to Armenia, visited the disaster areas and gave moral support to all the people. It is impossible to forget this."[40]

By January 1989 the Karabagh movement had come to a temporary halt, with the positions of the government and the committee completely opposed. Gorbachev was firm in his refusal to change republic borders but equally committed to reform for Karabagh. Nineteen eighty-eight was the year he had been forced to recognize the nationality issue as one of the most serious on the Soviet agenda. In January 1989 he told a meeting of intellectuals that "at some stage we began to rest on our laurels, believing that all questions had been resolved. There was even a proposal to begin the virtual fusion of nations. At one time I managed only with great difficulty to withstand pressure from certain men of science who were trying to force this dangerous directive into the Party Program now in effect. . . ." He indicated that various solutions were possible, but nothing that leads to "the kindling of nationalistic passions" or "national isolation and exclusiveness." He favored the "national" but not the "nationalistic."[41] Most importantly, he would use whatever means at his disposal to preserve and enhance the prestige and power of the Communist party.

Before his arrest in early January, Ashot Manucharian gave an interview from hiding to L'Express and wrote up his own account of what had happened since the earthquake. He noted his surprise that foreign news reports referred to the Karabagh movement as "narrowly nationalistic." "In reality," he explained, "starting from the question of Karabagh, the thrust of the movement quickly broadened into a democratic, anti-mafia campaign. And that is the reason for the fierce attacks on our Committee. The point is that the Soviet mafia is found within the political power structure." The mafia survives because of the principle of appointing officials from above and would be eliminated by real democratic choice.[42] For the Karabagh Committee nothing short of full democratization would be acceptable.

In mid-January 1989 Karabagh was placed under a special administration. A committee, chaired by Volskii and directly responsible to the central Soviet government, replaced the local soviet. This interim solution to the Karabagh issue only dealt with one of the demands of the Armenians—the end of the sixty-five-year-long Azerbaijani domination of Karabagh. The issues of full democratization remained. Repression of the democratic movement in Armenia only further radicalized the population, and, as in Poland, the government was eventually compelled to open a dialogue with the popular forces for reform.

13 Looking toward Ararat: The Diaspora and the "Homeland"

In their discussions of the historical roots and evolution of nationalism, theorists and historians of national movements have for the last few decades been emphasizing the constructed nature of "the ethnic" and the importance of intellectual and political interventions in the process of nationality formation. If the application of a less essentialist approach to nationality has been helpful in historicizing the making of nations even when the familiar ingredients of linguistic and religious culture, shared history, and territory are present, how much more inventive must the role of intellectuals, activists, and politicians be in the creation of self-conscious diaspora communities.

Two meanings of diaspora immediately come to mind. As a simple demographic declarative, diaspora can refer to anyone living outside their putative "homeland." Diaspora, Webster tells us, comes from the Greek term *diaspeirein*, to scatter, which in turn is related to *speirein*, to sow. Originally it referred to the dispersion of Greek communities outside Hellas and of the Jews from Palestine. Attributed to a self-conscious community, diaspora can be narrowed to refer only to communities formed to maintain a relation, whether real or imagined, with their homeland. Millions of people live outside their original ethnic homelands (some 60 million in the Soviet Union alone and most of the American population), but diaspora in this stricter sense means more than just exiles or emigrants and refers to those uprooted and resettled who continue to hold on to some reference to their land of origin. The idea of an *original* "homeland," though not necessarily with the legally constituted "homeland" of the present, is fundamental to the process of forming cohesive and conscious diaspora communities. Whether a relationship with the existing "homeland" is maintained or has been broken, whether that relationship and that "homeland" exists only on the level of myth, the acceptance or rejection of that presence very often becomes a key element in the construction of the diaspora community. A sense of loss, a longing to return, or an acceptance of the impossibility of return can all contribute to the construction of a diaspora community.

Though diasporas, formed as the result of conquest and forced migration, existed long before nation-states, the ubiquity of modern states largely based on core ethnicities has had profound effects on diasporas. With the most ancient diasporas—the Greek, Jewish, and Armenian—the problematic relation with nation-states has led to a pull in two directions: return and merger with the homeland, on the one hand; self-definition and distance, on the other. From another direction diasporas have influenced nation-states. The dramatic military and political formation of nation-states in Europe in the nineteenth century often originated with exiled intellectuals and diaspora political movements, and in their creation the new states both contained dispersed communities of other peoples and left new diasporas of their compatriots outside the new polity.

As difficult as the construction of coherent and self-conscious diaspora communities may be, the conceptualization and formation of the larger "imagined community" of the whole diaspora is even more problematic. Despite its evident fractures and formlessness, the diaspora, even in its most inchoate and amorphous form, has been available as a refuge for the exile and the refugee, as a political and economic resource for those left in the homeland. Itself an act of imagination and intellectual and political construction, the diaspora, like the nation-state, has at key moments taken on a political salience that states have had to acknowledge. Khachig Tololyan, editor of the new journal *Diaspora,* has called diasporas "exemplary communities of the transnational moment" in history. Even as peoples struggle for nationhood both in their homelands and diasporas, existing nation-states are beginning to "confront the extent to which their boundaries are porous and their ostensible homogeneity a multicultural heterogeneity." In the present context, "transnational communities are sometimes the paradigmatic Other of the nation-state and at other times they are its ally, lobby, or even, as in the case of Israel, its precursor."[1]

Armenians speaking of the diaspora adopt the ancient Hebrew word *galut* into their *gaghut* (colony) and the Greek *speirein* into *spiurk* (diaspora) or *spiurkahaiutiun* (Armenian diaspora). Dispersion and exile have been a near constant in the two-and-a-half millennia history of the Armenians. Only once in their past was the entire Armenian plateau unified under a single Armenian ruler, and the division of the plateau by empires to the west (Roman, Byzantine, Ottoman) and to the east and south (Iranian, Arab) resulted in frequent dispersions of parts of the population. After the Seljuk invasions of the eleventh century, Armenians in significant numbers moved north into the Georgian kingdoms and south to form eventually a diaspora principality, later kingdom, of Cilician Armenia. The success of this migration and longevity of the Kingdom of Lesser Armenia transformed an exile realm into part of what many Armenians regarded as their core territory. From the disappearance of Armenian polities in the late Middle Ages, Armenians living outside the Armenian plateau benefited from greater mobility and relative security and prosperity (in Safavid Iran, Muscovite and Petrine Russia, Europe, India, Southeast Asia) and formed merchant networks, printed the first Armenian books and newspapers, and through the efforts of clerical scholars (most importantly, the Mekhitarist fathers in Venice and Vienna of the eighteenth and early nineteenth centuries) helped to generate a new national consciousness. For Armenians the diaspora was the source of wealth and ideas that stimulated organization and self-awareness within the homeland.[2]

When the Armenian Question was first raised in international diplomatic circles just over 100 years ago, Armenians, neither in the diaspora nor in the Ottoman and tsarist empires, had yet formulated any political consensus on their future political existence. With no general agreement on whether Armenia would be an independent, sovereign state or autonomous regions within multinational empires, the national movement split between those radicals who favored an independent socialist state (Hnchaks) and the majority of political activists (Dashnaks and liberals) who pragmatically opted for autonomy. In the subsequent quarter-century, as Armenian political life underwent a series of reversals—massacres, revolutions in both Turkey and Russia, a genocidal campaign to eradicate the Armenians from their historic homeland—the leading political party, the Armenian Revolutionary Federation (Dashnaktsutiun or ARF), accepted the need for independence. With the end of the First World War, the Russian Civil War, and the Turkish Nationalist war, the only portion of historic Armenia under any kind of Armenian political control was the formerly Persian, later Russian corner of Transcaucasia that had come under Soviet power. A new diaspora had been formed of deported peoples from eastern Anatolia, as well as a relatively compact population of refugee Armenians in the Soviet republic. For the next seventy years the Armenian Question was posed in a new form: was Armenia to be Soviet and tied to the fate of Communist Russia, or was it possible at some future moment for Armenia to be reunited and sovereign under another government?

The choice for or against Soviet Armenia was a harsh and difficult one for most diaspora Armenians. Today just under 50 percent of the world's Armenians live in the Armenian republic, another 20 to 25 percent live in other parts of what was the Soviet Union, and somewhere between one-third and one-quarter of all Armenians live in the diaspora outside the former USSR.[3] The great majority of Armenians outside the "homeland" have preferred some (or any) alternative to the often harsh "socialist" regime established in Erevan late in 1920. At least two distinct political discourses competed within the diaspora: one accepting Soviet Armenia as the legitimate (or only possible) Armenian homeland; another rejecting it as a pseudo-state that could not embody Armenian national aspirations. Even when recognizing that without Soviet protection the Armenians may have ceased to exist on any portion of the Armenian plateau, a large part of the diaspora maintained a political and cultural distance from their brethren inside the Soviet Union. The Dashnaktsutiun, which had briefly ruled Armenia from 1918 to 1920, engaged at different times in more or less active resistance against the Soviet system, and though by the 1970s the party had accommodated itself to the persistence of Soviet power, the legacy of antagonism never faded. Except for a small group of leftist sympathizers and those thousands who "returned" to Armenia after the Second World War, most diaspora Armenians remained embarrassed by the fact that Armenia was a Soviet republic and tried to avoid the political difficulties this fact presented. Though more and more segments of the diaspora made their peace with "Armenia" as it existed, they never embraced the particular political form under which it was governed. Armenian "Zionism," so to speak, always remained a minority movement, and until the advent of the Karabagh movement, the earthquake of December 1988, and the declaration on Armenian sovereignty and independence in 1990, Armenians around the world remained a complexly fractured people, pulled further apart by the cold war division of East and West.

While attitudes toward Soviet Armenia have been central to Armenian identities in the period since the establishment of the republic, Armenian self-representations have also by their position as a subordinate minority living among dominant alien peoples. Whether within the Muslim world against which Armenians insulated themselves by a sense of Christian superiority or within European cultures with which they both felt kinship and from which they maintained a discrete distance, diaspora Armenians have been pulled from one direction by the demands of their own ethnic and religious culture and from the other by the pressures or attractions of the dominant *otar* (foreign) culture.

Three modes of adaptation have been utilized by diaspora Armenians. At one extreme, some Armenians reject as much as possible any involvement with the dominant culture and civilization and live almost entirely within the Armenian community. They feel their Armenianness as either something natural and unchosen or as an obligation not to be questioned. The logic of this position would be *hairenadartsutiun* (return to the fatherland), but political differences with the Soviet regime have kept many of these nationally conscious Armenians "in exile." At the other extreme there are Armenians who have thrown off their ties to ethnic culture and acculturated or even assimilated into the dominant culture. Particularly among North American Armenians, where intermarriage has reached levels of 90 percent and the loss of the Armenian language is nearly complete, association with Armenians or identification with Armenia has been on a steady, accelerating decline. Many of these "Armenians" are already ceasing to be part of the Armenian diaspora in any meaningful sense. In between these two poles are the majority of diaspora Armenians, who are involved both in Armenian community affairs and in the political and cultural world of the dominant society. In Nikola Schahgaldian's useful phrase, "They consider Armenian ethnicity as a voluntary form of association that does not conflict with their economic, social, and political integration into the host countries."[4] It is from this group that the diaspora communities, with their roots both in ethnic solidarities and in the politics of accommodation with the larger non-Armenian world, find their principal leaders, intellectuals, and constituents.

The 1920s–1940s: Rebuilding Diaspora Communities

Estimates differ as to the number of Armenians killed or displaced by the Turkish deportations and massacres of 1915–1922. They range from 600,000 to about 1,500,000. According to Justin McCarthy, a demographer sympathetic to Turkish denial of the genocide, Muslims made up 83 percent of the Anatolian population in 1912 (13,700,000) and 97.4 percent in 1922 (11,200,000). They suffered a decline in overall population of 18.5 percent. Non-Muslims were 17 percent (2,800,000) of Anatolia in 1912 and 2.6 percent (300,000) in 1922, a drop of 89.2 percent.[5] Hundreds of thousands of survivors made their way to Russia, Lebanon, Syria, Egypt, France, and the United States, where the principal post-genocide colonies of Armenians were formed. The first years after the war were marked by migrations from refugee camps into the towns of the Middle East and the cities of the United States and France, some movement to Soviet Armenia, and the relief efforts of various charitable organizations, Near East Relief, and the League of Nations.[6] The push of the Kemalist forces into Cilicia in 1922 ended any hope of retaining that region as an Armenian enclave under French protection, and with the stabilization of Ataturk's regime, supported both by Soviet Russia and the United States (after the Lausanne Treaty) Anatolian Armenians were forced to face a future of exile.

Though each diaspora community has its own peculiarities, its own history of resistance and accommodation, the complex divisions of the diaspora Armenians in the post-genocide period can be illustrated in the story of one of the most successful communities, the Armenian diaspora in Lebanon. The community, first, included Armenians who had lived in Lebanon before the genocide, primarily Catholics who had fled persecution by Apostolic Armenians in the nineteenth century. Their primary identity was with Catholicism, and by the twentieth century they had lost the use of the Armenian language and spoke Arabic, or, to a lesser extent, French, and intermarried with the Maronites.[7] These first Armenian settlers were joined at the turn of the century by a second immigration, this time of more ethnically conscious Apostolic Armenians. The two communities coexisted, but separately, and the newcomers were more receptive to Armenian nationalism. By 1904 the Dashnaktsutiun had established a local party committee in Beirut.

The third immigration, 1915–1922, was made up of genocide survivors, orphaned, without resources, living in refugee camps. About 200,000 survivors reached the Syrian desert and settled secretly in the districts of Aleppo, Damascus, and in the villages of Hawran. But the economic blockade of Mount Lebanon, the persecution and partial deportation of Lebanese Armenians by the Ottomans, the removal of the local Christian (Armenian) governor, Hovhannes Pasha Guyumjian, and the abolition of the *mutassarafiyah* (autonomy under Christian governorship) regime in 1915 made further immigration to Lebanon impossible until the defeat of the Ottoman armies in 1918. The tens of thousands who entered Lebanon after the war were divided linguistically, socially, and religiously. Cilician Armenians, who made up the bulk of the Lebanese Armenians, were largely Turkish-speaking and had a larger representation of middle-class elements as well as a high percentage of Catholic and Protestants among them. Among the Marashtsis, for example, 25 percent were Catholic and 15 percent Protestant.[8] Central and western Anatolian Armenians also spoke Turkish, knew little Armenian, and also had some fairly well-to-do members and a significant number of Catholics and Protestants. But the Armenians from historic Armenia, eastern Anatolia, still retained Armenian and were among the poorest of the immigrants and almost entirely members of the Armenian Apostolic church.

Rich and poor, city folk and mountaineers, Catholic and Apostolic, divided by region and language, the Armenians of Lebanon were extraordinarily fragmented. As Schahgaldian eloquently puts it: "Armenian refugee camps in Lebanon in the 1920s and 1930s brought together in every day contact the proud mountaineer of Sasun with the urbane and cosmopolitan Armenian of Izmir, the Armenian-speaking peasant of Van with the Turkish-speaking merchant of Adana, the fanatically religious Catholic of Ankara with the equally religious Apostolic of Erzurum."[9] Living and associating with people from their own village, town, or region, the refugees organized about thirty patriotic or locality organizations *(hairenak'tskanner)*. Identity was local rather than national (*"Vor deghatsi ek?"*—"What place are you from?"), religious rather than politically nationalist. Even when they left the camps to build more permanent settlements, as the Cilician Armenians first attempted around Beirut in the early 1930s (Nor Sis, Nor Hajen, Nor Marash, Nor Adana), they grouped together with their compatriots from the same town.[10] Confessional loyalties submerged national identities and even regional attachments. Catholic and Protestant Armenians especially were more concerned with internal religious and communal matters than with general problems of Armenians. Schahgaldian concludes:

> ... political relations among Lebanon's diaspora Armenians and their traditional leadership were initially predicated not on membership in the same

nation, nor even on the same home town or geographic area, but on religious affiliations within a given single subgroup. Thus, conscious loyalties rarely went beyond the rival Catholic, Protestant and Apostolic "locality groups," which were structurally manifested by the so-called "Compatriotic Unions." Armenian national consciousness, on the other hand, was the least likely area in which diaspora locality groups found their identity or sense of belonging. . . . This type of ethnic and cultural fragmentation hindered the development of pan-Armenian institutions among non-Apostolic diaspora Armenians and caused each religious group to act as if it were a different nationality.[11]

In its attempt to unite Armenians around the Apostolic church, the Apostolic clergy met resistance both from rival religious authorities and secular political leaders with a tradition of anticlericalism. Only when Armenians began to feel threatened by the dominant Muslim population and were forced to become players in Lebanese and Middle Eastern politics were the internal divisions among Armenians overcome and a more coherent and cohesive community built. In the mid-1920s Sunni Muslim leaders agitated against the settlement of Armenians in Lebanon, while Maronite Christians supported their coming. In 1926 Druze rebels in Syria attacked and destroyed Armenian refugee camps, forcing the inhabitants to flee to Lebanon. Maronites, increasingly insecure about the growing Muslim threat, favored the entry of Armenian Catholics into the local representative council (1929).

The state authority, in this case the French mandatory authorities, helped define the community and empower the Armenian clerical leaders. In 1924 the French officially granted most Armenian refugees Lebanese citizenship and recognized the Supreme Patriarch of the Cilician See, now located in Lebanon, as the spiritual leader of the local Armenian community. Four years later they recognized Armenians as one of Lebanon's official confessional groups and invited Patriarch Sahak to come from Jerusalem to head the Apostolic community as Catholicos. The next year the bishoprics of Aleppo, Damascus, and Cyprus were placed under the Catholicos, thus making Lebanon the center of Armenian Christianity in the Middle East, eventually eclipsing the patriarchates of Istanbul and Jerusalem.

Within the Armenian community itself, the defeated Dashnak leaders of the Armenian republic, who found their greatest support among those Armenian refugees from eastern Anatolia, began to build a political base in Lebanon. A central committee was set up in Beirut, and a newspaper, *Nor Piunik* (New Phoenix), began to appear in 1924. At first the Dashnaks thought of the recent immigrants as a nation in temporary exile that should be ready to return to its homeland as soon as political conditions permitted.[12] They attempted in the 1920s to undercut the patriotic societies, which they considered to be "useless weeds," and mobilize Armenians around issues of socialism and nationalism, organizing anti-Turkish and anti-Soviet operations. Success was elusive, however, as a report to Dashnak headquarters abroad indicated:

> The masses are confused and pessimistic. . . . Our party suffers from the fact that for the first time in recent history, the ARF has lost its influence among the masses. . . . Party members are split ideologically and otherwise. . . . Religious heads, exploiting the mentality of the refugees, continually try to disrupt and neutralize secular bodies and extend their rule over them. . . .[13]

After failing to attract broad support, the Dashnaks adopted a new strategy in the second half of the decade that emphasized mass education in the national spirit. The expectations that Europe would come to the aid of Armenia and that Bolshevism's victory would be temporary both had to be abandoned, and the Dashnaks reluctantly began to see themselves as a party of the diaspora. Using the issue of preservation of the Armenian language, they set up secular schools, campaigned against Turkish and Arab influences among the Armenians, created a teachers' training school, and founded a number of national cultural institutions associated with the party. Their project was to create "true Armenians," men and women who knew their mother tongue and felt deeply about the national cause (hai tade). "The Armenian, especially the Apostolic, was taught in school and elsewhere, to regard himself as a member of a superior ethnic group."[14] Boundaries were created between Armenians and otarner, and the spontaneous process of otaratsum ("foreignization") was reversed. In carrying out this "sacred mission," the party both created for itself a new constituency and forged a community of ethnically conscious Armenians who over time would be able to act in greater concert.

Through its newspapers, charitable organizations, publishing house, and active intervention in the community, the Dashnaktsutiun overpowered its rivals in the Armenian community and became the leading force both organizing and representing the disparate Armenians of Beirut. From an originally working-class base, the party gained support among affluent Armenians as well. In 1926 Dashnaks swept the elections to the communal council set up to govern the local Armenians. In the 1930s the party backed the efforts of Arab nationalists toward independence, thus gaining new allies and learning to maneuver in the intricate communal politics of Lebanon. In 1937 they won well over 90 percent of the votes in parliamentary elections. Now a much more conservative party, muting its anticlerical and socialist rhetoric and excluding women from its membership, the Dashnaktsutiun displaced its rivals, and in thirty-one electoral contests in Lebanon from 1926 through the 1970s candidates backed by the Dashnaks won all but three. From 1954 the party dominated the Catholicosate of Cilicia, located in Antelias, and the prelates "became little more than political appointees of the best organized Armenian political party in Lebanon—the Armenian Revolutionary Federation."[15]

"The Lebanese Armenian community," writes Khachig Toloyan,

> was a particularly successful story of the overcoming of intracommunal divisions. Both the active intervention of the Dashnaktsutiun and the peculiar

context of Lebanese communal politics worked to bring the bulk of Armenians in the country together around a shared political vision. Arab governments and their colonial masters (British and French) welcomed the Armenians' ability to care for themselves. The result in Lebanon (where the confessional state has always been weak) was the creation of Armenian enclaves with Armenian mayors in which the principal language of daily life is Armenian, where separate hospitals and old-age homes exist, as does an Armenian college; there are designated Armenian seats in Parliament, for which the Dashnags fight and usually win electoral battles against other factions.[16]

Community-building was carried out by "an exile government in the Armenian polity," a political class that won loyalty by providing its constituents with services. Though it could not achieve its original goals of liberating and governing Armenia itself, the Dashnaktsutiun carried out productive cultural work and political organization, "which preserves, invigorates and invents the concepts, narratives and symbols that empower exiles to live on as a collectivity, or at least to represent their situation as such to themselves and others."[17]

The Politics of Exile: Relations with Soviet Armenia, 1920s–1950s

The divisions among Armenians predate the East-West conflict of the postrevolutionary years. For half a millenium eastern Armenia (Persian, Russian, Soviet) and western Armenia (the Ottoman Empire) were separated by international borders, hostile political regimes, and frequent warfare. Eastern or Transcaucasian Armenians developed their own dialects of Armenian, a closer relation to the central See of Echmiadzin, and cultural ties with Russia and northern Europe. Western or Turkish Armenians, on the other hand, lived in a significantly more repressive and insecure political environment, though they maintained some autonomy within the *Ermeni millet* under the rule of the Patriarch of Constantinople. They developed their own dialects or adopted Turkish and were culturally oriented toward Istanbul and southern Europe. Each community developed its own political and social elites, and through the nineteenth century power in the community shifted from the old clerical leadership to the wealthy merchants and manufacturers (the *amira* and *sarafs* of Istanbul, the *mokalakebi* of Tiflis), who in turn were challenged, first, by the reformist intelligentsia and by the turn of the century by secular revolutionaries, the Hnchaks and, most impressively, the Dashnaks.

Once eastern Armenia came under the control of the Communists, the territorial and political interests of Caucasian Armenians were subordinated to those of the Soviets. Because of Lenin's support for the anti-imperialist struggles of the Muslim East, Soviet Armenia soon gave up its claims to Turkish Armenia in the 1921 treaties of Kars and Moscow. Defeated and displaced by the Bolsheviks, the Dashnaktsutiun opposed these "anti-national" policies and adopted a vehement hostility toward the new regime. Until 1924 an exile government functioned in France, and after France's recognition of the Kemalist republic, the Dashnaks maintained what was known as the *Patvira-kutiun* (Delegation) in Paris until 1965.[18] An attempt to end the enmity between the Dashnaks and the Communists, at a meeting in Riga in July 1921, failed when both the ARF bureau and the Soviet government refused to ratify the agreement.

Politically active Armenians were deeply divided between those more conciliatory toward the Soviets and those militantly opposed. In a dramatic reversal early in the 1920s, the former prime minister of independent Armenia, Hovhannes Kachaznuni, "defected" to Soviet Armenia, explaining his choice in a pamphlet, *The Dashnaktsutiun Has Nothing More to Do.*" The Hnchaks, who considered themselves a Social Democratic party, defended Soviet Armenia as the practical answer to the Armenian Question, a secure state backed by a powerful Russian ally. Their view was shared by the Ramkavar (Democratic Liberal) party, a diaspora organization that was at one and the same time opposed to socialism but supportive of the only existing Armenian state.

The pull toward Armenia, even in its Soviet incarnation, and the fear of *otaratsum* (denationalization) proved irresistible for many. When the Soviet government invited repatriation, 28,000 refugees, mostly from Greece, Iraq, and Istanbul, some from France and the USA, settled in Soviet Armenia in the first decade. The Norwegian explorer and humanitarian Fridtjof Nansen, as League of Nations' High Commissioner of Refugees, worked assiduously to convince the league to finance the repatriation of Armenians to Soviet Armenia. "There is, in fact," he argued,

> in this little Republic a national home for the Armenians at last, and I ask the members of the Assembly whether they sincerely and earnestly believe that any other national home can be hoped for. I believe I know the answer which their consciences will give, and I appeal to the Assembly to approve this one effort to carry out all the promises which have been made in the past concerning a national home for the Armenian nation.[19]

Ultimately the loan was not given, but from 1929 to 1937, 16,000 more refugees arrived in Armenia, mostly from Europe and financed by the Soviet government.[20] The small numbers of pro-Soviet sympathizers in the diaspora (e.g., the *Hai ognutian komite* [Armenian Aid Committee] in the United States) did their part by organizing support groups and raising money for Armenia.[21] Even the anti-Soviet political parties in the diaspora supported the repatriation movement through fundraising and organization, though both sides launched polemics against the other.

Ironically, the period of rising sympathy and support for the USSR coincided with the height of Stalinist repression—the persecution of the Armenian church, the purging of the first generation of Armenian Communist leaders, attacks on cultural nationalism, and the abrupt end to emigration. In the 1930s the Dashnaktsutiun suffered a decline in popularity and influence in many diaspora communities. Various pro-Soviet organizations, like the *Garmir Khatch* (Red Cross), and leftist activists organized public activities (chorus concerts; Red weddings, christenings, and funerals to replace church services) to engender support for Soviet Armenia.[22] HOG, and the Armenian Progressive League *(Harajdimakanner)* out of which it emerged, were closely associated with separate Armenian sections of Communist parties. They remained a minority movement within Armenian communities and suffered from governmental pressure. In 1934, for example, after organizing one of the last groups of repatriates to Soviet Armenia, the HOG in France was disbanded by the government. In the United States the Progressives were later placed on the attorney general's list of subversive organizations.

The inability to reconcile differences within Armenian political circles on the issue of the homeland tore at the efforts to unify communities, even as those communities were rebuilding after the catastrophe of the genocide. Through the 1920s and 1930s, the political struggles were fought out in the major diaspora institution, the church. Even before Armenia was Soviet, Armenians fought among themselves about political influence in parish councils. As early as 1919–1920, the Dashnaks ejected the old Ramkavar board of the Holy Cross Church in Los Angeles and refused to recognize the authority of the Primate in Worcester, Massachusetts. A decade later, as Stalin carried out his brutal revolution from above in the Soviet Union, the new Primate of the North American Diocese, Bishop Ghevond Turian, began a campaign against Dashnak influence in the church. On July 2, 1933, the bishop refused to speak at the Armenian Day celebration at the Chicago World's Fair until the tricolor flag of the independent republic was removed. He wrote to *Banvor* (Worker), the newspaper of HOG, that he considered the tricolor "a manifestation of revolt and disdain against the state organization of present Armenia." A month later Archbishop Tourian was beaten by a group of young Armenians. The diocesan convention opened in New York City on September 1, and only one-third of the delegates supported the Primate. Tourian and his faction retreated to the Hotel Martinique and refused to give up their control of the American church. Catholicos Khoren in Echmiadzin, Soviet Armenia, ruled that Archbishop Tourian was his rightful representative, but many churches refused to obey his order. On the day before Christmas, 1933, while the Primate celebrated mass in the Soorp Khach Church in New York, he was knifed to death by assassins. Though the Dashnaktsutiun officially denied any connection to the affair, nine members of the party were convicted of the murder.[23] The American Armenian church was in *de facto* schism, and the trauma of the division reverberated through the communities and split friends and families. In most major American cities to the present time Armenians still attend rival churches allied either to the Ramkavar or Dashnak parties, subordinate either to the Catholicos in Echmiadzin or to his rival in Antelias, Lebanon.

The zenith of pro-Soviet feeling in the diaspora was reached during the

Second World War. As anti-Soviet propaganda was dampened in the Allied countries and the Soviet media hailed the anti-fascist nations of the West, the great majority of diaspora Armenians rallied to the Allies. Hnchaks, Communists, and Ramkavars worked together in a united front, and Committees in Defense of the Armenian Question were formed throughout the diaspora. Cleric Tiran Nersoyan published his tract *The Christian Approach to Communism* in London in 1942.[24]

The Dashnaktsutiun, while remaining "dedicated to the destruction of Soviet rule, the liberation of Armenia, and the reunion of Turkish and Russian Armenia, . . . maintained a high degree of silence during the war years."[25] The party formed its own defense committees that competed with those of the parties more sympathetic to the USSR. Some cooperation between the Dashnaks and other parties occurred in Lebanon, where the election of the Catholicos in May 1943 was a rare example of national consensus.[26] Hnchaks, Communists, and Dashnaks put forth joint lists of candidates in that year's parliamentary elections as well. Yet serious disputes divided the Dashnak leadership, and several rival central committees, in Lebanon, Syria, and elsewhere, appeared. Some Dashnak leaders favored an Allied victory, but a right-wing faction of the party in Europe split off and actively joined the Nazis in the war on the Soviet Union. Organized by the Armenian National Council in Berlin, which in turn was sponsored by the German Ministry of the Eastern Occupied Areas, the pro-Nazi Dashnaks signed an agreement, made public in 1943, to allow Germany to establish a protectorate over a self-governing Armenia.[27] Though carried out by only a fraction of the Dashnaktsutiun, the pro-Nazi activity opened the party to accusations of collaboration, which became a central theme of the popular exposé by John Roy Carlson, *Undercover*.[28]

In its desperate struggle for survival the Soviet government quickly made a number of concessions to the Armenian church, which became the major link between Soviet Armenia and the diaspora. Within a month of the German invasion of the USSR, the Supreme Religious Council of the Echmiadzin Catholicosate issued an appeal for unity with the church and the homeland:

> There is not foothold for the Armenian people outside Soviet Armenia and outside the Armenian Apostolic Church as headed by the All-Armenian Catholicosate in Echmiadzin. To aid the Soviet Union is to aid the fatherland. The victory of the USSR is the victory of the Armenian people as well. Each Armenian who is concerned with the progress of the Armenian people must assist Soviet Armenia. Long live the Armenian spirit of national resistance which will defeat the savage enemy and make our nation live on.[29]

In late 1942 some of the closed churches in Armenia were reopened, and exiled clergy returned from Siberia. In April 1943 the Council of Ecclesiastical Affairs was created, and a seminary and printing press were allowed in Echmiadzin. A year later Gevork Cherekjian, who had been the acting head of the church since the violent death of the last Catholicos in 1938, was received by Stalin in the Kremlin.

Armenian diaspora and Soviet interests most completely coincided at the very end of the Second World War and in the brief interlude before the cold war. Shortly after the Yalta Conference, the Soviet government initiated a campaign to encourage Armenian settlement in the Armenian republic and to recover Armenian irredenta in eastern Turkey. On June 7, 1945, Foreign Minister Molotov told the Turkish ambassador to Moscow that the USSR demanded a revision of the Soviet-Turkish border in the region of Kars and Ardahan. Stalin's policy reversed Lenin's agreement with Turkey to give up any Armenian claims against the new Kemalist state and removed one of the most serious impediments to the Soviet Armenian state's defense of Armenian national interests. This change in policy occurred almost simultaneously with the gathering of lay and clerical delegates to the congress in Echmiadzin to elect a new Catholicos (June 16–25). After his unanimous election, Gevork VI sent a letter to Stalin supporting the repatriation of diaspora Armenians and the return of Armenian lands in Turkey.[30]

Political forces in the Armenian diaspora now possessed a powerful emotional issue to mobilize their communities. A novel opportunity had risen for the first time since 1920 to resolve the Armenian Question in both its territorial and demographic aspects with a single solution. Though Soviet policy was aimed more exactly at weakening British influence in the Middle East than at justice for the Armenians, most of the diaspora parties—and religious organizations with the exception of the Armenian Catholics who remained silent on the territorial issue and actively hostile to emigration—fell in line behind the Soviet promise of a larger Armenian state. Pro-Soviet diaspora organizations, especially the Apostolic church, organized repatriation drives, supported petitions for the return of Armenian territory to the USSR, and made appeals directly to the US State Department. Nearly 100,000 diaspora Armenians, mostly from the Middle East, migrated to Soviet Armenia.

Stalin's policy backfired when both Turkey and Iran rejected Stalin's demands and quickly found support from the United States.[31] The cold war division of the world was established along the Arax River, the border between Soviet Armenia and Turkey. Those diaspora Armenians who had backed the Soviet initiative soon found themselves in the unenviable position of living in one political camp and supporting the policy of the other.

The old divisions within the diaspora not only reemerged but deepened into irreconcilable differences. For a time after the war the Dashnaktsutiun, still suffering from serious splits within the leadership, wavered between accommodation with the popular enthusiasm for the Soviet Union and its traditional opposition. Even before the war, the party had cooled its initial enthusiasm for repatriation. When Soviet Armenian officials stipulated that "progressive" elements should organize the repatriation drive, powerful Dashnak leaders, particularly in Lebanon and Syria, turned against emigration and what they perceived as Soviet interference in the affairs of the diaspora. Many of them had been pro-Axis in the war and saw Soviet Armenia as an alien state. Schahgaldian writes of them:

> These were mostly middle-aged, middle-level party functionaries whose ancestors had lived in the diaspora for centuries. To be sure, they were mostly Armenian-speakers, yet they were raised in Turkish-speaking families and neighborhoods. To them, Armenian nationalism meant the preservation of the Church, the continuation of local "Armenian" customs, and was largely confused with anti-Turkism.[32]

At the fourteenth Congress of the Dashnaktsutiun, held in Cairo in September 1947, this wing of the party dominated and came out against emigration "as long as the territorial expansion of Armenia remained unrealized."[33] The common electoral politics of Dashnaks and the Marxist parties in Lebanon collapsed just before the 1947 elections, and by the end of the year dozens of activists were killing each other in the streets of Beirut.

By the late 1940s the lines of division were drawn once again between Dashnaks on one side and anti-Dashnaks (Ramkavars, Hnchaks, neutrals [chezok]) on the other. When San Francisco restauranteur George Mardigian and the Dashnak-backed Armenian Relief Society assisted thousands of Armenian "displaced persons," former Soviet citizens who preferred the Germans to the Soviets, to come to the United States in the late 1940s, anti-Dashnak Armenians refused to participate. The Dashnaktsutiun organized a lecture tour of the collaborationist General Dro Ganayan to help fund the settlement of the "DPs" in America. Appealing to the new generation of English-speaking Armenians, both sides started their own thick journals: the short-lived *Armenian Affairs* of those more sympathetic to Soviet Armenia; and the long-running *Armenian Review,* supported by the Dashnaktsutiun.[34]

As the cold war grew colder, the Left, condemned as fellow travelers, lost its influence among diaspora Armenians. Armenian "progressives" merged quietly with the anti-Dashnak communities. In the United States the Ramkavars became the major political opposition to the Dashnaks; in Lebanon both the Ramkavars and Hnchaks increased their popularity and effectiveness. The Dashnaktsutiun, on the other hand, became the beneficiary of a renewed anti-Communist politics. In 1951 the fifteenth World Congress called for close "cooperation and alliance with all anti-Communist and anti-Soviet forces," among which were included the "ruling forces" of the "Free World."[35] In Lebanon a group that called itself "True Dashnaks" left the party in 1953 to form an opposition around the newspaper *Azdarar* (Monitor), and in the next few years the conservative leadership of the Dashnaktsutiun purged hundreds of its more moderate members.

In 1956 the Dashnaktsutiun maneuvered the election of the Primate of Aleppo, Zareh Payaslian, to the Catholicosate of Cilicia, and a *de facto* schism of the Armenian Apostolic church was created both in Lebanon and throughout the diaspora. Dashnaks and their adversaries took to the streets of Beirut, gunning down their opponents. The elections of 1957, once again carried by the Dashnaks, led to more bloodshed, and as Lebanon went through a brief civil war in 1958—in which the Dashnaks sided with the Christian forces in Lebanon, while the anti-Dashnaks gravitated toward the Muslims—another sixty Armenians were killed before a truce was arranged between the Hnchaks and Dashnaks.

Partisanship had always been an important part of the political culture of diaspora Armenians, but during the cold war it further divided communities and even families into hostile, self-contained groups. Armenianness was re-served for members of one's own subcommunity. Marriage or even communi-cation across the divisional lines between the Dashnaks and anti-Dashnaks was nearly impossible. Yet, even as each party and religious organization articulated its principal tasks as preservation of the culture and "holding on to our youth," the increasingly archaic concerns of the old leaders found less and less resonance in younger people. Conflict over support or rejection of the one Armenian "state" that existed reduced focus on other Armenian is-sues, most importantly the question of western Armenia. The Dashnaks, allied as they were in the cold war with the anti-Soviet policies of the United States, were limited in their ability to criticize America's Turkish ally. The energy spent on intracommunal infighting was not available for the kind of earlier community building that had characterized the first decades of the post-geno-cide diaspora. As a result younger Armenians either moved out of Armenian life into the dominant cultures or in extreme cases, as in the Middle East, demonstrated their rejection of the old politics with a new, violent commit-ment to the Armenian cause through terrorism.

The Road to Reconciliation, 1960s–1980s

Despite the intense conflicts that followed the global schism in the Arme-nian Apostolic church, the lines of conflict among Armenians began to blur in the next several decades. In part this was the result of the post-Stalinist reforms in the USSR, which permitted contacts between the diaspora and Soviet Armenia. In 1962 students from abroad began studying in Erevan, and in April of that year Armenia permitted a limited repatriation of diaspora Armenians to begin. The Soviet government tried to lessen tensions with the diaspora by issuing a newspaper, *Hayreniki dzain* (Voice of the Fatherland), especially for Armenians living abroad. Within the country concessions to Armenian national feelings, the building of monuments to the genocide and to the victory over the Turks at Sardarabad, greater freedom of expression, and less overt antagonism toward the Dashnaktsutiun, all contributed to a lessening of the hostility between diaspora subgroups. Many now demanded greater cooperation of the political parties, joint social and cultural events, and the end of the religious schism. In the Lebanese parliamentary elections of 1960, the Dashnaktsutiun, which recently had purged its more extremely conservative leaders, easily beat the anti-Dashnak coalition (Ramkavars, Hnchaks, and independents), but neither winners nor losers engaged in the kind of hyperbolic rhetoric that had characterized their contests in the recent past.

The movement toward greater unity, both within the diaspora and between the diaspora and Soviet Armenia, was greatly aided by the growing awareness of an old issue, now renewed and freshly articulated, that united all politically conscious Armenians—the genocide of 1915. The spontaneous demonstrations of Soviet Armenians in April 1965, demanding recognition of the genocide by their own government, and the continuing and intensifying campaign by official Turkish agencies to deny that a genocide had occurred stimulated greater interest in the issue. A new discourse around the genocide developed, along with ritual observances on April 24, conferences and institutes for study of the genocide, and political action to have European and American governments recognize the "forgotten Holocaust." The Dashnaktsutiun softened its anti-Soviet tone and argued once again that the main enemy was Turkey and that the principal task of the diaspora was raising the issue of Armenian irredenta and recognition of the genocide.

As a powerful mobilizing theme, the genocide resonated within broader discourses of ethnic self-assertion and the revival of attention to the Jewish Holocaust. Yet even as it brought Armenians of different political camps together, the inability of the political campaigns to effect any change in the attitude of the Turkish government—except to stimulate its efforts at denial—created a new militancy among radicalized young people in the Middle East. Once again a strong sense that action must be taken before the "nation" disappears led small groups of revolutionaries, influenced by the resistance of the Palestinians, to form the Armenian Secret Army for the Liberation of Armenia (ASALA) in 1975.[36] Soon followed by other groups, the Justice Commandos and the Armenian Revolutionary party, the "terrorists" assassinated both Turkish diplomats and officials as well as Dashnak political leaders. The shock value of the initial assassinations wore off quickly, and by the mid-1980s internal fighting within the organizations over tactics and personalities led to the decline of Armenian "terrorist" activities. Like the cold war polarization on the issue of Soviet Armenia, so the harsh choice between politics and revolutionary warfare divided Armenians rather than bringing them together around a common vision.

By the 1970s political developments in the Middle East made the future of Armenian communities increasingly precarious. Besides the civil war in Lebanon, repression in Syria and Turkey, and Muslim fundamentalism in Iran, a generally inhospitable environment for traditional Armenian business pursuits stimulated emigration from the region, primarily to the United States. By the 1980s the two principal centers of Armenian life were the Soviet republic and the scattered communities in California and other parts of North America. The one certainty for Armenians was that life within the borders of one or the other superpower was the best guarantee for the future. Within the American-Armenian community the issue of assimilation versus retention of Armenian culture and language led to efforts to revitalize the Armenian community. Armenian day schools were opened throughout the country; more than a half-dozen university chairs in Armenian studies were endowed; the number of newspapers increased, particularly in English; a political representation was established in Washington through the ecumenical Armenian Assembly; and a unique intellectual center, the Zoryan Institute, attempted to link Armenian intellectuals in a common effort to rethink problems facing the diaspora. These efforts at community-building were at one and the same time novel in their adoption of American modes of organization and traditional in their concerns. Though American Armenians did not become effective political players in the way that Lebanese Armenians had become before 1975, they managed to be well-positioned by the 1980s, both intellectually and financially, to react to the unforeseen opportunities and potential catastrophe that opened with the Karabagh events of 1988.

The Current Crisis

If rather than the simple release of objective cultural essences, the formation of diaspora communities, like the formation of nations, has been a product of political intervention and cultural creativity, the current crisis holds the double meaning of danger and opportunity. Tradition was never anything just given but something actively "preserved," indeed "invented." The construction of communities was always a matter of forging internal solidarities and understandings and defining the external boundaries. Diaspora communities in particular were voluntary polities insofar as they were consciously constituted. And within them the intense struggles for authority, power, and influence have been at one and the same time both divisive and defining. Clergy and political activists, independent intellectuals and businessmen, teachers and poets—all have pressed their less-than-convincing claims to leadership in the community. Temporary coalitions and systems of patronage brought together people of prestige and influence who were able for a time to gain a broad legitimacy within a given constituency. But no one group or person has been able to bind the factions together, to overcome the regional, religious, and political differences, even within one community, not to mention within the diaspora as a whole. Neither in its parts nor its whole has the Armenian diaspora been able to act in a concerted way, with a single voice, and its influence on the homeland has been far less than it might have been. But the very idea that a diaspora community or a whole diaspora could (or should) act in concert or harmony may be as mythic as it would be for a nation-state.

Around the issue of the genocide first, and later in its efforts to aid Armenia after the earthquake of December 7, 1988, the diaspora found a number of common interests that both overrode the grossest divisions within the diaspora and linked it vitally with the Armenian republic. As the Armenians of Armenia moved steadily toward independence, the same suspicions and confusions about the future of Armenia arose in the diaspora. Far less enthusiasm for independence was expressed at first by diaspora political movements, including the Dashnaktsutiun, than by the Armenian National Movement (HHSh) within the republic. While Armenia exaggerated the potential of the diaspora to help it along its uncertain path, the diaspora—with some notable exceptions, like the Armenian General Benevolent Union and a few daring entrepreneurs—marked time, unable to settle old issues that have for so long prevented it from uniting its efforts. The Armenian government officially recognized the diaspora as a part of the larger Armenian nation and invited it to full citizenship. The appointment of Raffi Hovannisan, a lawyer and activist from the American diaspora, as the first minister of foreign affairs of independent Armenia, symbolically reaffirmed the interconnectedness of the two parts of a nation so long severed. What is new in the current situation, and most hopeful for the future, is the general consensus in the diaspora at the moment that the Republic of Armenia under its current government *is* the Armenian homeland, a legitimate state with which relations are to be maintained, a nation to be protected and aided. Though return to the homeland is far less an aspiration for most diaspora Armenians than at times in the past, there is another sense of return that is being widely felt at this moment—the sense that the Armenian language, Armenia's history, its unique Christian faith, and the fate of the diaspora are all bound up with the stories that will be told in the one Armenia left to its people.

14 Armenia on the Road to Independence, Again

The Gorbachev initiatives have been usefully described as a triple revolution—at one and the same time a political revolution leading from authoritarianism to democracy; an economic revolution transforming a state-run command economy into some kind of market-based economy; and an anticolonial revolution turning a Russian-dominated empire into a new confederation of sovereign states. Democratization, marketization, and decolonization occurred simultaneously and with effects from one process deeply influencing, shaping, and distorting the progress of the others. From the beginning the Gorbachev reformers had insisted that greater freedom in society and liberalization of the political sphere were essential to jump-starting the failing economy. Yet the devolution of power and the consequent collapse of the Communist party led to rival centers of power, the infamous "war of laws," and the elimination of any "verticality of power," disruptive strikes and demonstrations, and the rise of nationalist challengers to central state authority. The explosion of ethnic nationalism at the same time undermined central economic plans, disrupted transport and inter-republic trade, and created a new autarkic mentality about economics. Nationalism allied with environmentalism closed down enterprises that in some cases represented key sources of energy, foreign exchange, or supply to other industries. Behind all other developments, like a specter haunting the best-laid plans of the reformers and democrats, the accelerating decline of the economy intensified national hatreds and encouraged more conservative forces to resist further democratization and decentralization. The revolution began as a reform of the economy, but failing in the realm of economics, it led to the collapse of the Soviet Union and the creation of more than a dozen "independent" states.

The disintegration of the Soviet empire and implosion of its self-proclaimed "socialist" system have been variously interpreted as an inevitable failure of an impossible utopia, the successful result of Reagan's strategy of economic and military overload imposed by the United States on a weakening Soviet economy, or the product of the natural rise of popular aspirations for democracy and freedom. The entire experience of the seventy-four years of the Soviet system is now read by many as flawed from the start, and the mammoth transformations that accompanied industrialization, urbanization, and the victory over fascism have been overwhelmed by the numbing revelations of Stalinist mass murders, the grinding degradation of a corrupt and hierarchical Brezhnevian conservatism, and the evident revulsion with Soviet-style socialism in the peripheries of the empire. Whatever the long-range causes of the collapse and the short-term errors of the Gorbachev team, the more intermediate (and often neglected) reasons for failure lie in the long years of the Brezhnev regime when the Soviet leadership neglected the signs of decay, already evident in the late 1970s, and rejected reforms in favor of a consolidation of power based on military strength and political conformity. The turning point at which the Soviet bloc did not turn was in 1968, when Communist reformers in Czechoslovakia attempted to build a more democratic socialism, only to have their experiment crushed by Soviet tanks. Retrenchment at home and in Eastern Europe, coupled with detente with the West and a military buildup, were amalgamated into a stop-gap plan for lumbering into the 1980s.

By the early 1980s the Brezhnevian system was grinding to a halt. Economic growth, which had been a consistent characteristic of the Soviet system since the early years of Stalinism, had by the early 1970s begun to decelerate. The extensive growth strategy that was part of the Stalin system no longer worked, and various reforms to improve productivity only prolonged the agony. Growth rates of 8 percent (in rate of net material product or goods produced) in the late 1960s fell to just over 3 percent by the early 1980s. Though the rise in oil prices in the 1970s greatly aided the Soviets, who were the second largest exporter of oil in the world, the secular decline in the domestic economy could not be reversed. At the same time, the international context put great pressure on the Soviet system to reform in order to compete effectively with the more developed West (and Japan) in technology, economic growth, and military capability.

The long years of Brezhnev's reign, which soon would be dubbed the "period of stagnation [*zastoi*]," were characterized—on the political level—by a deep conservatism, an unwillingness to embark on fundamental reform, a remarkable stability and continuity in the leadership, and a vigorous and confident military and foreign policy. But at a deeper social and economic level the enormous changes that had continued to affect Soviet society— urbanization, greater mobility, cultural and technical literacy, higher consumer expectations—were also undermining that political system and the economic machine. Basically, an educated, mobile, expectant society had been created in the Soviet Union by Stalinism and the post-Stalinist bureaucratic economic system. With the end of mass terror and the worse excesses of the police state, a civil society had emerged in the USSR but with no place to go.

A deep, dull, persistent conflict developed between the stagnant state structure and the society created by the system. The rewards and security of the system were taken for granted, but frustrations arose from the impossibility of realizing one's ambitions and, given the undemocratic political order and the petrified ideology of Marxism-Leninism, of full expression of one's opinions and interests.[1] The population was pushed into ever less satisfying labors. For most Soviet citizens work was not something they valued. Increasingly, the private sphere of life, one's friends and family, had become most important. In the Brezhnev years it became more difficult for people to move out of their social class. Society was frozen as parents tried to pass privileges on to their children. The scarcity of consumer goods led to the widespread development of black and gray markets, of beating the system by working around it, by cheating, bribing, holding back goods and distributing them to friends and relatives. No one could make it without cheating, as indicated by a Soviet curse: "May you be forced to live on your salary."

Among the non-Russian peoples, now about one-half the Soviet population, newly compact, conscious, coherent nations had emerged, with their own cultural and political agendas at variance with the Soviet central authorities. Among non-Russians the feeling grew that they did not have equal access to the privileges of the system (though for local elites this was certainly not true) and that their republics were particularly disadvantaged. A conviction was widespread that without Russian encumbrance they would fare much better economically.

Gorbachev's triple revolution—democratization, marketization, decolonization—stimulated a series of mass national movements for greater autonomy and democracy. In terms of their eventual success in dismantling the hypercentralized Soviet federation and undermining the rule of local Communist parties, these movements were the initiators of a series of national democratic revolutions, the first massive manifestations of which occurred in Armenia. The Armenian Revolution began as a protest movement in 1987–1988, focused on ecology and the question of Karabagh, and within six months created a potent national opposition to the rule of the Armenian Communist party. Already by May 1988, the Karabagh Committee expanded its political horizon to include the question of democracy in Armenia. Important figures unwilling to go along with these more radical demands—including Zori Balayan, Silva Kaputikian, and Igor Muratian—left the committee, which was soon joined by new people, like Levon Ter Petrosian, much more critical of Communist rule.[2] This formative period, from February through December 1988, may be considered the first stage of the growing revolution.

With the old Armenian Communist leadership fundamentally opposed to *perestroika* and completely discredited among the population, the choices for

Moscow in Armenia were between a weak reform tendency within the ruling party or the powerful but increasingly anti-Communist democratic movement. By December effective power in the republic was devolving into the hands of the Karabagh Committee, and Gorbachev decided to shore up Communist rule. The arrest of the leaders of the democratic movement launched the second stage of the Armenian Revolution—the attempt of the old authorities to rule without the nation—which lasted until the release of the committee members at the end of May 1989.

Gorbachev faced a double political challenge in 1988–1989: repeated attempts by the conservatives in the party to limit *glasnost* and prevent electoral reform within the party; and the explosion of popular nationalism, first among the Armenians, followed by the Baltic peoples. The first challenge, signalled by the infamous Nina Andreevna letter in April, was quickly squelched, and at the Nineteenth Party Conference in June Gorbachev pushed through a proposal for multi-candidate elections to a new parliament, the Congress of People's Deputies. These elections, though limited in their representativeness, proved to be the hammer blow to the monopoly of power by the Communist party. While they provided a new forum and base of support for Gorbachev, the open political process rapidly eroded the instrument of power that he had hitherto relied on. Gorbachev was torn between preserving and reforming the party, on the one hand, and creating political alternatives that eventually undermined the Communists, on the other.

The awakening of political society throughout the Soviet Union in 1988–1989 intensified the Gorbachevian dilemma. He could encourage the movement toward greater democracy, and thereby threaten the Communists' monopoly on power, or resort to force and violence to contain the aroused population within acceptable limits and thereby undermine his own plans for democratization. Within the party these alternative strategies were fiercely debated, with reformers like Aleksandr Yakovlev and Boris Yeltsin pulling Gorbachev to the Left and greater democracy and conservatives like Yegor Ligachev holding the line for discipline and order.

With the contested elections to the Congress of People's Deputies in 1989, the view long held by many Western Sovietologists that the Soviet people were incapable of democratic politics had to be laid to rest. Whatever the effects of the authoritarian political culture of the tsarist and Stalinist past, millions of Soviets participated in the creation of a real parliamentary system, defeating the *apparat* in many elections, shaking the authority of the party, and gaining a new confidence that they would be able to rule themselves. When the Congress of People's Deputies opened in June 1989, independent deputies went on the offensive, blaming the country's leaders for the massacre of nineteen Georgian demonstrators two months earlier. In a skillful display of parliamentary leadership, Soviet-style, Gorbachev managed to hold the political center and keep his coalition together, but the Moscow intelligentsia and other elements of the "Left" split off to form their own faction. Television coverage of the Congress had an electrifying effect on the Soviet population. A largely depoliticized population was given a new political education. Power was demystified and the people animated.

The second challenge—the revolt of the Soviet nations—could not be contained within the imperial structure of the USSR, and over the next three years mobilized non-Russians tore the fragile fabric of the Union to shreds. The protests of the Armenians of Nagorno-Karabagh against Azerbaijani rule, like the national culturalist and democratizing movements in the Baltic republics, began in the spirit of *perestroika* but evolved quickly into anti-Communist coalitions for democracy and national sovereignty. Gorbachev's attempts to compromise with the Armenians, proposing enhanced autonomy for Karabagh but within Azerbaijan, satisfied neither Armenians nor Azerbaijanis, and a long and inconclusive war erupted between the two peoples. The attempt to break the back of the nationalists by arresting the principal leaders proved that repression was as ineffective as compromise.

Each tentative step by the Gorbachev team toward a new political system was threatened by escalating demands from the republics. In Armenia the attempt by the Communist party to rule without the popular representatives of the national movement only worsened the political crisis. In March 1989 many voters boycotted the general elections. Massive demonstrations started up again in early May demanding the release of the members of the Karabagh Committee, and in the elections to the Congress of People's Deputies in May Armenians chose people identified with the Karabagh cause.[3] Party chief Suren Harutiunian made a number of gestures to win over popular sentiment. He agreed that May 28, the day the Dashnaktsutiun had proclaimed Armenian independence in 1918, should be recognized as the anniversary of the restoration of Armenian statehood. The tricolor flag that had been identified with that republic (and by many with the Dashnaktsutiun) was accepted as the national flag of Armenia. Finally, on the last day of May the Karabagh Committee members and Igor Muratian were released after their case was transferred to the Armenian Procurator General's office. Demonstrations greeted their arrival in Erevan.

The third stage of the Armenian Revolution (June–October 1989) was marked by a kind of condominium of the Communists and the nationalists. For six months the Armenian Communist leadership and the national movement worked as uncomfortable allies, much as the popular fronts and Communists were operating in the Baltic republics. Already emerging as the most important of the movement's leaders, the philologist Levon Ter Petrosian made it clear that the committee had a broader vision than merely the solution of the Karabagh question. Ultimately determined to bring full democracy and independence to Armenia, the trajectory of the movement would bring it into head-on collision with the party.

In June the mushrooming unofficial organizations joined together to form the Pan-Armenian National Movement (*Haiots Hamazgayin Sharzhum,*

HHSh), and the government gave them official recognition. Ter Petrosian praised Harutiunian's defense of Armenian national interests at the Congress of People's Deputies in an interview in *Le Monde* and stated his belief that the interests of the Armenian Communist party and the HHSh were converging. Though the Karabagh Committee did not have "any intentions to take the place of the official leadership at the moment," he emphasized, it had already emerged as a key player in Armenian politics. In June members of the Karabagh Committee were invited to participate, along with writer Zori Balayan, in sessions of the Supreme Soviet, where they displayed a distinct pragmatism. When Balayan spoke of the threat to Armenia from Pan-Turkism and the need to rely on the traditional friendship with Russia, Ter Petrosian read the committee's official statement dismissing the relevance of Pan-Turkism at the present time and condemning the raising of such a volatile issue that prejudiced the case for Artsakh (Karabagh).[4] In public rallies Ter Petrosian argued that raising other territorial issues was dangerous and that Armenia' claims were democratic, not racist or expansionist. In the diaspora the Dashnak organ *Droshak* sided with Balayan and labeled Ter Petrosian's views "dangerous."

The Azerbaijani-Armenian conflict escalated steadily in the summer and fall of 1989. Both the HHSh and the newly formed Azerbaijani Popular Front (APF) called for abolition of the special administration, headed by Gorbachev's deputy Arkadii Volskii. The Armenians held to their position that Karabagh must become part of the Armenian republic, and radical Azerbaijanis called for the abolition of Karabagh autonomy altogether. As hundreds of thousands of Azerbaijanis demonstrated in Baku, the blockade of Karabagh and Armenia tightened. Karabagh Armenians responded by electing their own National Council, which on August 23 declared the secession of Karabagh from Azerbaijan and its merger with Armenia. Daily armed clashes were reported in Karabagh; strikes initiated by the APF shut down much of Baku; and the nationalists in Azerbaijan demanded a declaration of sovereignty, recognition of the APF, and the dismantling of the Volskii Committee. In September the Azerbaijani authorities succumbed to the pressure from the Popular Front and declared Azerbaijan a sovereign republic within the USSR.

The Armenian Supreme Soviet then further escalated the conflict by declaring the Karabagh National Council the sole legitimate representative of the Karabagh people. The Azerbaijani Supreme Soviet responded by abrogating the autonomy of Karabagh and Nakhichevan. Though all of these decisions were ultimately declared invalid by the USSR Supreme Soviet, neither republic, both of which were still governed by Communist parties, was willing to obey directives from Moscow on the Karabagh issue.

On November 28, in frustration at its inability to bring the parties together, the USSR Supreme Soviet voted 348–5 to replace the Special Administration Committee in Karabagh with an administration subject largely to Azerbaijan. Even the Baltic deputies, who generally supported the Armenian position in the Karabagh question, voted with the majority. The Supreme

Soviet authorized creation of a special "organizing committee" at the republic level made up equally of Armenians and Azerbaijanis and, at the same time, restored the Nagorno-Karabagh provincial Soviet and its executive committee (suspended by the January 12, 1989, decree). The Union Monitoring and Observation Commission, which was subordinate to the Supreme Soviet of the USSR, would supervise the sociopolitical situation, and special troops from the USSR Ministry of Internal Affairs would remain until conditions normalized. A new law was to be worked out within two months to guarantee the full development of Karabagh. No changes in the demographic situation were to be permitted.

Neither side was satisfied. Demonstrations were held both in Erevan and Baku against the resolution. The Armenian Supreme Soviet rejected Moscow's decision and on December 1 declared Karabagh a part of Armenia. Forty thousand demonstrators were mobilized on December 5 to surround the Supreme Soviet building and demand the end of colonialist practices, the abolition of Article Six of the Soviet Constitution, which gave the Communist party a leading political role, and the renaming of the republic, "Republic of Armenia." By the late fall of 1989 the cooperative relationship between the Armenian Communist authorities and the HHSh had come to an end, and the movement was accelerating its efforts toward democratization and independence. The fourth stage of the Armenian Revolution (October 1989–August 1990) saw an open contest for power between the nationalists and the Communists.

Events within the Soviet Union were overtaken by the fall of Communist governments in Eastern Europe at the end of 1989. The demise of the Soviet external empire profoundly affected non-Russians within the Soviet Union, legitimizing their drive for sovereignty and independence. In January, under HHSh pressure, the Armenian Supreme Soviet revised the republic's constitution and gave itself the power to validate USSR laws. Central state authority withered, and the writ of the Kremlin could only be enforced by police and soldiers. But after the Tbilisi killings and the volatile reaction from the Congress of People's Deputies, Gorbachev restrained the use of armed force against protesters, except in the most extreme interethnic warfare and to prevent secession from the Soviet Union.

By 1990 Gorbachev's strategy to reform the political structure while preserving a renewed Communist party had led to a deep polarization of Soviet politics. His policies had failed to revive the stagnating Soviet economy and instead threatened the unity of the Soviet Union. His extraordinary foreign policy successes were generally acknowledged, but inside the USSR he was faced by ever more frequent and ever more threatening crises. In Transcaucasia, as in the rest of the disintegrating Soviet Union, the cycle of economic decline and radicalized politics fed on each other. Both the incomplete political reform, in part democratic, in part preserving the old structures, and the national revolts had negative effects on the economy. From 1988 the terms of foreign trade had grown worse. Imports continued to grow, and supplies of convertible currency dried up. By the end of 1989 the USSR had a gross external debt in hard currency of $54 billion. Oil and coal production began to fall in 1989. The following year national material production fell by an estimated 4 percent, while GNP fell by about 2 percent. Only the service sector grew. Wages and salaries increased by 12 percent, but open and repressed inflation accelerated in 1990. Oil production continued to decline, and oil exports fell by nearly 20 percent in 1990.[5] In Armenia hundreds of thousands of people, both victims of the earthquake and refugees from Azerbaijan and other parts of the Soviet Union, remained homeless or inadequately housed, while the blockade by Azerbaijan prevented the rebuilding of the regions hit by the earthquake.

After more than two years of the Karabagh conflict, Armenians had moved from being one of the most loyal Soviet nations to complete loss of confidence in Moscow. They perceived a pro-Azerbaijani slant to official media coverage that treated both sides as equally just in their claims and equally culpable for the cascading violence. Gorbachev's unwillingness to grant Karabagh to Armenia and his failure to end the blockade convinced people that the Kremlin calculated political advantage in backing the Muslims. In Armenia the Communist party, under Suren Harutiunian, was torn between the Kremlin's refusal to allow the merger of Karabagh with Armenia and the growing popular movement that would be satisfied with nothing less.

In Azerbaijan the Communist party was faced by a massive opposition, which the Popular Front barely controlled. Early in the new year, 150,000 Azerbaijanis demonstrated in Baku for open borders. In Nakhichevan Soviet border guards refrained from restricting movement back and forth into Iran. In Lenkoran, south of Baku, local officials had little real authority. Suddenly, on January 13, 1990, as a quarter of a million Azerbaijanis listened to speeches in the central square in Baku, groups of young people broke away and began running through the city beating and killing Armenians. Two days later the central Soviet government declared a state of emergency in Azerbaijan and launched a series of maneuvers, first in Karabagh and other areas, and then toward Baku. On January 20, as the Popular Front organized a haphazard defense of the city, the Soviet army stormed Baku, killing hundreds. Most Armenians were evacuated, and the military restored the power of the Communist party of Azerbaijan and repressed the Popular Front.

Representatives of the HHSh were invited by Baltic democrats to Riga to discuss the Karabagh issue with leaders of the Azerbaijani Popular Front, but the weakness of the APF, its inability to control the crowds in Baku, and the news that APF Delegates had entered Armenian villages near Karabagh demanding that its inhabitants leave their homes led to the collapse of the talks after two days. What had begun as a peaceful constitutional movement for Armenian rights in Karabagh had, by the spring of 1990, degenerated into a guerilla war between two nations in the southern Soviet Union.

With the Communist party in rapid decline and the popular nationalist forces far from united, a vacuum of power could be felt in Armenia. Allied intellectually and politically with the democratic opposition that had formed in Russia around Yeltsin, the Armenian National Movement was committed to dismantling the Communist system, preparing for eventual political independence, and marketizing the economy. With the resignation of Harutiunian as first secretary of the Armenian Communist party (April 6, 1990) and the elections of the spring and summer of 1990, the old political elite gradually made way for a new political class that had matured in the two years of the Karabagh movement. At first Communists and their opponents appeared equally strong at the polls, and Ter Petrosian spoke of a possible coalition government. But by late July it became clear that the non-Communists would win a parliamentary majority. After several rounds of voting, the newly elected Armenian parliament chose Levon Ter Petrosian instead of the new Communist chief Vladimir Movsesian as its chairman.

With the HHSh in power and the Communists in opposition, a fifth stage of the Armenian Revolution was reached—the transition from Soviet-style government to an independent democratic state. The leading writers within the Armenian National Movement had steadily combatted the Russian orientation of the Communist party and the centrist political forces (Ramkavars, Hnchaks) in the diaspora. Instead of the long-held view that Armenia could not become an independent state in face of the dangers of Pan-Turkism, that it required protection from the Russian or Soviet state, the HHSh argued that Armenians must abandon their reliance on a "third force," rethink their traditional hostility toward and fear of the Turks, and be prepared to create their own independent state by themselves now that the opportunity had arisen. These views echoed those long expressed by the leading diaspora party, the Dashnaktsutiun, though with significant differences.[6] The HHSh was prepared to deal more directly and forthrightly with the Turks and believed that the question of Armenian lands in Turkey had to be deferred until the issue of full sovereignty and independence was resolved.

The new government faced a nearly complete collapse of order in the republic. Buildings had been seized by armed men in Erevan, and several independent militias operated in Erevan as well as on the Azerbaijani frontier. Frustrated by the Azerbaijani blockade and determined to defend their republic and Karabagh, Armenia *fedayees* (a term that recalls the revolutionaries of the turn of the century) raided arsenals and police stations to arm themselves for the coming battles. Armenians were convinced that the Soviet army was aiding the deportation of Armenians from villages in Azerbaijan outside of Karabagh—Azat, Kamo, Martunashen, Getashen—and the guerillas massed in the easternmost province of Armenia, Zangezur, prepared to aid their countrymen across the border in Azerbaijan. In April 1990 a crowd attempted to storm the KGB building in the capital, and a month later Soviet troops clashed with Armenian irregulars at the Erevan railroad station. Twenty-four were killed. In July Gorbachev issued an ultimatum demanding that the independent militias of Armenia be disarmed within fifteen days and threatening military intervention if they did not comply. Ter Petrosian's government set out itself to disarm the independent militias and restore order in Erevan.

As Armenians fought Armenians and the new national leadership tried to establish its authority, Armenia formally declared its intention to become a sovereign and independent state (August 23, 1990) with Karabagh an integral part of the new Republic of Armenia.[7] The Armenian nation was defined broadly to include, not only those on the territory of the republic, but the worldwide diaspora as well. And the government set out to redefine Armenian national interests, recognizing but laying aside for the moment the painful question of the Armenian genocide and seeking improved relations with Turkey and Iran.

In its first months, the non-Communist government of Armenia acted as a fireman in a burning building. First, Azerbaijanis surrounded Getashen; then in early September, Soviet Ministry of the Interior (MVD) troops worked with Azerbaijanis to remove Armenians from the villages of Armavir, Azat, and Kamo. Police searched houses in Stepanakert aided by the Soviet army. The Armenian Supreme Soviet declared on September 5, 1990 that the Soviet MVD must redeploy its troops along the borders of Karabagh, Shahumian, and Getashen and called for lifting of the blockade in those regions. That same day, the Azerbaijani leader, Ayaz Mutalibov, said that his government would abolish Karabagh's autonomy if Moscow did not help get rid of "bandit formations." His government cancelled local elections in Karabagh and cut off gas to Armenia. On September 12, Ter Petrosian, his prime minister Vazgen Manukian, and Communist party chief Vladimir Movsesian met in Moscow with Mutalibov, Prime Minister Hasan Hasanov, President Gorbachev, Prime Minister Ryzhkov, and Rafik Nishanov. The USSR and Azerbaijani sides rejected Armenian demands that the Soviet army be withdrawn from Armenian towns and villages and a demarcation line be created between Armenians and Azerbaijanis. Gorbachev had clearly sided with the Communists in Azerbaijan, against the non-Communists in Armenia.

The political evolution of Armenia and Azerbaijan moved in precisely opposite directions in the fall of 1990. In Armenia the new government attempted to extend democratic rule while reducing Communist party power in enterprises, institutes, and the military. Late in October the Supreme Soviet passed a law on privatization of the economy. Ter Petrosian was wary about Gorbachev's efforts to renew the federation through the signing of a new union treaty. In contrast, in Azerbaijan the Communist party won an overwhelming victory in the September elections to the republic's Supreme Soviet, reducing the Popular Front to an insignificant political force. A close working alliance developed between Gorbachev and Mutalibov, who like most of the other Muslim Communist leaders in the southern republics supported the Kremlin's plan for a union treaty to bind up the fragmenting union.

Gorbachev's revolution-from-above was spinning out of control by the fall of 1990, and former supporters of the Soviet president feared that democracy would soon fall victim to social chaos and political conservatism. Unwilling to break with his allies within the Communist apparatus, Gorbachev first moved toward the reformers in July, accepting the radical 500-day program for economic reform, only to turn against the reformers and toward the "Right" in the fall. The only effective means at the president's disposal were the army, the KGB, and the Communist bureaucracy. In the "war of laws" waged between the central Soviet government and the republics, even presidential degrees were not enforced locally. As Soviet political scientist Andranik Migranyan put it, "There is no verticality of power." The restructuring of the central government in December 1990—a stronger presidency combined with a new Council of the Federation with policymaking powers, a Cabinet of Ministers, and a consultative Security Council—and the increase of power in the hands of Gorbachev could not resolve the fundamental political problem in the USSR: the relationships between the center and the peripheries, most importantly the union republics. Faced with the breakup of his country, Gorbachev offered greater autonomy to the republics through a new union treaty, but the first draft, published in November 1990, found few takers. Ter Petrosian had warned that a union treaty was possible but not on the basis of the existing constitution or government, and he found this draft unacceptable. While in the United States in September, the Armenian president made it clear that he favored a confederation of equal, sovereign states.

Similarly, the emerging political leader of the Russian republic, Boris Yeltsin, believed that the political logic of the Gorbachev government was to wreck the republics' sovereignty and sabotage radical reforms. "The so-called revolution from above has ended. The Kremlin is no longer the initiator of the country's renewal or an active champion of the new. The processes of renewal, blocked at the level of the center, have moved to the republics. . . . The Union has lost at least six republics as a result of its policy of pressure. . . ."[8] Gorbachev called for "firm power" and proposed a referendum on "a Union of sovereign states with a new division of authority, but a single state nevertheless." The results in each republic would be a final verdict, and if a republic decided to leave the Union, the law on secession adopted in April 1990 would apply.

Through December and the first months of 1991 Gorbachev remained allied with the conservatives. Shaken by the defections of his closest allies, Edvard Shevardnadze and Aleksandr Yakovlev, he equivocated when violence was used against Lithuanians and Latvians in January. The Council of the Federation in Moscow sent a delegation, which included Armenia's president, Levon Ter Petrosian, to Vilnius to negotiate, but the very evening of the day they arrived, January 12–13, shootings resulted in thirteen people killed. Massive demonstrations were held in Moscow protesting the Baltic repressions. The Right pulled back, and the elected governments of the Baltic republics remained in power.

While Gorbachev struggled to stave off the collapse of his state, a second draft of his union treaty was published on March 9, just a week before the planned referendum. But the Baltic republics, Moldova, Armenia, and Georgia, refused to take part in either negotiations or the referendum. Only the nine Slavic and Muslim republics were willing to work, warily, with Gorbachev. As early as January, the Armenian parliament, led by the HHSh, had decided not to participate in the referendum, whose results, they held, would be binding on the whole of the Soviet Union and contradict the rights of republics to self-determination.[9] Prime Minister Manukian dismissed the whole process as "a political game, a temporary maneuver."[10] At the beginning of March the Armenian Supreme Soviet announced that the republic would hold its own referendum on September 21 to comply with the Soviet law on secession.

The new draft treaty proposed that the Union was to be a federation, with federal laws supreme, one currency, a federal budget, and taxes. The republics were to be responsible for setting the rules for secession from the Union and accepting new members into the Union. The center was to control implementation of security, war and peace, and foreign policy, but the strategy for state security and determination of foreign policy and defense policy, as well as the compilation and monitoring of the budget, would be joint responsibilities of the center and the republics. The ownership of property, resources, and lands was to be shared by center and republics, and republic laws were to be considered in implementation of use.

On March 17, the referendum was held in the nine Slavic and Muslim republics, while the six determined to be independent sat it out. Though support for Yeltsin was strong in Russia, where his proposal for an elected presidency passed overwhelmingly, Gorbachev could be satisfied with a 76.4 percent vote overall for the union. His greatest support came from the countryside and the more conservative republics in Central Asia. Ninety-two percent of Azerbaijani voters voted for the union, and in Nagorno-Karabagh a majority came out for the union.

With what he considered a mandate on union, Gorbachev was now prepared to reassess his political alliances. On April 23, he met at a dacha with the leaders of the nine Slavic and Muslim republics and worked out an agreement on dealing with the current crisis. They agreed to finalize the draft of the union treaty, draft a constitution for the union of sovereign states within six months after the signing of the treaty, and carry out new elections for the union political bodies. The 9 + 1 agreed that Latvia, Lithuania, Estonia, Moldavia, Georgia, and Armenia could independently decide whether to sign the union treaty but pointedly made it clear that those republics signing would be granted most-favored nation status in economic relations.

The April 23 agreement was a decisive move by Gorbachev toward the positions advocated by Yeltsin, both in the area of economic reforms and in the concessions made to the sovereign republics. But the USSR president was still walking a tightrope between conservative forces that believed that the union treaty gave too much power to the republics and the more independent-minded republics that would make no concessions on their sovereignty. On May 21, the USSR Supreme Soviet expressed its dissatisfaction with the 9 + 1 agreement and proposed a renovated federation of Soviet republics with a socialist system for all of them. Only three weeks later did the Supreme Soviet of the USSR adopt, with reservations, the draft of the union treaty.

Through the spring Armenia paid a high price for its moves toward independence. In May Soviet paratroopers landed at Erevan airport to protect Soviet defense installations in Armenia, without notifying the Armenian government of the movement. Fighting broke out on the border of Armenia and Azerbaijan, and Armenians accused Soviet troops of once again deporting Armenians from Getashen (Chaikend) and Martunashen in Azerbaijan. The Azerbaijanis claimed only that documents were being checked and that armed militants were in the area, but eyewitnesses told of beatings and people being forced to sign documents that they were willing to leave their villages. Ter Petrosian issued a statement on May 6: "To all intents and purposes, the Soviet Union has declared war on Armenia."[11] A village inside Armenia (Voskepar in the Novemberyan district) was destroyed by invading MVD troops under Azerbaijani control. Combat continued in the Goris district where six villages were entered by hostile soldiers. In retaliation Armenians in Dilijan disarmed sixty Soviet soldiers and held them hostage.

Ter Petrosian told *Moscow News* that Armenia saw no solution to its problems other than independence. Having chosen a legitimate way of seceding from the Union, through a referendum, Armenians wanted no confrontation with the Soviet Union. Independence would allow Armenia to receive direct economic assistance from other countries. "The Armenian diaspora will assume the part of both a serious mediator and a large-scale investor. So . . . the status of least favoured nation with which the non-aligned republics are being threatened may not work in relation to Armenia." He went on to state that "Armenia does not at all rule out the possibility of joining the would-be Union if the latter does not use its power like a 16th Republic to suppress the rights of sovereign states. . . . [T]he 9 + 1 agreement has left the door open for a future membership in the Union." He reminded the readers that it was not Armenia that backed away from the Union but the Union that backed away from Armenia, "leaving it one on one with its problems."[12]

Just a month before the planned referendum on independence, the Armenian president made it clear that he understood the economic legacies of the empire Armenia was leaving. The six republics that were moving toward full independence remained highly dependent on the Soviet market and on Soviet supplies of raw material. Altogether they represented only 7.2 percent of the Soviet population, while the nine made up over 92 percent. Highly interlocked economically, the share of national material product of each republic delivered to the other republics ranged from 31 to 67 percent. Only the Russian republic was relatively self-sufficient, sharing only 18 percent (1988).[13] None of the Soviet republics was integrated into the world economy. Foreign exports made up only 1 percent of national material production in Armenia or Kirgizia, only 9 percent in Russia. Raw materials were exported only from Russia, Ukraine, and Belorussia in significant amounts.[14]

Ethnically the most homogeneous of Soviet republics, Armenia was perhaps the most unfortunate economically—with nearly a quarter of the population homeless, the victims of both political and natural earthquakes. Armenia had a population of about 3,283,000. Its neighbor Azerbaijan numbered 7,029,000, and Georgia 5,449,000. With less than 16 million people, Transcaucasia represented just under 6 percent of the whole Soviet population. Armenia made up only 1.1 percent of the Soviet population, produced only 0.9 percent of the USSR's national material product (NMP) (1.2 percent in industry, 0.7 percent in agriculture), retained 1.4 percent of the state budget revenue, delivered 63.7 percent of its NMP to other republics, and exported 1.4 percent abroad. It was highly integrated into the Soviet economy. Its exports flowed almost entirely to other parts of the Union, and its imports came from its sister republics. Along with Estonia and Tajikistan, Armenia had the highest level of imports of any Soviet republic. Forty percent of all enterprises in Armenia were devoted to defense and were in particular trouble.

With the union treaty about to be signed, Gorbachev left for a vacation in the Crimea in late August. Fearful that the union treaty meant the end of the Soviet Union as they hoped to preserve it, and angry at Yeltsin's decree removing Communist party organizations from places of work, the conservative leaders of the army, KGB, and the party decided to act. On the morning of August 19, the world awoke to hear the stunning news that a self-proclaimed Emergency Committee had overthrown Gorbachev and taken control of the Soviet government. For three tense days the forces loyal to Yeltsin and the democratic movement withstood the threats from the *putchisti*. In his Crimean isolation Gorbachev refused to give in to the coup organizers, and after a strained stalemate the army and police refused to obey the plotters. The coup collapsed and with it the last hopes of a union treaty.

While Azerbaijan's Mutalibov had welcomed the coup, and Georgia's president Zviad Gamsakhurdia vacillated, Ter Petrosian resolutely opposed the plotters. The Armenian government called publicly for restraint, and Ter Petrosian phoned Yanaev, Yazov, Kryuchkov, and Pugo to discover their views about Karabagh. Ten Soviet generals arrived in Erevan and tried to persuade Ter Petrosian to introduce a state of emergency in Armenia. The republic's defense committee secretly resolved to have the republic's legal armed forces go underground and wage guerilla warfare. Prime Minister Manukian predicted the coup would collapse within two or three months.

The new political environment created by the failed coup provided both opportunities and dangers. Ter Petrosian, who believed that Gorbachev's personnel blunders, indecisiveness, and concessions to the Right were to blame for the coup, was overjoyed by the political defeat of the conservatives. Armenian leaders hoped that a more powerful Russia under Yeltsin would provide the economic and political support that the central government under Gorbachev had denied them. At the same time there was an awareness that some kind of relationship, particularly in the realm of economics, was essential between Armenia and whatever remained of the Soviet Union.

The Communist leaders of Azerbaijan, discredited by their backing of the coup, played the nationalist card as they had in the preceding few years, posing as the defender of the homeland against Armenian pretensions. They quickly suppressed the Popular Front and organized an election in which Mutalibov ran as the only real candidate for president. The continuing Armenian presence in mountainous Karabagh and surrounding villages, still a thorn in the side of all Azerbaijanis, even the more democratic elements of the Popular Front, provided a unifying motive for the political elite and a lever by which the center or Russia could influence Azerbaijani politics. Left to the mercy of an Azerbaijan unchecked by Soviet restraints, the Armenians there had no options except active resistance or emigration. Fighting continued through the fall into the winter, despite efforts by Yeltsin and Kazakhstan's Nursultan Nazarbayev to broker an agreement on Karabagh between Ter Petrosian and Mutalibov in late September. The crisis heated up briefly in November when a helicopter crashed in Karabagh and the Azerbaijanis labeled the event an act of Armenian terrorism. Azerbaijan's parliament debated war measures against Armenia and voted to annul the autonomous status of Karabagh.

Within the first two months of the failed coup Armenians went to the polls twice: the first time on September 20 to reaffirm the commitment to independence; the second on October 16 to elect Levon Ter Petrosian president of the republic. Receiving 83 percent of the votes cast, Ter Petrosian now had a popular mandate to carry out his vision of Armenian independence and self-sufficiency. Among the defeated candidates the long-time militant Paruir Hairikian received 7.2 percent of the vote; Sos Sarksian, the Dashnak candidate, 4.3 percent; and the others—Zori Balayan, Raphael Ghazarian, and Ashot Navasartian—less than .5 percent each.[15]

As the power of the central state rapidly withered away through the fall of 1991, almost all the Soviet republics established themselves as independent states. At the same time a series of attempts were made to resurrect some form of central authority or at least linkages between republics. Gorbachev tried in vain to resurrect the union treaty, but interrepublic cooperation could only be achieved on the economic level. In early October ten republics, including Armenia, agreed to an economic treaty, though only eight (including Armenia) actually signed it on October 18.[16] At the Kremlin ceremony Ter Petrosian stated that the Treaty on an Economic Community signified qualitatively new relations between independent states. In this treaty, for the first time in seventy-four years, political considerations have given way to purely economic ones. Deep-seated processes of development are being freed of ideological fetters and can proceed normally, and "that is why Armenia signed this treaty."[17]

Early in November Gorbachev brought seven republics—Russia, Belorus, Kazakhstan, Azerbaijan, Kyrgyzstan, Tajikistan, and Turkmenistan—together in an agreement to work toward a new confederation, the Union of Sovereign States.[18] Ominously for its success, the second-largest republic, Ukraine, was absent, preparing for its own referendum on independence. Within two weeks the effort was scuttled when the leaders of the seven republics decided to refer the issue back to their parliaments.[19] On December 1, Ukraine's citizens voted overwhelmingly for independence, and a week later, on December 8, the leaders of the three Slavic republics—Yeltsin, Kravchuk, and Shushkevich—announced that the USSR had ceased to exist and that a commonwealth had been set up by the three republics to which other republics were invited to join. An economic declaration linked the three republics in a common currency system and a joint economic program. Gorbachev was stunned by what he considered an illegal act. Left out of the negotiations, the chief spokesman for the Central Asian republics, Nazarbayev, was dismayed by the preemptive move by the Slavic republics. In Erevan, however, Ter Petrosian offered "full support" for the initiative and signaled Armenia's intention to join the new commonwealth. The Armenian voters of Karabagh responded to the collapse of the Soviet Union with overwhelming support for a referendum for independence (December 10).

The positive effects of the revolutionary transformations that took place in the second half of 1991 in the Soviet Union were more than matched by the anxiety shared alike by the former Soviet peoples and many Europeans and Americans that economic collapse and militant nationalism will lead to unprecedented instability in the international order. For all its faults, Soviet-style Communism and imperialism had managed a rough peace throughout the Soviet empire, both within the USSR and along its borders, that precluded interethnic warfare and interstate hostilities. Yet while the erosion of Pax Sovietica led to enormous uncertainty and confusion about the future of the non-Russian peoples of the Soviet periphery, the end of the cold war presented a dangerous opportunity for self-definition and determination that had been denied to most of these nationalities since the end of the Russian Civil War. Like the Baltic republics, Ukraine, and others, Armenia seized that opportunity to shape its own future. With a new confidence born of the conviction that Armenians did not need a "third force" to achieve their independent statehood, the post-Communist government of the Republic of Armenia combined a cautious pragmatism with a bold faith that it could construct its own stability and prosperity in the troubled and treacherous world in which it was forced to live.

Notes

PREFACE

1. Stuart Hall, "Ethnicity: Identity and Difference," *Radical America* XXIII, 4 (October–December 1989), p. 19.

INTRODUCTION

1. Anthony D. Smith, *The Ethnic Origins of Nations* (Oxford: Basil Blackwell, 1986), p. 2.

2. Gerard J. Libaridian, ed., *Armenia at the Crossroads: Democracy and Nationhood in the Post-Soviet Era. Essays, Interviews and Speeches by the Leaders of the National Democratic Movement in Armenia* (Watertown, MA: Blue Crane Books, 1991), p. 108.

3. Among the few exceptions to this bleak picture are the investigation of the last years of the Erevan khanate by George Bournoutian, the studies of the revolutionary movement by Louise Nalbandian and Anahide Ter Minassian, the encyclopedic works on the independent Armenian republic by Richard Hovannisian, and the analyses of Soviet Armenia by Mary Matossian and Claire Mouradian. (See the bibliography at the end of this volume.)

4. This argument has been made quite convincingly about another ancient and dispersed people, the Jews. "The successes of the group, and its past glory, are linked to its essence, just as the failure and misdeeds of adversary groups are to theirs. Present national consciousness is projected back into the past. . . . All of history is reconstructed as a function of a single project: the constitution of the ethnic-national group as it exists today." Maxime Rodinson, *Cult, Ghetto, and State: The Persistence of the Jewish Question,* trans. Jon Rothschild (Thetford, Norfolk: Al Saqi Books, 1983), p. 127.

5. Ełishe, *History of Vardan and the Armenian War,* trans. and commentary by Robert W. Thomson (Cambridge, MA: Harvard University Press, 1982).

6. This view of the nation as an "imagined community" is influenced by much of the writing on nationality and nationalism by Anthony D. Smith, Benedict Anderson, Eric J. Hobsbawm, and others.

7. Kevork Bardakjian, *The Mekhitarist Contribution to Armenian Culture and Scholarship* (Cambridge, MA: Harvard College Library, 1976).

8. Thomson, "Introduction," Ełishe, *History of Vardan and the Armenian War,* p. 2.

9. Moses Khorenats'i, *History of the Armenians,* trans. and commentary by Robert W. Thomson (Cambridge, MA: Harvard University Press, 1978), p. 69.

10. Nicholas Adontz, *Armenia in the Period of Justinian: The Political Conditions Based on the Naxarar System,* trans. and annotated by Nina G. Garsoian (Lisbon: Calouste Gulbenkian Foundation, 1970).

11. See, most importantly, Moses Khorenats'i, *History of the Armenians.*

12. Smith, *Ethnic Origins of Nations,* pp. 21–41.

13. Leonardo P. Alishan, "Crucifixion without 'The Cross': The Impact of the Genocide on Armenian Literature," *Armenian Review* XXXVIII, 1 (Spring 1985), p. 29.

14. Thomson, "Introduction," Ełishe, *History of Vardan and the Armenian War,* p. 25.

15. The poet Rafael Patkanian (1830–1892) writes of Vardan's love for the soil *(hogh)* of his motherland *(mayreni)* in his poem *The Death of the Valiant Vardan Mamikonian.* Ibid., p. 51.

16. On the *millet* system, see Benjamin Braude and Bernard Lewis, eds., *Christians and Jews in the Ottoman Empire: The Functioning of a Plural Society,* 2 vols. (London: Holmes and Meier, 1982). See, particularly, the essay on the origins of the Armenian patriarchate by Kevork B. Bardakjian, "The Rise of the Armenian Patriarchate of Constantinople," in volume I, pp. 89–100.

17. Smith, *Ethnic Origins of Nations,* pp. 96–97.

1. ARMENIA AND ITS RULERS

1. Karl W. Deutsch, *Nationalism and Social Communication: An Inquiry into the Foundations of Nationality,* 2nd ed. (Cambridge, MA: MIT Press, 1966).

2. Ibid., pp. 70–71.

3. Karl W. Deutsch, *Nationalism and Its Alternatives* (New York, 1969), p. 14.

4. Ibid., p. 78.

5. Karl W. Deutsch, "Are Our Models of Nationalism Western and Provincial? Nationalism in Different World Regions" (Unpublished lecture, Harvard University, November 1980).

6. Deutsch, *Nationalism and Its Alternatives,* p. 19.

7. On geographical influences on Armenia history, see Frédéric Macler, *Quatre conférences sur l'Arménie* (Paris, 1932), pp. 5–61. For an analysis of medieval Armenia's social structure and political divisions, see Nicholas Adontz, *Armenia in the Age of Justinian: The Political Conditions Based on the Naxarar System,* trans. and ed. by Nina Garsoian (Lisbon: Calouste Gulbenkian Foundation, 1970).

8. The travel account of H.F.B. Lynch [*Armenia: Travels and Studies,* 2 vols. (London: Longmans, Green, 1901; Beirut: Khayats, 1965)] remain among the most informative sources contrasting the life of Armenians in Turkish and Russian Armenia.

9. The best introduction in English to the early history of Armenian political movements is Louise Nalbandian, *The Armenian Revolutionary Movement: The Development of Armenian Political Parties through the Nineteenth Century* (Berkeley: University of California Press, 1963). A vast literature of partisan histories and highly informative memoirs exists in Armenian. The best account of the history of the Armenian Revolutionary Federation (Dashnaktsutian) remains Mikayel Varandian, *H. H. Dashnaktsutian batmutiun,* 2 vols. (Paris: Navarre, 1932; Cairo: Husaber, 1950).

10. Hagop Barsoumian, "Economic Role of the Armenian Amira Class in the Ottoman Empire," *Armenian Review* XXXI, 3/123 (March 1979), pp. 310–16.

11. Ronald Grigor Suny, *The Making of the Georgian Nation* (Bloomington and Stanford: Indiana University Press and Hoover Institution Press, 1988), pp. 113–43.

12. Ronald Grigor Suny, "Populism, Nationalism and Marxism: The Origins of Revolutionary Parties among the Armenians of the Caucasus," *Armenian Review* XXXII, 2/120 (June 1979), p. 136.

13. Cited in Deutsch, *Nationalism and Its Alternatives*, p. 3.

14. James Etmekjian, *The French Influence on the Western Armenian Renaissance, 1843–1915* (New York: Twayne, 1964), pp. 94–161.

15. A. D. Sarkissian, *History of the Armenian Question to 1885* (Urbana: University of Illinois Press, 1938); William L. Langer, *The Diplomacy of Imperialism*, I (New York: Alfred Knopf, 1951).

16. Anahide Ter Minassian, "Le mouvement révolutionnaire arménien, 1890–1903," *Cahiers du monde russe et soviétique* XIV, 4 (October–December 1973), pp. 536–607.

17. Cited in Roderic Davison, *Reform in the Ottoman Empire, 1856–1876* (Princeton University Press, 1963), p. 42.

18. Ibid., p. 60.

19. S. J. and Ezel Kural Shaw, *History of the Ottoman Empire and Modern Turkey*, II (Cambridge: Cambridge University Press, 1977), p. 260. See also, Bernard Lewis, *The Emergence of Modern Turkey* (Oxford: Oxford University Press, 1961), p. 204.

20. Michael Harris Haltzel, "The Reaction of the Baltic Germans to Russification during the Nineteenth Century" (Ph.d. diss., Harvard University, 1971), p. 113.

21. Ibid.

22. For a fuller discussion of Russian views of the Armenians, see Ronald Grigor Suny, "Images of the Armenians in the Russian Empire," in *The Armenian Image in History and Literature*, Richard G. Hovannisian (Malibu: Undena, 1981), pp. 105–37.

23. Richard G. Hovannisian, *Armenia on the Road to Independence, 1918* (Berkeley: University of California Press, 1967), pp. 41–42.

2. IMAGES OF THE ARMENIANS IN THE RUSSIAN EMPIRE

1. See *Armiano-russkie otnosheniia v XVII v.*, I (Erevan, 1955), passim.

2. Laurence Lockhart, *The Fall of the Safavid Dynasty and the Afghan Occupation of Persia* (Cambridge, 1958).

3. Cited in P. T. Arutiunian, *Osvoboditel'noe dvizhenie armianskogo naroda v pervoi chetverti XVIII veka* (Moscow, 1954), p. 238.

4. See Alan W. Fisher, *The Russian Annexation of the Crimea, 1772–1783* (Cambridge, 1970), passim. For an excellent analysis of Russian imperial expansion and integration in the late eighteenth century, see Marc Raeff, "The Style of Russia's Imperial Policy and Prince G. A. Potemkin," in G. N. Grob, ed., *Statesmen and Statecraft of the Modern West* (Barre, MA, 1967), pp. 1–52.

5. *Kavkazskii sbornik*, I (Tiflis, 1876), pp. 139–93.

6. A. S. Pushkin, "Puteshestvie v Arzrum vo vremia pokhoda 1829 goda," in *Sochineniia v trekh tomakh*, III (Moscow, 1974), p. 557.

7. Ronald G. Suny, "Russian Rule and Caucasian Society in the First Half of the Nineteenth Century: The Georgian Nobility and the Armenian Bourgeoisie, 1801–1856," *Nationalities Papers* VII, 1 (Spring 1979), pp. 53–78; *The Making of the Georgian Nation* (Bloomington and Stanford: Indiana University Press and Hoover Institution Press, 1988), pp. 63–95.

8. *Akty sobrannye Kavkazskoiu arkheograficheskoiu kommissieiu*, ed. A. P. Berzhe

(Tiflis, 1866), I, p. 436 (doc. no. 548) [henceforth cited as *Akty*]; reprinted in *Prisoedinenie vostochnoi Armenii k Rossii: Sbornik dokumentov, I (1801–1813)*, ed. Ts. P. Agaian (Erevan, 1972), p. 66.

9. N. I. Badriashvili, *Tiflis, I, Ot osnovaniia goroda do XIX v.* (Tiflis, 1934), p. 124.

10. *Akty*, I, p. 185.

11. Ibid., p. 329.

12. Ibid., p. 101–102.

13. Sh. A. Meskhiia, *Goroda i gorodskoi stroi feodal'noi Gruzii XVII–XVIII vv.* (Tbilisi, 1969), p. 232.

14. In his *Putevoditel' po Kavkazu*, G. V. Vaidenbaum wrote that "in the ethnographic sense Tiflis is, and it seems has been for a long time, an Armenian town. Georgians lived there only in a service capacity: they were military commanders, court officials, living with their grand retinues of nobles of various degrees, domestic servants, and peasants tending the gardens of their lords. They were only temporarily or accidentally inhabitants of the city. They usually lived on their dynastic estates. The real citizens of the city or *mokalaki* . . . i.e., the various kinds of craftsmen and traders, were Armenians who made up the majority of the population of Tiflis. . . . Georgians never had an inclination toward urban life nor were tied to it by occupation." [Quoted in *Putevoditel' po Tiflisu*, ed. K. N. Begichev (Tiflis, 1896), p. 40.]

15. Pushkin, *Sochineniia*, III, p. 538.

16. Dmitrii Bakradze and Nikolai Berzenov, *Tiflis v istoricheskom i etnograficheskom otnosheniiakh* (St. Petersburg, 1879), pp. 101–102.

17. *Obozrenie rossiiskikh vladenii na Kavkaze* (St. Petersburg, 1836), pp. 197–99.

18. Alfred J. Rieber, *The Politics of Autocracy: Letters of Alexander II to Prince A. I. Bariatinskii, 1857–1864* (Paris, 1966), p. 70.

19. Ibid., p. 104.

20. Ibid., p. 104, n. 1.

21. Ibid.

22. A. M. Amfiteatrov, *Armianskii vopros* (St. Petersburg, 1906), p. 47.

23. S. Maksimov, *Russkiia gory i kavkazskie gortsy* (n.p., 1873), p. 56.

24. P. I. Kovalevskii, *Kavkaz*, I (St. Petersburg, 1914), p. 234.

25. Sir Oliver Wardrop, *The Kingdom of Georgia: Travel in a Land of Women, Wine and Song* (London, 1988), pp. 13–14.

26. P. A. Zaionchkovskii, *Krizis samoderzhaviia na rubezhe 1870–1880 godov* (Moscow, 1964), p. 324. See also H. Heilbronner, "Alexander III and the Reform Plan of Loris-Melikov," *Journal of Modern History* XXXIII, 4 (December 1961), pp. 384–97.

27. Hugh Seton-Watson, *The Russian Empire, 1801–1917* (Oxford, 1967), p. 268.

28. P. A. Zaionchkovskii, *Rossiiskoe samoderzhavie v kontse XIX stoletiia (Politicheskaia reaktsiia 80-kh – nachala 90-kh godov)* (Moscow, 1970), p. 310.

29. K. P. Pobedonostsev, *Pis'ma Pobedonostseva k Aleksandru III*, II (Moscow, 1926), pp. 113–17; cited in Robert F. Byrnes, *Pobedonostsev: His Life and Thought* (Bloomington, 1968), p. 196.

30. William L. Langer, *The Diplomacy of Imperialism, 1890–1902*, 2nd ed. (New York, 1960), p. viii.

31. Anahide Ter Minassian, "Le mouvement révolutionnaire arménien, 1890–1903," *Cahiers du monde russe et soviétique* XIV, 4 (October–December 1973), p. 567.

32. Ibid., p. 588.

33. Ibid.

34. Aleksei Karpovich Dzhivelegov, *Armiane v Rossii* (Moscow, 1906), pp. 16–20.

35. Ibid., p. 25n.
36. *Russkii vestnik* XLVIII, 5 (May 1903), p. 253.
37. Ibid., p. 254.
38. Ibid., XLVII, 12 (December 1902), pp. 617–18.
40. Quoted in G. M. Tumanov, *Zametki o gorodskom samoupravlenii na Kavkaze* (Tiflis, 1902), p. 85.
41. *Russkii vestnik* XLVII, 12 (December 1902), p. 627.
42. Nikolai Nikolaevich Mazurenko, *Gruzino-armianskie pretenzii i zakavkazskaia revoliutsiia* (Kiev, 1906), p. 27.
43. A. Liprandi, *Kavkaz i Rossiia* (Kharkov, 1911), pp. 9–10.
44. Ibid., p. 46.
45. M. Gor'kii, *O kavkazskikh sobytiiakh* (Geneva, 1905), in M. Gor'kii, *Sobranie sochinenii v tridtsati tomakh* (Moscow, 1953), XXIII, p. 337.
46. Maxim Gor'kii, ed., *Sbornik armianskoi literatury* (Petrograd, 1916); Valerii Briusov, ed., *Poeziia Armenii s drevneishikh vremen do nashikh dnei* (Moscow, 1916).
47. Iu. A. Veselovskii, *Ocherki armianskoi literatury, istorii i kul'tury* (Erevan, 1972), p. 34.
48. I. I. Vorontsov-Dashkov, *Vsepoddanneishii otchet za vosem' let upravleniia Kavkazom* (St. Petersburg, 1913), p. 6.
49. Ibid., p. 7.

3. THE EMERGENCE OF THE ARMENIAN PATRIOTIC INTELLIGENTSIA IN RUSSIA

1. For an informed and critical review of the historiography on nationalism, see Geoff Eley, "Nationalism and Social History," *Social History* VI, 1 (January 1981), pp. 83–107.
2. The language here refers to two seminal works: Eric Hobsbawm and Terence Ranger, *The Invention of Tradition* (Cambridge: Cambridge University Press, 1983), and Benedict Anderson, *Imagined Communities: Reflections on the Origin and Spread of Nationalism* (London: Verso, 1983).
3. Eley, "Nationalism and Social History," p. 90.
4, Miroslav Hroch's *Die Vorkampfer der nationalen Bewegung bei den kleinen Volkern Europas* (Prague, 1968) and *Social Preconditions of National Revival in Europe: A Comparative Analysis of the Social Composition of Patriotic Groups among the Smaller European Nations* (Cambridge: Cambridge University Press, 1985) are the basic works. This particular formulation is from Miroslav Hroch, "The Social Composition of the Czech Patriots in Bohemia, 1827–1848," in Peter Brock and H. Gordon Skilling, eds., *The Czech Renascence of the Nineteenth Century: Essays Presented to Otakar Odlozilik in Honour of His Seventieth Birthday* (Toronto, 1970), pp. 33–52 (p. 39). See also Hroch, "How Much Does Nation Formation Depend on Nationalism?" *East European Politics and Societies* IV, 1 (Winter 1990), pp. 101–15, and Eley, "Nationalism and Social History," p. 100.
5. Hroch, "Social Composition," p. 39.
6. *The Life and Adventures of Joseph Emin, an Armenian. Written in English by Himself* (London, 1792); reprinted and edited by Amy Apcar, *Life and Adventures of Emin Joseph Emin 1726–1809 Written by Himself* (Calcutta, 1918), p. 58.
7 Ibid., pp. 141–42.
8. Later, in the early nineteenth century, the Mekhitarists expanded and improved the dictionary, then the *Nor Haikazian Bararan* (1836–1837). The work of the early

compilers of dictionaries was an essential part of the creation of national consciousness. Eley writes: "Language is less a prior determinant of nationality than part of a complex process of cultural innovation, involving hard ideological labour, careful propaganda and a creative imagination: dictionaries and elementary primers are among the earliest and most important cultural artifacts of a national tradition" ("Nationalism and Social History," p. 91).

9. Three volumes (Venice, 1784–1786); English translation: Michael Chamchian, *History of Armenia from B.C. 2247 to the Year of Christ 1780 or 1229 of the Armenian Era*, 3 vols., trans. Johannes Avdall (Calcutta: Bishops College Press, 1829). For a brief appreciation of the Mekhitarist efforts at "enlightenment," see Kevork B. Bardakjian, *The Mekhitarist Contributions to Armenian Culture and Scholarship* (Cambridge, MA: Harvard College Library, 1976).

10. A major interpretation and analysis of social and intellectual developments among Armenians in the Russian Empire was written by the Marxist David Ananoun (David Ter Danielian), *Rusahayeri hasarakakan zarkatsume*, 3 vols. (Baku, 1916; Echmiadzin, 1922; Venice, 1926).

11. There is a great deal of literature on the early relations of Armenians and the Russian Empire and on the annexation of eastern Armenia, one of the topics promoted in Soviet scholarship. Besides the Western study by George Bournoutian, *Eastern Armenia in the Last Decades of Persian Rule, 1807–1828: A Political and Socioeconomic Study of the Khanate of Erevan on the Eve of the Russian Conquest* (Malibu, CA: Undena, 1982), see V. R. Grigorian, *Erevani Khanutiune XVIII dari verjum (1780–1800)* (Erevan, 1958); A. R. Ioannisian, *Prisoedineniia Zakavkaz'ia k Rossii i mezhdunarodnye otnosheniia v nachale XIX stoletiia* (Erevan, 1958); Zh. A. Ananian, *Armianskaia koloniia Grigoriopol'* (Erevan, 1969); L. A. Pogosian, *Armianskaia koloniia Armavira* (Erevan, 1981); V. Parsamian, *Hayastane XIX dari arajin kesin* (vol. 7 of the *Hai zhoghovordi patmutiun*) (Erevan, 1960).

12. For an overview of Russo-Armenian relations in the nineteenth century, see Ronald Grigor Suny, "Images of the Armenians in the Russian Empire," in Richard G. Hovannisian, ed., *The Armenian Image in History and Literature* (Malibu, CA: Undena, 1981), pp. 105–37.

13. Information on Armenian education in the first half of the nineteenth century can be found in a very useful but disorganized monograph, S. G. Areshian, *Armianskaia pechat' i tsarskaia tsenzura* (Erevan, 1957).

14. On Gabriel Patkanian, see Areshian, *Armianskaia pechat'*, pp. 44–54; Shushanik Nazarian, "Gabriel Patkaniani kiankn u grakan-hasarakan gotsuneutiune (1830–1860–akan tt.)," *Banber Matenadarani* 3 (1956). Much of the information on Patkanian and Nalbandian came from an unpublished paper by Sarkis Shmavonian, a portion of which was edited into his article: "Mikayel Nalbandian and Non-Territorial Armenian Nationalism," *Armenian Review* XXXVI, 3/143 (Autumn 1983), pp. 35–56.

15. The Literature on Nalbandian is extensive. His complete works are available in Armenian: Mikayel Nalbandian, *Erkeri likatar zhoghovatsu*, 4 vols. (Erevan, 1940–1948); and selected works in Russian: M. Nalbandian, *Izbrannye filosfskie i obshchestvenno-politichskie proizvedeniia* (Moscow, 1954). One of Nalbandian's most important writings has been translated into English, along with an analysis, by Leon D. Megrian, "Mikayel Nalbandyan and His Tract 'Agriculture as the True Way,'" *Armenian Review* XXVII, 2/106 (Summer 1974), pp. 160–77. For biographical information, see A. M. Injikian, *Mikayel Nalbandiani kianki ev gortsuneutian taregrutiune* (Erevan, 1954); and S. K. Daronian, *Mikael Nalbandian: Problemy tvorchestva i literaturnykh sviazei* (Erevan, 1975).

16. Nalbandian, *Erkeri*, II, p. 65. The translations of Nalbandian's works are taken from the unpublished manuscript by Sarkis Shmavonian.

17. Ibid., IV, p. 45; Injikian, *Mikayel Nalbandiani kianki,* p. 78: Letter to Grigor Saltikian, June 1, 1857.
18. Nalbandian, *Erkeri,* pp. 452–55.
19. Ibid.

4. POPULISM, NATIONALISM, AND MARXISM

1. "Le mouvement révolutionnaire arménien, 1890–1903," *Cahiers du monde russe et soviétique* XIV, 4 (October–December 1973), p. 554.
2. *droeba,* no. 3, 1872; G. I. Megrelishvili, *Gruzinskaia obshchestvenno-ekonom-icheskaia mysl' vtoroi poloviny 19 veka i nachala 20 veka,* II (Tbilisi, 1959), pp. 61–62.
3. The members, led by a teacher Arsen Kritian (1850–1910) and Petros Haikazuni (1839–1927), managed for six years to avoid detection by the police until exposed by an unsympathetic bishop in April 1875. Forty-three members of the Aleksandropol society were arrested, along with a number of participants in a sister society, the "Office of Love for the Fatherland" *(Kontora hairenaits),* which had been set up the year before in Karaklis by Hambartsum Balasaniants (1840–1900). [For information on these groups, see V. A. Parsamian, *Pervoe zhandarmskoe delo v Aleksandropole* (Erevan, 1936); and his *Istoriia armianskogo naroda, 1801–1900 gg. Kniga pervaia* (Erevan, 1972), pp. 298–301.] Little is known about the group's activities or its aims, except that its leaders dreamed of a free Armenia. The members distributed portraits of Mikayel Nalbandian to students, read his more nationalist verses, and were familiar with the ideas expressed in his work *Agriculture as the True Path (Erkragortsutiune vorpes ughigh janaparh),* a copy of which was discovered among Kritian's papers by the police. The Aleksandropol group has the distinction as the first organization in eastern Armenia that advocated the liberation of Armenia, a precursor to the Armenian revolutionary movement of a decade later.
4. Artsruni had inherited great wealth from his father and as a young man studied in Moscow, Geneva, and Heidelberg where he was awarded the doctorate of philosophy. In his obituary for Artsruni, the writer Aleksandr Shirvanzade pictured him as the leader of a third generation of the Armenian nineteenth-century intelligentsia. The "enlighteners" of the first generation—Khachatur Abovian, Mikayel Nalbandian, and Stepan Nazariants—had given way to men who saw the only salvation for Armenians coming from the national church. But Artsruni, influenced by the Russian "men of the Sixties," revived the earlier "progressive" tendency, writing about the despotism of Armenian men within the family, demanding freedom for women, urging industrial development for Transcaucasia, and, in general, touting the virtues of Western liberalism and enterprise. (Shirvanzade, "Grigorii Artsruni," *Novoe obozrenie,* no. 3097, December 24, 1892). For additional information on Artsruni, see Kh. G. Gulanian, *Ocherki istorii armianskoi ekonomicheskoi mysli xix veka* (Moscow, 1955), pp. 226–88; and Leo, *Grigor Artsruni* (3 vols.) (Tiflis, 1901–1904).
5. S. T. Arkomed (Gevork Gharajian), *Pervaia gruppa revoliutsionerov armian na Kavkaze* (Tiflis, 1929), pp. 7–14.
6. Ruben Khanazatian recalled the day that his relatives read in *Mshak* about Article LXI of the Berlin Treaty and sadly concluded that Armenia's case could be brought forcefully before the Great Powers only if the Turkish Armenians followed the Bulgarian example and promoted an insurrectionary movement. Ruben Khan-Azat, "Hai Heghapokhakani Husherits," *Hairenik Amsakir* 8 (56) (June 1927), p. 62.
7. Arkomed, *Pervaia gruppa,* p. 13.
8. A. Snegireva, "Revoliutsionnye organizatsii gruzinskikh narodnikov," in *Istoriia klassovoi bor'by v Zakavkaz'i: Sbornik statei. Kniga pervaia,* ed. M. Zhakov, S. Sef, and G. Khachapuridze (Tiflis, 1930), p. 29.

9. Khan-Azat, "Hai Heghapokhakani Husherits," p. 64.

10. Kristapor Mikayelian noted that *Narodnaia volia* was very influential among Caucasian youth in the early 1880s. The ideal of Russian, Georgian, and Armenian students was international socialism, and they united in common organizations. "Bekorner im husherits," *Hairenik Amsakir* II, 10 (August 1924), p. 56.

11. Khan-Azat, vol. 8, p. 64.

12. Mikayelian, "Bekorner im Husherits," p. 56; Louise Nalbandian, *The Armenian Revolutionary Movement: The Development of Armenian Political Parties through the Nineteenth Century* (Berkeley: University of California Press, 1963), p. 137.

13. Mikayelian, "Bekorner im Husherits," p. 57.

14. Nalbandian, *Armenian Revolutionary Movement*, p. 138. Leaving the Caucasus for Moscow or St. Petersburg did not require that Armenian students give up their interest in the liberation movement, for in the north, too, circles existed in semi-secrecy. In April, 1882, four Armenians studying in Moscow formed a "Union of Patriots" *(Hairenaserneri Miutiun)* whose leader Nerses Abelian (1855–1933) willingly acknowledged his indebtedness to the *Mshakakanner:* "At the beginning of the 1880s, Armenian public opinion, after the bitter disillusionment of the Treaty of Berlin and its Article 61, centered its attention on internal work in order to prepare a mass movement whose aim would be the liberation of the Armenian working population of Turkish Armenia from the Sultan's yoke. The heralds of this idea were the newspaper *Mshak* and its talented directors, Artsruni and Raffi" [from Abelian's memoirs, cited in V. A. Parsamian, *Istoriia armianskogo naroda (1801–1900 gg.)*]. *Kniga Pervaia* (Erevan, 1972), p. 308. Like the *Mshakakanner* in Tiflis, the Moscow-based Union of Patriots directed their propaganda efforts toward Turkish Armenia. In 1883–1884 the union joined with Abraham Dastakian and other former members of his Tiflis circle and published an illegal newspaper, *Azatutian avetaber* (Herald of Freedom), which warned Armenians that liberty could be won only with the sacrifice of their own blood and not by reliance on the Western powers. While emphasizing the primacy of political independence for Turkish Armenia, the paper also advocated social reform: "the cornerstone of the people's freedom is its economic independence" (Nalbandian, *Agriculture as the True Path*, pp. 142–43). The flavor of Russian populist thought is evident in their call for communal ownership of property. Another group known as *Haiaser* or *Azgaser* (Patriot) existed in Erevan in the early 1880s and was discovered by the police when a certain T. Mgerian slapped the face of the Russian inspector of the Erevan classical high school for calling him *Armiashka*. Mgerian was arrested, but within a day 5,000 rubles bail was raised to free him. The police then carried out searches in Erevan and in the homes of Artsruni and Raffi in Tiflis to uncover the hidden ties between the Erevan patriots and the Tiflis liberals. Although a connection could not be effectively established, enough evidence was gathered to create in the tsarist bureaucracy a lingering suspicion that the Armenian intelligentsia was involved in a far-reaching conspiracy that involved separatist ambitions and plans for the unification of eastern and western Armenia. The schools were seedbeds for such ideas. It was not long before the government took drastic action against the educational system of the Armenians.

15. Mikayelian, "Bekorner im Husherits," p. 58. Nalbandian, *Armenian Revolutionary Movement*, p. 139.

16. Arkomed, *Pervaia gruppa* pp. 23–27.

17. Gevork Gharajian (S. T. Arkomed), a teacher who witnessed the closing of such a school in Ganja (Elisavetpol'), remembered the arrival of the local inspector of school, Orlov, accompanied by police and soldiers, his order to the teachers and pupils to leave the school, and the tears of some of the children as they were forced out. The experience so embittered the young teacher that he decided to assassinate the school

inspector. As a member of Mikayelian's circle in Tiflis, he secured the approval of his comrades, but the assassination was never carried out. (Ibid., p. 27.)

18. Ibid., pp. 51–66.

19. Kristapor Mikayelian moved to Moscow in 1885 and studied Russian until his return to Tiflis in 1887. Arkomed claims that in this period Mikaielian drifted away from populism toward increasing concern with Turkish Armenia and a solution to the Armenian Question through diplomatic means. Gabo Mirzoian (d. 1902) and Khachatur Malumian were moving toward liberalism again with the Armenian Question central to their concerns. Malumian worked with *Mshak* until 1898 when he joined the *Dashnaktsutiun* and left for Geneva where he wrote for *Droshak*. He was killed by the Turks in the massacres of 1915. "Sandal" was sympathetic to anarchism, and he and Gharajian maintained that the Armenian Question was a matter exclusively for the Armenians in Turkey. The sixth member of the group, Konstantin Melikian, died in 1887, and his political outlook remains unknown. (Arkomed, *Pervaia gruppa*, pp. 36–37.)

20. The principal western Armenian advocate of Armenian liberation in this period was Mkrtich Portugalian (1848–1923), a liberal democrat who published the newspaper *Armenia* in Marseilles from 1885. Armenian students in the Caucasus and Western Europe, excited by the first Armenian paper free from censorship, were encouraged by its articles to consider forming a revolutionary political party. Portugalian himself hesitated to establish such a party. In Van a group of his former students set up the first Armenian political party, the Armenakans, in 1885, but students in Europe did not learn of the party's existence for another ten years.

21. S. T. Arkomed, *Za rubezhom. Istoricheskie zametki. Period studentchestva ot 1886 g. do 1890 g. Chast' 1.* (Tiflis, 1929), pp. 12–13.

22. Ibid., p. 61.

23. When it was completed, he sent it off to the liberal Armenian editor, Mkrtich Portugalian, for publication in *Armenia*, but Portugalian rejected the text and it was lost. Gharajian writes that the translation was not published for lack of funds. (Ibid., p. 32.)

24. S. T. Arkomed, *Za rubezhom*, p. 8.

25. Khan-Azat, "Hai Heghapokhakani Husherits," p. 71.

26. A seventh member of the group, Levon Stepanian, was at the time of the founding in Montpellier studying; after his graduation in the winter of 1887, he joined his comrades in Geneva. Nalbandian, *Armenian Revolutionary Movement*, p. 208.

27. Both Nazarbekian and Gharajian wrote articles for the first issue of *Hnchak*, but when his article was rejected by the others Gharajian broke with the group. What prompted this rejection is unknown, but Gharajian's progressive drift toward Marxism, a tendency not yet shared by the other members of *Hnchak* group, may have led to the rejection. Gharajian soon returned to the Caucasus where he hoped to form social democratic circles. Plekhanov suggested creating a "Caucasian Social Democratic Union," but Gharajian felt that cadres for such an organization were lacking. (S. T. Arkomed, *Za rubezhom*, p. 33.) When Gharajian crossed the border into Russia, most of his books were confiscated by the customs officer. The *Communist Manifesto* was torn to pieces, but he was allowed to keep the French edition of *Capital*. (Ibid., pp. 61–62.) Sometime later he read the first issue of Plekhanov's Geneva-based journal *Sotsial-Demokrat*, which had appeared in 1888. In his excitement, he sent off a warm letter to Plekhanov which ended: "Hail the arrival of Eastern Social Democracy!" (S. T. Arkomed, *Rabochee dvizhenie i sotsial-demokratiia na Kavkaze (s 80-kh gg. po 1903 g.)* [Moscow-Petrograd, 1923], p. 20.)

28. Khan-Azat, "Hai Heghapokhakani Husherits," V. 9, p. 55.

29. The relationship of Marxism and Populism in Russia at this time has been dealt

with in a very suggestive article by Richard Pipes, "Russian Marxism and the Populist Background: The Late Nineteenth Century," *Russian Review* XIX, 4 (October 1960), pp. 316–37. Pipes argues that "in the 1880's and 1890's inside Russia the Populist circles were deeply affected by Marxism, while Marxist circles were heavily under Populist influence, with Populism exerting its influence on the theoretical one" (p. 330). For another interpretation of the emergence of Russian Marxism from Populism, see Leopold H. Haimson, *The Russian Marxists and the Origins of Bolshevism* (Cambridge, MA: Harvard University Press, 1955), Part I.

30. Khan-Azat, "Hai Heghapokhakani Husherits," V. 9, p. 55.

31. Ibid., p. 57.

32. On *Eritasart Haiastan,* see Mikayelian, "Bekorner im husherits," pp. 60–62; Nalbandian, *Armenian Revolutionary Movement,* pp. 145–48.

33. Khan-Azat, "Hai Heghapokhakani Husherits," V. 10, pp. 65–66, 71.

34. Ibid., p. 68.

35. The radicals included Rostom Zarian, Aram Nazaretian, Hovsep Arghutian, Khachatur Malumian, N. Matinian, S. Makhumian, Hakop Kocharian, Tigran Hovhannesian, Ervant Taghianosian, Harutiun Iusufian, Galagszian, Vardges Kajaznuni, Martin Shatirian, Aleksandr Petrosian, and Others. (Ibid., V. 11, pp. 127–28.)

36. Ibid., pp. 128–29. Khanazatian compared Kalantar's approach to socialism to that of the Russian Populist Burtsev to whom political liberation was the primary goal and socialism only secondary.

37. Khanazatian reported ironically that now the young Armenian intellectuals could say: "While we are still socialists, following the example of the Russian revolutionaries, we are temporarily setting aside socialism." (Ibid., p. 129.)

38. Ibid., p. 128.

39. Ibid., V. 12, p. 126.

40. Sarkis Gugunian (1866–1913), the son of poor peasants, was educated at the Nersesian Jemaran in Tiflis and spent the later years of the 1880s in St. Petersburg where he made contact with Polish and Bulgarian students. He returned to Tiflis in the spring of 1890 and decided to form a volunteer band to march into Turkey. He managed to find money, weapons, and 125 young men to engage in this mission, which Anahide Ter Minassian calls "a summit of revolutionary romanticism" (p. 567). At first, the Dashnaks supported the expedition, but they soon abandoned the project. On September 23, 1890, the force set out toward Turkey but was soon attacked by Cossacks and arrested. The leaders were tried and exiled to Siberia. Their exploits and martyrdom made them the heroic subjects of legends and songs. [Ter Minassian, "Le mouvement révolutionaire arménien," pp. 566–68. Nalbandian, *Armenian Revolutionary Movement,* pp. 155–61; Mikaiel Varandian, *H. H. Dashnaktsutian Patmutiun,* I (Paris, 1932), pp. 69–77.]

41. Varandian, *H. H. Dashnaktsutian,* pp. 59–60.

42. Khan-Azat, "Hai Heghapokhakani Husherits," VI, 2 (62), pp. 122–23.

43. Ibid., p. 120.

44. Ibid., pp. 122–23. The first central committee of the Dashnaktsutiun included Kristapor Mikayelian, Simon Zavarian, Abraham Dastakian, Hovhannes Loris-Melikian, and Levon Sargsian. (Varandian, *H. H. Dashnaktsutian,* p. 64.)

45. Khan-Azat, "Hai Heghapokhakani Husherits," VI, 2 (62), p. 121.

46. Varandian, *H. H. Dashnaktsutian,* p. 63.

47. "Manifest H. H. Dashnaktsutian," in *Droshak "Hai Heghapokhakan Dashnaktsutian" Organ, 1890–1897* (n.p., 1958), p. i.

48. Khan-Azat, "Hai Heghapokhakani Husherits," VI, 4 (64) (February 1928), pp. 124–25; Nalbandian, *Armenian Revolutionary Movement,* pp. 163–64.

49. Nalbandian, *Armenian Revolutionary Movement,* p. 217.

5. LABOR AND SOCIALISM AMONG ARMENIANS IN TRANSCAUCASIA

1. Louise Nalbandian, *Armenian Revolutionary Movement: The Development of Armenian Political Parties through the Nineteenth Century* (Berkeley: University of California Press, 1963), p. 164.

2. Simon Vratzian, "The Armenian Revolution and the Armenian Revolutionary Federation," *Armenian Review* III, 3 (11) (Autumn: October 1950), p. 16.

3. When Ruben Khanazatian, the Hnchak who had negotiated with the Dashnaks about merger, arrived in Geneva early in 1891, he found that his fellow Hnchaks were much less willing to compromise than he had been in order to form a single revolutionary federation. The Geneva Hnchaks had received complaints from party members that Dashnaks treated them poorly and were convinced that the Dashnaktsutiun was in the hands not of the socialists Mikayelian and Zavarian but of non-socialist nationalists. [Ruben Khan-Azat, "Hai Heghapokhakani Husherits," *Hairenik Amsakir* VI, 4 (64) (February 1928), pp. 124–25; Nalbandian, *Armenian Revolutionary Movement*, pp. 163–64.] Avetis Nazarbekian, the leader of the Hnchaks in Geneva, disapproved of the first circular of the Dashnaktsutiun, the *Droshaki Trutsik Tert*, no. 1, the contents of which are unknown to us. After lengthy discussions the Hnchaks decided to end their agreement with the Dashnaks and communicated their intentions in *Hnchak* issues on May 18 and June 5, 1891, in which, as Louise Nalbandian points out, they claimed that no union of the two parties had ever taken place. (Nalbandian, *Armenian Revolutionary Movement*, p. 217.)

4. Avetis Nazarbek, "Zeitun," *Contemporary Review* LXIX (April 1896), pp. 513–28.

5. In his massive work, *The Diplomacy of Imperialism, 1890–1902* (Cambridge, MA: Harvard University Press, 1935), William L. Langer is particularly harsh in his judgments of the Hnchaks. He is convinced that their "leaders were quite prepared to have thousands of their fellow-countrymen massacred in order to force intervention by the European powers and in order to raise from the ruins of the Ottoman Empire a new Armenian socialist state" (p. 163). While there is evidence that individual Hnchaks may have held such callous views (see, for example, pp. 157–58), in fact Hnchak policy with its overt socialism de-emphasized reliance on Western intervention and counted on the armed resistance of the Armenian people themselves to create an independent and united Armenia. Their revolutionary efforts did result in extremely vicious responses from the Turks, but their policy was not cynically directed toward such a response but rather toward self-defense and the development of a revolutionary struggle. The mistake of the Hnchaks may have lain in their underestimation of the resilience of the Turkish government and in overestimation of their own strength. Langer's account rests on the assumption that the Turkish massacres of the Armenians were provoked by the revolutionaries who had little support among the Armenians themselves. But such an argument neglects analysis of the causes of the revolutionary movement itself, the situation of the Armenians in the Turkish Empire, or the fact that massacres had occurred long before the Hnchaks arrived on the scene. The clash between the Turkish rulers and their subject peoples arose from the refusal of significant groups within the ruled to acquiesce any longer to the oppressive material and political situation in which they lived. Langer argues consistently from the point of view of the Turkish rulers and excuses their excesses. While discussing the government-organized reprisals for the Dashnak seizure of the Ottoman Bank, in which 6,000 Armenians were killed in Constantinople by Turkish mobs, Langer writes "The troops conducted

themselves well and took little if any part in the proceedings. They merely looked on while the carnage took place" (p. 324).

6. Ibid., p. 197.

7. Ibid., p. 164.

8. Report no. 5561, quoted in Anahide Ter Minassian, "Le mouvement révolutionaire arménien, 1890–1903," *Cahiers du monde russe et soviétique* XIV, 4 (October––December 1973), p. 578.

9. Ibid., pp. 578–80.

10. Ibid., p. 581.

11. E. Aknouni, *Political Persecution: Armenian Prisoners of the Caucasus (A Page of the Tzar's Persecution)* (New York, 1911), pp. 12–13.

12. G. M. Tumanov, *Kharakteristiki i vospominaniia. Zametki kavkazskogo khronikera*, III (Tiflis, 1907), p. 66.

13. An observer of this development of nationalism in the Caucasus, the Social Democrat Gevork Gharajian wrote in 1910: "Ten or fifteen years ago . . . except for the 'Dashnaktsutiun' and 'Hnchak' parties and a few small bourgeois groups in Armenian society preoccupied with resolution of the national question in Turkish Armenia, and also the weak manifestation of national-chauvinist attitudes and feelings among the noble landholding elements of the Georgian and Muslim populations, the national question did not exist in the Caucasus as a mass social phenomenon. Workers and, in part, the peasant masses of the Transcaucasian peoples did not then know national strife, did not set up national barriers between themselves, and only in *ertoba* (Georgian for "unity") did they see their social-economic and political liberation. Only with the development of capitalism and the differentiation of economic and property relations in Caucasian society did national disagreements and objectives take on an increasingly sharp character in the following years." (S. T. Arkomed, *Rabochee dvizhenie i sotsial-demokratiia na Kavkaze (s 80-kh gg. po 1903 g.)* (Moscow-Petrograd, 1923), pp. 3–4.]

14. Tumanov, II, pp. 22–24.

15. Ibid., III (Tiflis, 1913), pp. 73–74.

16. Ter Minassian, "Mouvement révolutionaire arménien," pp. 572–73.

17. Ibid., p. 573; see Gharajian above, note 13.

18. Ter Minassian, "Mouvement révolutionaire arménien," pp. 597–99. Except for the workers in the railroad yards of Tiflis, those in Georgia (Tiflis and Kutaisi provinces) were primarily artisans. Georgians made up 42 percent of the nonagricultural work force in these provinces, Armenians 24 percent, and Russians 11 percent. In some industries, like tobacco and chemicals, Armenian workers made up the majority of the work force; Georgians made up a majority only in textiles and in the wineries. In general workers were mixed by nationality in factories, but occasionally an Armenian businessman would prefer hiring his own countrymen and countrywomen. For figures on workers in the Georgian provinces see Mio Kantere, "Utochnennye dannye o chislennosti i sostave rabochikh promyshlennosti Gruzii kontsa XIX nachala X vekov," *Matsne*, 1969, n. 1 (46), p. 82.

19. *droeba*, no. 15, 1872.

20. Ter Minassian, "Mouvement révolutionaire arménien," p. 599.

21. S. T. Arkomed, *Rabochee dvizhenie*, pp. 46–47.

22. Ts. P. Agaian et al., *Ocherki istorii kommunisticheskoi partii Armenii* (Erevan, 1967), p. 22.

23. S. T. Arkomed, *Rabochee dvizhenie*, pp. 43–44.

24. Ter Stepanian was killed in 1896 by the Dashnaks, according to V. Nevskii, *Ocherki po istorii rossiiskoi kommunisticheskoi partii*, I (Leningrad, 1925): pp. 496–500.

25. Members of this group included A. Khazhakian, S. Ter-Simonian, P. Mnatsakanian, S. Khanoian, S. Martikian, G. Sadatian, A. Muradian, Simon Zavarian, N. Madi-

nian, Kh. Malumian, and others. Others became Hnchaks, and some, like Khumarian, Khanoian, Martikian, and Mnatsakanian, eventually joined the Bolsheviks.

26. G. S. Khumarian, *Ashot Khumarian* (Erevan, 1971), pp. 7–8.

27. Ibid., p. 10.

28. Nevskii, p. 500. Anahide Ter Minassian quotes Khumarian as saying that "the socialism of the Association was far from the scientific socialism of Marx" ("Mouvement révolutionaire arménien," p. 577, n. 36).

29. Ter Minassian, "Mouvement révolutionaire arménien," p. 591.

30. For information on Palian (Balian) and the *Handes,* see Gerard Libaridian's "The Socialist Review *Handes* and Its Significance in the development of Armenian Political Thought," an unpublished paper presented to the Middle East Studies Association convention in Los Angeles, November 1976; also Kh. Gulanian, *Marksistskaia mysl' v Armenii (v kontse XIX-nachale XX veka)* (Erevan, 1967), pp. 51–55.

31. See Nalbandian, *Armenian Revolutionary Movement,* pp. 176–78, for details; also Great Britain, *Correspondence Respecting the Disturbances at Constantinople in August 1896,* Parl. Pub., 1897, vol. CI (Accounts and Papers), c. 8303, Turkey No. 1.

32. From the Dashnak program, cited by Ter Minassian, "Mouvement révolutionaire arménien," p. 583.

33. Ibid., p. 582.

34. Mikayel Varandian, *H. H. Dashnaktsutian Patmutiun,* I (Paris, 1932), p. 103.

35. Among them were V. G. Kurnatovskii, I. I. Luzin, S. Ia. Francheski, V. K. Rodzevich-Belevich, M. I. Malinin, N. G. Poletaev, S. Ia. Alliluev, and A. Ia. Krasnova (Ts. P. Agaian *Ocherki istorii kommunisticheskoi partii Armenii,* p. 18).

36. The young Stepan Shahumian wrote in 1900 to the newspaper *Taraz* praising the editor of *Murj,* Avetis Areskhanian, for his "many-sided and objective study of the phenomena of social life." [Letter to *Taraz,* no. 10, 1900; quoted in A. Voskerchian, *Stepan Shaumian i voprosy literatury* (Moscow, 1959), p. 25. This letter by Shahumian is excerpted by Voskerchian but has not been reproduced in any of the collections of Shahumian's letters or writings.]

37. For an excellent discussion of this period in the history of Russian socialism, see Allan K. Wildman, *The Making of a Workers' Revolution: Russian Social Democracy, 1891–1903* (Chicago: University of Chicago Press, 1967).

38. Wildman writes: "Reports from Odessa, Tiflis, and Rostov, and minor ripples from still more remote regions (Yaroslavl, Kostroma, Tver, Saratov, and Tula) during the next two years complete the impression of the uninterrupted diffusion of the technique of economic agitation to all corners of the Empire." (*Making of a Workers' Revolution,* p. 80.)

39. *Rabochee delo,* 1899, nos. 2–3; S. T. Arkomed, *Rabochee dvizhenie,* pp. 47–48.

40. S. T. Arkomed, *Rabochee dvizhenie,* pp. 47–48.

41. The leaders of the group were Haik Pilosian (H. Adamian), an Armenian from Turkey working in Enfiajian Tobacco Factory, and Garegin Kozikian (Esalem), a custodian employed by the Armenian Welfare Society. Other members included the dyer Melik Melikian, known as "Dedushka," Asatur Kakhoian (Banvor Khecho), a worker in Adel'khanov's shoe factory; the Social Democrat Gevork Gharajian; railroad workers, Kh. Kesheshian, Grigor Mkrtumian, and A. Ter-Harutiunian, workers from Bozarjian's tobacco plant, Aleksandr Vardanian, and Petros Tavlushian (Ts. P. Agaian *Ocherki istorii kommunisticheskoi partii Armenii,* pp. 95–96).

42. Ter Minassian, "Mouvement révolutionaire arménien," p. 596.

43. Ibid., pp. 596, 598.

44. Ts. P. Agaian *Ocherki istorii kommunisticheskoi partii Armenii,* p. 26; Ter Minassian, "Mouvement révolutionaire arménien," p. 597.

45. See Wildman, *Making of a Workers' Revolution,* pp. 215–16; also Leopold H. Haimson, *The Russian Marxists and the Origins of Bolshevism* (Cambridge, MA: Harvard University Press, 1955), pp. 120–21.

46. Ter Minassian, "Mouvement révolutionaire arménien," p. 595.

47. None of the reports of the 1899 celebration mentions any but Georgian speakers. Filip Makharadze, *Ocherki revoliutsionnogo dvizheniia v Zakavkaz'e* (Tiflis, 1927), p. 72; S. Talakvadze, *K istorii kommunisticheskoi partii Gruzii. Chast' I. (Dva perioda)* (Tiflis, 1925), p. 29.

48. The Armenian Social Democrat Gharajian, writing later under the name S. T. Arkomed, complained that the Georgians, who had more Social Democratic activists among their workers than did the Armenians, directed "their strength and energy . . . almost exclusively toward the Georgian proletariat." (*Rabochee dvizhenie*, pp. 52–53.) Arkomed goes so far as to claim that the "particularism" of the Georgian Social Democrats "drove many Armenian workers away from active participation in the revolutionary workers' movement." (Ibid., note to second edition, p. 179.) Since many Armenian workers understood Georgian, some Social Democrats reasoned, all propaganda and literature could be in the Georgian language. (Ibid., pp. 179–80). But many Armenian workers from the countryside did not understand any but their own language and thus could read only the nationalist press. The Dashnaks and Hnchaks, on the other hand, remained suspicious of the multi-national labor movement and "boycotted" the Social Democratic organizations, and this led Armenian workers to have to make the choice between an "internationalist" movement dominated by Georgians or the nationalist movement of their own people.

Not surprisingly Armenian Social Democrats found it extremely difficult to recruit Armenian workers into their party. For a long time the Tiflis Committee was unable to find a single Armenian typesetter who would work on a leaflet in the Armenian language, and ultimately a Georgian printer agreed to learn enough Armenian to set the leaflet. Gharajian-Arkomed himself tried in 1901 to organize a meeting of Armenian printers to discuss the views of the Social Democrats, but an old Hnchak printer disrupted the gathering by demanding that the Social Democrats explain their position on the liberation of Turkish Armenia. Gharajian's comrades attempted to convince the workers that the task of the Social Democrats was to organize a workers' party in the Caucasus and that the revolution in Turkey was the business of Turkish Armenians. Apparently this view was unacceptable to the printers and the meeting broke up in disagreements. (*Ibid.*, p. 54.)

49. The Azeri Social Democrats soon found themselves in a multinational socialist movement dominated by men and women of other nationalities, and this led to the establishment in 1904 of an Azerbaijani Social Democratic organization, *Himmat* (Endeavor), tied loosely to the RSDRP. For a recent treatment of *Himmat*, see Tadeusz Swietochowski, "The Himmat Party: Socialism and the National Question in Russian Azerbaijan, 1904–1920," *Cahiers du monde russe et soviétique*, XIX, 1–2 (January–June 1978), pp. 119–142.

50. *Iskra*, no. 6, July 1901.

51. When the second Tiflis Committee was elected, Gevork Gharajian was chosen as the sole Armenian member. Five Georgians, a Russian, and a Ukrainian made up the rest of the Committee which was arrested *en masse* on February 15, 1902.

52. Its members included the young Stepan Shahumian, later a leading Bolshevik in Transcaucasia and in 1917 a member of the Bolshevik Central Committee; Bogdan Knuniants, later a Bolshevik and still later a Menshevik-liquidationist; Arshak Zurabian (Zurabov), who became a Menshevik and an elected deputy to the Second State Duma; Ashot Khumarian, S. Khanoian, M. Melikian, R. Dashtoian, D. Shahverdian, A. Erzinkian, and others. (Ts. P. Agaian, *Ocherki istorii Kommunisticheskoi partii Armenii*, p. 34.)

53. Stepan Shaumian, *Izbrannye proizvedeniia*, I (Moscow, 1957), p. 17.

54. Ibid., pp. 17–18.

55. The Manifesto was sent to the editors of *Iskra,* and the young Vladimir Lenin

wrote a brief critique of their position on the national question. [*Iskra*, no. 33, February 1, 1903; V. I. Lenin, *Polnoe sobranie sochinenii* (5th edition) (Moscow, 1972), VII, pp. 102–106]. Lenin pointed out an inconsistency between proposing a federal solution to the national problem and rejecting the formation of politically autonomous national units. Opposed himself to federalism, Lenin suggested that the Union drop the demand for federation and limit itself to a demand for a democratic republic. "It is not the business of the proletariat to *preach* federalism and national autonomy, not the business of the proletariat to put forth such demands which inevitably become demands to create autonomous *class* states." (p. 105.)

56. Shaumian, *Izbrannye* proizvedeniia, I, p. 14.

57. For a discussion of the history of Armenian Marxism after the crisis of 1903, see Anaide Ter Minassian, "Aux origines du marxisme arménien: les spécifistes," *Cahiers du monde russe et soviétique*, XIX, 1–2 (January–June 1978), pp. 67–117.

6. RETHINKING THE UNTHINKABLE

1. Bernard Lewis, *The Emergence of Modern Turkey* (Oxford: Oxford University Press, 1961; 2nd edition, paperback, 1968), p. 329.

2. Ibid., p. 330.

3. The "provocation thesis" is explained at length and criticized in the illuminating article by Robert Melson, "A Theoretical Inquiry into the Armenian Massacres of 1894–1896," *Comparative Studies in Society and History* XXIV, 3 (July 1892), pp. 481–509.

4. Stanford and Ezel Kural Shaw, *History of the Ottoman Empire and Modern Turkey*, II (Cambridge: Cambridge University Press, 1977), pp. 315–16.

5. Ambassador Elekdag's letter was reprinted in *The Armenian Mirror-Spectator*, January 26, 1985, pp. 2, 15.

6. Salahi R. Sonyel, "Yeni Belgelerin Isigi altinda Ermeni Techcirleri—Armenian Deportations: A Re-appraisal in the Light of New Documents," *T.T.K. Belleten* c. XXXVI, no. 141, January 1972, pp. 31–69 (Turkish and English); Gwynne Dyer, "Turkish 'Falsifiers' and Armenian 'Deceivers': Historiography and the Armenian Massacres," *Middle Eastern Studies* XII, 1 (January 1976), p. 101.

7. Benjamin Braude and Bernard Lewis, "Introduction," Braude and Lewis, eds., *Christians and Jews in the Ottoman Empire: The Functioning of a Plural Society, Volume I: The Central Lands* (New York: Holmes and Meier, 1982), pp. 3–4.

8. Ibid., p. 7.

9. Roderic H. Davison, *Reform in the Ottoman Empire, 1856–1876* (Princeton: Princeton University Press, 1963), pp. 115–16.

10. Great Britain, *Parliamentary Papers. Accounts and Papers, Turkey*, for the years 1877 through 1881; A. O. Sarkissian, *History of the Armenian Question to 1885*, Illinois Studies in the Social Sciences, XXXV, 80 (Urbana: University of Illinois Press, 1938). Sarkissian used the thirty volumes of records of the Armenian National Assembly in Istanbul, "a true mine of information on Armenian affairs in Turkey." [*Adenakerutiunk Azkayin Zhoghovoi, 1870–1914* (Constantinople, 1870–1914).]

11. *Adenakerutiunk Azkayin Zhoghovoi*, September 17/29, 1876, pp. 207–208; cited in Sarkissian, *History of the Armenian Question to 1885*, p. 40.

12. William L. Langer, *The Diplomacy of Imperialism* I (New York: Knopf, 1935), p. 160. On this passage Norman Ravitch states that Langer's "labelling of the Armenian movement as *national-socialist* can hardly be considered a slip of the pen." ["The Armenian Catastrophe: Of History, Murder & Sin," *Encounter* LVII, 6 (December 1981), p. 76, n16.]

13. Ruben Khan Azat, "Hai heghapokhakani husherits," *Hairenik amsakir* V, 10 (58) (August 1927), p. 65.

14. On the importance of considering perceptions and projections, see Melson, "A Theoretical Inquiry into the Armenian Massacres of 1894–1896."

15. On the Dashnaktsutiun, see Gerard J. Libaridian, "Revolution and Liberation in the 1892 and 1907 Programs of the Dashnaktsutiun," in R. G. Suny, *Transcaucasia, Nationalism and Social Change: Essays in the History of Armenia, Azerbaijan, and Georgia* (Ann Arbor: Michigan Slavic Publications, 1983), pp. 185–96.

16. See, for example, the thoughtful essay by Stepan Astourian, "The Armenian Genocide: An Interpretation," *History Teacher* XXIII, 2 (February 1990), pp. 111–60.

17. Mark Sykes, *Through Five Turkish Provinces* (London, 1900), p. 80; see also Robert Adelson, *Mark Sykes, Portrait of an Amateur* (London: Jonathan Cape, 1975), p. 65.

18. Carter V. Findley, *Bureaucratic Reform in the Ottoman Empire: The Sublime Porte, 1789–1922* (Princeton: Princeton University Press, 1980), p. 221.

19. Cited in M. S. Lazarev, *Kurdskii vopros (1891–1917)* (Moscow: Nauka, 1972), p. 40.

20. The British traveler H.F.B. Lynch paints an unflattering picture of the Hamidiye in his *Armenia, Travels and Studies, II, The Turkish Provinces* (London, 1901; reprint: Beirut: Khayats, 1965), pp. 4–5.

21. Stephen Duguid, "The Politics of Unity: Hamidian Policy in Eastern Anatolia," *Middle Eastern Studies* IX, 2 (May 1973), pp. 139–55.

22. Letter of Sir P. Currie to the Earl of Kimberley, Great Britain, Foreign Office, *Turkey, no. 1 (1895), (Part I) Correspondence Relating to the Asiatic Provinces of Turkey, Part I. Events at Sassoon, and Commission of Inquiry at Moush* (London, 1895), pp. 8–10.

23. Ibid., pp. 20–21.

24. Melson, "A Theoretical Inquiry into the Armenian Massacres," pp. 503, 509.

25. Less understandable than the sultan's justifications of his actions is the defense of those policies by Western historians. William Langer, for example, writes: "Whether Abdul Hamid deserves the black reputation that has been pinned to him is a matter of debate. If he was 'the bloody assassin' and the 'red Sultan' to most people, he was the hard-working, conscientious, much harassed but personally charming ruler to others. Those who have spoken for him have pointed out that the Sultan felt his Empire threatened by the Armenians, who, he knew, or at least believed were in league with the Young Turks, the Greeks, Macedonians, etc. They believe that Abdul Hamid was the victim of what we moderns call a persecution complex." (*The Diplomacy of Imperialism*, I, p. 159.)

26. Justin McCarthy, "Foundations of the Turkish Republic: Social and Economic Change," *Middle Eastern Studies* XIX, 2 (April 1983), pp. 139–51. The figures for the *kaza* (district) are lower than the non-Muslim figure for the town would be, because of the larger representation of Muslims in the surrounding peasantry.

27. Ibid., pp. 143–44, 148.

28. Donald Quataert, *Social Disintegration and Popular Resistance in the Ottoman Empire, 1881–1908* (New York-London: NYU Press, 1983), p. 79. The Union of Employees of the Anatolian Railroad, which briefly flourished in 1908 before the Minister of the Interior outlawed unions and prohibited strikes, was largely a non-Muslim affair.

29. Feroz Ahmad, *The Young Turks: The Committee of Union and Progress in Turkish Politics, 1908–1914* (Oxford: Oxford University Press, 1969), pp. 154–55.

30. Stanford and Ezel Kural Shaw, *History of the Ottoman Empire and Modern Turkey*, II, p. 315.

31. Ibid., pp. 315–16.

32. Sinasi Orel and Sureyya Yuca, *Ermenilerce Talat Pasaya Atfedilen Telegraflarin Gercek Yuzu* (Ankara, 1983); Turkkaya Ataov, *The Andonian Documents Attributed to Talat Pasha Are Forgeries* (Ankara, 1984); Kamuran Gurun, *Ermeni Dosyasi* (Ankara, 1982); *The Armenian File: The Myth of Innocence Exposed* (New York: St. Martin's Press, 1985), pp. 237–39.

33. Vahakn N. Dadrian, "The Naim-Andonian Documents on the World War I Destruction of Ottoman Armenians: The Anatomy of a Genocide," *International Journal of Middle East Studies* XVII, 3 (August 1986), pp. 311–60.

34. Aram Andonian, comp., *The Memoirs of Naim Bey: Turkish Official Documents Relating to the Deportations and Massacres of Armenians* (London: Hodder and Stoughton, 1920), pp. 49–51. Shakir was a major figure in the organization and implementation of the Armenian genocide. He was a member of a small secret committee formed by the CUP in 1914 called the Special Organization (Teshkilati Mahsusa) that was charged with carrying out the exterminations. (This information comes from British intelligence reports cited by Dadrian, "The Naim-Andonian Documents," p. 351, fn. 53, and confirmed by the Turkish historian Dogan Avcioglu.)

35. Ibid., pp. 51–52.

36. Ibid., pp. 52–53.

37. Ibid. p. 54. Three other telegrams from Talaat to Aleppo should be mentioned: September 3 (16), 1915—"We recommend that the operations which we have ordered you to make shall be first carried out on the men of the said people and that you shall subject the women and children to them also. Appoint reliable officials for this"; September 29 (October 12), 1915—"We hear that some of the people and officials are marrying Armenian women. We strictly prohibit this, and urgently recommend that these women shall be picked out and sent away"; November 29 (December 6), 1915— "Destroy by secret means the Armenians of the Eastern Provinces who pass into your hands there." (Ibid., pp. 54–55.)

38. One might mention a few of the documentary sources on the genocide: Arthur Beylerian, *Les grandes puissances, l'Empire Ottoman, et les Arméniens dans les archives françaises (1914–1918: Recueil de documents)* (Paris: Université de Paris I, 1983); *The Armenian Genocide: Documentation, I* (Munich: Institut für Armenishche Fragen, 1987); Leslie A. Davis, *The Slaughterhouse Province: An American Diplomat's Report on the Armenian Genocide, 1915–1917*, ed. Susan K. Blair (New Rochelle, NY: Aristide D. Caratzas, 1989). See also Richard G. Hovannisian, *The Armenian Holocaust: A Bibliography Relating to the Deportations, Massacres, and Dispersion of the Armenian People, 1915–1923* (Cambridge, MA: National Association for Armenian Studies and Research, 1978).

39. Henry Morgenthau, *Ambassador Morgenthau's Story* (Garden City: Doubleday, Page, 1918, 1919; reprint: Plandome, NY: New Age, 1975), pp. 344–45.

40. Ibid., pp. 345, 347.

41. Ibid., pp. 351–52.

42. Ibid., pp. 337–38.

43. Bernard Lewis, *The Emergence of Modern Turkey*, p. 356.

7. ARMENIA AND THE RUSSIAN REVOLUTION

1. Alexander Khatissian, "The Memoirs of a Mayor," *Armenian Review* III, 4 (8) (December 1949), p. 108.

2. *Rech'*, no. 109, May 11, 1917; cited in S. M. Dimanshtein, ed., *Revoliutsiia i national'nyi vopros*, III (Moscow, 1930), p. 401.

3. For a discussion of the war and peace issue in 1917, see Rex A. Wade, *The*

Russian Search for Peace, February–October, 1917 (Stanford: Stanford University Press, 1969).

4. Richard G. Hovannisian, *Armenia on the Road to Independence, 1918* (Berkeley: University of California Press, 1967), p. 79.

5. Ibid., p. 81.

6. *Baku,* no. 87, April 22, 1917.

7. Firuz Kazemzadeh, *The Struggle for Transcaucasia (1917–1921)* (New York: Philosophical Library, 1951), pp. 54–64.

8. Hovannisian, *Armenia on the Road to Independence,* p. 97.

9. Ibid., p. 98.

10. Ibid., p. 100.

11. For details on the events leading to Transcaucasian independence, see Kazemzadeh, *The Struggle for Transcaucasia,* pp. 79–105; and Zourab Avalishvili, *The Independence of Georgia in International Politics, 1918–1921* (London: Headley Brothers, 1940), pp. 26–29.

12. The American Secretary of State Robert Lansing rejected the appeals of his consul in Tiflis, Felix Willoughby Smith, for aid. (Hovannisian, *Armenia on the Road to Independence,* p. 118.)

13. Ronald Grigor Suny, *The Baku Commune, 1917–1918: Class and Nationality in the Russian Revolution* (Princeton: Princeton University Press, 1972), pp. 214–24.

14. Ibid., p. 211.

15. For the difficulties facing the new Armenian Republic, see Hovannisian, *Armenia on the Road to Independence,* pp. 190–94, 207–15.

16. For an evaluation of the conflicting pressures on the Armenian Republic, see Richard G. Hovannisian, "Dimensions of Democracy and Authority in Caucasian Armenia, 1917–1920," *Russian Review* XXXIII, 1 (January 1974), pp. 37–49.

17. Hovannisian, *Armenia on the Road to Independence,* pp. 212–13.

18. Richard G. Hovanissian, *The Republic of Armenia, I: 1918–1919* (Berkeley: University of California Press, 1971), p. 130.

19. Cited in Hovannisian, *Republic of Armenia,* p. 128.

20. The unity of the Armenian delegations in Paris was an alliance of convenience. The underlying conflicts within the Armenian community remained. In February 1919, for example, a congress of western Armenians met in Erevan and made it clear that they wanted Boghos Nubar Pasha to head the future government of united Armenia, not the Dashnak leaders of the Erevan republic. That same month the Armenian National Congress in Paris also took a hesitant and conditional approach toward the Armenian republic, preferring that a united Armenian state be dominated by non-Caucasian Armenians. In his article "Exile Government in the Armenian Polity," Khachig Tololyan argues that the tensions between the delegations reflected a deep bifurcation in the transnational Armenian nation: "The Armenian solution [two delegations] was a damaging compromise. The contestants needed each other. The bourgeois elite could not openly challenge the leaders of the longed-for state, whose existence was joyfully celebrated by its constituency, whether in salons or survivors' camps. In turn, the Dashnags were a party in control of a government that had to have help from those leaders who remained relatively wealthy in the overseas diaspora or Transcaucasus." [*Journal of Political Science* XVIII, 1 (Spring 1990), p. 137.]

21. James B. Gidney, *A Mandate for Armenia* (Kent, OH: Kent State University Press, 1967), p. 237.

22. Stanley E. Kerr, *The Lions of Marash: Personal Experiences with American Near East Relief, 1919–1922* (Albany: State University of New York Press, 1973), pp. 195–96.

23. Richard G. Hovannisian, "Armenia and the Caucasus in the Genesis of the

Soviet-Turkish Entente," *International Journal of Middle East Studies* IV, 2 (1973), p. 147.

24. Richard Pipes, *The Formation of the Soviet Union: Communism and Nationalism, 1917–1923* (Cambridge, MA: Harvard University Press, 1954, 1957), pp. 229–33.

8. BUILDING A SOCIALIST NATION

1. Dean C. Tipps, "Modernization Theory and the Comparative Study of Societies: A Critical Perspective," *Comparative Studies in Society and History* XV, 2 (March 1973), p. 210.

2. Clifford Geertz, "The Integrative Revolution: Primordial Sentiments and Civil Politics in the New States," in C. Geertz, ed., *Old Societies and New States* (New York, 1963), pp. 105–57.

3. S. V. Kharmandarian, *Armianskaia SSR v pervyi god novoi ekonomicheskoi politiki (1921–1922)* (Erevan, 1955), p. 26.

4. Oliver Baldwin, *Six Prisons and Two Revolutions: Adventures in Trans-Caucasia and Anatolia, 1920–1921* (Garden City, NY: Doubleday, Page, 1925), pp. 33–34.

5. B. A. Bor'ian, *Armeniia, mezhdunarodnaia diplomatiia i SSSR*, II (Moscow-Leningrad, 1929), p. 126.

6. Firuz Kazemzadeh, *The Struggle for Transcaucasia (1917–1921)* (New York: Philosophical Library, 1951), p. 328.

7. V. I. Lenin, *Polnoe sobranie sochinenii*, 5th ed., XLIII (Moscow, 1970), pp. 198–200.

8. Bor'ian, *Armeniia*, II, p. 319; Edward Hallett Carr, *The Bolshevik Revolution, 1917–1923*, I (New York: MacMillan, 1951), p. 394.

9. On the controversy over the Transcaucasian federation and nationality policy, see Moshe Lewin, *Lenin's Last Struggle*, trans. A. M. Sheridan Smith (New York: Pantheon, 1968), pp. 43–63; Ronald Grigor Suny, *The Making of the Georgian Nation* (Bloomington and Stanford: Indiana University Press and Hoover Institution Press, 1988), pp. 209–25.

10. Mary Kilbourne Matossian, *The Impact of Soviet Policies in Armenia* (Leiden: E. J. Brill, 1962), p. 52.

11. Ibid., p. 58.

12. Ibid., p. 59.

13. Ibid., pp. 63–73.

14. Fridtjof Nansen, *Armenia and the Near East* (New York: Duffield, 1928), p. 225.

9. STALIN AND THE ARMENIANS

1. Leon Trotsky, *Stalin: An Appraisal of the Man and His Influence* (New York: Harper & Brothers, 1941), p. 393.

2. For a historiographical review of the relationship of Bolshevism and Stalinism, see Stephen F. Cohen, "Bolshevism and Stalinism," in Robert C. Tucker, ed., *Stalinism: Essays in Historical Interpretation* (New York: W. W. Norton, 1977), pp. 3–29.

3. Mary Kilbourne Matossian, *The Impact of Soviet Policies in Armenia* (Leiden: E. J. Brill, 1962), pp. 102–103.

4. Ibid., p. 104.

5. Ibid., p. 108.

6. Ibid., p. 105.

7. Ibid., p. 106.

8. *Sotsialisticheskoe stroitel'stvo Armianskoi SSR (1920–1940 gg.). Statisticheskii sbornik* (Erevan, 1940), p. 42.

9. Ibid.; Matossian, *Impact of Soviet Policies*, p. 108.

10. *Sotsialisticheskoe stroitel'stvo*, p. 48.

11. Ibid., p. 47.

12. Matossian, *Impact of Soviet Policies*, p. 115.

13. Ibid., p. 116.

14. Ibid., p. 174.

15. *Sotsialisticheskoe stroitel'stvo*, p. 12.

16. Ibid., p. 9; Matossian, *Impact of Soviet Policies*, p. 139.

17. Matossian, *Impact of Soviet Policies*, p. 190.

18. Victor Zaslavsky, "The Ethnic Question in the USSR," *Telos*, no. 45 (Fall 1980), pp. 51–52.

19. S. Frederick Starr, *Melnikov: Solo Architect in a Mass Society* (Princeton: Princeton University Press, 1978), pp. 218–23.

20. *Kommunist* (Erevan), September 14, 1943; cited in Matossian, *Impact of Soviet Policies*, pp. 165–66.

21. David Marshall Lang and Christopher J. Walker, *The Armenians*, Minority Rights Group Report no. 32 (London: Minority Rights Group, 1976), pp. 12–13.

22. Matossian, *Impact of Soviet Policies*, p. 167.

23. Ibid., p. 168.

24. For a Western discussion of these events, see Alexander Werth, *Musical Uproar in Moscow* (London: Turnstile Press, 1949).

10. RETURN TO ARARAT

The author thanks Ara Sarafian for his research assistance in preparing this chapter.

1. Bruce Robellet Kuniholm, *The Origins of the Cold War in the Near East: Great Power Conflict and Diplomacy in Iran, Turkey, and Greece* (Princeton: Princeton University Press, 1980), p. xx.

2. The Montreux Convention of 1936, which both the USSR and Great Britain had signed, allowed warships of various nations to pass through the straits, but if Turkey were at war, its government could determine unilaterally which warships could pass through. The convention also allowed Turkey to fortify the straits.

3. OSS, Research and Analysis Branch, R & A no. 1968, April 14, 1944, p. 7.

4. *Foreign Relations of the United States*, 1944, V, p. 881; Churchill, *Triumph and Tragedy*, vol. 6 of *The Second World War* (Boston: Houghton Mifflin, 1948–53), pp. 80–81.

5. *Foreign Relations*, 1945, VIII, pp. 1229–31.

6. Ibid., pp. 1234–36.

7. *Foreign Relations*, 1946, VII, p. 802.

8. Ibid., 1945, V, p. 253.

9. Kuniholm, *The Origins of the Cold War in the Near East*, p. xx.

10. Armenian version of the letter in K. Lazian, *Haiastan ev hai date* (Cairo, 1957), p. 353; French translation, in Claire Mouradian, "L'immigration des Arméniens de la diaspora vers la RSS d'Arménie, 1946–1962," *Cahiers du Monde russe et soviétique* XX, 1 (January–March 1979), p. 80.

11. *Foreign Relations*, 1946, VII, p. 807.

12. *Time*, December 31, 1945, p. 22.

13. Khrushchev, appalled by the whole affair, was highly critical of Beria and Stalin for not foreseeing that "Turkey would respond to our demand by accepting American

support. So Beria and Stalin succeeded only in frightening the Turks right into the open arms of the Americans. Because of Stalin's note to the Turkish government, the Americans were able to penetrate Turkey and set up bases right next to our borders. . . . Thus, thanks to his inflexibility and the psychic disturbance which came over him at the end of his life, Stalin ruined our relations with the Turks. Turkey has allowed the US to have military bases on its territory ever since." (*Khrushchev Remembers: The Last Testament,* trans. and ed. Strobe Talbott [Boston: Little, Brown and Company, 1974], pp. 295–96.)

14. *Time,* p. 23.

15. Quoted in Kuniholm, *The Origins of the Cold War in the Near East,* p. 270.

16. Foreign Relations, 1946, VII, pp. 806, 808.

17. Truman, *Memoirs* (Garden City, NY: Doubleday, 1955–56), vol. I, pp. 551–52; this episode is not mentioned in Byrnes's memoirs [James Francis Byrnes, *All in One Lifetime* (New York: Harper & Brothers, 1958)].

18. *Foreign Relations,* 1946, VII, pp. 805–806. An important telegram, Deptel 1210 of 21 [29] December, has not been published.

19. Ibid., p. 806.

20. Ibid.

21. Ibid., pp. 808–809.

22. Ibid., pp. 810–11.

23. Ibid., p. 812.

24. Ibid., pp. 815–16.

25. Ibid., pp. 816–17.

26. Ibid., p. 817.

27. Ibid., p. 819; on March 18, Wilson received a secret letter, dated February 27, 1946, about the situation in Turkey from the Secretary of State; this letter has not been printed. (Ibid., p. 820.) A few days later, March 23, Wilson reiterated his views on Soviet intentions to "break down this present independent Turkish Government and to establish in its place a vassal or 'friendly' regime in Turkey" (Ibid., p. 821).

28. Kuniholm, *The Origins of the Cold War in the Near East,* pp. 332–34.

29. Department of State, Office of Research and Intelligence," Notes on Armenian National Aspirations and on the Soviet Claims to the Eastern Provinces of Turkey," March 12, 1946, no. 3523.2, pp. 18–19.

30. Ibid., p. 4.

31. Ibid., pp. 10–11.

32. Ibid., p. 15.

33. Ibid., pp. 15, 17.

34. Ibid., pp. 18–19.

35. Ibid., appendix, p. 4; MS Department of State, file 860j.01/633, quoted by G. H. Hickworth, *Digest of International Law* (Washington, 1940), I, p. 322.

36. *Foreign Relations,* 1946, VII, pp. 827–29.

37. Ibid.., pp. 857–58.

38. Ibid., pp. 893–97.

39. Truman's speech has been reprinted in Kuniholm, *The Origins of the Cold War in the Near East,* pp. 434–39.

40. Ibid., p. 895.

41. From a personal conversation with Tiran Nersoyan, October 11, 1970.

42. "In exaggerating the Soviet threat against Iran and Turkey and in misinterpreting the Greek civil war, the United States exerted its economic power in such a way as to further divide the world. Yet aid to Greece and Turkey provided Americans with another 'lesson.' As Truman explained it in 1952, 'We helped the Greeks to defeat a Communist invasion of their soil, and our aid has kept Turkey free and independent.'

The vaguely defined containment doctrine served as the rationale for American intervention on a global scale thereafter." [Thomas G. Paterson, *Soviet-American Confrontation: Postwar Reconstruction and the Origins of the Cold War* (Baltimore: Johns Hopkins University Press, 1973), p. 206.]

11. THE NEW NATIONALISM IN ARMENIA

1. Mary Kilbourne, *The Impact of Soviet Policies in Armenia* (Leiden: E. J. Brill, 1962), p. 201.

2. Levon Mikirtichian, "Aksel Bakounts as the Champion of the True Concept of the Popular Basis of Literature in Soviet Armenia," *Caucasian Review* VII (1958), p. 90.

3. Matossian, *Impact of Soviet Policies,* p. 202.

4. "Teenagers' Organization in Armenia," *Caucasian Review* IV (1957), p. 140.

5. Gerhard Simon, "Nationalismus und Nationalitätenpolitik in der Sowjetunion seit Stalin," *Berichte des Bundesinstitute für ostwissenschaftliche und internationale Studien* XXXIV (1979), p. 34.

6. "Kh" = *khnami* (in-law); "ts" = *tsanot* (acquaintance); and "b" = *barekam* (friend or relative).

7. Gertrude Schroeder Greenslade, "Transcaucasia since Stalin: The Economic Dimension," in Ronald Grigor Suny, ed., *Transcaucasia, Nationalism and Social Change: Essays in the History of Armenia, Azerbaijan, and Georgia* (Ann Arbor, MI: Michigan Slavic Publications, 1983), Table 1, p. 399.

8. Ibid.

9. Ibid., Table 2, p. 401.

10. Ibid.

11. Ibid.

12. Ibid.

13. Ann Sheehy and Elizabeth Fuller, "Armenia and Armenians in the USSR: Nationality and Language Aspects of the Census of 1979," *Radio Liberty Research Bulletin* XXIV, 24 (3072), June 13, 1980 (RL 208/80), p. 1.

14. *Vestnik statistiki,* no. 6 (1980), p. 46.

15. Ibid., no. 11 (1980), p. 61.

16. Ibid., no. 1 (1980), p. 72.

17. Sheehy and Fuller, "Armenia and Armenians in the USSR," p. 2.

18. Ibid., p. 3.

19. *Vestnik statistiki,* no. 11 (1980), p. 61.

20. Ibid.

21. Ibid., p. 67.

22. Ann Sheehy, "Data from the Soviet Census of 1979 on the Georgians and the Georgian SSR," *Radio Liberty Research Bulletin* XXIV, 19 (3067), May 9, 1980 (RL 162/80), p. 2.

23. *Radio Liberty Research Bulletin* XXII, 48 (2992), December 1, 1978 (RL 269/78).

24. *Arkhiv samizdata* 3076, p. 1.

25. Anatolii N. Yamskov, "Ethnic Conflict in the Transcaucasus: The Case of Nagorno-Karabagh," Working Paper, no. 118, Center for Studies of Social Change, New School for Social Research (New York, May 1991), p. 11.

26. Ibid.

27. Ibid., pp. 7–9.

28. *Vestnik statistiki,* no. 10 (1980), p. 70.

29. A copy of this letter is in my possession, thanks to Dr. Vahakn N. Dadrian, who made the English translation.

12. NATIONALISM AND DEMOCRACY

1. *Nagornyi Karabakh, Istoricheskaia spravka* (Erevan: Izdatel'stvo Akademii nauk Armianskoi SSR, 1988), pp. 32–33.

2. Ibid., p. 33.

3. Elizabeth Fuller, "Is Armenia on the Brink of an Ecological Disaster?" *Radio Liberty Research*, RL 307/86, August 5, 1986; "Armenian Authorities Appear to Yield to 'Ecological Lobby,'" ibid., RL 130/87, March 30, 1987; "Armenian Journalist Links Air Pollution and Infant Mortality," ibid., RL 275/87, July 14, 1987 (on Zori Balayan's article in *Literaturnaia gazeta*, no. 26, June 24, 1987); and "Mass Demonstration in Armenia against Environmental Pollution," ibid., RL 421/87, October 18, 1987.

4. *Izvestiia*, January 6, 1987; *Current Digest of the Soviet Press* [henceforth CDSP] XL, 1, February 3, 1988, p. 17.

5. *Pravda*, January 18, 1988; CDSP, XL, 3, February 17, 1988, p. 5.

6. *Izvestiia*, January 6, 1987; CDSP, XL, February 3, 1988, p. 17.

7. Jackie Abramian, "An Interview with Zori Balayan," *Armenian Weekly*, July 16, 1988, p. 7.

8. *New York Times*, March 11, 1988, p. 4.

9. *Pravda*, March 21, 1988.

10. *Izvestiia*, July 14, 1988, p. 3; CDSP, XL, 28, August 10, 1988, pp. 18–19.

11. *Izvestiia*, July 5, 1988, p. 6; CDSP, XL, 28, August 10, 1988, p. 16.

12. *Izvestiia*, July 12, p. 3; CDSP, XL, 28, August 10, 1988, p. 18.

13. Other members of the committee included his colleague, Samson Kazarian, a teacher in the same school; Hambartsum Galstian, a researcher in Erevan City Soviet's sociological research laboratory; Rafael Kazarian, a corresponding member of Armenian Academy of Sciences; Vano Siradeghian, a member of Armenian Writers' Union; Levon Ter Petrosian, a doctor of philology; Samvel Gevorkian, television commentator; Aleksan Hakopian, a researcher in the Institute of Oriental Studies of the Academy of Sciences; Vazgen Manukian, an instructor at Erevan State University; Babken Araktsian, department head at the university; David Vardanian, a senior researcher at the solid-state branch laboratory; and Igor Muradian, a senior researcher at the Armenian Gosplan Economic Planning Research Institute.

14. *Izvestiia*, July 22, 1988, p. 6; CDSP, XL, 30, August 24, 1988, p. 17.

15. *Pravda*, July 21, 1988, p. 6; CDSP, XL, 30, August 24, 1988, p. 16.

16. *Pravda* and *Izvestiia*, July 20, 1988; CDSP, XL, 29, August 17, 1988, pp. 1–11, 31–32.

17. *La Vanguardia;* discussed in Bohdan Nahaylo, "Vitalii Korotych on 'Undemocratic' Conditions in Ukraine, on Sumgait, and on 'Pamyat,'" *Radio Liberty Research*, RL 400/88, September 5, 1988.

18. *Izvestiia*, July 22, 1988, p. 6; excerpts in CDSP, XL, 30, August 14, 1988, pp. 16–17.

19. *Pravda*, July 25, 1988, p. 8; CDSP, XL, 30, August 24, 1988, pp. 18–19.

20. Bill Keller, "Soviet Region Hit by New Ethnic Unrest and Strike," *New York Times*, September 16, 1988.

21. "Armenian Strikers Hold Rally," *New York Times*, September 21, 1988.

22. Bill Keller, "Parts of Armenia are Blocked off by Soviet Troops," *New York Times*, September 23, 1988.

23. *Pravda*, September 28, 1988, p. 6; CDSP, XL, 39, October 26, 1988, p. 10.

24. *Pravda*, October 4, 1988, p. 6; CDSP, XL, 39, October 26, 1988, p. 11.

25. *Pravda,* October 2, 1988, p. 6; CDSP, XL, 39, October 26, 1988, p. 11.

26. *Krasnaia zvezda,* November 26, 1988, p. 6; CDSP, XL, 48, December 28, 1988, p. 11.

27. *Izvestiia,* November 25, 1988, p. 3; CDSP, XL, 48, December 28, 1988, p. 9.

28. *Komsomol'skaia pravda,* November 27, 1988, p. 2; CDSP, XL, 48, December 28, 1988, p. 11.

29. Felicity Barringer, "1,400 Arrests Reported in Tense Armenian Capital," *New York Times,* November 29, 1988.

30. *Bakinskii rabochii,* November 27, 1988, p. 3; CDSP, XL, 48, December 28, 1988, p. 14.

31. *Krasnaia zvezda,* December 24, 1989; CDSP, XL, 52, January 25, 1989, pp. 9–10. Panakhov was arrested in late December 1988.

32. *Pioner Azerbaidzhana,* November 25, 1988; *Komsomol'skaia pravda,* December 1, 1988, p. 4; CDSP, XL, 48, December 28, 1988, p. 12.

33. *Bakinskii rabochii,* December 3, 1988, p. 4; CDSP, XL, 48, December 28, 1988, p. 15.

34. "Address of Soviet Leader: 'We Are One Family,'" *New York Times,* November 28, 1988.

35. *Pravda* and *Izvestiia,* December 4, 1988, pp. 1, 3; CDSP, XL, 49, January 4, 1989, pp. 13–14.

36. *Pravda* and *Izvestiia,* December 2, 1988, pp. 1–3; CDSP, XL, 51, January 18, 1989, pp. 16, 27.

37. *Bakinskii rabochii,* December 3, 1988, p. 4; CDSP, XL, 48, December 28, 1988, p. 15.

38. Manucharian was released when he said that as an elected member of the Armenian Supreme Soviet he had immunity, and he immediately went into hiding.

39. *Pravda,* December 12, 1988, pp. 1–2; CDSP, XL, 50, January 11, 1989, p. 4.

40. *Pravda,* December 16, 1988, p. 8, carried the complete text of a 1,000-word address by Vazgen to Armenian believers.

41. *Pravda,* January 8, 1989; CDSP, XLI, 1, February 1, 1989, pp. 7–8.

42. Ashot Manucharian, "How it Happened," *The Armenian Mirror-Spectator,* April 8, 1989, pp. 8, 10. This report was originally written on December 18, 1988. Manucharian himself had defeated a member of the mafia in the parliamentary elections. He was then offered 100,000 rubles if he would give up the campaign. Later he received death threats.

13. LOOKING TOWARD ARARAT

1. Khachig Tololyan, "The Nation-State and Its Others: In Lieu of a Preface," *Diaspora* I, 1 (Spring 1991), pp. 3–7.

2. Fernand Braudel, *The Wheel of Commerce,* vol. II, trans. Sian Reynolds (New York: Harper & Row, 1982), pp. 122–24, 154–59.

3. Estimates of the diaspora population are not very reliable. Nikola Schahgaldian attempted a compilation in his dissertation:

	1926	1940	1976
Soviet Armenia	750,000	1,100,000	2,600,000
USSR (rest of)	820,000	1,050,000	1,400,000
USA and Canada	120,000	200,000	500,000

Lebanon	50,000	110,000	250,000
Iran	140,000	130,000	180,000
France	35,000	70,000	150,000
Syria	115,000	100,000	130,000
Turkey	125,000	110,000	125,000

(Nikola Bagrad Schahgaldian, "The Political Integration of an Immigrant Community into a Composite Society: The Armenians in Lebanon, 1920–1974," Columbia University, Ph.d. in Political Science, 1979, p. 47.)

4. Ibid., p. 90.

5. Justin McCarthy, "Foundations of the Turkish Republic: Social and Economic Change," *Middle Eastern Studies* XIX, 2 (April 1983), pp. 139–51.

6. Fridtjof Nansen, *Armenia and the Near East* (New York: Duffield and Co., 1928).

7. Schahgaldian, "The Political Integration of an Immigrant Community," p. 52.

8. Ibid., p. 79.

9. Ibid., p. 79.

10. For detailed information, much of it in encyclopedic form, on Armenians in Lebanon, see Sisak H. Varzhapetian, *Haiere Libanani mej: Hanragitaran libananahai gaghuti*, 5 vols. (first published in three parts: Beirut, 1951; reissued 1981–1983 [vol. 1, 5: Hamazgayini Vahe Setian tparan, 1982–1983; vols. 2, 3: Beirut: Sevan Press, 1981; vol. 4: Fairlawn, NJ: Rosekeer Press, 1983]).

11. Schahgaldian, "The Political Integration of an Immigrant Community," p. 84.

12. Ibid., p. 1.

13. Cited in ibid., p. 155.

14. Ibid., p. 172.

15. Ibid., p. 140.

16. Ibid., p. 141.

17. Khachig Toloyan, "Exile Government in the Armenian Polity," *Journal of Political Science* XVIII, 1 (Spring 1990), pp. 125–26.

18. Ibid., p. 139.

19. Kathryn Davis, *The Soviets at Geneva* (Geneva, 1934), p. 41.

20. V. H. Meliksetyan, *Arevmtahayeri brnagaghte ev spirukahayeri hayrenadardzutiune Sovetakan Hayastan* (Erevan, 1975), pp. 170–72; Schahgaldian, "The Political Integration of an Immigrant Community," p. 93. The immigration was ended in 1937 and not resumed until after World War II.

21. My father, George Suny, remembers selling Soviet Armenian candy to sympathetic Jewish merchants when Armenian shopkeepers close to the Dashnaktsutiun refused to buy.

22. The composer and ethnomusicologist Grikor Mirzoev Suni, for example, organized concerts in which the singers sang about the building of socialism in the USSR, ending up with the Internationale, all the while wearing gowns adorned with the sickle and hammer.

23. *The New York Times,* September 5, 1933, p. E19; December 5, 1933, p. 3; December 25, 1933, p. 3; *Armenian Mirror-Spectator,* April 3, 1935. For an account sympathetic to the Dashnaktsutiun, see Sarkis Atamian, *The Armenian Community: The Historical Development of a Social and Ideological Conflict* (New York: Philosophical Library, 1955), pp. 358–75.

24. Bishop Tiran Nersoyan, *A Christian Approach to Communism* (London: Frederick Muller, 1942).

25. Vahe A. Sarafian, "The Soviet and the Armenian Church," *Armenian Review* VIII, 2 (30) (Summer 1955), p. 97.

26. Archbishop Garegin Hovsepyan, the Apostolic Primate of North America, was

elected when the Dashnaks withdrew their candidate, though they controlled the majority of votes in the Electoral Conclave. (Schahgaldian, "The Political Integration of an Immigrant Community," p. 192.)

27. John Roy Carlson, "The Armenian Displaced Persons: A First-Hand Report on Conditions in Europe," *Armenian Affairs* I, 1 (Winter 1949–1950), p. 19.

28. John Roy Carlson, *Undercover* (New York: E. P. Dutton, 1943).

29. Translation in Schahgaldian, "The Political Integration of an Immigrant Community," pp. 96–97; the appeal was published in most Armenian diaspora newspapers; see, for example, *Zartonk* (Beirut), August 12, 1941.

30. An Armenian version of the letter can be found in K. Lazian, *Hayastan ev Hay tade* (Cairo, 1957), p. 353; French translation in Claire Mouradian, "L'immigration des Arméniens de la diaspora vers la RSS d'Arménie, 1946, 1962," *Cahiers du Monde russe et soviétique* XX, 1 (January–March 1979), p. 80.

31. For a more detailed account of Soviet policy toward Turkey and the Armenian irredenta at the end of World War II, see Ronald Grigor Suny, "Return to Ararat: Armenia in the Cold War," *Armenian Review* XLII, 3/167 (Autumn 1989), pp. 1–19, reproduced in this volume as chapter 10.

32. Schahgaldian, "The Political Integration of an Immigrant Community," p. 107.

33. Ibid., p. 108.

34. *Armenian Affairs,* called "a journal of Armenian studies," was edited by the pro-Soviet Charles Vertanes and featured in its first issue a long "exposé" of the Mardigian efforts on behalf of the displaced persons by John Roy Carlson, "The Armenian Displaced Persons," *Armenian Affairs* I, 1 (Winter 1949–1950), pp. 17–34. It ceased publication after three issues in the fall of 1950. *The Armenian Review* first appeared in the winter of 1948, edited by Reuben Darbinian, and continues to the present time.

35. Cited in Schahgaldian, "The Political Integration of an Immigrant Community," p. 208.

36. In 1973 the seventy-three-year-old Gurgen Yanikian, a victim of the Armenian genocide, lured two Turkish diplomats to a meeting in Santa Barbara where he killed them. This event inspired younger Armenians to engage in "propaganda of the deed."

14. ARMENIA ON THE ROAD TO INDEPENDENCE, AGAIN

1. In his book *The Gorbachev Phenomenon,* Moshe Lewin writes: "One thing is clear: Soviet society needs a state that can match its complexity. And in ways sometimes overt, sometimes covert, contemporary urban society has become a powerful 'system maker,' pressuring both political institutions and the economic model to adapt. Through numerous channels, some visible, some slow, insidious, and imperceptible, Soviet urban society is affecting individuals, groups, institutions, and the state. Civil society is talking, gossiping, demanding, sulking, expressing its interests in many ways and thereby creating moods, ideologies, and public opinion." Moshe Lewin, *The Gorbachev Phenomenon: A Historical Interpretation* (Berkeley: University of California Press, 1988), p. 146.

2. Gerard J. Libaridian, *Armenia at the Crossroads: Democracy and Nationhood in the Post-Stalin Era* (Watertown: Blue Crane Books, 1991), p. 75n.

3. Actor Sos Sarksian, journalist Garen Simonian, writer Sero Khanzadian, and the Russian ethnographer Galina Starovoitova were elected to the Congress of People's Deputies.

4. Libaridian, *Armenia at the Crossroads,* pp. 151–56.

5. "The traditional centrally planned system has largely collapsed, but has not

been replaced by a functioning market system. The progressive breakdown is perhaps most visible at the retail level, with few goods to be found in state shops, barter becoming common and black markets and the dollarization of the economy spreading rapidly. Meanwhile, policy making in the republics has been characterized by growing autonomy. In a climate of deepening shortages, republics have become increasingly unwilling to trade with each other except on a barter basis." *The Economy of the USSR: A Study Undertaken in Response to a Request by the Houston Summit: Summary and Recommendations* (Washington, D.C.: The World Bank, 1991), pp. 10–11.

6. See the parallel articles by Rafael Ishkhanian of the Karabagh Committee and Khajak Ter Grigorian of the Bureau of the Dashnaktsutiun, in Libaridian, *Armenia at the Crossroads,* pp. 9–38, 137–42. Both writers contrast those Armenian heroes of the past who favored a Russian orientation (e.g., Israel Ori, Joseph Emin, Archbishop Hovsep Arghutian, Dr. Zavriev, General Antranik, Zori Balayan, Silva Kaputikian) unfavorably with those who proposed self-reliance (e.g., Davit Beg, Aram Manukian, Nzhdeh), though they do not use all the same examples.

7. Libaridian, *Armenia at the Crossroads,* pp. 107–10.

8. *Izvestiia,* December 20, 1990; *Current Digest of the Soviet Press* [CDSP] XLII, 52, January 30, 1991, pp. 4–5.

9. Elizabeth Fuller, "The All-Union Referendum in the Transcaucasus," *Report on the USSR,* III, 13, March 29, 1991, p. 3.

10. Ibid.

11. CDSP, XLIII, no. 18, p. 9.

12. *Moscow News,* no. 23, June 9–16, 1991, pp. 8–9.

13. *The Economy of the Soviet Union,* p. 11.

14. The RSFSR exports 73 percent of the oil and gas from the USSR, Ukraine and Belorussia another 10 percent. "If traded goods were valued at world market prices, the Russian Republic would have a large trade surplus with the rest of the world while virtually all the other republics would reportedly record a trade deficit" (Ibid., p. 11).

15. *The Armenian Mirror-Spectator,* October 26, 1991, pp. 1, 16.

16. Ukraine and Moldova signed the economic treaty on November 4.

17. *Izvestiia,* October 19, 1991; CDSP, XLIII, no. 42, November 20, 1991, p. 1.

18. *New York Times,* November 15, 1991.

19. *New York Times,* November 26, 1991.

Bibliography of Books and Articles in Western Languages on Modern Armenian History

Afanasyan, Serge, *L'Arménie, l'Azerbaijan et la Géorgie de l'indépendance à l'instauration du pouvoir soviétique (1917–1923)* (Paris: Editions L'Harmattan, 1981).

———, *La victoire de Sardarabad, Arménie 21–29 mai 1918* (Paris: Editions L'Harmattan, 1985).

Aftandilian, Gregory, *Armenia, Vision of a Republic: The Independence Lobby in America* (Boston: Charles River Books, 1981).

Alishan, Leonardo: "Crucifixion without 'the Cross': The Impact of the Genocide on Armenian Literature," *Armenian Review* XXXVIII, 1 (1985), pp. 27–50.

Andonian, Aram, comp., *The Memoirs of Naim Bey: Turkish Official Documents Relating to the Deportations and Massacres of Armenians* (London: Hodder and Stoughton, 1920).

Arlen, Michael, *Passage to Ararat* (New York: Farrar, Straus & Giroux, 1975).

Arménie-Diaspora, Mémoire et Modernité, special issue of *Les Temps Modernes* XLIII, 504–506 (July–September 1988).

Arpee, Leon, *The Armenian Awakening: A History of the Armenian Church, 1820–1860* (Chicago: University of Chicago Press, 1909).

Arslanian, Artin, "Britain and the Question of Mountainous Karabagh," *Middle Eastern Studies* XVI, 1 (January 1980), pp. 92–104.

———, "British Wartime Pledges, 1917–18: The Armenian Case," *Journal of Contemporary History* XIII (1978), pp. 517–30.

———, "Dunsterville's Adventures: A Reappraisal," *International Journal of Middle East Studies* XII, 2 (September 1980), pp. 199–216.

———, "The British Decision to Intervene in Transcaucasia during World War I," *Armenian Review* XXVII, 2–106 (Summer 1974), pp. 146–59.

———, and Nichols, Robert L., "Nationalism and the Russian Civil War: The Case of Volunteer Army-Armenian Relations, 1918–20," *Soviet Studies* XXXI, 4 (October 1979), pp. 559–73.

Aslan, Kevork, *Armenia and the Armenians from the Earliest Times until the Great War (1914)* (trans. Pierre Crabites) (New York: MacMillan, 1920).

Aspaturian, Vernon V., *The Union Republics in Soviet Diplomacy: A Study of Soviet Federalism in the Service of Soviet Foreign Policy* (Geneva: E. Droz, 1960).

Astourian, Stephan, "The Armenian Genocide: An Interpretation," *History Teacher* XXIII, 2 (February 1990), pp. 111–60.

———, "The Sykes-Picot Agreement Revisited: Behavioral Models and Diplomatic History," *UCLA Journal of Middle Eastern Studies* III (1987), pp. 1–36.

Atamian, Sarkis, *The Armenian Community: The Historical Development of a Social and Ideological Conflict* (New York: Philosophical Library, 1955).

Azarya, Victor, *The Armenian Quarter of Jerusalem* (Berkeley: University of California, 1984).

Baldwin, Oliver, *Six Prisons and Two Revolutions: Adventures in Trans-Caucasia and Anatolia, 1920–1921* (Garden City, NY: Doubleday, Page and Co., 1925).

Bamberger, Joan, "Family and Kinship in an Armenian-American Community," *Journal of Armenian Studies* III, 1 (1986–1987), pp. 76–86.

Bardakjian, Kevork B., *Hitler and the Armenian Genocide*, Zoryan Institute Special Report no. 3 (Cambridge, MA: Zoryan Institute, 1985).

———, *The Mekhitarist Contributions to Armenian Culture and Scholarship* (Cambridge, MA: Harvard College Library, 1976).

Barratt, Glynn R., "A Note on the Russian Conquest of Armenia (1827)," *Slavonic and East European Review* L, 120 (July 1972), pp. 386–409.

Barsoumian, Hagop, "Economic Role of the Armenian Amira Class in the Ottoman Empire," *Armenian Review* XXXI, 3–123 (March 1979), pp. 310–16.

Barth, Frederik, *Ethnic Groups and Boundaries: The Social Organization of Culture Difference* (Boston: Little, Brown, 1969).

Bauer-Manndorff, Elisabeth, *Armenia: Past and Present* (Lucerne: Reich Verlag, 1981; New York: Armenian Prelacy, 1981).

Beylerian, Arthur, "L'échec d'une percée internationale: Le mouvement national arménien (1914–1923)," *Relations internationales,* no. 31 (Autumn 1982), pp. 351–71.

———, *Les grandes puissances, L'empire Ottoman, et les Arméniens dans les archives française 1914–1918: Recueil de documents* (Paris: Sorbonne, 1983).

Blackwell, Alice Stone, *Armenian Poetry* (Boston: Atlantic Printing Co., 1917).

Bliss, Edwin Munsell, *Turkey and the Armenian Atrocities* (Philadelphia: Keystone, 1896).

Bournoutian, George A., *Eastern Armenia in the Last Decades of Persian Rule, 1807–1828: A Political and Socioeconomic Study of the Khanate of Erevan on the Eve of the Russian Conquest* (Malibu, CA: Undena, 1982).

Braude, Benjamin, and Lewis, Bernard, *Christians and Jews in the Ottoman Empire: The Functioning of a Plural Society,* 2 vols. (New York: Holmes and Meier, 1982).

Bryce, James, *Transcaucasia and Ararat* (London: MacMillan, 1896; reprint: New York: Arno Press, 1970).

Buheiry, Marwan, "Herzel and the Armenians," *Journal of Palestine Studies* VII, 1 (Autumn 1977), pp. 75–97.

Buxton, Noel, and Buxton, Harold, *Travels and Politics in Armenia* (London: John Murray, 1914).

Carlson, John Roy, *Undercover* (New York: E. P. Dutton, 1943).

Chalabian, Antranig, *General Andranik and the Armenian Revolutionary Movement* (Southfield, MI; A. Chalabian, 1988).

Chamchian, Michael, *History of Armenia from* B.C. *2247 to the Year of Christ 1780 or 1229 of the Armenian Era,* 3 vols., trans. Johannes Avdall (Calcutta: Bishops College Press, 1827).

Corbyn, F. C., "The Present Position of the Armenian Nation," *Journal of the Royal Central Asian Society* XIX, 4 (October 1932), pp. 587–616.

A Crime of Silence. The Armenian Genocide: The Permanent Peoples' Tribunal (London: Zed Books, 1985).

Dadrian, Vahakn, "The Naim-Andonian Documents on the World War I Destruction of Ottoman Armenians: The Anatomy of a Genocide," *International Journal of Middle East Studies* XVIII, 3 (August 1986), pp. 311–60.

———, "The Role of Turkish Physicians in the World War I Genocide of Ottoman Armenians," *Holocaust and Genocide Studies* I, 2 (1986), pp. 169–192.

———, "The Structural and Functional Components of Genocide: A Victimological Approach to the Armenian Case," in Israel Drapkin and Emilio Viano, eds., *Victimology* (Lexington, MA: D. C. Heath, 1974), pp. 123–36.

Davis, Leslie A., *The Slaughterhouse Province: An American Diplomat's Report on the Armenian Genocide, 1915–1917*, ed. Susan K. Blair (New Rochelle, NY: Aristide D. Caratzas, 1989).

Davison, Roderic, "The Armenian Crisis, 1912–1914," *American Historical Review* LIII, 3 (April 1948), pp. 481–505.

———, *Reform in the Ottoman Empire, 1856–1876* (Princeton: Princeton University Press, 1963).

Dedeyan, Gerard, ed., *Histoire des arméniens* (Paris: Privat, 1982).

Dekmejian, R. H., "Soviet-Turkish Relations and Policies in the Armenian SSR," *Soviet Studies* XIX, 4 (April 1968), pp. 510–25.

De Morgan, Jacques, *History of the Armenian People*, trans. by Ernest F. Barry (Boston: Hairenik Press, n.d.)

Des Pres, Terrence, "On Governing Narratives: The Turkish-Armenian Case," *The Yale Review* LXXV, 4 (October 1986), pp. 517–31.

Deutsch, Karl W., *Nationalism and Social Communication: An Inquiry into the Foundations of Nationality* (New York and Cambridge, 1953).

———, *Nationalism and Its Alternatives* (New York, 1969).

Djemal Pasha, *Memories of a Turkish Statesman, 1913–1919* (London: Hutchinson and Co., n.d.)

Duguid, Stephen, "The Politics of Unity: Hamidian Policy in Eastern Anatolia," *Middle Eastern Studies* IX, 2 (May 1973), pp. 139–155.

Duncan, Charles, *A Campaign with the Turks in Asia*, 2 vols. (London: Smith, Elder, 1855).

Dzeron, Manoog B., *Village of Parchanj: General History (1600–1937)* (Fresno, CA: Panorama West Books, 1984).

Elliott, Mabel Evelyn, *Beginning Again at Ararat* (New York: Fleming H. Revell, 1924).

Etmekjian, James, *The French Influence on the Western Armenian Renaissance, 1843–1915* (New York: Twayne, 1964).

Gaspard, Armand, *Le combat arménien: Entre terrorisme et utopie, Lausanne, 1923–1983* (Lausanne: L'Age d'Homme, 1984).

Gidney, James B., *A Mandate for Armenia* (Kent, OH: Kent State University Press, 1967).

Gocek, Fatma Muge, *East Meets West: France and the Ottoman Empire in the Eighteenth Century* (Oxford: Oxford University Press, 1987).

Goshgarian, Geoffrey, "Eghishe Charents and the 'Modernization' of Soviet Armenian Literature," *Armenian Review* XXXVI, 1 (Spring 1983), pp. 76–88.

Greene, Frederick Davis, *Armenian Massacres or The Sword of Mohammed* (Philadelphia: American Oxford, 1896).

Hamalian, Arpi, "The Shirkets: Visiting Pattern of Armenians in Lebanon," *Anthropological Quarterly* XLVII (1974), pp. 71–92.

Hautiunian, Abraham H., *Neither to Laugh nor to Weep: A Memoir of the Armenian Genocide*, trans. Vartan Hartunian (Boston: Beacon Press, 1968).

Hepworth, George Hughes, *Through Armenia on Horseback* (London: Isbister and Co., 1898).

Hewsen, Robert H., "The Meliks of Eastern Armenia, A Preliminary Study," *Revue des études arméniennes*, N.S., IX (1972), pp. 255–329.

——, "The Meliks of Eastern Armenia, II," *Revue des études arméniennes*, N.S., X (1973–1974), pp. 281–303.

——, "The Meliks of Eastern Armenia, III," *Revue des études arméniennes*, N.S., XI (1975–1976), pp. 219–43.

Hoogasian-Villa, Susie, and Kilbourne Matossian, Mary, *Armenian Village Life before 1914* (Detroit: Wayne State University Press, 1982).

Hovannisian, Richard G., "Armenia and the Caucasus in the Genesis of the Soviet-Turkish Entente," *International Journal of Middle East Studies* IV, 2 (April 1973), pp. 129–47.

——, *Armenia on the Road to Independence, 1918* (Berkeley: University of California Press, 1967).

——, "Dimensions of Democracy and Authority in Caucasian Armenia, 1917–1920," *Russian Review* XXXIII, 1 (January 1974), pp. 37–49.

——, "Russian Armenia: A Century of Tsarist Rule," *Jahrbücher für Geschichte Osteuropas* XIX, 1 (March 1971), pp. 31–48.

——, "Simon Vratzian and Armenian Nationalism," *Middle Eastern Studies* V, 3 (October 1969), pp. 192–220.

——, *The Armenian Holocaust: A Bibliography Relating to the Deportations, Massacres, and Dispersion of the Armenian People, 1915–1923* (Cambridge, MA: Armenian Heritage Press, 1978).

——, ed., *The Armenian Image in History and Literature* (Malibu: Undena Press, 1981).

——, ed., *The Armenian Genocide in Perspective* (New Brunswick, N.J.: Transaction, 1986).

——, *The Armenian Republic*, vols. I and II (Berkeley: University of California Press, 1971–1982).

Hovannisian, Richard G., Shaw, Stanford J., and Shaw, Ezel Kural, "Forum: The Armenian Question," *International Journal of Middle East Studies* IX, 3 (August 1978), pp. 379–400.

Indjeyan, Lazare, *Mirage arménien et Miradors* (Paris: La Pensée Universelle, 1980).

Institut für Armenische Fragen, *The Armenian Genocide, I: Documentation* (Munich: Institut für Armenische Fragen, 1987).

Jernazian, Ephraim K., *Judgment Unto Truth: Witnessing the Armenian Genocide*, trans. Alice Haig (New Brunswick, N.J.: Transaction, 1990).

Kalfaian, Aris, *Chomaklou: The History of an Armenian Village*, trans. Krikor Asadourian (New York: Chomaklou Compatriotic Society, 1982).

Kasbarian-Bricout, Beatrice, *La société arménienne au XIX siècle* (Paris: La Pensée Universelle, 1981).

——, *Les Arméniens au XXe siècle* (Paris: Editions L'Harmattan, 1984).

Kayaloff, Jacques, *The Battle of Sardarabad* (The Hague: Mouton, 1973).

Kazanjian, David, and Kassabian, Anahid, "Naming the Armenian Genocide: The Quest for 'Truth' and a Search for Possibilities," *New Formations*, no. 8 (Summer 1989), pp. 81–98.

Kazemzadeh, Firuz, *The Struggle for Transcaucasia (1917–1921)* (New York: Philosophical Library, 1951).

Kehayan, Nina, and Kehayan, Jean, *Rue du prolétaire rouge: Deux communistes français en Urss* (Paris: Editions du Seuil, 1978).

Kerr, Stanley Elphinstone, *The Lions of Marash: Personal Experiences with American Near East Relief, 1919–1922* (Albany: State University of New York Press, 1973).

Khatissian, Alexander, "The Memoirs of a Mayor," *Armenian Review* II, 3-7 (Autumn 1949), pp. 40–47; 4-8 (Winter 1949–1950), pp. 104–16; III, 1-9 (Spring 1950), pp. 87–106; 2-10 (Summer 1950), pp. 78–92; 3-11 (Autumn 1950), 97–115; 4-12 (Winter 1950–1951), pp. 106–13.

Kloian, Richard D., *The Armenian Genocide: News Accounts from the American Press: 1915–1922* (Berkeley: Anto Printing, 1980).

Krikorian, Mesrob K., *Armenians in the Service of the Ottoman Empire, 1860–1908* (London, 1978).

———, "The Armenian Church and the WCC: A Personal View," *The Ecumenical Review* XL (July/October 1988), pp. 411–17.

Kuper, Leo, *Genocide: Its Political Use in the Twentieth Century* (New Haven: Yale University Press, 1981).

Kurkjian, Vahan M., *A History of Armenia* (New York: Armenian General Benevolent Union, 1958).

Lang, David Marshall, *The Armenians, A People in Exile* (London: George Allen & Unwin, 1981).

Lang, David Marshall, and Walker, Christopher J., *The Armenians*, Minority Rights Group Report no. 32 (London: Minority Rights Group, 1976).

Langer, William L., *Diplomacy of Imperialism 1890–1902,* 2 vols. (New York: Alfred Knopf, 1935; 2nd ed.: 1951).

Leart, Marcel, *La Question arménienne—à la lumière des documents* (Paris: A. Challamel, Librairie Maritime et Coloniale, 1913).

Lepsius, Johannes, *Armenia and Europe: An Indictment* (London: Hodder and Stoughton, 1897).

Lewis, Bernard, *The Emergence of Modern Turkey* (Oxford: Oxford University Press, 1961).

Libaridian, Gerard J., ed., *Armenia at the Crossroads: Democracy and Nationhood in the Post-Soviet Era: Essays, Interviews and Speeches by the Leaders of the National Democratic Movement in Armenia* (Watertown, MA: Blue Crane, 1991).

———, *The Karabagh File: Documents and Facts on the Question of Mountainous Karabagh, 1918–1988* (Cambridge, MA: Zoryan Institute, 1988).

Lynch, H. F. B., *Armenia: Travels and Studies,* 2 vols. (London: Longmans, Green, 1901; Beirut: Khayats, 1965).

Malcom, Vartan, *The Armenians in America* (Boston: Pilgrim Press, 1919).

Malkasian, Mark, "The Disintegration of the Armenian Cause in the United States, 1918–1927," *International Journal of Middle East Studies,* XVI, 3 (August 1984), pp. 347–65.

Maloumian, Armand, *Les fils du goulag* (Paris: Presse de la Cité, 1976).

Matossian, Mary Kilbourne, *The Impact of Soviet Policies in Armenia* (Leiden: E. J. Brill, 1962).

Mazian, Florence, *Why Genocide? The Armenian and Jewish Experiences in Perspective* (Ames: Iowa State University Press, 1990).

Megrian, Leon, "Mikayel Nalbandyan and His Tract 'Agriculture as the True Way,'" *Armenian Review* XXVII, 2/106 (Summer 1974), pp. 160–77.

Melson, Robert, "A Theoretical Inquiry into the Armenian Massacres of 1894–1896," *Comparative Studies in Society and History* XXIV, 3 (July 1982), pp. 481–509.

Mikirtichian, Levon, "Aksel Bakounts as the Champion of the True Concept of the Popular Basis of Literature in Soviet Armenia," *The Caucasian Review* VII (1958), pp. 60–90; VIII (1959), pp. 41–69.

Miller, Donald E., and Miller, Lorna Touryan, "Armenian Survivors: A Typological Analysis of Victim Response," *Oral History Review* X (1982), pp. 47–72.

Mirak, Robert, "Armenian Emigration to the United States to 1915 (I): Leaving the Old Country," *Journal of Armenian Studies* I, 1 (Autumn 1975), pp. 5–42.

———, "Armenians," in Stephen Thernstrom, ed., *Harvard Encyclopedia of American Ethnic Groups* (Cambridge, MA: Harvard University Press, 1980), pp. 136–49.

———, "On New Soil: The Armenian Orthodox and Armenian Protestant Churches in the New World to 1915," in Randall M. Miller and Thomas D. Marxik, eds., *Immigrants and Religion in Urban America* (Philadelphia: Temple University Press, 1977), pp. 138–61.

———, *Torn Between Two Lands: Armenians in America, 1890 to World War I* (Cambridge, MA: Harvard University Press, 1983).

Missakian, Jirayr, *Searchlight on the Armenian Question* (Boston: Hairenik, 1930).

Morgenthau, Henry, *Ambassador Morgenthau's Story* (Garden City, NY: Doubleday, Page, 1918; reprint: Plandome, NY: New Age, 1975).

Mouradian, Claire, *De Staline à Gorbatchev, Histoire d'une république soviétique: L'Arménie* (Paris: Editions Ramsay, 1990).

———, "L'immigration des Arméniens de la diaspora vers la RSS d'Arménie, 1946–1962," *Cahiers du monde russe et soviétique* XX, 1 (January-March 1979), pp. 79–110.

Nalbandian, Louise, *The Armenian Revolutionary Movement: The Development of Armenian Political Parties Through the Nineteenth Century* (Berkeley: University of California Press, 1963).

Nansen, Fridtjof, *Armenia and the Near East* (New York: Duffield, 1928).

Nassibian, Akaby, *Britain and the Armenian Question, 1915–1923* (London: Croom Helm, 1984).

Nersoyan, Bishop Tiran, *A Christian Approach to Communism* (London: Frederick Muller, 1942).

Norman, C. B., *Armenia and the Campaign of 1877* (London: Cassell, Petter, and Galpin, n.d.)

O'Grady, Ingrid, "Ararat, Etchmiadzin, and Haig (Nation, Church, and Kin): A Study of the Symbol System of American Armenians," (Ph.d. dissertation: Catholic University, 1979).

Ormanian, Malachia, *The Church of Armenia*, trans. A. Marcar Gregory (London: A. R. Mowbray, 1912).

Oshagan, Vahe, "Cultural and Literary Awakening of Western Armenians, 1789–1915," *Armenian Review* XXXVI, 3 (Autumn 1983), pp. 57–70.

———, "Literature of the Armenian Diaspora," *World Literature Today* LX, (Spring 1986), pp. 224–28.

———, *The English Influence on West Armenian Literature in the Nineteenth Century* (Cleveland: Cleveland State University, 1982).

Papazian, K. S., *Patriotism Perverted* (Boston: Baikar Press, 1934).

Pasdermadjian, Garegin, *Why Armenia Should Be Free* (Boston: Hairenik, 1918).

Phillips, Jenny King, "Symbol, Myth, and Rhetoric: The Politics of Culture in an Armenian-American Population" (Ph.d. dissertation: Boston University, 1978).

Piotrowski, Thaddeus M., *The Armenian Diaspora in Manchester, N.H.* (Manchester, NH: no pub., 1977).

Pipes, Richard, *The Formation of the Soviet Union: Communism and Nationalism, 1917–1923* (Cambridge, MA: Harvard University Press, 1954; revised edition: 1964; New York: Atheneum, 1968).

Rakowska-Harmstone, Teresa, "The Dialectics of Nationalism in the USSR," *Problems of Communism* XIII, 3 (May-June 1974), pp. 1–22.

Ravitch, Norman, "The Armenian Catastrophe: Of History, Murder & Sin," *Encounter* LVII, 6 (December 1981), pp. 69–84.

Safran, William, "Diasporas in Modern Societies: Myths of Homeland and Return," *Diaspora* I, 1 (Spring 1991), pp. 83–99.

Salt, Jeremy, "Britain, the Armenian Question and the Cause of Ottoman Reforms: 1894–96," *Middle Eastern Studies* XXVI, (July 1990), pp. 308–28.

Sanasarian, Eliz, "Gender Distinction in the Genocidal Process: A Preliminary Study of the Armenian Case," *Holocaust and Genocide Studies* IV, 4 (1989), pp. 449–61.

Sanjian, Avedis K., "Status of Armenian Studies," *Bulletin for the Advancement of Armenian Studies* I, 1/2 (Autumn-Winter 1963), pp. 3–31.

———, *The Armenian Communities in Syria under Ottoman Dominion* (Cambridge, MA: Harvard University Press, 1965).

Sarkissian, A. O., *History of the Armenian Question to 1885*, Illinois Studies in Social Sciences, XXII, 3–4 (Urbana: University of Illinois Press, 1938).

Sarkissian, Karekin, "The Armenian Church," in A. J. Arberry, ed., *Religion in the Middle East, I* (Cambridge: Cambridge University Press, 1969), pp. 482–520.

Sarkisyanz, Manuel, *A Modern History of Transcaucasian Armenia: Social, Cultural, and Political* (Leiden: E. J. Brill, 1975).

Schahgaldian, Nikola, "Political Integration of an Immigrant Community into a Composite Society: The Armenians in Lebanon, 1920–1974" (Ph.D. dissertation: Columbia University, 1979).

Shaw, Stanford Jay, and Shaw, Ezel Kural, *History of the Ottoman Empire and Modern Turkey*, 2 vols. (Cambridge: Cambridge University Press, 1976–1977).

Shaginyan, Marietta Sergeevna, *Journey through Soviet Armenia* (Moscow: Foreign Language Publishing House, 1954).

Sheehy, Ann, and Fuller, Elizabeth, "Armenia and Armenians in the USSR: Nationality and Language Aspects of the Census of 1979," *Radio Liberty Research Bulletin* XXIV, 24 (3072), June 13, 1980 (RL 208/80).

Smith, Anthony D., *The Ethnic Origins of Nations* (Oxford: Basil Blackwell, 1986).

Stone, Frank Andrews, *Academies for Anatolia: A Study of the Rationale, Program and Impact of the Educational Institutions Sponsored by the American Board in Turkey: 1830–1980* (Lanham, MD: University Press of America, 1984).

Suny, Ronald Grigor, *Armenia in the Twentieth Century* (Chico, CA: Scholars Press, 1983).

———, *The Baku Commune, 1917–1918: Class and Revolution in the Russian Revolution* (Princeton: Princeton University Press, 1972).

———, "Incomplete Revolution: National Movements and the Collapse of the Soviet Empire," *New Left Review*, no. 189 (September/October 1991), pp. 111–26.

———, *The Making of the Georgian Nation* (Bloomington and Stanford: Indiana University Press and the Hoover Institution Press, 1988).

———, "The Revenge of the Past: Socialism and Ethnic Conflict in Transcaucasia," *New Left Review*, no. 184 (November-December 1990), pp. 5–34.

———, ed., *Transcaucasia, Nationalism and Social Change: Essays in the History of Armenia, Azerbaijan, and Georgia* (Ann Arbor: Michigan Slavic Publications, 1983).

Sutton, Peter, "A View of Soviet Armenia," *Contemporary Review* CCXLVI (May 4, 1985), pp. 251–54.

Tala'i, Vered, "Social Boundaries within and between Ethnic Groups: Armenians in London," *Man* XXI, 2 (1986), pp. 251–70.

———, "The Circumscription of Ethnicity: A Case Study of the London Armenian Community," *Ethnic and Racial Studies* IX, 2 (1986), pp. 211–18.

Tashjian, James H., *The Armenians of the United States and Canada* (Boston: Hairenik, 1947).

Ter Minassian, Anahide, *La Question arménienne* (Roquevaire: Editions Parentheses, 1983).

———, *La République d'Arménie* (Paris: Editions Complexe, 1989).

———, "Le mouvement révolutionnaire arménien, 1890–1903," *Cahiers du monde russe et soviétique* XIV, 4 (October-December 1973), pp. 536–607.

———, *Nationalism and Socialism in the Armenian Revolutionary Movement* (Cambridge, MA: Zoryan Institute, 1984).

Ternon, Yves, *La cause arménienne* (Paris: Editions du Seuil, 1983).

———, *Les Arméniens, Histoire d'un genocide* (Paris: Editions du Seuil, 1977).

Thorossian, H., *Histoire de la littérature arménienne, des origines jusqu'à nos jours* (Paris: n.p., 1951).

Tololyan, Khachig, "Cultural Narrative and the Motivation of the Terrorist," *The Journal of Strategic Studies* X, 4 (December 1987), pp. 217–33.

———, "Exile Government in the Armenian Polity," *Journal of Political Science* XVIII, 1 (Spring 1990), pp. 124–47.

———, "Martyrdom as Legitimacy: Terrorism, Religion, and Symbolic Appropriation in the Armenian Diaspora," in Paul Wilkinson and Alasdair Stewart, eds., *Contemporary Research on Terrorism* (Aberdeen: Aberdeen University Press, 1987), pp. 89–103.

———, "The Nation-State and Its Others: In Lieu of a Preface," *Diaspora* I, 1 (Spring 1991), pp. 3–7.

———, "The Role of the Armenian Apostolic Church in the Diaspora," *Armenian Review* XLI, 1/161 (Spring 1988), pp. 55–68.

Toynbee, Arnold J., *Armenian Atrocities: The Murder of a Nation* (London: Hodder and Stoughton, 1915).

———, ed., *The Treatment of Armenians in the Ottoman Empire: Documents Presented to Viscount Grey of Fallodon by Viscount Bryce* (London: Sir Joseph Causton and Sons, 1916; reprint: Beirut: G. Doniguian, 1972).

Tsimhoni, Daphne, "The Armenians and the Syrians: Ethno-religious Communities in Jerusalem," *Middle Eastern Studies* XX, 3 (July 1984), pp. 352–59.

Vertanes, Charles, *Armenia Reborn* (New York: The Armenian National Council of America, 1947).

Vratsian, Simon, *Armenia and the Armenian Question*, trans. James G. Mandalian (Boston: Hairenik, 1943).

———, ed., *Bank Ottoman: Memoirs of Armen Garo, The Armenian Ambassador to America from the Independent Republic of Armenia*, trans. Haig T. Partizian (Detroit: Armen Topouzian, 1990).

Walker, Christopher J., "Armenia: A Nation in Asia," *Asian Affairs* XIX (February 1988), pp. 20–35.

———, *Armenia, the Survival of a Nation* (Beckenham, Kent: Croom Helm, 1980; New York: St. Martin's Press, 1980).

———, ed., *Armenia and Karabagh: The Struggle for Unity* (London: Minority Rights, 1991).

Yeghenian, A. Y., *The Red Flag at Ararat* (New York: The Womans Press, 1932).

Yeghiayan, Vartkes, trans., *Armenian Political Trials, Proceedings I: The Case of Soghomon Tehlirian* (Los Angeles: A.R.F. Varantian Gomideh, 1985).

Index

RONALD GRIGOR SUNY is Alex Manoogian Professor of Modern Armenian History at the University of Michigan. A specialist in the history of the non-Russian peoples of the Soviet Union, he is author of *The Baku Commune, 1917–1918: Class and Nationality in the Russian Revolution* and *The Making of the Georgian Nation* and editor of *Transcaucasia, Nationalism and Social Change* and *The Russian Revolution and Bolshevik Victory*.